Pasts at play

Series editors: Anna Barton, Andrew Smith

Editorial board: David Amigoni, Isobel Armstrong, Philip Holden, Jerome McGann, Joanne Wilkes, Julia M. Wright

Interventions: Rethinking the Nineteenth Century seeks to make a significant intervention into the critical narratives that dominate conventional and established understandings of nineteenth-century literature. Informed by the latest developments in criticism and theory the series provides a focus for how texts from the long nineteenth century, and more recent adaptations of them, revitalise our knowledge of and engagement with the period. It explores the radical possibilities offered by new methods, unexplored contexts and neglected authors and texts to re-map the literary-cultural landscape of the period and rigorously re-imagine its geographical and historical parameters. The series includes monographs, edited collections, and scholarly sourcebooks.

Already published

Engine of modernity: The omnibus and urban culture in nineteenth-century Paris
Masha Belenky

Spain in the nineteenth century: New essays on experiences of culture and society
Andrew Ginger and Geraldine Lawless

Instead of modernity: The Western canon and the incorporation of the Hispanic (c. 1850–75)
Andrew Ginger

Creating character: Theories of nature and nurture in Victorian sensation fiction
Helena Ifill

Margaret Harkness: Writing social engagement 1880–1921   Flore Janssen and Lisa C. Robertson (eds)

Richard Marsh, popular fiction and literary culture, 1890–1915: Re-reading the fin de siècle
Victoria Margree, Daniel Orrells and Minna Vuohelainen (eds)

Charlotte Brontë: Legacies and afterlives   Amber K. Regis and Deborah Wynne (eds)

The Great Exhibition, 1851: A sourcebook   Jonathon Shears (ed.)

Interventions: Rethinking the nineteenth century   Andrew Smith and Anna Barton (eds)

Counterfactual Romanticism   Damian Walford Davies (ed.)

Pasts at play

Childhood encounters with history in British culture, 1750–1914

Edited by Rachel Bryant Davies and
Barbara Gribling

Manchester University Press

Copyright © Manchester University Press 2020

While copyright in the volume as a whole is vested in Manchester University Press, copyright in individual chapters belongs to their respective authors, and no chapter may be reproduced wholly or in part without the express permission in writing of both author and publisher.

Published by Manchester University Press
Oxford Road, Manchester M13 9PL

www.manchesteruniversitypress.co.uk

British Library Cataloguing-in-Publication Data
A catalogue record for this book is available from the British Library

ISBN 978 1 5261 2889 8 hardback
ISBN 978 1 5261 7182 5 paperback

The publisher has no responsibility for the persistence or accuracy of URLs for any external or third-party internet websites referred to in this book, and does not guarantee that any content on such websites is, or will remain, accurate or appropriate.

Typeset
by New Best-set Typesetters Ltd

We dedicate this volume to

Rosemary Mitchell

and

Bennett Zon

in grateful acknowledgement of their generous support and encouragement from which we, and many other early career scholars, have greatly benefited.

Contents

List of figures	*page* ix
List of contributors	xii
Acknowledgements	xiv

Introduction: pasts at play   1
Rachel Bryant Davies and Barbara Gribling

Part I: Biblical and archaeological pasts   23

1 Noah's Ark-aeology and nineteenth-century children   25
Melanie Keene

2 Bringing Egypt home: children's encounters with ancient Egypt in the long nineteenth century   48
Virginia Zimmerman

Part II: Classical pasts   69

3 Didactic heroes: masculinity, sexuality and exploration in the Argonaut story of Kingsley's *The Heroes*   71
Helen Lovatt

4 'Fun from the Classics': puzzling antiquity in *The Boy's Own Paper*   96
Rachel Bryant Davies

Part III: Medieval and early modern pasts   123

5 Youthful consumption and conservative visions: Robin Hood and Wat Tyler in late Victorian penny periodicals   125
Stephen Basdeo

6 A tale of two ladies? Stuart women as role models for Victorian and Edwardian girls and young women   142
Rosemary Mitchell

Contents

Part IV: Revived pasts — **165**

7 Tarry-at-home antiquarians: children's 'tour books', 1740–1850 — 167
M. O. Grenby

8 Playing with the past: child consumers, pedagogy and British history games, c. 1780–1850 — 193
Barbara Gribling

9 Re-enacting local history in the Stepney Children's Pageant, 1909 — 221
Ellie Reid

Appendix A: A list of 'tour books' — 244
M. O. Grenby

Appendix B: A list of British history-themed toys and games — 250
Barbara Gribling

Index — 254

Figures

0.1 *Wallis's New Game of Universal History and Chronology* (London: J. Wallis, 1840). Courtesy of Princeton University Library   2

0.2 Close-up of medallion playing spaces from *Wallis's New Game of Universal History and Chronology* (London: J. Wallis, 1840), including the first ship which appeared in Europe brought from Egypt by Danaüs, the founding of the Kingdom of Egypt, the wooden horse entering Troy and jousting knights. Courtesy of Princeton University Library   3

0.3 Close-up of medallion playing spaces from *Wallis's New Game of Universal History and Chronology* (London: J. Wallis, 1840), including Adam and Eve, Noah's Ark, Homer, Caesar in Britain, Egbert, Greenland discovered, gardening introduced, London Bridge and children forbidden to be sold by their parents. Courtesy of Princeton University Library   3

0.4 Close-up of central medallion from *Wallis's New Game of Universal History and Chronology* (London: J. Wallis, 1840), showing new royal portraits of Victoria, and the railway line. Courtesy of Princeton University Library   5

0.5 Toy theatre souvenir sheet, 'Skelt's Favorite Horse Combats', depicting two combats staged at Astley's Amphitheatre in London – the top combat from *Wallace, the Hero of Scotland* (1815) and the lower combat from *The Giant Horse, or Siege of Troy* (1833)   16

1.1 A painted wooden Noah's Ark, c. 1830, given by Miss M. M. Wyley, from Malvern. © Victoria and Albert Museum   27

1.2 Children playing with a Noah's Ark set. Print, illustration by Arthur Boyd Houghton, engraved by the Dalziel Brothers, made for Dora Greenwell's poem 'Noah's Ark', in *Home Thoughts and Home Scenes*, an anthology of popular verse published in 1865. © Victoria and Albert Museum   29

Figures

1.3	Metamorphic print, 'The Wonders of the Ark', 1845. Children could turn a paper dial to control the boarding of animals. © The Bodleian Libraries, The University of Oxford, John Johnson Collection: Puzzle Pictures Folder 3 (7)	37
2.1	Illustration by H. R. Millar from E. Nesbit's *The Story of the Amulet* (London: T. Fisher Unwin, 1906), 'In the Middle of a Wall was a Mummy Case', showing a group of children looking at a mummy case in a room in an Edwardian house. © Reproduced by kind permission of the Syndics of Cambridge University Library	60
2.2	'Little Jack Horner' from *Mother Goose in Hieroglyphics* (Boston: Brown, Taggard & Chase, 1849), p. 5	64
3.1	Illustration for *The Heroes*, first edition, by Charles Kingsley himself. From C. Kingsley, *The Heroes, or, Greek Fairy Tales for my Children* (Cambridge: Macmillan, 1856), p. 54	82
4.1	An initial capital letter using a medieval boy-knight to illustrate an article about the popularity of Latin, Greek and classical antiquity: 'Odd Fellow', 'Still more fun from the Classics', *Boy's Own Paper* (17 March 1883), p. 398	106
4.2	Cartoon of anachronistic classical figures: Anon., 'Fun from the Classics', *Boy's Own Paper* (11 March 1893), p. 38	109
4.3	Comically updated cartoons: Anon., 'Fun from the Classics', *Boy's Own Paper* (13 April 1895), p. 448	111
5.1	First number of George Emmett's *Robin Hood*, p. 1	131
5.2	*The Sword of Freedom; or, The Boyhood Days of Jack Straw*, c. 1870, issue 2, p. 2	132
6.1	Queen Henrietta Maria with Charles I and sons, after Anthony Van Dyck, from Agnes and Elizabeth Strickland, *The Lives of the Queens of England* (London: Colburn and Co. 1845–1848), VIII, title page	145
6.2	'Lord and Lady Russell', illustration to H. A. F., 'Lady Rachel Russell', *Chatterbox* (14 July 1873), p. 260. © Reproduced by kind permission of the Syndics of Cambridge University Library	153
7.1	John Penrose Jnr to John Murray II, 7 December 1829. Manuscript note of the itinerary for a planned children's tour book: ten towns and cities, nine castles, five churches and cathedrals, five stately homes, three natural attractions and probably three industrial sites (two Cornish tin and copper mines, and 'Ivy Bridge' in Devon, most likely for its paper mills). National Library of Scotland (MSS. 40,938, fo. 25r)	169

Figures

7.2	Frontispiece to [Samuel Clarke], *Reuben Ramble's Travels Through the Counties of England* (London: Darton & Clark, n.d.). Published by Darton from the 1840s. © British Library Board	178
7.3	Illustration for Monmouthshire, [Samuel Clarke], *Reuben Ramble's Travels in the Midland Counties of England* (London: Darton & Clark, n.d.). Published by Darton from the 1840s. © British Library Board	179
7.4	Page from [Ann and Jane Taylor], *City Scenes: or, A Peep into London, for Good Children* (London: Darton and Harvey, 1809). © British Library Board	183
8.1	Cover of *An Historical Game of England* (London: Didier and Tebbett, 1804). Courtesy of Princeton University Library	196
8.2	*Historical Amusement. A New Game* (London: N. Carpenter, 1850–1855). © Victoria and Albert Museum	197
8.3	Anon., 'Richard III' card, *Historical Cards*, c. 1809. © Museum of Childhood, Edinburgh	199
8.4	Close-ups of circles from *Historical Pastime or a New Game of the History of England from the Conquest to the Accession of George the Third* (London: J. Harris and J. Wallis, 1803). Courtesy of Princeton University Library	204
8.5	Close up of the central spiral including contemporary events added in the 1820s editions and additions made to the first Queen Victoria edition. *Historical Pastime. A New Game of the History of England* (London: J. Passmore, c. 1850). © Adrian Seville, private collection	208
8.6	A comparison of circles in *Historical Pastime*, 1803 and *Historical Pastime*, 1824. Courtesy of Princeton University Library	209
9.1	'John Stow and London Children', Stepney Children's Pageant, May 1909, Whitechapel Gallery. © Whitechapel Gallery Archive	226
9.2	'The Empress Maud. The Blind Beggar of Bethnal Green and his Daughter. The Coming of William the Conqueror', *Daily Graphic* (5 May 1909), p. 4. © The Bodleian Libraries, The University of Oxford, N2288 b. 17, v. 78	227
9.3	'Queen Elizabeth and Ladies in Waiting', Stepney Children's Pageant, May 1909, Whitechapel Gallery. © Whitechapel Gallery Archive	228

Contributors

Stephen Basdeo is a Lecturer at Richmond: The American International University. He is interested in all aspects of eighteenth- and nineteenth-century social and cultural history, although his research has led to a few areas of focus: he has recently written a book on post-medieval portrayals of Wat Tyler, and another on representations of Robin Hood from the early modern period onwards. He is currently writing *Heroes of the British Empire*, due for release in 2020.

Rachel Bryant Davies is Lecturer in Comparative Literature at Queen Mary University of London. She previously held an Addison Wheeler Research Fellowship in Classics with the Centre for Nineteenth-Century Studies at Durham University. Her first monograph, *Troy, Carthage and the Victorians* and anthology *Victorian Epic Burlesques* analysed contests over the popularisation of the Trojan War epics, especially in circus and burlesque performances. Her forthcoming monograph, *Greco-Roman Antiquity in British Children's Culture, c. 1750–1914* investigates how children's earliest encounters with idealised classical role models embedded Greco-Roman antiquity in private and public life.

M. O. Grenby is Professor of Eighteenth-Century Studies and Dean of Research and Innovation for the Faculty of Humanities and Social Sciences at Newcastle University. He is the author of books on children's literature, child readers, and eighteenth-century fiction, and is author or editor of many essays, scholarly editions and edited collections, as well as co-producer of innovative digital tools designed to engage children and young people with heritage.

Barbara Gribling is a Research Associate in Children's Literature and Culture at Newcastle University, having previously been a Junior Research Fellow in the Department of History at Durham University. Her book on *The Image of Edward the Black Prince in Georgian and Victorian England* (2017) and essay on 'The Dark Side of Chivalry' (2016) explored the contested nature of the medieval past in Victorian Britain. Her new work investigates children's everyday experiences with British history and heritage from 1750 to 1945 in two separate projects: the first focusing on children's encounters with built heritage and the second on childhood medievalism.

Melanie Keene is a Fellow of Homerton College, Cambridge in History and Philosophy of Science. She is the author of *Science in Wonderland: The Scientific Fairy Tales of Victorian Britain* (2015). Her work has explored children's engagement with science from astronomy-themed board games to scientific instruments to the Crystal Palace dinosaurs. Her new research investigates science in juvenile periodicals and medical education in schools.

Helen Lovatt is Professor of Classics at the University of Nottingham. She has worked on the epic tradition in both Latin and Greek literature, publishing *Statius and Epic Games: Sport, Politics and Poetics in the Thebaid* (2005), *The Epic Gaze: Vision, Gender and Narrative in Ancient Epic* (2013) and a co-edited work *Epic Visions* (2013) with Caroline Vout. She currently works on classical reception, resulting in her co-edited volume *Classical Reception and Children's Literature: Greece, Rome and Childhood Transformation* (2018) with Owen Hodkinson.

Rosemary Mitchell is Professor of Victorian Studies and Deputy Director of the Leeds Centre for Victorian Studies at Leeds Trinity University. She is also associate editor for the *Journal of Victorian Culture*. She is the author of *Picturing the Past: English History in Text and Image, 1830–1870* (2000), journal articles in *Nineteenth-Century Contexts*, *Clio*, *Women's History Review* and the *Journal of Victorian Culture*, as well as ten book chapters and over 150 biographical entries for *The Oxford Dictionary of National Biography*.

Ellie Reid is a Local Studies Librarian at Oxfordshire History Centre. She has been a contributor to the Arts and Humanities Research Council-funded project 'The Redress of the Past: Historical Pageants in Britain 1905–2016' and has published on historical pageants and their material culture.

Virginia Zimmerman is Professor of English at Bucknell University. Her publications include *Excavating Victorians* (2008) and essays in *Configurations*, *Journal of Literature and Science*, *Victorian Periodicals Review*, *BRANCH*, *Children's Literature* and *The Lion and the Unicorn*. She has also published a novel for children, *The Rosemary Spell* (2015).

Acknowledgements

This collection of essays has its roots in our first conversation, back in December 2015, at Durham's railway station. The editors are indebted to Bennett Zon, who first suggested that we meet to discuss our shared interested in children's culture of the long nineteenth century and historical pastimes.

That meeting resulted in a conference, *Packaging the Past for Children, c. 1750–1914*, hosted by the Centre for Nineteenth-Century Studies at Durham University in July 2016. We are grateful to Andrew Moss for his assistance in organising the event, and to the Faculty of Arts and Humanities, Durham University, for the financial support which enabled us to bring people together and begin this conversation. We would also like to extend thanks to the delegates who attended the panel, 'Pasts at Play: Packaging History for Child Consumers' at the 2016 British Association of Victorian Studies conference in Cardiff, thoughtfully chaired by Rosemary Mitchell, which helped the editors think through the project.

We thank Matthew Frost and the series editors at Manchester University Press for their efficiency and understanding, and the anonymous readers for their helpful comments. We would also like to thank Jessica Cuthbert-Smith for her expert copyediting.

The volume would not be illustrated without the generous financial support of the Marc Fitch Fund: thank you.

On a personal note, Rachel would like to thank Robin Hellen and Barbara would like to thank Annie Moore and Marthe Tholen for their ongoing support and encouragement.

Introduction: pasts at play

Rachel Bryant Davies and Barbara Gribling

In 1814, John Wallis, one of the earliest pioneers of children's educational games, created his *New Game of Universal History and Chronology*. The game reflected burgeoning interest in play, new forms of didactic media and the vogue for historical knowledge. Our cover image shows a portion of this best-selling board game, which enabled players to travel through time by re-enacting events and demonstrating their modern relevance. Wallis's game, reissued in 1840, gets to the core of this volume: the intersection of childhood, play, and the juxtaposition of different pasts, from the biblical creation through to the reigning British monarch (Figure 0.1).

Players of Wallis's *New Game of Universal History and Chronology* progress through a traditional spiral route: as they moved around the board, they re-enact the events depicted in the medallions which mark each playing space. Players journey through finely detailed scenes, portraits and symbols which miniaturise standard iconography. Miniature, 'Lilliputian'-size books, games and toy-theatre sets were particularly marketed for children from the late eighteenth century as the affordability of printing technologies spurred the new demand for a children's publishing market. Wallis exploits this association to contrast with the vast scale of universal history. Following contemporary fascination with universal history, the game embraces mythical, legendary and religious traditions alongside world history harnessed to British nationalist didacticism: the aim of the game is to be 'appointed First Lord of the Treasury'.[1]

Many of the medallions showcase the different pasts discussed in the chapters in this book, beginning from the Bible: the cover depicts Noah's Ark (also medallion No. 3), and the spiral begins with a portrait of Adam and Eve in the Garden of Eden (Figure 0.1; Figure 0.3). Textual medallions note the 'Kingdom of Egypt' (No. 6) and 'Letters first invented by Memnon the Egyptian'

1

Pasts at play

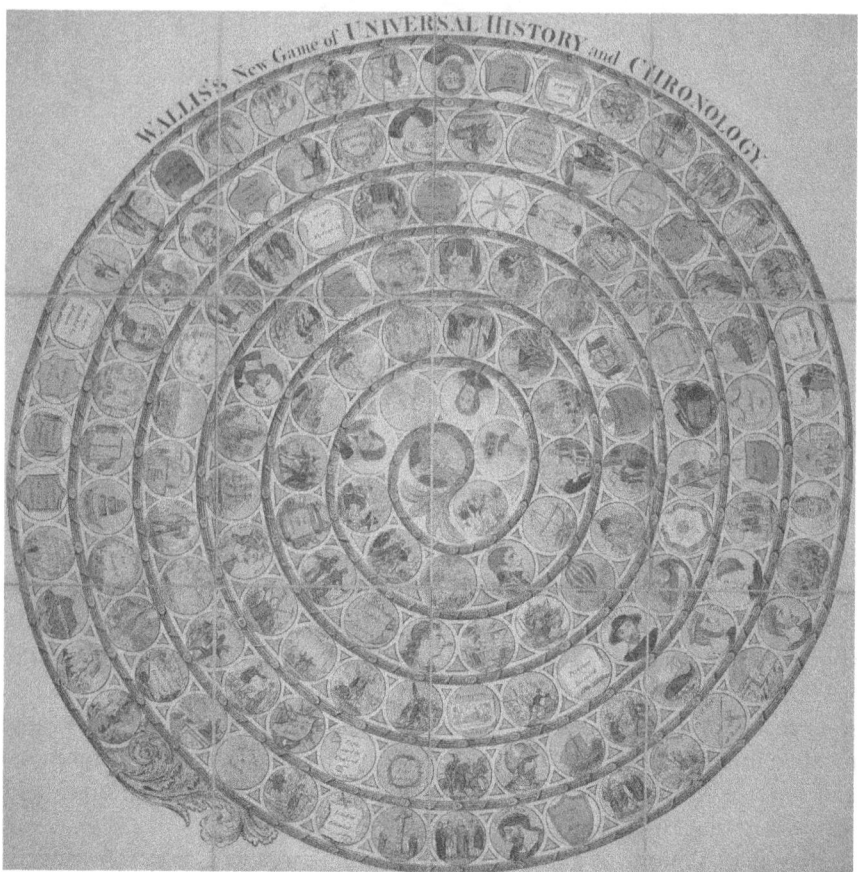

0.1 *Wallis's New Game of Universal History and Chronology* (London: J. Wallis, 1840). Courtesy of Princeton University Library.

(No. 8) while a pictorial medallion shows the 'First ship to appear in Europe brought from Egypt by Danaüs' (No. 12).[2] The classical past was amply represented, as evident in Figures 0.2 and 0.3, for example the foundation of Athens and Rome was noted (Nos. 11 and 18), along with the flourishing of major figures (e.g. Homer, No. 16) and noteworthy battles (Trojan War, No. 13; 'Civil War in Rome', No. 31).[3]

The transition from classical to medieval is instantaneous: in No. 51, the Romans evacuate Britain, but the game flouts convention by jumping directly to medieval concepts of archery and knighthood ('Archery introduced to Britain' in No. 52 and 'Knighthood' in No. 55), rather than the chronological periodisation and progression of monarchies: here, the Saxons do not appear until No. 66 (Figure 0.3). While major national events are represented, such as the

Introduction: pasts at play

0.2 Close-up of medallion playing spaces from *Wallis's New Game of Universal History and Chronology* (London: J. Wallis, 1840), including the first ship which appeared in Europe brought from Egypt by Danaüs, the founding of the Kingdom of Egypt, the wooden horse entering Troy and jousting knights. Courtesy of Princeton University Library.

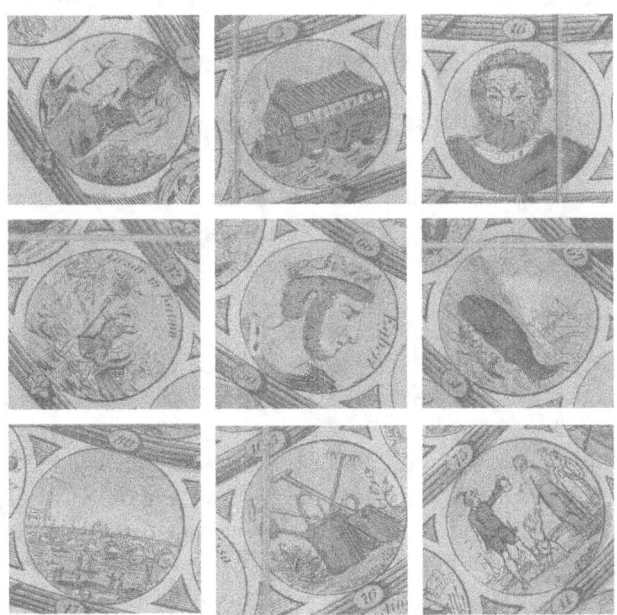

0.3 Close-up of medallion playing spaces from *Wallis's New Game of Universal History and Chronology* (London: J. Wallis, 1840), including Adam and Eve, Noah's Ark, Homer, Caesar in Britain, Egbert, Greenland discovered, gardening introduced, London Bridge and children forbidden to be sold by their parents. Courtesy of Princeton University Library.

Roman and Norman conquests of Britain ('Britain first invaded by Julius Caesar', No. 32; 'Battle of Hastings', No. 76) and the rule of Elizabeth I (No. 110 is the Destruction of the Spanish Armada), the game also aimed to familiarise children with key historical sites embracing national built heritage (e.g. Tower of London, No. 77; creation of London Bridge, No. 80) and including the modern industrial landscape (e.g. 'Coalmines discovered in Newcastle', No. 90) as an historical landmark (Figure 0.3).

The game's attempts at universality are equally selective and perhaps unexpected in a Georgian and Victorian game: for example, in addition to 'Greenland discovered and the whale fishery established by the Norwegians' (No. 67) and 'America discovered by Columbus' (No. 101), other surprises include a watering can (prominent on the cover of this book) which represents 'Gardening introduced from the Netherlands, whence vegetables used to be imported' (No. 103) (Figure 0.3).[4] As 'imported' (to Britain) suggests, the focus remains distinctly national. This is emphasised through the rulebook, which asks players to read about historical events – including some that may have been unfamiliar, both then and now, but were seen as essential to universal history. Recent British history is afforded less explanation within this game (and it is noticeable that Scottish events are almost entirely omitted), whereas ancient Greece and Rome, and modern political events in, for example, Prussia, Russia and Sweden, are described in greater detail.[5]

The role of this historical 'crib' is also unusual: Wallis's rules for this game *explicitly* require reading of the historical crib as part of landing on specific medallions.[6] The possession of knowledge is rewarded, while needing to read up on a forgotten or unfamiliar event is sometimes framed as a penalty; for instance, ignorance of Homer is expensive, costing a player tokens.[7] This balance between requisite and provided knowledge, summed up in Wallis's advertising catchphrase 'amusing and instructive', is a theme many of our chapters explore. An example of the playfulness in contemporary children's publishing, and of the particular national target market, is No. 75, which celebrates 'Children forbidden by the English law to be sold by their parents!' (Figure 0.3).[8]

This market is specifically addressed by the revamped board of the 1840 edition.[9] Whereas the spiral of the 1814 edition culminated in a portrait of George IV as Prince Regent, this later version expanded his space into a gallery of Kings and Queens, including Queen Victoria. The central area of this 1840 edition of Wallis's *New Game of Universal History and Chronology* culminated not with a monarch, however, but with a steam train (Figure 0.4). At first sight, the railway line seems to erupt out of more traditional historical models of cyclical history and so might appear to epitomise the Victorian narrative of linear, teleological historical progression (as epitomised by the floorplan of the Crystal Palace at Sydenham, which moved from ancient art to modern technology).[10] However, players would actually end up moving

Introduction: pasts at play

0.4 Close-up of central medallion from *Wallis's New Game of Universal History and Chronology* (London: J. Wallis, 1840), showing new royal portraits of Victoria and the railway line. Courtesy of Princeton University Library.

backwards and forwards through time and space, repeatedly revisiting some events and skipping over others. Updated central images were not, in themselves, an unusual revision – but the railway train running through a cutting is a much more radical addition and symbol of a new, modern, Victorian age.

In playing with different pasts and juxtaposing the present in one game, *Wallis's Universal History* offers a practical example of how children routinely encountered multiple pasts and reveals how ephemeral and often-overlooked archival material can reveal intersections between children's culture and history. This game is a convenient single artefact that expresses how children's everyday experiences of juxtaposed pasts were made relevant to their present. As an expensive commodity, it only offers one perspective: the elite home schoolroom of early nineteenth-century Britain. Yet, as the chapters in this volume reveal, multiple pasts were often experienced simultaneously in different ways and through different media, by boys and girls across the social classes and throughout the long nineteenth century, for the purpose of amusement and instruction.[11]

It is this intersection between pasts and present in childhood culture that this volume seeks to explore: how does comparing and assessing multiple pasts help us understand their unique cultural work in the British imagination? What was the significance of encountering pasts juxtaposed or individually? And how can visual, material and performance cultures enhance our understanding of pasts at play? These timely questions grow out of controversies emerging from the burgeoning of interest in the uses of the past, consumer culture and childhood, as these are approached by different disciplines in isolation. Yet the intersections between these approaches need to be examined in order to understand the complex relationships between the competing pasts co-existing in nurseries and at school, on bookshelves or in toy cupboards, and in the theatres and museums, where they were simultaneously experienced by children.

The critical field: the uses of the past and children's culture

Scholars from different disciplines have been investigating the question of how the Victorians and Edwardians engaged with the past; this was the topic of a Leverhulme-funded research project, 'Past vs. Present: Abandoning the Past in an Age of Progress' (Cambridge Victorian Studies Group, 2006–2011).[12] More recently, the ERC-funded 'The Bible and Antiquity in Nineteenth-Century Culture' project (CRASSH, Cambridge, 2012–2017) as well as 'Redress of the Past: Historical Pageants in Britain, 1905–2016' project (AHRC; KCL) have emphasised the legacy of different pasts.[13] Alongside these projects, there has been a sustained scholarly interest in classical reception and medievalism[14] – and an increased awareness of different sorts of sources and encounters with the past.[15]

In the past decade, there has also been a developing literature on the ways in which specific pasts have been revived and used in British culture, from the ancient Egyptian to the Tudor and the Stuart past.[16] In particular, children's versions of Greco-Roman antiquity is a rapidly developing area within the field of classical reception, as borne out by the ERC-funded project at the University of Warsaw, 'Our Mythical Childhood'.[17] Childhood medievalism has also become a popular way to assess the reinvention and experience of the medieval past.[18] However, many studies tend to emphasise popular culture after 1914.

Children's culture has increasingly been pinpointed as a means to nuance narratives of everyday encounters with the past and to measure the temperature of historical consciousness in wider society.[19] Jackie Horne's recent study *History and the Construction of the Child in Early British Children's Literature* charts the emergence of history as a genre essential for children to know.[20]

Within the history of childhood and children's literature, children's consumption, children's historical adventure novels and children's periodicals have been significant areas of scholarly study.[21] Meanwhile, there is an emerging focus on material culture, the interactivity of reading and play, and different socio-economic experiences of childhood in historical contexts.[22]

Scope and methodology

The chapters in this volume build on all these approaches by illustrating the importance of integrating children as users of diverse, juxtaposed, pasts. Together, they encompass varied genres and media: sources are drawn from both elite and non-elite contexts and represent the range of material, visual, performative and textual cultures experienced by young consumers. In turn, the dialogue between these different sources as analysed from different disciplinary perspectives illuminates the cultural work of specific pasts. These chapters talk to three central themes emerging from recent scholarship in the uses of the past and history of childhood, as outlined above.

We have chosen to focus our chapters on one geographic space – Britain – in the period between 1750 and 1914, to chart the emergence of books and toys, puzzles and games produced specifically for boys' and girls' consumption: history was a pivotal theme in this educational entertainment market. Commercial children's books were published from around 1744; the first full-length book of original stories for children in English (Sarah Fielding's *The Governess* featuring Mrs Teachum) was not published until 1749. By the 1790s there was a vibrant market for children's educational products, led by the Newbery, Wallis and Darton families.[23] At the same time, spectacular entertainment such as circuses and exhibitions including the Crystal Palace ensured that a considerable overlap with adult popular culture persisted. By the start of the twentieth century, new trends emerged, with pageants becoming a popular form of participatory entertainment for children: 1914 offers an ideal endpoint for the volume since the advent of the First World War, bringing an embargo on German exports – including toys – brought about a clear shift in the children's market in Britain.

Themes and summaries

Our chapters encompass prehistoric, biblical and ancient pasts as well as different periods of British history. Our scope deliberately encompasses the variety of historical, mythical or imagined pasts at play during the long nineteenth century. We have arranged the chapters chronologically, as children often encountered them in history books, games and pastimes, such as *Wallis's New Game of Universal History and Chronology* (Figure 0.1) – as opposed to experiences of exhibitions and built heritage which could, as Virginia Zimmerman and M. O. Grenby show, be more muddled. This structure enables exploration of the 'cultural work' of individual periods as well as contrasting different approaches to the various categories of pasts distinguished during the nineteenth century – for example, archaeological, ancient, medieval and early modern. As we will reveal, issues of consumerism, knowledge and interaction are common to each chapter.

The collection begins with Part I, 'Biblical and archaeological pasts'. Melanie Keene's 'Noah's Ark-aeology and nineteenth-century children' uses Noah's Ark as the focal point to explore the intersections between the biblical and prehistoric past, scriptural didacticism and developing scientific concepts of palaeontology and evolution. Keene uses toy sets of Noah's Ark to enable comparison of different children's media: she compares, for example, advertising material for toys and reminiscences of playing with them, as well as instructions for making these toys in periodicals. The Ark, Keene argues, offered an opportunity to navigate moral values, social interactions, imaginative conjecture and even nascent consumerism as a means of learning scriptural and natural history.

Just as Keene explores the difference between actual and fictionalised encounters with Noah's Ark toys, Virginia Zimmerman's chapter examines real and fictional experiences of ancient artefacts spurred on by archaeological discoveries. In 'Bringing Egypt home: children's encounters with ancient Egypt in the long nineteenth century', Zimmerman exposes how ancient Egypt was just as prevalent in everyday experience as Noah's Arks, especially in the built environment and museums of London. As these artefacts made their way into homes through guidebooks and stories, they exacerbated the tension between the exotic appeal of Egypt as foreign 'other' and the common domestication of this past.

Moving on to Part II, 'Classical pasts', Helen Lovatt's chapter, 'Didactic heroes: masculinity, sexuality and exploration in the Argonaut story of Kingsley's *The Heroes*' highlights how the myth of Jason and the Golden Fleece became a staple of juvenile culture in Victorian Britain. She shows how the story of the Argonauts, previously associated with medieval tradition, was brought back into the canon of classical myth in 1855 by Kingsley, who reworked the ancient poem known as the *Orphic Argonautica*. In examining this 're-classicisation', Lovatt highlights how the choice of ancient source rehabilitates Jason as a moral, even arguably, Christian hero.

Controversy over what sorts of classical knowledge should be familiar to consumers of periodicals in the second half of the nineteenth century is also the subject of Rachel Bryant Davies's chapter, '"Fun from the Classics": puzzling antiquity in *The Boy's Own Paper*'. She examines the craze for interactive

Introduction: pasts at play

puzzles in children's periodicals, setting an eccentric series of grammatical riddles against the broader context of school stories and classical puzzles, which poked fun at both the Classics and formalised classical education. Initially intended to be consumed alongside Latin and Greek lessons, but marketed as leisure pastimes, these articles explicitly negotiated changes in traditional, classically dominated school curricula.

Periodicals are also linked to social change in both Stephen Basdeo's and Rosemary Mitchell's chapters, which represent consumption of 'Medieval and early modern pasts' in Part III. As in Bryant Davies's analysis of classical puzzles, Basdeo's chapter, 'Youthful consumption and conservative visions: Robin Hood and Wat Tyler in late Victorian penny periodicals', explores tensions in historical knowledge perceived as elite: his comparison of Robin Hood and his Merry Men, with the leaders of the Peasants' Revolt, Wat Tyler and Jack Straw, demonstrate that medievalism could be promoted in periodicals intended for boys – periodicals that were both cheap and conservative, such as 'penny dreadfuls'. These (anti-)heroes were, he argues, used less to promote political agendas than to promote morality and to dissuade juvenile readers from crime.

Mitchell's chapter, 'A tale of two ladies? Stuart women as role models for Victorian and Edwardian girls and young women', also draws on evidence from periodicals; this time those primarily aimed at girls and women (such as *Girl's Own*), contrasted with history books. Examining biographies of Queen Henrietta Maria and Rachel Russell, Mitchell reveals how these women – contrasted in their religious allegiances, political participation and national identities – were appropriated to promote domestic ideology and 'traditional' gender roles to middle-class audiences. Although both women were repeatedly translated into historical exemplars despite the inherent ideological challenges, the periodicals – as also shown by Bryant Davies and Basdeo – more easily and playfully blurred boundaries between didactic historical education and leisure.

This intersection between pedagogy and leisure is central to our final part, which explores how different media and forms of play offered new opportunities to engage with a variety of pasts simultaneously. Part IV, 'Revived pasts', begins with M. O. Grenby's 'Tarry-at-home antiquarians: children's 'tour books', c. 1740–1840' which charts the emergence of a new sub-genre of literature – the juvenile tour book – that emerged out of a desire to communicate historical, geographical and antiquarian knowledge to children. While Grenby highlights that elite children were active participants on tours of Britain and Europe, these 'tour books' enabled virtual travel for a wider range of children from elite and middle-class backgrounds. These books' emphasis on both past and modern heritage thus offered up an engaging lesson in nation-building and national pride.

Also exploring change across the publishing market, Barbara Gribling's chapter, 'Playing with the past: child consumers, pedagogy and British history games, c. 1780–1850', likewise identifies how new types of media impacted children's encounters with the past. It begins by identifying the emergence of a children's market for British history-themed toys and games before focusing on one of the most popular history games of the period – *Historical Pastime* (1803) – to explore shifting perceptions of history and requisite historical knowledge. She situates the emergence of these toys and games in an increased interest in play as a pedagogical tool, alongside a new focus on knowledge of British history as essential for children of all ages. Consumed by elite and middle-class children in homes and schools, these toys and games played with royalty, biography and significant 'scenes' to create informed citizens and patriotic character.

Moving into the Edwardian era, Ellie Reid's chapter, 'Re-enacting local history in the Stepney Children's Pageant, 1909', highlights how this event, advertised as the first historical pageant performed exclusively by children, was part of a larger educational mission: to engage local children with British history and heritage. The chapter illustrates the democratisation of history at the end of our period, with the 600 child participants drawn from local schools in London's East End. It also highlights how playful and performative modes of historical learning continued to be adopted – and adapted – as vehicles to engage children with historical events and characters seen to be locally and nationally significant. The chapter follows the story of the pageant from its origins in Edwardian 'pageant fever' and the desire of social reformers to create new educative opportunities for children. The Stepney pageant illustrates children's key role in pageant culture – both participating and shaping locally grounded versions of British history.

Congruences: consumerism, knowledge and interaction

Together, these chapters highlight three central themes: consumerism, knowledge and interaction. They demonstrate how different media, from games to guidebooks and puzzles to pageants, were created for and consumed by children. In so doing, this volume highlights an active and shifting market for history across the long nineteenth century. Each chapter grapples with pinpointing precisely what is it that children need to know about the past and exactly how it should be taught to, and experienced by, them. The chapters chart trends in requisite and provided knowledge, which vary not only by the expected gender, age group, and class of the target market, but also by the media at play and the specific past communicated. Tracking such tendencies through, for example, competing modes of morality and heroism illuminates the importance of different pasts and their cultural work for different constituencies.

Introduction: pasts at play

Play provides a dynamic lens through which to explore children's interaction with the past as a vehicle for instruction.

Wallis's *New Game of Universal History and Chronology* is, as we have demonstrated, a prime example of the process of commercialising knowledge, particularly, as the reworked 1840 edition of the game shows, by identifying and responding to consumer demand. This volume highlights the multiplicity of ways in which children encountered the past. Gribling, Keene and Bryant Davies analyse how playfulness was promoted in different media as the century progressed: from the toys and games which dominated in the first half of the century, through to interactive puzzles and 'how-to' pages which later proliferated in periodicals. Basdeo and Mitchell explore the intersections between the medieval and Stuart past as represented in novels and periodicals for boys and girls, respectively. This interaction between fiction and history is also present in Lovatt's exploration of how the Argonaut story is retold for juvenile and adult audiences. Zimmerman's chapter, meanwhile, contextualises fictional accounts of Egypt with the lived experiences of encountering artefacts in museums and around London. Grenby's chapter surveys the emergence of these types of juvenile encounters with heritage through guidebooks, particularly for buildings around Britain, through charting the development of the 'tour book' in the Georgian period. At the other end of our time span, Reid demonstrates how Edwardian children enacted national and regional heritage through local pageants.

All of these chapters see a concern with what constituted necessary historical knowledge and how best to foster historical consciousness. From the nursery to the schoolroom, the range of artefacts analysed here intersects with changing educational experiences. Some were consumed as part of more formal education: the games and 'tour books' discussed by Gribling and Grenby respectively were, most likely, often played and read as part of home lessons, whereas the Stepney pageant was organised in conjunction with schools. Other media relied on knowledge formed through more formalised schooling: Bryant Davies's study of grammatical riddles and stories of Latin classes illustrates how formal and informal education intersected in innovative and playful ways through children's periodicals. Both Keene and Bryant Davies investigate the pressures, particularly inherent for juvenile audiences, in the gaps between requisite and provided knowledge: even as new concepts of prehistory and evolution rendered once-familiar tenets of scriptural history and classical mythology uncertain, anachronistic jokes and riddles in Latin played with the need to puzzle over supposedly familiar, but actually unintelligible, names. Keene's Noah's Ark toys relied on scriptural knowledge, possibly gained through a Sunday school, while Basdeo, Mitchell, Lovatt and Zimmerman explore different ways in which family activities such as visiting museums or reading aloud promoted knowledge of the past.

Tracking what was expected to be known – requisite knowledge – and what explanations, clues and prompts needed to be provided, allows us to interrogate the sorts of pasts that were considered essential for children to know, what aspects of those pasts were important, and how this shifted across the century. Bryant Davies and Gribling illustrate how expectations regarding children's prior knowledge shifted across the period. In the late eighteenth and early nineteenth century, Gribling's survey of British history-themed toys illustrates changes in assumptions about what a child should know; while Bryant Davies shows that, in the late Victorian period, classical puzzles in periodicals became simpler and relied less on linguistic competence as the curriculum became more crowded.

The order in which different sorts of information should be encountered mattered. As Keene shows, commentators often emphasised that the Biblical narrative of Noah's Ark should be mastered before playing with any toy set or other derivative version; in contrast, Lovatt explains how Kingsley sets out in his preface to *The Heroes* that children should read his fictional retelling in the expectation of learning further classical mythology at school. Guidebooks are likewise concerned with prescribing the order of tours, as Grenby and Zimmerman show: 'tour books' offered a prescribed geographical route with maps (see Figure 7.3), while museum guides dictated a route around the artefacts but were often stereotyped as unintelligible for those without existing knowledge of the information they were, ironically, attempting to impart. Similarly, Reid's pageants were experienced in live performance in an order dictated by chronology.

In every case, the target audience impacted the shape and scope of children's encounters with the past. Price was closely linked to media: the games discussed by Gribling were an integral part of elite and middle-class children's education, while the number of cheaper periodicals discussed by Basdeo, Bryant Davies and Mitchell expanded in the later nineteenth century to include penny papers consumed by the middle and working classes. The 'tarry-at-home antiquarians' discussed by Grenby most likely read 'tour books' as aspirational, while Keene and Bryant Davies discuss how the conflict of 'high' and 'low' culture often led to spoofs. Reid's Stepney pageant, performed by East London school children, illustrates the democratisation of the past in the Edwardian era. Many of these encounters were set up for both boys and girls, despite the gendered differences in formal education: the toys, games, mythological books and pageants discussed here were marketed for both genders, whereas many of the periodicals targeted boys or girls (though were often read by both).[24]

The long nineteenth century saw the broadening of audiences for the past across class lines as well as new intersections between elite and popular culture. The breadth of our selection of chapters enables a comparison of audiences, from the more elite backgrounds of Georgian child antiquaries who explored

Introduction: pasts at play

heritage sites, to the predominantly working-class pageant performers. Our authors also interrogate key points of contention in childhood culture, broaching the relationship between child and adult audiences.

These chapters, as a group, also draw out tensions between the drive to domesticate and familiarise the past and its inherent 'otherness'. By 'domestic', we encompass literal meaning – artefacts for use in the home and everyday experience in terms of curriculum, pastime, environment – but also embrace notions of familiarity, suitability and British national or imperial identities. It has become a cliché that 'the past is a foreign country': the chapters in this volume negotiate the relationship between the British nineteenth-century present and national and 'othering' past narratives, which could both need domesticating.

Zimmerman's exploration of Egyptian mummies (and, punningly, the role of real and fictional mothers in pedagogy) introduces the theme of domesticating heritage through the example of Egyptian artefacts within London's built environment. These chapters expose the difference between the pasts of other countries and the British national and imperial past, which is further complicated through classical antiquity: Britain's own past was 'othered' (through accounts of the Roman conquest and Roman Britain), even as pasts of other countries (including ancient Greece and Rome) were domesticated through familiarity. This is illuminated by the contrast between Lovatt's analysis of the process by which Kingsley domesticated the Argonaut myth and Bryant Davies's examination of the assumption that the Greek and Roman past should be a natural, desirable part of everyday educational experience. On the other hand, Keene demonstrates how the biblical past is literally domesticated, but distanced by new scientific discoveries.

Zimmerman, Lovatt and Mitchell, albeit contrasting very different sorts of pasts, each explore more explicitly domestic ideologies. While Zimmerman examines the assimilation of ancient Egypt into the Victorian and Edwardian domestic sphere, Lovatt investigates how the relationship breakdown of Jason and Medeia – made famous by Euripides' tragedy *Medea* – was avoided by Kingsley, in favour of a more positive portrayal which challenges American models of heroism to rehabilitate Jason as a moral, muscular hero for domestic consumption, and Mitchell demonstrates the problematic domestic appropriation of two Stuart women as role models for Victorian women.

Competing models of heroism rendered historical events a battleground for debates about ideal role models; historical figures were used to promote ideas about religious, national and imperial characters. Whereas Lovatt and Basdeo interrogate masculine role models, focusing on the moral and political respectively, Mitchell contrasts two female role models who enabled the promotion of competing religious and political ideologies. Local pageants, as Reid shows, promoted local heroes and heroines.

Play, interactivity and interaction were critical to understanding children's encounters with the past across our period. The toys and games discussed in Gribling's chapter were explicitly interactive (and indeed, the interactivity was seen to be an essential part of the process of historical learning). As Bryant Davies (and Mitchell) demonstrate, in the Victorian era, the adult editors of periodicals were often overwhelmed with children's submitted puzzles and numbers of competitors sending in answers. Periodicals also, as Keene shows, included 'how-to' columns which provided instructions for children to make their own, cheap, versions of Noah's Ark. Reid's Edwardian pageants showcase how interactive and immersive engagement underpinned the educational and social mission of the pageant reformers, which reinforced knowledge through acting and action.

This interaction with the past was also facilitated by new kinds of media – the objects, performances and texts – that lent themselves to more playful encounters with the past. Zimmerman analyses how Victorian and Edwardian child protagonists drew on Egyptian artefacts to travel, both literally and imaginatively, to different times; while Grenby highlights how the 'tour book' enabled virtual tours of heritage sites. Yet these chapters also illustrate how play and production allowed for creative scope even within a prescriptive framework. Keene's exploration of Noah's Ark toys highlights how many children felt quite unencumbered by the need to stick to existing narratives when creating alternative stories about the past. This was not necessarily intentional subversion, whereas deliberately encouraged, prescriptive alterations are highlighted by Gribling's analysis of board games which enabled players to change the outcome of historical events such as the Wars of the Roses. Some of these games show children's inscriptions and graffiti, and even scrawled alterations recording players changing the rules.

Classical reception and medievalism at play

Such pastimes, such as *Wallis's New Game of Universal History and Chronology*, enabled children to mix up pasts and to play with narrative outcomes. The packaging of these multiple pasts for consumers highlights how children's toys and games hover irreverently between pedagogy and play, between consumption and creativity. As we have shown, each chapter tackles these intersections between consumerism, knowledge and interaction to illuminate the cultural work of a variety of different pasts. The different (inter)disciplinary perspectives in this volume highlight the far-reaching significance of children's culture and its importance as historical evidence. But what happens if one applies a collaborative, multidisciplinary approach – in our case, from the fields of classical reception and medievalism? Alongside our analysis of the Wallis game, another genre we have previously investigated in separate projects was toy theatre. Our individual archival experiences and analysis has convinced us that a collaborative approach (which complements individual discipline-focused projects) can yield new results, by taking us closer to understanding how children might have experienced simultaneous different pasts.

Whereas the Wallis game showcased how historical characters and events were deliberately juxtaposed in order to teach universal history and chronology through a mixture of pedagogy and play, the multiple pasts which co-existed in theatrical leisure culture was not primarily intended for didactic purposes. The toy theatre was another interactive genre which peaked in popularity at around the same time as the two editions of the Wallis game were produced in 1814 and 1840. Known as 'juvenile drama', toy-theatre sheets are comparable to merchandise surrounding modern films, bringing historical subject matter to life by re-creating contemporary theatrical performances for family play at home.

A case in point is 'Skelt's Favorite Horse Combats', which circulated in Britain from 1837 (Figure 0.5).[25] The two combats depicted represent entertainments staged at Astley's Amphitheatre in London, a venue which combined circus ring with theatrical stage and was immensely popular across all sectors of society. The top combat, from *Wallace, the Hero of Scotland* (1815), shows a tartan-bedecked knight goring his English opponent in the neck. The lower combat represents a duel between ancient Greek and Trojan warriors from *The Giant Horse, or Siege of Troy* (1833).[26]

Toy theatres are a fascinating repository of evidence for how the past was imagined, including developments in iconographic details which came to signify different periods.[27] There are obvious similarities in composition in the two illustrations on the Skelt sheet, but the artist has differentiated between the four different types of weapons and armour: Trojan, Greek, Scots and English. The great walls of Troy rise up behind the lower combat; the Scottish landscape above appears to be passed over in favour of a military camp. Many theatrical portraits set in the Middle Ages emphasise a romantic view of warfare, with pitched tents and fluttering flags, while the original *Siege of Troy* privileged picturesque ruins as backdrops for processions, battles and grand tableaux which bore little relation to the actual Homeric epic. Since producers sent artists to performances to capture scenic details, such sheets provide an insight into how the visual elements of performances – staging, scenery, props, costumes and actors – contributed to wider historical visions. The fact that this appears to be a newly commissioned engraving lends all the more weight to similarities in composition, while the decision to juxtapose these two medieval and ancient combats reflects a wider fascination with and reinventions of both the medieval and classical pasts in this period and how they intersected.[28]

Pasts at play

0.5 Toy theatre souvenir sheet, 'Skelt's Favorite Horse Combats', depicting two combats staged at Astley's Amphitheatre in London – the top combat from *Wallace, the Hero of Scotland* (1815) and the lower combat from *The Giant Horse, or Siege of Troy* (1833).

Introduction: pasts at play

Widening Wallis's spiral

This short example, along with our previous analysis of *Wallis's New Game of Universal History and Chronology*, reveals the potential of a different kind of framework for collaboration. Out of this volume also emerge several new directions for expanding the study of childhood and the uses of the past: engaging with different types of media, examining children as creators as well as consumers and widening the scope to adopt wider global perspectives. The chapters begin to draw out new types of media, but also approach media that have been extensively studied in new ways, such as looking at the full range of articles and interactive activities in periodicals as sources for assessing consumer knowledge and engagement.[29] While some of the chapters are able to engage directly with the issue of children as both creators and consumers, and children as active participants, there is further scope to study a wider range of children's creations and children's voices. The scope includes exploring different class, gender, age and ethnic backgrounds and is a burgeoning area for scholarly attention. However, it is not often extended to the uses of the past.[30] Finally, this book is deliberately focused on Britain because restricting the geographical scope enabled the chapters to encompass a wider range of genres and pasts, but an important next step would be to embrace global perspectives, including colonial and imperial contexts.

Wallis's New Game of Universal History and Chronology presents its chosen events as the entirety of the relevant past. Promoting play as vehicle for instruction, it embraces myth, legend, religious tradition and events classified as 'historical'. Its embodiment of the correlation between consumerism, knowledge and interaction sets up this volume to explore the rich diversity of pasts that animated nineteenth-century culture.

Notes

1 Anon., *Wallis's New Game of Universal History and Chronology*, 1814; Anon., *Explanation to Wallis's New Game*, p. 17.
2 Anon., *Explanation to Wallis's New Game*, p. 6.
3 Anon., *Wallis's New Game of Universal History and Chronology*, 1814.
4 Anon., *Explanation to Wallis's New Game*, pp. 11, 14.
5 The only exception is 'The kingdom of Caledonia, or Scotland, revives under Fergus' (No. 49): *ibid.*, p. 9.
6 For example, players who landed on No. 6 'Kingdom of Egypt', No. 18 'Rome founded' and No. 51 'The Romans evacuate Britain' were instructed to read more about these events. This was also true of modern political events concerning other countries.

7 Players who landed on No. 16 'Homer flourished' lost or profited from this special rule: 'If you can say who he [Homer] was, and what he wrote, receive 2 from each player; otherwise, place 6 on No. 13 [which the next player who landed there would gain], and learn there.' Anon., *Explanation to Wallis's New Game*, p. 6. See Bryant Davies, '"This is the Modern Horse of Troy"'.
8 Anon., *Explanation to Wallis's New Game*, p. 11. See Gribling, in Chapter 8 of this book. Another example of this playfulness can be found in Anon., *Explanation to the Royal Game of British Sovereigns*, p. 35, where children who landed on the winning circle were told 'Whoever arrives here first is declared winner, and is recommended to proceed immediately to the Publisher's, to purchase another Game, equally instructive and amusing'.
9 Anon., *Wallis's New Game of Universal History*, 1840.
10 See further, for example, Challis, 'Modern to Ancient'.
11 E.g. on the democratisation of history, see Melman, *Culture of History*, pp. 20–21; see here Chapters 1, 2, 4, 5 and 6, which all draw extensively on cheap print and Chapter 9 on pageants.
12 See Buckland and Qureshi, *Time Travellers*.
13 See the database by Bartie *et al.*, *Redress of the Past*, and Bartie *et al.*, *Restaging the Past*.
14 Jenkyns, *Victorians and Ancient Greece*; Turner, *Greek Heritage in Victorian Britain*; Vance, *Victorians and Ancient Rome*; Chandler, *A Dream of Order*; Dellheim, *Face of the Past*; Girouard, *Return to Camelot*; Alexander, *Medievalism*.
15 E.g. Goldhill, *Victorian Culture and Classical Antiquity*; Nichols, *Greece and Rome at the Crystal Palace*, and on burlesque theatre: Hall, 'Classical mythology in the Victorian popular theatre'; Monrós-Gaspar, *Cassandra the Fortune-teller*; Bryant Davies, *Troy, Carthage and the Victorians*; Vandrei, *Queen Boudica and Historical Culture in Britain*; Gribling, *The Image of Edward the Black Prince*.
16 E.g. Gange, *Dialogues with the Dead*; Zimmerman, *Excavating Victorians*; Dobson and Tonks, 'Ancient Egypt in nineteenth-century culture'; O'Malley, *From Archaeology to Spectacle in Victorian Britain*; Melman, *Culture of History*; Mandler, 'Revisiting the Olden Time'; Mitchell, 'Cavalier Children'; Mitchell, *Household Histories*; Worden, *Roundhead Reputations*.
17 E.g. Maurice, *Reception of Ancient Greece and Rome*; Marciniak, *Our Mythical Childhood*; Lovatt and Hodkinson, *Classical Reception and Children's Literature*.
18 E.g. Bradford, *Middle Ages in Children's Literature*.
19 Mitchell, *Picturing the Past*; Nichols, *Greece and Rome at the Crystal Palace*; Melman, *Culture of History*.
20 Horne, *History and the Construction of the Child*.
21 Denisoff, *Nineteenth-Century Child and Consumer Culture*; O'Malley, *Children's Literature, Popular Culture*; Roberts and Murnaghan, *Childhood and the Classics*. On periodicals, see e.g. Avery, *Childhood's Pattern*; Boyd, *Manliness and the Boys' Story Paper*; Dixon, 'Children's magazines and science'; Drotner, *English Children and their Magazines*; Lang, 'Childhood's champions'; Prince, 'Shakespeare in the Victorian Children's Periodicals'; Pooley, 'Children's writing and the popular press'; Sumpter, *Victorian Press and the Fairy Tale*.

Introduction: pasts at play

22 E.g. Briggs *et al.*, *Popular Children's Literature in Britain*; Grenby, *The Child Reader*; Gleadle, 'Juvenile Enlightenment'; Baxter and Ellis, *Nineteenth Century Childhoods*; Hopkins, *Childhood Transformed*.
23 E.g. Shefrin, *The Dartons*.
24 The 1870 Education Act made schooling compulsory for both boys and girls aged 5–12 in England and Wales.
25 See further, Bryant Davies, 'Through the Proscenium Arch'.
26 Both were popular toy-theatre options: *Wallace* (1822) had previously been adapted by three different publishers as a juvenile drama for miniature performance in table-top theatres at home; *Giant Horse* (1833) had been adapted by Orlando Hodgson in an especially large and beautiful set. See Bryant Davies, *Troy, Carthage and the Victorians*, pp. 47–124; Morton, 'The most efficacious patriot', p. 237.
27 Gribling, *The Image of Edward the Black Prince*, pp. 125–128; Bryant Davies, *Troy, Carthage and the Victorians*, pp. 47–124.
28 This engraving bears no resemblance to Orlando Hodgson's *Giant Horse* engravings. This suggests that Skelt commissioned new images to circulate in a cheaper format: halfpence for the sheet rather than the usual penny or tuppence for toy-theatre characters. The composition is more similar to theatrical portraits which were sometimes coloured and cut out like toy-theatre characters, but more often stuck into albums than manipulated on-stage.
29 Pooley, 'Children's writing and the popular press'.
30 Gleadle, 'Juvenile Enlightenment'; Eddy, 'The nature of notebooks'.

References

Alexander, M., *Medievalism: The Middle Ages in Modern England* (New Haven and London: Yale University Press, 2007).

Anon., *Explanation to the Royal Game of British Sovereigns Exhibiting the most Remarkable Events in each Reign, from Egbert, the First King, to that of His Present Majesty*. 3rd edn (London: E. Wallis, c. 1820) (1st edn 1810s).

Anon., *Explanation to Wallis's New Game of Universal History and Chronology* (London: John Wallis, 1814).

Anon., *Wallis's New Game of Universal History and Chronology* (London: J. Wallis, 1840).

Avery, Gillian, *Childhood's Pattern: A Study of the Heroes and Heroines of Children's Fiction 1770–1950* (London: Hodder and Stoughton, 1975).

Bartie, A., Caton, P., Fleming, L., Freeman, M., Hulme, T., Hutton, A. and Readman, P., Database: *The Redress of the Past: Historical Pageants in Britain, 1905–2016* (www.historicalpageants.ac.uk/pageants/).

Bartie, A., Fleming, L., Freeman, M., Hutton, A. and Readman, P. (eds), *Restaging the Past: Historical Pageants, Culture and Society in Modern Britain* (London: UCL Press, forthcoming).

Baxter, Jane Eva and Ellis, Meredith A. B., *Nineteenth Century Childhoods in Interdisciplinary and International Perspectives* (Oxford: Oxbow Books, 2018).

Boyd, Kelly, *Manliness and the Boys' Story Paper in Britain: A Cultural History, 1855–1940* (Basingstoke: Palgrave Macmillan, 2002).

Bradford, Clare, *The Middle Ages in Children's Literature* (New York: Palgrave Macmillan, 2015).

Briggs, Julia, Butts, Dennis and Grenby, Matthew (eds), *Popular Children's Literature in Britain* (Farnham: Ashgate, 2008).

Bryant Davies, Rachel, '"This is the Modern Horse of Troy": The Trojan Horse as Nineteenth-Century Children's Entertainment', in Katarzyna Marciniak (ed.), *Our Mythical Hope* (Warsaw: University of Warsaw Press, forthcoming).

Bryant Davies, Rachel, 'Through the Proscenium Arch', in Adelene Buckland and Sadiah Qureshi (eds), *Time Travellers: Victorian Perspectives on the Past* (Chicago: Chicago University Press, 2020).

Bryant Davies, Rachel, *Troy, Carthage and the Victorians: The Drama of Classical Ruins in the Nineteenth-Century Imagination* (Cambridge: Cambridge University Press, 2018).

Buckland, Adelene and Qureshi, Sadiah (eds), *Time Travellers: Victorian Perspectives on the Past* (Chicago: Chicago University Press, 2020).

Challis, Debbie, 'Modern to Ancient: Greece at the Great Exhibition and the Crystal Palace', in Jeffrey A. Auerbach (ed.), *Britain, the Empire, and the World at the Great Exhibition of 1851* (London: Routledge, 2016), pp. 173–190.

Chandler, Alice, *A Dream of Order: The Medieval Ideal in Nineteenth-Century English Literature* (Lincoln: University of Nebraska Press, 1970).

Dellheim, Charles, *The Face of the Past: The Preservation of the Medieval Inheritance in Victorian England* (Cambridge: Cambridge University Press, 1982).

Denisoff, Dennis (ed.) *The Nineteenth-Century Child and Consumer Culture* (Farnham: Ashgate, 2008).

Dixon, Diana, 'Children's magazines and science in the nineteenth century', *Victorian Periodicals Review*, 34:3 (2001), 228–238.

Dobson, Eleanor and Tonks, Nichola (eds), 'Ancient Egypt in nineteenth-century culture', *Nineteenth-Century Contexts: An Interdisciplinary Journal*, 40: 4 (2018), 311–315.

Drotner, Kristen, *English Children and their Magazines, 1751–1945* (New Haven: Yale University Press, 1988).

Eddy, Matthew, 'The nature of notebooks: how Enlightenment schoolchildren transformed the tabula rasa', *Journal of British Studies* 57:2 (2018), 275–307.

Gange, David, *Dialogues with the Dead: Egyptology in British Culture and Religion, 1822–1922* (Oxford: Oxford University Press, 2013).

Girouard, Mark, *The Return to Camelot: Chivalry and the English Gentleman* (New Haven and London: Yale University Press, 1981).

Gleadle, Kathryn, 'The juvenile Enlightenment: British children and youth during the French Revolution', *Past and Present*, 233:1 (2016), 143–184.

Goldhill, Simon, *Victorian Culture and Classical Antiquity: Art, Opera, Fiction, and the Proclamation of Modernity* (Princeton: Princeton University Press, 2011).

Grenby, M. O., *The Child Reader* (Cambridge: Cambridge University Press, 2011).

Gribling, Barbara, *The Image of Edward the Black Prince in Georgian and Victorian England: Negotiating the Late Medieval Past* (London: Royal Historical Society; Woodbridge: Boydell Press, 2017).

Hall, Edith, 'Classical mythology in the Victorian popular theatre', *International Journal of the Classical Tradition*, 5: 3 (1999), 336–366.

Hopkins, Eric, *Childhood Transformed: Working-Class Children in Nineteenth-Century England* (Manchester: Manchester University Press, 1994).
Horne, Jackie C., *History and the Construction of the Child in Early British Children's Literature* (London: Routledge, 2016).
Jenkyns, Richard, *The Victorians and Ancient Greece* (Oxford: Blackwell, 1980).
Lang, Marjory, 'Childhood's champions: mid-Victorian children's periodicals and the critics', *Victorian Periodicals Review*, 13:1/2 (1980), 17–31.
Lovatt, Helen and Hodkinson, Owen, *Classical Reception and Children's Literature: Greece, Rome and Childhood Transformation* (London: I.B. Tauris, 2018).
Mandler, Peter, 'Revisiting the Olden Time: Popular Tudorism in the Time of Victoria', in C. String and M. Bull (eds), *Tudorism: Historical Imagination and the Appropriation of the Sixteenth Century* (Oxford: Oxford University Press, 2011), pp. 13–35.
Marciniak, Katarzyna, *Our Mythical Childhood...: The Classics and Literature for Children and Young Adults* (Leiden: Brill, 2016).
Maurice, Lisa (ed.), *The Reception of Ancient Greece and Rome in Children's Literature: Heroes and Eagles* (Leiden and Boston: Brill, 2015).
Melman, Billie, *The Culture of History: English Uses of the Past 1800–1953* (Oxford: Oxford University Press, 2006).
Mitchell, Rosemary, 'Cavalier Children: Sentimental History and the Stuarts', in Susan Anderson, Rosemary Mitchell and Karen Sayer (eds), *Victorian Childhoods* (Leeds: Leeds Working Papers in Victorian Studies, c. 2010), pp. 131–142.
Mitchell, Rosemary, *Household Histories: Gender and Domesticity in Victorian Historical Cultures* (forthcoming).
Mitchell, Rosemary, *Picturing the Past: English History in Text and Image, 1830–1870* (Oxford University Press, 2000).
Monrós-Gaspar, Laura, *Cassandra the Fortune-teller: Prophets, Gipsies and Victorian Burlesque* (Bari: Levante, 2011).
Morton, Graeme, 'The most efficacious patriot: the heritage of William Wallace in nineteenth-century Scotland', *Scottish Historical Review*, 77:204 (1998), 224–251.
Nichols, Kate, *Greece and Rome at the Crystal Palace: Classical Sculpture and Modern Britain, 1854–1936* (Oxford: Oxford University Press, 2015).
O'Malley, Andrew, *Children's Literature, Popular Culture, and Robinson Crusoe* (Basingstoke: Palgrave Macmillan, 2012).
O'Malley, Shawn, *From Archaeology to Spectacle in Victorian Britain: The Case of Assyria, 1845–1854* (Farnham: Ashgate, 2012).
Pooley, Siân, 'Children's writing and the popular press in England 1876–1914', *History Workshop Journal*, 80:1 (2015), 75–98.
Prince, Kathryn, 'Shakespeare in the Victorian Children's Periodicals', in K. Chedgzoy, S. Greenhalgh and R. Shaughnessy (eds), *Shakespeare and Childhood* (Cambridge: Cambridge University Press, 2007), pp. 153–168.
Roberts, Deborah and Murnaghan, Sheila, *Childhood and the Classics: Britain and America, 1850–1965* (Oxford: Oxford University Press, 2018).
Shefrin, Jill, *The Dartons: Publishers of Educational Aids, Pastimes and Juvenile Ephemera, 1787–1876* (Los Angeles: Cotsen Occasional Press, 2009).
Sumpter, Caroline, *The Victorian Press and the Fairy Tale* (Basingstoke: Palgrave Macmillan, 2008).

Turner, Frank, *The Greek Heritage in Victorian Britain* (New Haven: Yale University Press, 1981).
Vance, Norman, *The Victorians and Ancient Rome* (Oxford: Blackwell, 1997).
Vandrei, Martha, *Queen Boudica and Historical Culture in Britain: An Image of Truth* (Oxford: Oxford University Press, 2018).
Worden, Blair, *Roundhead Reputations: The English Civil War and the Passions of Posterity* (London: Allen Lane, 2001).
Zimmerman, Virginia, *Excavating Victorians* (Albany: State University of New York Press, 2007).

Part I

Biblical and archaeological pasts

1

Noah's Ark-aeology and nineteenth-century children

Melanie Keene

Oh the wonderful Noah's Ark! It was not found seaworthy when put in a washing-tub, and the animals were crammed in at the roof, and needed to have their legs well shaken down before they could be got in, even there – and then, ten to one but they began to tumble out at the door, which was but imperfectly fastened with a wire latch – but what was THAT against it! Consider the noble fly, a size or two smaller that the elephant: the lady-bird, the butterfly – all triumphs of art! Consider the goose, whose feet were so small, and whose balance was so indifferent, that he usually tumbled forward, and knocked down all the animal creation. Consider Noah and his family, like idiotic tobacco-stoppers, and how the leopard stuck to warm little fingers; and how the tails of the larger animals used gradually to resolve themselves into frayed bits of string![1]

A leaky boat, wobbling out-of-scale animals, sticky childish fingers and fraying tails or tempers: the experience of playing with a Noah's Ark toy set was fondly remembered by many people growing up in the nineteenth century. As Charles Dickens captured in this characteristically exuberant prose for *Household Words*, certain specific material features of the Ark acted as a time machine to his middle-class readers, immediately transporting them back to nostalgic childhood days. Alongside the doll's house, rocking-horse, or spinning-top, Noah's Ark had found a home in the Victorian nursery as a popular commodity. More than just a toy, however, its intrinsic spiritual heft and ability to conjure a multi-layered series of pasts gave it additional power. In what follows, I explore a range of nineteenth-century children's playful encounters with the pasts of their Noah's Arks, whether engaging with Bible stories, extinct creatures, early human history or even with maritime engineering. The toy sets, I argue, provided a safe refuge in which to embark on imaginative or subversive excursions through space and time, their very domestic materiality

– with all those remembered physical sensations of its use – a familiar shelter from the storms of history.

When *Fun* sent up the Royal Academy as 'Noah's Ark-ademy' in 1868 (John Everett Millais was one of the giraffes), its comic cartoonist assumed that readers needed no further introduction to the biblical boat; moreover, the satirical piece had opened with the purchase of a toy ark.[2] Not only was the scriptural story well-known in the Christianised world of the imperial metropolis, but its visual iconography had settled on a series of stock images, bringing together boat, animals and deluge as punishment for sinfulness in contemporary depictions. Noah's Ark found itself an important and recurrent part of nineteenth-century culture, appearing across a wide range of media targeted at both adults and children: Bibles, conversational works, fiction, alphabets, games, natural history books, periodicals, picture books and – by the early twentieth century – film.[3] But perhaps its most significant presence in children's lives was as an embodied artefact: the numerous nineteenth-century Noah's Ark toy sets which survive today in private, local and national collections – from beautiful examples in London's V&A Museum of Childhood to lonely broken lions in family attics – attest to their vast historical popularity.[4] These toys retained relatively stable and identifiable shapes and contents across the long nineteenth century (see Figure 1.1): a painted wooden boat that more closely resembled a floating barn than a seagoing clipper and – nestled inside or marching across the carpet – matched pairs of wildly out-of-scale animals, identified by shape rather than decoration, and one or more robed human figures. Indeed, Noah's Ark toy sets were such a notable part of the consumer and domestic landscapes that even their characteristic process of manufacture was the subject of periodical articles, and of deposits at the Museum of Economic Botany at Kew. For instance, readers of *All the Year Round* learned in 1865 of the connections between the wood samples held in London, the German toy industry and the means by which individual Noah's Ark animals were standardised by being sliced off an 'endless ring of elephants', doves or donkeys.[5]

In this chapter, I will explore how Noah's Ark could be used as a means of playing, both figuratively and literally, with presents and pasts, and to facilitate moving between different types of media. Boys, girls and family groups, I will reveal, used this particular sacred story as a means of learning not only scriptural and natural history, but also how to navigate moral values, social interactions, imaginative conjecture and even nascent consumerism. I first outline the various ways in which children played with their arks, before taking each layered past (biblical, geological, zoological) in turn to investigate how these meanings were brought together. In the final section, a reappraisal of one children's book unites the chapter's themes and demonstrates connections between literary and material cultures of childhood. Throughout, we will see

1.1 A painted wooden Noah's Ark, c. 1830, given by Miss M. M. Wyley, from Malvern. © Victoria and Albert Museum.

how the Ark embodies the comic potential in the clash of canonical ancient and scriptural narratives with modern science and technology.[6] More than this, the following examples highlight the tensions between past and present in the evolving world of the nineteenth century, in which familiar forms could provide refuge, but also themselves mutate. Underpinning Dickens's remembered chaos and creativity of childhood encounters with Noah and his Ark, therefore, many pasts were at play.

'I play at them going in pairs':[7] Noah's Ark as a children's toy

Two-year-old Edith Robinson was, her father Phil declared, a toddler 'authority' on all things Noah's Ark, her (arguably superior) scribbled separate preface accompanying his to *Noah's Ark; or, 'Mornings at the Zoo'* (1882):

> I am of opinion that no one living can be considered a greater authority upon the subject of Noah's Ark than my daughter Edith, for on the occasion of her second birthday (last Thursday), we gave her a Noah's Ark, and her life ever since has been devoted to original researches into the properties of its various

inhabitants. Not only does she bathe and feed each individual of the menagerie every day, but she puts Noah and all his family, and as many of the Beasts as she can find, under her pillow every night. Moreover, she approaches her subject quite unprejudiced by previous information, and with a grasp that is both bold and comprehensive. This free, generous handling of the persons and animals that have come under her notice, convinces me, therefore, that the contents of this volume will receive from her a fairer introduction to the Public that I could expect from a more precisely critical pen.[8]

Like the main text of *Mornings at the Zoo*, itself a 'comic' reworking of Noah's Ark, this preface was played for laughs, but nevertheless Robinson's punning description of Edith's 'grasp' of the subject gives an insight into how children typically engaged with their toy sets. Edith treated the miniature animals as if they were real; was simultaneously protective and careless of the separate parts; and gave the set her focused attention, with her play being unencumbered by the need to stick to existing narratives. Though both 'Ark' and 'Beasts' are given the honour of capital letters, the sacred connotations are, for Edith, not of immediate concern, the biblical origins of her toy less pressing than their immediate sensory properties, familiar shapes and gifted preciousness.

Many nineteenth-century periodicals also depicted children playing with Noah's Ark toy sets and gave accounts of their being used; often sitting on the floor, setting out parades of animals with Noah overseeing (see Figure 1.2). Jack, the hero of an 1889 'Story of a Noah's Ark' in *Sunday at Home*, the long-running and popular Religious Tract Society periodical, was the lucky owner of five Noah's Arks, a collection he amassed in order of size and complexity (and – one imagines – price). 'First, I had the little ark with the straw roof – I bought it myself – then father gave me the big one last Christmas, and I got the others since.' An older child, Jack's play was more advanced than Edith's, though he had retained a similar affection for his toys; his Noah's Ark sets were to prove a prompt for motivating the plot of the story and Jack's re-evaluation of his relationships with family members as of more value than a material artefact. Jack also connected his Noah's Ark to its origins, as he restaged and recapitulated the biblical story: 'Sometimes I pretend the flood's coming, and I play at them going in pairs, just to see how many I have. But I never can think how Noah managed to arrange them inside.'[9] What was once a theological puzzle for early modern scholars had become a pragmatic problem for Victorian youth.[10]

The difficulties of keeping order or control over the contents of one's Noah's Ark were raised by several commentators. For E. Nesbit, who remembered her childhood Noah's Ark as one of a few key nursery artefacts, a firm imposition of toy taxonomy was essential: 'Keep the Noah's Ark animals in their Ark, and the bricks in their boxes, and when you are going to build don't get everything out at once and make a rubbish heap of it on the floor.'[11] Indeed, without

1.2 Children playing with a Noah's Ark set. Print, illustration by Arthur Boyd Houghton, engraved by the Dalziel Brothers, made for Dora Greenwell's poem 'Noah's Ark', in *Home Thoughts and Home Scenes*, an anthology of popular verse published in 1865. © Victoria and Albert Museum.

keeping things neat and tidy they were liable to break: one commentator in *Leisure Hour* in 1867 took a rather cynical view of the ark market, claiming that the rather fragile toys often need to be 'replaced by new ones', since the 'animals are awfully subject to fractures, dislocations, and decapitations, especially when packed together higgledy-piggledy in Noah's ark'.[12] The author found much humour in the combination of a lowly and common plaything with grandiose Latinate vocabulary and cod-medical diagnosis, waxing lyrical on how:

> the head of Noah [was] jammed fast between the hind legs of a rhinoceros, and Masters Shem, Ham, and Japhet, with their little Dutch wives, reposing topsy-turvey among the limbs, horns, snouts, and tails of unlimited *ferae naturae*, so that, when they have to be let out, they exhibit a doleful array of surgical cases beyond the medication even of the glue-pot.[13]

A certain amount of necessary repair was to be expected after a robust encounter with a boisterous youth, but these objects were just too flimsy: the author lamented that 'they are not made to endure, but to sell – to impart a fleeting pleasure to the youthful possessor, and then to vanish out of his sight and his remembrance, being replaced by new ones'.[14] The conversion to a one-off purchase rather than a family investment was particularly galling with Noah's Arks sets, which were more than just desirable consumer products: intergenerational heirlooms to be passed on from parents to children.

Thankfully, cheaper and more deliberately ephemeral alternatives, made of cardboard, glue and gummed paper, could be made and played through the booming juvenile periodical press, which often ran do-it-yourself columns.[15] For example, 'How I made a Noah's Ark' began as a story on a 'rainy day', where 'toys had been broken', whereupon Mother suggested the children 'try to *make* some' instead.[16] After this preface, the article turned into a how-to guide, with a page of the magazine itself being converted into a blueprint to be cut out. One could even play at Noah's Ark without a toy at all. 'Suggestions' from 'A Noah's Ark party' in the *Ladies' Home Journal* from 1903 for those seeking 'amusing entertainments for children': involves a 'pin the animal on the ark' game, with the different animals. Appropriate prize suggestions include 'giant galoshes, or a gingham umbrella, or a toy Noah's ark', and for those 'whose animals are voted to be in the most hazardous positions', 'tiny lobsters' are suggested as a 'delicately suggestive souvenir'.[17] 'Noah's Ark shadows' was suggested to amuse 'sick children', projecting either a 'Noah's ark [toy set], or a piece of paper cut to resemble one' onto a 'small white tablecloth on string'. Using hatpins and a candle, the animals could be manipulated such that they appeared to move into the Ark, and players were encouraged to add character to their scenario: 'A little objection on the part of the animals to enter … adds greatly to the amusement.'[18]

Rain was often associated with Noah's Ark and used as a prompt to begin discussions or activities, the specific form of weather transcending and connecting histories. For example, in 'A rainy-day game', it was 'when it rained and rained' that 'the children … happened to remember their old Noah's ark'. Inspired by these memories, the protagonists decided to create a new game where they would each have a different boat made from 'a big piece of common brown wrapping paper'. They would 'cut pictures of animals and birds and folks from the old papers and magazines and paste them on' and 'tell each other stories about our families and the animals, where they were rescued and all about it'. The children engaged in both sensory play ('O my! Hear it rain!') and imaginative re-enactment ('Maybe my captain is on land somewhere, trying now to get back to his ship!'). In the end, when 'the sun had come out', 'the seven big pieces of wrapping paper had seven different stories to tell'.[19] The child readers used the prompt of the rain and the existing knowledge they had about Noah and their toy set to construct their own narratives about their present surroundings through play, through reuse of materials from the home, and from past publications.

These numerous examples reveal how Noah's Ark sets were a common feature of nineteenth-century nurseries and came to be seen as a defining and treasured childhood toy. Fictional representations, as well as periodical articles such as party guides or do-it-yourself columns, suggest that children were encouraged to manipulate, rearrange and repurpose Noah's Ark through physical and imaginative play, dealing with common problems such as broken animals, jealous siblings or rainy days. But many of these games were far away from the original, religious, purpose of revisiting the flood story: to emphasise the consequences of sin, and the conviction of faith.

'We'd better have some preachin'':[20] Noah's Ark as biblical narrative

The 'BIBLE is no fit PLAY-THING FOR CHILDREN', preached an early American religious author.[21] But playthings based on the Bible could safely be recommended for even the most evangelical audience: one reason why Noah's Arks were so popular was their sanctioning (indeed, sanctifying) as a suitably devout plaything for the Sabbath, a well-loved passage of the Old Testament manifest in miniature. Children remembered these restrictions on their playful activities later in their lives: for a 'Miss Lyall' and her family, it had been decreed that they 'mayn't have [their] dolls or toys on Sunday', and Alison Utley's brother could play only with a Noah's Ark on Sundays.[22] Such restrictions did not pass without acerbic comment: for the author of 'Children's Sundays', writing in the *Saturday Review* in 1870, 'the recipe for avoiding sin without loss of pleasure is simple. The parent should buy a couple of hundred wooden bricks and a Noah's ark, and with that simple machinery he may set the wiles of the tempter at defiance.'[23] Rather than a coherent attempt to reinforce modes of appropriate behaviour in Christian communities, the Noah's Ark set was perceived as a means of having one's cake and eating it.

Not all commentators were so cynical, and Noah's tale became a favoured means of inculcating moral and spiritual values of particular significance to Christian and Jewish audiences, with many retellings in religious story books, hieroglyphic Bibles, stand-alone illustrations, and poems, across the full range of children's media.[24] Accounts varied in presenting parts of the tale or the whole narrative, and in how it was tied in to wider doctrine. For instance, religious presentations of the story could foreground faith (the Ark as a metaphor for Christian belief, and Jesus as an Ark); devotion and thankfulness to God (who had kept Noah safe); or the importance of refraining from sin. These different formats operated together to reinforce and affirm the plot and wider meanings of the story, as children approached them with various combinations of pre-existing knowledge about characters and events. As with other contemporary games and activities, such as puzzles in periodicals, children were expected to bring a significant amount of knowledge with them. The order in which information was encountered mattered enormously for some commentators: it was clear that the Bible version had to be mastered first, before playing with any toy set or other derivative version:

> But I have been supposing all along that you know all about the original Noah's ark; if you do not, I would not allow any of you to have the toy till you had learned the account given by Moses in the Book of Genesis. It is full of interest, not only for the account itself of the building of the ark, of the safety of those who were enclosed, of the deluge that covered the earth, but far more, as showing that while our heavenly Father hates sin, He is full of love, and ready to save those who love and serve Him.[25]

A material artefact such as the Noah's Ark set was a means by which the important messages of divine love and interest could be repeated and internalised, as evoked in Dora Greenwell's poem, 'Noah's Ark', which accompanies an engraving in *Home Thoughts and Home Scenes* (1865): 'Now does childish play/ That sweet tale rehearse' (Figure 1.2).[26] Many children's interactions with their Noah's Arks remained pious or even twee (in the spirit of the poem), but accounts also present distracted and bored players; for instance, the child in the background who is not engaging with the toy set like the other children, but is staring listlessly out at the viewer. Play could also be irreverent: in a *Messenger* article from 1878 on 'Playing Noah's Ark' the children took 'this tub for a Nark', took on the roles of Noah, walked the animals into the tub 'two by two' and registered them.[27] The overtly ill-spoken children knew that religion was an important part of Noah's Ark but were not sure of the details:

'We'd better have some preachin', I fink;/Noah probably did, I guess'. The central message of sin and redemption was repurposed with live animals at hand, as their pet 'kittens' and 'Old Rover' end up cast as the 'wicked folks/A'left out of the Nark'.[28]

Like the use of rain in earlier examples, Noah's Ark was combined with appropriate aspects of the surrounding natural and domestic environments to lend verisimilitude to the children's playful activities: for the finale, the tub on the edge of the kitchen sink fell in to create an effect which was *'truly'* a flood.[29] As has been shown in scholarly work on hymns in this period, Victorian children were not passive recipients of doctrine, but active agents responding to and reinterpreting material as they re-enacted well-known biblical passages.[30] Deploying their pets as characters in the story, and making the kitchen sink stand in for the floodwaters, the children took liberties with the story, making mistakes and jokes that contributed to their own reimagined version. Perhaps this was not canonical, but it had enough of a recognisable connection back to the familiar aspects of the Bible verse that – to the children, if not to a religious authority figure – it counted as 'Playing Noah's Ark', the title of the article itself. Recent scholarship has explored the ways in which the performances children enacted using toy theatres permitted the creation of alternative interpretations of familiar scenes or stories, as well as demonstrating a 'simultaneous awareness' of 'multiple spaces, temporalities, and contexts during a performance'.[31] The self-awareness of the children playing with their 'Nark' reveals how they could move between the past of the Noah story and their present context in sophisticated ways belied by their rather unsophisticated speech.

Due to the many ways in which children's active engagement with tales and toys was fraught with the potential for reinterpretation for pragmatic, entertaining, or just forgetful reasons, religious presentations of Noah's story required careful management and framing to ensure the 'correct' lesson was being learned.[32] For example, an 1841 conversational work – a dialogue format that was standard in juvenile pedagogy – between 'little Fanny Ackland' and her mother presented a discussion about a Noah's Ark set that had been given to Fanny by her grandmother. Fanny demonstrated good awareness of the object with which she had been presented: it was a 'proper' toy for Sunday and was something she was already familiar with from her Bible. But this was not sufficient for the author, Mrs Bourne, who used a conversational exchange to demonstrate the richness of the Noah passage for teaching a wide variety of religious messages, and also that children's own interpretations or analysis should be curtailed and not permitted to run on without interruption:

> 'Oh, mamma,' said Fanny, 'I know I shall be entertained by looking at, and placing the figures; but what can it teach me? I know all about Noah's ark already.'

> 'I know,' said Fanny, 'that it was built by Noah, at the command of God Almighty, that he and his family might be saved, when the rest of the world was destroyed by the deluge, and—'
>
> 'Stop, my dear,' interrupted Mrs. Ackland, 'there is much to be learnt from what you have already said.' Fanny looked surprised.[33]

For Mrs Ackland, even the briefest of discussions of Noah's Ark could unlock a wealth of educational and doctrinal possibility. However, by the late 1870s, as educational responsibility was increasingly state-controlled and centralised, the toy epitomised, for some, an outmoded past form of religiously determined instruction and play:

> *Lady Customer.* 'My little Boy wishes for a Noah's Ark. Have you one?'
> *Toyman.* 'No, M'um, no. We've given up keeping Noah's Harks since the School Boards come in. They was considered too Denominational, M'um!'[34]

Throughout the nineteenth century, Noah's Ark toys and tales were of central importance in teaching biblical history and content. Children were encouraged to, first, learn the relevant passage from Genesis, and then re-encounter its characters, imagery and plots in a range of other media. But children's own agency was liable to lead them into interpretations that were too far away from biblical scripture, and texts and images exploited ways of managing how their young audiences reflected on, reworked and remembered Noah.

Antediluvian animals: Noah's Ark and geology

That the biblical flood was an historical event was assumed in almost all children's presentations of Noah's Ark across the long nineteenth century, and it could be used as a shorthand for the very earliest ages of the earth.[35] For John Marshall's 1818 *Chronological Star of the World* game of instruction and amusement, Noah's Ark is the second event in the history of the world, preceded only by the Garden of Eden; *Wallis's New Game of Universal History and Chronology* (discussed in the Introduction to this volume) similarly included Noah's Ark as an actual historical event.[36] Noah himself often appeared in children's texts as an historical figure, 'the first person of whose life we have any lengthened account', and the model for all future biographies. Therefore, it is unsurprising that some of the representations of children's play in periodical stories adhere to historical accuracy – for instance, Jack from *Sunday at Home* emphasised that Noah's wife 'only likes goat's milk – they never had tea in the real ark'.[37] New disciplines such as biblical geography and archaeology drew heavily on the story of Noah and his Ark in their attempts to trace the legacy and origins of scriptural narratives as specifically historical documents that related to past events in the Middle East, which could be correlated with present remains or regions. Possible sites for the flood were scouted, just as the locations for other events from the Bible were sought, and the idea that the flood related to a past environmental event gained currency. Alongside an emphasis on the historical landscapes across which Noah navigated or on which he finally disembarked, the people on the Ark were also used as a racialised explanation for human differences: that the descendants of Noah's sons map on to geographic variation – Ham (Africa), Shem (Asia) and Japhet (Europe). Works such as Lyman Coleman's *An Historical Text Book and Atlas of Biblical Geography* (1849) not only used the flood as an uncontested marker of the end of the first historical era, but also carved up the known Hebrew world into three regions named for the 'sons' of the three brothers.[38] Noah's descendants, then, had constructed a family empire that spanned the globe.

The nineteenth century was not only an era in which biblical history and geography were rethought, but also a period of significant change in how the history of the earth was understood: all of a sudden there was much more time to play with. The flood became a key part of the new discipline of geology, which swept up older antiquarianism with new fossil finds and reconfigured the meaning of what were called 'antediluvian' remains: they had been organisms that perished in the flood. Even when expert practice moved on from flood and fire catastrophism to graduated processes, the term remained in use throughout the second half of the century to describe extinct creatures, such as the antediluvian animals – or monsters – sculpted for the expanded Sydenham Crystal Palace display, which opened in 1854. Walking down to the landscaped lake, visitors travelled back in time to reach the prehistoric spectacle that had been reconstructed to appear as if alive before their very eyes. Many children's stories about these animals connected them explicitly either to the flood or to the Ark itself:

Then the antediluvians loomed into sight,

Peter knew them quite well, so he did not take fright;

But when all around him these huge monsters stood,

He felt rather thankful there HAD been a Flood.[39]

For instance, in a story written for the *Crystal Palace Children's Annual* for Christmas 1899 (a thinly disguised marketing brochure), a boy, Cyril, who has indulged rather too much at the tea room dreams that the palace turns into the Ark and the monsters (now alive, and chasing him) cannot get in. Cyril's dream had been prefigured through frequent references to Noah's Ark toy sets throughout the prologue and discussion of the various sights of Sydenham, as well as in an earlier conversation between Cyril and his uncle:

> 'Uncle, are those the ante-ante-what-you-may-call-ems that Noah wouldn't take into his ark?'
>
> 'So we are told, my boy, and I can quite believe it. How would you like to be shut up for forty days and forty nights with such companions?'
>
> 'Ugh – it would be disagreeable, wouldn't it,' with a shiver. 'But, Uncle Tom, were these animals found here after the flood?'[40]

The story plays around with the slightly archaic terminology of 'antediluvian', or 'ante-ante-what-you-may-call-ems', off-hand remarks on how the creatures were not able to get on the Ark, as well as with the limits of Uncle Tom's knowledge, as he is unable to answer Cyril's question: 'Uncle Tom, whose knowledge of scriptural and zoological history is limited, thinks it high time to beat a retreat to the interior of the Palace; besides, it is getting chilly, and so right glad are they both to reach Lyons' Refreshment Room.'[41] The passage thus played around with the expected knowledge of its readers in relation to both palaeontology and Noah's Ark (as well as the real purpose of both a visit and the story, to make the most of the tea room).

By the Edwardian era, authors were still having fun with Noah and the dinosaurs. E. Boyd Smith's picture book *The Story of Noah's Ark* (1905) introduced new discoveries of large American species of dinosaurs to provide an updated version of why extinct creatures were not on the Ark, in a humorous attempt to use the flood to make sense of the fossil record: a sauropod breaks the walkway on to the Ark; and a list of extinct creatures who refused to enter the boat.[42] Indeed, size had been a recurring theme in both analyses of Noah's Ark and also Victoria's Britain, with bigger empire, monsters, machines – and boats – than ever before. Or maybe not quite ever: commentators on the new steamships constantly compared them to the Ark, such as in *Young Folks*: 'Noah's Ark was 81,662 tons burden. This equals the tonnage of about eighty-one first-rate ships of war. It was 547 feet long, eighty-one feet broad, and fifty-four feet high, making 2,730,782 solid feet.'[43] This comparison was not missed by the comic press, who depicted steamship passengers as animals lined up two by two, for instance in J. J. Grandville's *Un Autre Monde* of 1844.[44] So Boyd Smith's humour was perhaps not as original as it was hailed to be by contemporary reviewers, who lauded one 'of the most deliciously comical books of the season. Who would have imagined that Noah and his ship and his vast and variegated zoological collection, viewed with modern eyes, would be so funny?'[45]

'Look at the monkey':[46] the animals of Noah's Ark

Many nineteenth-century children first encountered Noah's Ark through its animals: toy sets, prints, models and books that foregrounded the fauna in their depictions (see Figures 1.1 and 1.3) – and could be used for teaching

1.3 Metamorphic print, 'The Wonders of the Ark', 1845. Children could turn a paper dial to control the boarding of animals. © The Bodleian Libraries, The University of Oxford, John Johnson Collection: Puzzle Pictures Folder 3 (7).

the names and appearances of different beasts and birds. Even when comically out of proportion (as Dickens had remarked in my opening extract), estimations of the overall shape and characteristics of different creatures, from long neck to spindly legs, could be figured out from the most rough-hewn of toy sets.

Accounts also remark on how part of children's enlivening play with Noah's Ark sets was to mimic the sounds of its animals:

> Sophia Isaac Holland kept a detailed journal to chart her son Thurstan's development from his birth in February 1836. She recorded that he began learning his letters in Autumn 1838: 'a few letters now each day', his parents making a start by imitating the cries of the animals from a Noah's Ark.[47]

A later poem on Noah's Ark in *St Nicholas* magazine revolved around the importance of sounds in resurrecting the Ark's animal inhabitants so they can join in the ludic fun: 'We'll wake them up, and make them play/... And bears shall growl, and nags shall neigh.'[48] Others tried, unsuccessfully, to bring the animals to life: in a *Punch* limerick, a reference to a Noah's Ark toy set is a comment on the inert nature of the bought animals:

> There was a Young Lady of Sark
>
> Who bought such a pretty Noah's Ark
>
> But flung it away
>
> On the very next day
>
> Because the blue dogs wouldn't bark.[49]

The use of toy animals such as blue dogs was one way to connect Noah's Ark to natural history, but could it be used to teach about *real* animals as well? *A Picture Book for a Noah's Ark* (1852) thought it could, being dedicated 'To every little boy or girl who has a Noah's Ark'.[50] The author introduced a brief outline of the Noah story in its opening pages, directing readers to 'the seventh chapter of Genesis' if they wanted further information. The main motivation of the text was not religious, but rather zoological, its pages providing a comprehensive natural history guide in a descending hierarchy of animals from lion to beetle. The selection of which species to include was justified in the preface: 'We are not told how many creatures were with Noah. I have described some of those with which we are most familiar, in order that you may know the history of those animals which are generally included in the toy "Noah's Ark".'[51]

The toy, therefore, rather than the biblical account, determined which 200 animals were covered in the abbreviated bestiary, each entry comprising a small illustration at the top of a page, followed by a paragraph of description.

By bringing together a representative (one, rather than two, this time) of each species, the pages of the book were themselves converted into an Ark, just as zoological gardens or museums were also analogised to the Ark, and their keepers to Noah.[52] From the *Athenaeum*, the book received warm if not effusive praise, a reviewer commenting that it contained 'a good deal of natural history very well adapted to the infant understanding'.[53] However, the *Literary Gazette* was much more critical, arguing that the text was too beholden to the past and had not kept up with new developments in scientific understanding:

> WHEN will writers of Natural Histories for children learn something about the science which they profess to make the theme of their stories? Here is a new one as full of popular errors as any sent forth in times gone by. ... Surely it is time that the right interpretation ... should be taught children in natural history as well as in astronomy. They are not told now that the earth stands still, and that the sun moves round it. Why teach them what is equally error?[54]

The reviewers' use of an astronomical comparison helps highlight beliefs that by the 1850s the nascent life science disciplines were entering a new era of research and practice that would mark a move away from the traditional subject of natural history.

However, other authors used Noah's Ark to argue against introducing modern scientific ideas to children: for examples, *Kind Words for Boys and Girls* used an 1866 article on Noah's Ark toys to attack evolutionary theories. It does not matter, 'to us', the author wrote, 'how wisely some foolish men talk when they say that man has come from a monkey, for our men never were monkeys, and are not a bit like them'.[55] Rather facile comparisons were made between the different primates on the boat, in a parody of comparative anatomy, as the reader was asked to compare 'our Noah and his three sons with the monkey – why, they have nothing in common'. The text directed readers to look at the 'splendid long great-coats' and 'high-crown hats' of the people, and 'then look at the monkey, and then tell me if you can see any resemblance'. The reviewer temporalised these evolutionary anxieties with an impossible wish to return to a past before such Darwinian explanations were afoot: 'It is a good thing that the idea [of evolution] never entered the monkey's head; and it would have been just as well if it had never entered anyone else's.'[56]

The Ark's animal inhabitants were, therefore, an enduringly popular feature of the story, and one which gained greater prominence when converted into a toy set or illustrated natural history book. Far from just being used to talk about a past assembled zoological collection, they also provided a means through which current anxieties over changes in scientific understandings of life on earth – and the appropriateness of teaching this to children – could be negotiated.

Biblical and archaeological pasts

A Noah's Ark-aeological narrative: Noah's Ark and children's literature

Comic writer and editor Tom Hood's *From Nowhere to the North Pole: A Noah's Ark-æological Narrative* (1875) not only provides an apposite subtitle to bring together the layered meanings of this particular toy set, but also serves as a useful overview of the themes of this chapter.[57] The work has usually been discussed only in its relation to Lewis Carroll's *Alice* (with which a reviewer's confusion led to a priority dispute) or to other nursery literature classics such as *The Water Babies*, yet its origins also lay in children's material culture as a contribution to Hood's intended book 'to be called "Toys of the World"'.[58] *From Nowhere* was to be his posthumous offering instead, a collaboration with artists E. C. Barnes and W. Brunton, as engraved by the Brothers Dalziel.[59] In its combination of childish play, animation of toy characters, attention to materiality, discussions of modernity and technology, zoology and anthropology, and picaresque narrative of discovery, peril and rescue, it is an ambitious exploration of the redemptive powers of story-telling, and of the Ark itself.

Hood's story opens with the birthday of spoilt protagonist Frank, who not only already owned 'one of the largest Noah's Arks that ever bothered a bishop or disconcerted a Darwin', but 'added to the stock' that day with some of his many celebratory presents.[60] (Seemingly an 'embarrassing number', as Henry Blackburn, reviewing the book, commented.[61]) Motifs that we have seen were common throughout children's engagement with Noah's Ark sets in both prose and images recur, as 'Frank set out all the procession of animals, and then, sitting down in the centre, set himself to contemplating them.'[62] The physical form of the Ark as an anchor for imaginative wonderings was re-emphasised with the reader's attention repeatedly being drawn to the material properties of the animals, including their proportions and practicalities: 'It kept Frank amused for a short time to set the animals up, because some of them would tumble down in such an absurd way.'[63] Frank's hubris as well as his somewhat cruel nature is captured in his relationship with his toy set: although the reader has already been assured that this is 'one of the largest', and by implication best, of the arks, our antihero was not satisfied, and 'began to fancy he could improve on them, or even design others of a superior kind. He found fault with them on various grounds.'[64]

The story deftly weaves together foreshadowing of the adventures and fantastical creatures Frank is soon to encounter (as he 'fell to picturing some of the marvellous creatures he could invent … And then his fancy wandered off into a sort of pantomime dreamland'[65]) with an emphasis on the limitations of his character, as revealed in his treatment of the toys. Echoing the displacement onto animals as more usually seen in moralising children's fiction, where one's attitude and behaviour towards lesser creatures reveals true personality, Frank laughs 'aloud' at the 'funny figures' of Noah and his family; even before the figures of Noah's family come alive, it is hinted that they are more than they appear, since they 'carried sensitive bosoms under their coats of paint'. From its early pages, Hood's narrator sets up the true purpose of his tale: to remould Frank's emotions and attitudes.[66]

Much of the central part of *From Nowhere* leaves Noah's Ark behind, following Frank's travels through 'fairydom' as he enters different realms and encounters an array of strange creatures. Nevertheless, many settings and characters are clearly connected back to his own domestic experiences and are inspired by objects or events from his recent past; for instance, a Germanic-sounding land for broken toys, or the Wallpaperites, caricatures that Frank has drawn on the fading paper of his bedroom walls. Frank also meets new kinds of animals: 'the queerest assembly of four-footed creatures you ever saw … it was as if you had shaken up the Zoological Gardens and the Natural History collection at the British Museum in a bag, until you broke everything into bits, and had then glued the pieces together haphazard in the dark.'[67]

Noah's Ark, therefore, continues to frame his experience of nature: although it is the zoo and museum which are mentioned, the description recalls the more usual broken and glued pieces of a Noah's Ark set which he had imagined creating in the early pages of the story, making hybrid forms such as: 'Zeca-melobra', 'Batonkey', 'Kangarillo', 'Monkape', 'Pigorselope' and even 'Lepuni-corn'.[68] The horrific consequences of Frank's attempt to design unnatural conjoined creatures echo evolutionary concerns over the status of missing links and in-between forms (as famously realised in the productions of Shelley's Frankenstein and H. G. Wells's Dr Moreau). The language Hood's narrator uses is also drawn from the vocabularies of evolutionary adaptation and natural theology, referencing both 'fitness' and design: Frank 'could not but remember that, when he had laughed at the animals in Noah's Ark, and fancied he could invent better ones, he had not proceeded to construct them with any regard to the mutual fitness of the various portions he had designed to join together'.[69] Layers of authority move outwards from the text: in the miniaturised world of the novel's childish play, Frank is the omniscient creator; the commenting narrator reserves an even more overarching perspective; the reader is the final judge of Frank's thoughts and actions.

It is not until chapter 13 that *From Nowhere* returns to 'Noah's notion of the matter', when it is revealed that Noah and his family are aware of the journey on which Frank had been about to be taken when taking leave of them earlier in the book.[70] At this point, having been fully immersed in several episodes of unlikely occurrences and outlandish characters, the treatment of the Noah's Ark toy as enlivened figures is unsurprising to the reader. During a conversation about what the group plans to do, Noah argues that it is the 'duty' of himself and his sons 'as Noah's Arkitects and gentlemen to plan some means of assisting him'.[71] Noah is revealed as the driving organisational and moral force, and his Ark converted into a steam-powered vessel capable of the rescue mission, echoing the common comparisons between the Ark and new Victorian maritime technology and exploration: 'The means are at hand in the shape of the ark, which will take us in safety through the dangers of the Arctic Ocean. We must ... at once steam off northward.'[72] Imperial context and agendas are also apparent during passages featuring Noah and his sons in conversation and during the voyage, which are notable for their racist language and characterisation. Drawing on the common trope from biblical geography and history that the descendants of Ham, Shem and Japhet map onto racial differences, the speech and personality of the three sons is clearly demarcated along stereotypically racist lines. After the toys had arrived at the North Pole, 'hurrying over the snow to his rescue', Frank reverts to babyhood, unable to walk, and is 'wrapped up in thick blankets' in a 'warm corner' of the ship for the voyage home, once again evocatively described, although it is unclear how long the passage takes.[73] Upon their safe arrival, Noah channels the moral of the story in his sermon to Frank: 'I hope this will be a warning to you. Be more considerate of others, less stuck-up with ideas of your own cleverness and superiority, and be, in short – a gentleman!', to which Frank responds: 'I shall, I hope, be a better boy after this', and Frank feels that 'it has done me good'.[74] It transpires that only half an hour has elapsed for the entirety of Frank's adventures: just as the book plays with ideas of space and scale in its shifting geographies and characters, so too does it inhabit an alternative dimension of time.

Within a deceptively frivolous narrative, *From Nowhere* therefore foregrounded the Ark's past religious connotations as a source of shelter and comfort, of salvation and redemption. Unlike that of Carroll's *Alice*, to which it has been compared, Frank's adventure was a narrative of moral and spiritual development, facilitated not just through the educational encounters of his adventure, but by the symbolic and actual help of – specifically – a Noah's Ark set. Like dream-worlds, nightmares and fiction, play is revealed as a sheltered space in which the extraordinary can occur, teaching lessons which can be brought back to the real world once the story is over. However, this play does not occur in *From Nowhere*, despite what the title might suggest: it is structured around existing objects and preoccupations, and necessarily is freighted with such a multi-layered past. Particularly for Noah's Arks, then, children such as Frank were encouraged to use their toys to think about wider consequences and contexts, to choose actions and priorities, and to negotiate between past, present and future.

Tail-piece: conclusion

We have loved Noah's ark from childhood, and we love it still.[75]

Noah's Arks were used to embody layered pasts and interconnected presents for nineteenth-century children. Exposing and considering what one might term Noah's Ark-aeology, and analysing just some of its numerous appearances in nineteenth-century anglophone children's literature and culture, has demonstrated how such objects and their surrounding stories and activities were simultaneously means of invoking actual, mythological, moral and personal pasts. In playing with these objects, children were encouraged to engage in complex and potentially contradictory activities: despite the constraints of the arc of Noah's story, there were many different ways with which it could be interpreted by young audiences. Equipped with a ready-made consumer product, a homespun toy or even just their imaginations, children could re-enact familiar biblical narratives. They could also begin to question the received stories of historical figures or launch into new animal adventures, simply enjoy trying to fit all the small parts into the small compass of the boat, or testing its seaworthiness in the bathtub. On a domestic scale they wrestled with significant questions over the past, present and future.

Some contemporary commentators had been jokingly pessimistic as to the future of Noah's Arks, seeing their inevitable defeat by chemistry sets in the battle of childhood boxes: 'Noah's arks will assume the form of chemical-experiment boxes: the beasts and birds will turn to rows of labelled reagents, and Noah and his family, sticks, little round hats and all, will be transformed into test-tubes and spirit lamps.'[76] But while chemistry sets did become very popular, so too remained the pre-packaged boat, animals and humans. Indeed, Noah's Arks proved (perhaps unsurprisingly) able to weather the deluge of new childish consumer products in the late nineteenth century, its story, connotations and physical form able to adapt to shifting interpretations, and to new media – from picture books to film.[77] Children embarking on Noah's Ark-aeology revealed layers of biblical, historical, geological or zoological pasts: but always came back to the material object and particular story at the centre of this matrix, with meaning as a personal past, passed on as presents to future generations.

Notes

1 [Dickens], 'A Christmas tree', p. 291.
2 Anon., 'Noah's Ark-ademy'.
3 See, for example: Dalton, *Children's Bibles in America*; England, '"The Water's Round My Shoulders"'; Piehl, 'Noah as survivor'; Shepherd, '"Noah's beasts were the stars"'.

4   Brown, *The British Toy Business*.
5   As discussed in Anon., 'Noah's Arks', *All the Year Round*, p. 259.
6   For comic anachronisms, see Chapter 4.
7   Moncrieff, 'The story of a Noah's Ark'.
8   Robinson, *Mornings at the Zoo*, pp. v–vi.
9   Moncrieff, 'The story of a Noah's Ark'.
10 Bennett and Mandelbrote, *Garden, the Ark, the Tower, the Temple*.
11 Nesbit, *Wings and the Child*, pp. 168–169.
12 Anon., 'A word on toys', p. 617.
13 *Ibid.* See Chapter 4 for more on the uses of Latin in-jokes.
14 *Ibid.*
15 This can be compared with advice on making hobby-horses out of 'sticks at hand' and 'next time you play with your wooden *toy* horse … remember the wooden Troy one': Anon., 'Toys', *Kind Words for Boys and Girls* (11 January 1866), p. 12: see Bryant Davies, '"This is the Modern Horse of Troy"'.
16 E. M. W., 'How I made a Noah's Ark'.
17 More Marsh, 'A Noah's Ark party'.
18 Hapgood, 'Ways of amusing sick children'.
19 Fox, 'A rainy-day game'.
20 Anon., 'Playing Noah's Ark'.
21 *The Children's Bible* (Philadelphia: Andrew Steuart, 1763), quoted in Dalton, *Children's Bibles*, p. 237.
22 Quoted in Brown, *British Toy Business*, p. 54.
23 Anon., 'Children's Sundays', p. 375.
24 See Dalton, *Children's Bibles*. For a good introductory survey to material in the Cotsen collection, see: https://blogs.princeton.edu/cotsen/2012/07/noahs-art-designing-arks-for-children [accessed 19/04/2020].
25 Anon., 'Toys', *Kind Words for Boys and Girls* (25 January 1866), p. 29.
26 Greenwell, 'Noah's Ark'.
27 Anon., 'Playing Noah's Ark', p. 6.
28 *Ibid.*
29 *Ibid.*
30 Clapp-Itnyre, *British Hymn Books for Children*.
31 Hofer-Robinson, '"Kaleidoscopes of changing pictures"', p. 60.
32 See Dalton, *Children's Bibles*.
33 Bourne, *[A Companion to the] Noah's Ark*.
34 Anon., 'Toys and their teaching'.
35 See Dalton, *Children's Bibles*.
36 Marshall, *Chronological Star of the World*.
37 Anon., 'A story of a Noah's Ark', *Sunday at Home*, p. 124.
38 Coleman, *An Historical Text Book and Atlas*, Map II.
39 Robinson, *Peter's Paradise*, p. 14.
40 Bridgman, 'Cyril's Christmas Dream', p. 16.
41 *Ibid.*
42 Boyd Smith, *Story of Noah's Ark*.

43 Anon., *Young Folks*, p. 238.
44 Grandville, *Un Autre Monde*, facing p. 285.
45 Anon., 'The story of Noah's Ark', *Watchman*.
46 Anon., 'Toys', *Kind Words for Boys and Girls* (25 January 1866).
47 In Grenby, *The Child Reader*. From Gaskell and Holland, *Private Voices*, pp. 95–96.
48 Anon., 'Noah's Ark', *St Nicholas* (April 1903).
49 Anon., 'Nursery rhymes'.
50 Anon., *A Picture-book for a Noah's Ark*, [p. v].
51 Ibid., [p. vi].
52 See Bennett and Mandelbrote, *The Garden, the Ark, the Tower, the Temple*.
53 Anon., 'A Picture Book for a Noah's Ark' (review), *Athenaeum*.
54 Anon., 'A Picture-book for a Noah's Ark' (review), *Literary Gazette*.
55 Anon., 'Toys', *Kind Words for Boys and Girls* (25 January 1866).
56 Ibid.
57 Hood, *From Nowhere to the North Pole*.
58 Ibid.
59 Blackburn, 'On some illustrated gift books', p. 154.
60 Hood, *Nowhere*, p. 6.
61 Blackburn, 'On some illustrated gift books', p. 154.
62 Hood, *Nowhere*, p. 6.
63 Ibid., p. 7.
64 Ibid., p. 9.
65 Ibid., p. 10.
66 Ibid., pp. 11–13.
67 Ibid., p. 95.
68 Ibid.
69 Ibid., pp. 101–102.
70 Ibid., p. 203.
71 Ibid., p. 204.
72 Ibid., p. 205.
73 Ibid., pp. 222–223.
74 Ibid., pp. 225–226, p. 231.
75 Anon., 'Toys', *Kind Words* (25 January 1866), p. 29.
76 [Smith], 'A little talk about science and the mountebanks', p. 146.
77 Shepherd, '"Noah's beasts were the stars"'.

References

Anon., *A Picture-book for a Noah's Ark* (1852).
Anon., 'A Picture Book for a Noah's Ark' (review), *Athenaeum* (4 September 1852), p. 942.
Anon., 'A Picture-book for a Noah's Ark' (review), *The Literary Gazette* (28 February 1852), p. 204.
Anon., 'A word on toys', *Leisure Hour* (1 September 1867), pp. 615–618.
Anon., 'Children's Sundays', *Saturday Review* (19 March 1870), pp. 375–376 (p. 375).

Anon., 'Noah's Ark', *St Nicholas* (April 1903) p. 450.
Anon., 'Nursery rhymes', *Punch* (14 February 1863), p. 63.
Anon., 'Noah's Arks', *All the Year Round* (5 April 1865), pp. 257–260.
Anon., 'Playing Noah's Ark', *Messenger* (5 June 1878), p. 6.
Anon., 'The Noah's Ark-ademy', *Fun* (2 May 1868), p. 88.
Anon., 'The story of a Noah's Ark', *Sunday at Home* (1 January 1899), pp. 123–130.
Anon., 'The story of Noah's Ark', *Watchman* (7 December 1905), p. 13.
Anon., 'Toys', *Kind Words for Boys and Girls* (11 January 1866), p. 12.
Anon., 'Toys', *Kind Words for Boys and Girls* (25 January 1866), p. 29.
Anon., 'Toys and their teaching', *Punch* (7 December 1878), p. 255.
Anon., *Young Folks* (31 December 1881), p. 238.
Bennett, Jim and Mandelbrote, Scott, *The Garden, the Ark, the Tower, the Temple*: Biblical Metaphors of Knowledge in Early Modern Europe (Oxford: Bodleian Library, 1998).
Blackburn, H., 'On some illustrated gift books', *London Society* (27 February 1875), pp. 149–156.
Bourne, Mrs, *[A Companion to the] Noah's Ark, Being Conversations between a Mother and her Children, on the Animals contained in the Ark* (London: T. Allman, 1841).
Boyd Smith, E., *The Story of Noah's Ark* (London: Archibald Constable, 1905).
Bridgman, Cunningham, 'Cyril's Christmas Dream', *Crystal Palace Children's Annual, Christmas 1899* (Sydenham, 1899), p. 16.
Brown, Kenneth D., *The British Toy Business: A History since 1700* (London: Hambledon Press, 1996).
Bryant Davies, Rachel, '"This is the Modern Horse of Troy": The Trojan Horse as Nineteenth-Century Children's Entertainment', in Katarzyna Marciniak (ed.), *Our Mythical Hope* (Warsaw: University of Warsaw Press, forthcoming).
Clapp-Itnyre, A., *British Hymn Books for Children, 1800–1900: Re-tuning the History of Childhood* (London: Ashgate, 2016).
Coleman, L., *An Historical Text Book and Atlas of Biblical Geography* (Philadelphia: Claxton, Remsen and Haffelfinger, 1874; new edition 1849).
Dalton, R. W., *Children's Bibles in America: A Reception History of the Story of Noah's Ark in US Children's Bibles* (London: Bloomsbury T&T Clark, 2016).
[Dickens, C.], 'A Christmas tree', *Household Words*, 39 (1850), pp. 289–295.
England, E., '"The Water's Round my Shoulders, and I'm – GLUG! GLUG! GLUG!": God's Destruction of Humanity in the Flood Story for Children', in Caroline Vander Stichele and Hugh S. Pyper (eds), *Text, Image, and Otherness in Children's Bibles: What Is in the Picture?* (Atlanta: Society of Biblical Literature, 2012), pp. 213–239.
E. M. W., 'How I made a Noah's Ark', *Child's Companion* (1 May 1880), p. 72.
Fox, Frances Margaret, 'A rainy-day game', *Youth's Companion* (12 September 1918), p. 465.
Gaskell, Elizabeth and Holland, Sophia, *Private Voices: The Diaries of Elizabeth Gaskell and Sophia Holland*, ed. J. A. V. Chapple and Anita C. Wilson (Keele: Keele University Press, 1996).
Grandville, J. J., *Un Autre Monde* (Paris: H. Fournier, 1844).
Greenwell, Dora, 'Noah's Ark', in Jean Ingelow et al. (eds), *Home Thoughts and Home Scenes* (London: Routledge, Warne, and Routledge, 1865).

Grenby, Matthew, *The Child Reader: 1700–1840* (Cambridge: Cambridge University Press, 2011).

Hapgood, Ruth, 'Ways of amusing sick children', *Pictorial Review* (October 1905), p. 39.

Hofer-Robinson, J., '"Kaleidoscopes of changing pictures": representing nations in toy theatre', *Journal of Victorian Culture*, 23 (2018) 45–63.

Hood, T., *From Nowhere to the North Pole: A Noah's Ark-æological Narrative* (London: Chatto & Windus, 1875).

Marshall, John, *The Chronological Star of the World, An Entertaining Game* (London: John Marshall, 1818).

Moncrieff, Mrs Scott, 'The story of a Noah's Ark', *Sunday at Home* (1 January 1899), pp. 123–130.

More Marsh, Marie, 'A Noah's Ark party', *Ladies' Home Journal* (November 1903), p. 55.

Nesbit, E., *Wings and the Child* (London: Hodder and Stoughton, 1913).

Piehl, K., 'Noah as survivor: a study of picture books', *Children's Literature in Education*, 13:2 (1982), 80–86.

Robinson, George H., *Peter's Paradise: A Child's Dream of the Crystal Palace* (London: Simpkin, Marshall & Co., [1890]).

Robinson, P., *Noah's Ark; or, Mornings in the Zoo* (London: Sampson Low, Marston, Searle, & Rivington, 1882).

Shepherd, D., '"Noah's beasts were the stars": Arthur Melbourne Cooper's Noah's Ark (1909)', *Journal of Religion & Film*, 20:1 (2016), 1–27.

[Smith], Albert, 'A little talk about science and the mountebanks', *Mirror of Literature, Science, and Amusement* (1841), pp. 146–148.

2

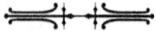

Bringing Egypt home: children's encounters with ancient Egypt in the long nineteenth century

Virginia Zimmerman

The anonymous author of 'At the British Museum', published in Charles Dickens's *All the Year Round* in August 1869, describes the visit of a group of working-class families to the British Museum: adults and children alike are bewildered, perplexed and puzzled.[1] The author asserts that while the 'man of education is thoroughly provided for at the British Museum, to the less well-educated, the Museum is an appalling enigma.'[2] Though the visitors carry a guidebook, they are nonetheless baffled by the displays of antiquities and natural history. The author pays particular attention to the group's confusion in the Egyptian gallery: 'they are not happy among the relics of Ancient Egypt; the scarabæus and amulets tell them nothing they can understand.'[3] The description of this encounter presents Egyptian antiquities as alien and mystifying, and the author asks 'whether the noble galleries and priceless curiosities stored in them should continue a sealed book to the vast majority of those visiting them'.[4] This chapter examines how the sealed book of ancient Egypt was opened, especially to an audience of children, through the strategic use of familiar, domestic language and imagery.

The nineteenth century is bracketed by two military operations in Egypt: Napoleon's campaign (1798–1801) and the 1882 British invasion, part of the Anglo-Egyptian War, that launched the so-called veiled protectorate (1882–1914). These events kept modern-day Egypt in the public eye and put forward, in the news and popular media, the subordination of Egypt to British might. Indeed, as Judith Pascoe asserts, 'enthusiasm for all things Egyptian … was fueled by Nelson's 1798 victory over Napoleon at the Battle of the Nile':[5] thus, Egyptomania is inextricable from British nationalism. These military operations in Egypt also occasioned archaeological excavations, which produced intriguing artefacts as well as narratives of adventure. These artefacts and narratives made prominent contributions to popular culture, bringing the stories and the stuff of Egypt into Britain.[6] Moreover, British literature of the nineteenth century frequently swaddled ancient Egypt in the domestic wrappings of nursery or fireside settings. The displays of Egyptian collections in the British Museum, the Egyptian Hall in Piccadilly and the Egyptian Court at the Crystal Palace in Sydenham empowered visitors who experienced ancient Egypt as part of the London landscape. From encounters in museums and other public displays, to didactic and popular texts, the British replaced bewildering, alien elements of Egyptian antiquities with accessible, familiar elements, essentially bringing Egypt home.

In *On Exhibit: Victorians and their Museums*, Barbara J. Black argues, 'the museum served to legitimate Britain's power at home and across the globe'.[7] She goes on to describe how collecting artefacts is empowering: 'the self initially collects out of curiosity for an other … yet possession ultimately empowers the self because the very act of collecting demystifies the unknown'.[8] Black describes the 'centrality of museums in the lives of nineteenth-century children'. She elaborates: 'Many etchings of nineteenth-century museum scenes portray an art-loving crowd diverse not only in gender and class but also in age. Whether with parents or with school classes, children stand prepared to be educated by the museum's holdings.'[9]

While the public exhibitions at the Egyptian Hall, Crystal Palace and British Museum were not designed specifically for children, children were certainly among the many visitors to these London sites. When visiting exhibitions of Egyptian artefacts, children learned the pertinent history, certainly, but they also learned to view ancient Egypt as a recognisable feature of London life. From mummies displayed in museums to the garish façade of the Egyptian Hall in Piccadilly to Cleopatra's Needle erected on the Thames Embankment in 1877, a child could not walk though London without encountering Egyptian art and artefacts. Indeed, Ancient Egypt was not so much packaged as plastered all over nineteenth-century London.

Ancient Egypt was not only a feature of public life in nineteenth-century London. It also made its way into the private space of the home, through books and images that made pyramids and hieroglyphs familiar even to those children who might never have access to exhibitions and museums. This chapter examines a range of texts, including didactic narratives, museum guides, popular fiction and nursery rhymes, in each of which Egypt is domesticated in one way or another. Guides to the Egyptian galleries at the British Museum highlight recognisable items, such as shoes, and the description of the Egyptian Court at the Crystal Palace merges an ancient temple with a Victorian monument to Victoria and Albert. In both cases, artefacts from a distant time and place are described in contemporary, domestic terms. Likewise, the didactic narratives of Sarah Atkins and Maria Hack deploy descriptions of archaeological adventures to teach familiar lessons of industry, morality and religion. In *The Story of the Amulet* (1906), E. Nesbit sends her child protagonists back in time to ancient Egypt, populating antiquity with modern-day children and their belongings; later, an Egyptian priest abandons his rightful time and place to take up permanent residence in twentieth-century London. In each instance, the text brings ancient Egypt into the present, into Britain and, often, into the home. In so doing, Britain (even its children) is shown conquering and domesticating the past.

'A sealed book'? exhibiting Egypt at the British Museum

The British Museum was one of the most renowned sites to display Egyptian artefacts. While some visitors were undoubtedly confused, as described in *All the Year Round*, others found their visits edifying. A variety of guides attempted to give visitors a robust understanding of the items on display and allowed those unable to visit to enjoy a sort of virtual tour facilitated by ekphrastic descriptions. The author of 'At the British Museum' describes 'a sharp lad of twelve' who carries 'the green guide-book in his own hand, and [is] puzzling himself over the names and descriptions it gives';[10] but, for many, guidebooks made the items on display accessible. In his guides to the Egyptian Rooms, Ernest Wallis Budge, Keeper of Egyptian and Assyrian Antiquities, writes of the fourth room, Table Case F, 'On the west side of this case is exhibited a large and important series of Egyptian amulets, i.e., objects and ornaments which were worn to protect the human body, either living or dead, from baleful influences and from the attacks of visible and invisible foes.'[11] He describes the purpose of the amulets and goes on to describe their appearances. Though Budge was not writing for children, and one could imagine the sharp lad of twelve finding his laborious descriptions overwhelming, his expertise was repackaged specifically for young people in E. Nesbit's children's novel *The Story of the Amulet* (1906). Nesbit consulted with Budge regarding the representation of ancient Egypt in her time-travel adventure, drew from his knowledge in the description of the titular artefact and dedicated the novel to him. She even repackaged Budge himself in the archaeologist character in her novel – the 'learned gentleman' – and sends her child protagonists, on multiple occasions, into the museum.

Juvenile guides to the British Museum were also available; however, their emphasis was often not on the antiquities but rather on the museum holdings as material evidence for biblical stories. Unlike Budge's guide, Anne Chapman's 1849 pamphlet, *The First Visit to the British Museum*, provides no description or explanation of the items on display. Instead, her aim is 'to bring under notice a certain number of interesting objects … to prevent confusion and fatigue to young minds, and to impress them with the goodness and wonderful works of God'.[12] In a short letter to children printed on the title page, Chapman explains: 'The multitude of objects contained in the British Museum would tend rather to confuse than enlighten your young minds: I have therefore selected only things for your notice, as you are in the daily habit of referring to in your Bibles.'[13] She lays out her catalogue in two columns. Headings indicate the room or gallery: in the left column are listed select items with their locations (usually a case number); in the right column, Chapman provides references to relevant passages of scripture. For example, in the Ethnographical Room, an Egyptian water bottle is displayed in Case 10, Shelf i: Chapman refers visitors to Genesis 24:13, 'Behold, I stand here by the well of water; and the daughters of the men of the city come out to draw water.'[14] Yet, only the citation, not the verse itself, is included; thus, Chapman either assumes her reader knows the Bible well and will summon the verse from memory when prompted, or she imagines child visitors carrying their Bibles with them when they visit the museum. With the Bible in hand, Chapman would likely assert, that sharp lad of twelve would not have been so puzzled.

Chapman's assumption that children will be familiar with the Bible offers a different way of domesticating the stuff of the past. The water bottle sitting on display before the child perhaps makes the verse from Genesis more accessible, and the verse from Genesis gives meaning to the water bottle, making it a thing the child recognises from a text he already knows. The selection of items Chapman includes in her guide foregrounds familiar objects of everyday use. For example, in the Egyptian Room, cases 20–21 contain, among other personal items, some shoes. Chapman references Joshua 5:15: 'And the captain of the Lord's host said unto Joshua, Loose thy shoe from off thy foot; for the place whereon thou standest is holy. And Joshua did so.'[15] Other domestic items that appear in the catalogue are mirrors, a yoke, writing materials, spoons, bricks, nails, linen cloth, musical instruments, spindles and assorted jewellery.[16] Though Chapman makes no explicit connection between the past and contemporary domestic life, the items she lists would certainly have been familiar to children. In this way, despite its brevity and simplicity, the pamphlet effectively brings the Egypt of the Bible into the present and into the very English space of the British Museum.

A more extensive assessment of Egyptian antiquities as illustrative of the Bible is offered in Philip Henry Gosse's *The Monuments of Ancient Egypt: And their Relation to the Word of God* (1847). In his preface, Gosse describes his aim to show how these monuments are 'illustration[s] of the Word of God'.[17] Thus, like Chapman, he packages the past in biblical wrappings, presenting children with a text that reinforces their religious education and presents the foreign in familiar terms. Gosse also relies on secular domestic images in his description of ancient Egypt. He catalogues images of private life depicted in tombs, such as 'the steward ... taking account of the stored corn [and] ladies and gentlemen ... seen assembled at convivial parties'.[18] Referencing everyday activities diminishes the distance between past and present. Gosse even asserts we may 'derive an acquaintance with the private life of Egyptians of 3000 years ago, perhaps more exact than we possess of our own ancestors in the times of the Edwards and the Henries'.[19] In other words, Gosse posits that ancient Egypt may be more familiar than British history, and he and Chapman both rely on the Bible to ensure that familiarity.

The Crystal Palace: visiting Egypt in London

Offering an extreme form of familiarity, the Crystal Palace in Sydenham invited visitors to an 'Egyptian Court' in the London suburbs. In Edmund Evans's children's book *Sydenham Sinbad* (1857), Fred, an admired young man, recounts to a group of children his visits to various exhibits at the Crystal Palace. Each visit is presented as a journey, one chapter per destination. The book is an amalgam of an adventure tale, modelled on the original story of Sinbad, and, at the end, a typical catalogue that offers extensive description of what visitors can expect to see. The first journey is to the Egyptian Court, but Fred's description suggests an actual journey to Egypt: 'It was on a fine afternoon last holiday time that not being disposed to read and having nothing particular to do I made up my mind instead of idling about to go to Egypt and be home to tea.'[20] It is only much later in the book, after several journeys have been recounted, that Fred invites the children to guess how it is he travelled all the way to Egypt in an afternoon, and they reveal they had already worked out he was talking about the Crystal Palace.

Fred explains that his narrative is drawn from what he saw at the Crystal Palace but also from information he gleaned from reading:

> The accounts of my travels were made up partly of what I saw there with an eye prepared by reading, mind you, and partly of what is familiar to me in books of travel history and antiquities. I wanted to make you all interested, or more interested than before, in the wonderful things the great Glass Palace of Art contains and, in an attempt to do that, I blended all the information I could think of in any way related to the different Courts.[21]

In an earlier exchange, he invites the children to recall Egyptian antiquities they had seen at the British Museum: 'Amy, Hetty, Bella, Bob, all of you! You have seen Egyptian sculptures in the British Museum.'[22] Thus, he also draws on this other exhibition space with which both his fictional audience and Evans's audience of readers are presumably familiar. Drawing on a range of encounters with ancient Egypt, Fred demonstrates how pervasive such encounters were in nineteenth-century England.

Even as Fred pretends to have been far away in Egypt, he emphasises connections between that ancient civilisation and life at home:

> 'Talking of home,' resumed Fred, 'turning round towards the Temple near which I stood, I could not help thinking that there is no nation of antiquity whose remains place us so much at home with the inhabitants as Egypt ... This is partly because some of the secrets disclosed by the excavations and discoveries of travellers show us that their domestic ways were very much like our own.[23]

Fred's assertion that ancient Egypt is familiar is not actually supported by his descriptions of his supposed visit to the past. It seems to be a rhetorical gesture meant to prompt his audience to seek evidence for the connection. Even if they struggle to find parallels to Victorian domestic life in the journey to Ancient Egypt, they cannot miss the amalgam of two disparate times and places in the design of the court. At the conclusion of Fred's first journey, the Egyptian scene morphs into the very English scene of the Crystal Palace:

> Above the columns there was an inscription which I was enabled to translate though it was in hieroglyphics, and it seemed to me that here was the old trick of erasing one monarch's name and substituting another. For what do you think the inscription said? It said that in the seventeenth year of the reign of Victoria, the Ruler of the Waves, this Temple or Palace ... was erected ... It was very strange to meet the name of our own Queen on an Egyptian Temple, and what was stranger still I heard at this very moment a band playing 'Rule Britannia.' All over this part of the Temple, I found the names of our Queen and Prince Albert and of King Ptolemy on the lintels and on the sides. Now the conjunction of Victoria and Ptolemy was ... very peculiar indeed, and perhaps you will not know what to make of it, though, after I have told you I made the journey to Egypt in the very boots I have on, you will have no right to be surprised at anything.[24]

The Crystal Palace made the past accessible in a diachronic jumble of Egyptian and English carvings. As such, the past was both framed by, and understood in relation to, the present. For child readers of *Sinbad* and child visitors to the Crystal Palace at Sydenham, this conflation of past and present, Egyptian and British, makes the ancient and foreign immediate and familiar. Moreover, as children read about visits to other times and places and as they visit other courts themselves, they learn to find the familiar in the past more generally.

Experiencing Egypt at the Egyptian Hall

While the British Museum displayed actual artefacts and the Egyptian Court at the Crystal Palace was a careful reproduction, the 1821–1822 exhibition of Giovanni Battista Belzoni's finds at the Egyptian Hall in Piccadilly offered a mix of actual archaeological material and careful recreations, displayed in a most appropriate venue: 'The central façade was crowned by a huge cornice supported by sphinxes and two colossal nude statues. ... Alongside the door were stubby lotus columns, and hieroglyphs bespeckled every free surface. ... The words LONDON MUSEUM [were] carved beneath the feet of Isis and Osiris.'[25] The Egyptian Hall was the perfect place to display the artefacts gleaned from Belzoni's travels in Egypt (1816–1819), described in his *Narrative of the Operations and Recent Discoveries within the Pyramids, Temples, Tombs and Excavations in Egypt and Nubia*, so popular it went through nine editions between 1821 and 1841. The exhibition was an immediate triumph: on the first day alone, 1,900 visitors came to see Belzoni's Egyptian artefacts.[26] Along with a scale model of the tomb of Seti I, which Belzoni excavated in 1817, the exhibition featured careful recreations of painted reliefs from the tomb. There were full-sized reproductions of the Entrance Hall and the Hall of Beauties, and fourteen cases displayed an assortment of authentic antiquities, including mummies.[27] Thus, reproductions and real artefacts were mingled together in the Egyptian Hall, which, like the Egyptian Court, brought ancient Egypt to Victorian London.

A description of a visit to Belzoni's exhibition, published in *The Times* on 30 April 1821, emphasised how 'The low roof and the lamp-light sought to re-create Belzoni's first impression as he entered the tomb.'[28] Much as Fred characterises his journey to Egypt in *Sydenham Sinbad*, Belzoni sought to offer Londoners the opportunity to step from Piccadilly directly into a distant space and time. He brought ancient Egypt home to England and wove it into the fabric of modern life. Richard D. Altick discusses an article published in the *Literary Gazette* in March 1822 in which Countess Blessington describes 'schoolboys [who] impishly discover likenesses of one another in the monstrous deities'.[29] Her tone is often satirical, but the description can be taken at face value. Children attended the exhibit and, in seeking familiar images in foreign carvings, they brought a spirit of play to their encounter with the past. Blessington references child visitors again when she recounts a governess inadequately answering her charges' questions, a child asking what a pyramid is, and a mother incorrectly identifying the body of water in a model.[30] Like the Egyptian galleries and the Egyptian Court, Belzoni's exhibition packaged the past, making representations of and relics from ancient Egypt a familiar and accessible part of the London landscape. As with the British Museum and the Crystal Palace, the exhibition was not exclusively for children; however, as Countess Blessington suggests in her description of the Egyptian Hall, children may be particularly adept at domesticating the ancient past.

Egypt at home

While many children enjoyed the opportunity to visit antiquities or impressive reproductions, others settled for encounters with Egypt in the comfort of their homes. As Barbara Black points out, children were encouraged to make museums at home, but even without collections on display in the drawing room or nursery, the past was made available through literature.[31] *Sydenham Sinbad*, for instance, depicts children at home, learning about ancient Egypt, and offers both child characters and child readers a fictional journey to Egypt through Fred's fantastical narrative. Other didactic works take a more realistic approach, dramatising fireside lessons. In *Victorian Popularizers of Science*, Bernard Lightman observes how many educational texts of the early century centred on 'a maternal figure who imparted knowledge in a domestic setting'.[32] In 'Science for Women and Children: The Dialogue of Popular Science in the Nineteenth Century', Greg Myers describes how these dialogues fictionalise the transmission of knowledge: 'in a sense, they are not about science, but about representing science'.[33] In addition to a domestic setting being deployed to make science accessible, domestic objects and processes are pressed into the service of educating young people at home. In 'Domestic science: making chemistry your cup of tea', Melanie Keene explains the appeal of focusing on the familiar: 'in their imagination, children could traverse the far reaches of the globe, searching out leaves in exotic lands and china from China, all whilst remaining in the safety of their familiar domestic surroundings'.[34] The discussions of Egypt in these didactic texts may only loosely be categorised as science, but Myers's point holds. In *Winter Evenings, or Tales of Travelers* (1818) and *Fruits of Enterprize Exhibited in the Adventures of Belzoni in Egypt and Nubia* (1824), Maria Hack and Sarah Atkins, respectively, present cosy domestic scenes in which children learn about ancient Egypt and contemporary archaeological excavations from their mothers. The exotic elements of the adventures are softened by the domestic setting and by the emphasis on the familiar. Moreover, information about Egypt is combined with a discussion of middle-class values, in particular British values of industry and honesty.

In *Fruits of Enterprize*, Atkins repackages Belzoni's narrative for a juvenile audience. The lesson begins as Mamma seeks to resolve a conflict: Laura has been drawing 'tiresome' pyramids, while Bernard wants her to help him draw a very domestic image, a cart in the lane. Mamma aims to show Bernard how interesting Egypt is, and so all the children are gathered in the library to listen to an account of Belzoni's travels and excavations. In this way, Egypt is brought into the home, framed by domestic space and family relationships. Throughout the account, Mamma and the children make the foreign familiar: Bernard says the Temple of Haron would have been a delightful place to play hide and seek, Mamma observes the pyramids are about the same height as St Paul's Cathedral and Bernard recites Jane Taylor's well-known 'A Child's Hymn of Praise' as he expresses relief that in England they are not expected to worship cats and crocodiles.[35] Atkins keeps the emphasis on the home by returning at chapter breaks to the business of that space. For instance, at the start of the fourth chapter, she sets the scene, highlighting domestic space and family relationships: 'Evening came. The curtains were drawn; the candles lighted; and the juvenile party seated around their mother. "Mother always fulfills [sic] her promise," whispered Bernard to Emily: "we need not put her in mind of Belzoni."'[36] In a particularly striking and extended conjunction of domestic and alien, the second chapter begins with the children repairing damage done to their garden. Performing work analogous to the work of excavation, they dig in the English soil, almost literally bringing Belzoni's labour home. When Mamma praises their work, Bernard replies, 'It was Belzoni who first taught me to exert it! You know I saw what he gained by perseverance, so I thought I would follow his example, and not give way to despair.'[37] The gardening interlude reveals the children have already learned important lessons about excavation and industry.

Indeed, Mamma and the children return throughout the narrative to what they call 'our favourite motto': *Labor omnia vincit*.[38] The repeated application of this familiar refrain – work conquers all – is another way of domesticating Belzoni's experiences in Egypt. A common school motto, then as now, the phrase would have been well known to most English school children and encourages readers to associate Belzoni's abilities and adventures with his youth. Indeed, Atkins concludes her account with a discussion of how Belzoni's success is rooted in his childhood. Owen, Bernard and Laura's brother, remarks:

> Belzoni was quite a boy when his attention was first turned to the science of hydraulics; otherwise he might never have gone into Egypt ... Had he not done so, the great pyramid might have remained unopened a thousand years longer; the tomb of Psammuthis ... might never have been explored, and we should never have heard this amusing narrative of Belzoni's discoveries in Egypt and Nubia. How much depends on our youthful pursuits.[39]

Pascoe observes that 'Belzoni, the Italian émigré, becomes in Atkins's account, and perversely, a paragon of English determination.'[40] Certainly, Atkins presents Belzoni as an example of the benefits of hard work, particularly hard work performed by children, and what is alien about Egypt is subordinated to the English values woven throughout the tale.

Atkins's *Fruits of Enterprize* may be the best-known early account of Egyptian excavation published for juveniles, but it is not the only one, nor was it the first. Hack's *Winter Evenings*, in four volumes, is organised by evenings, each offering a different story told by Mrs B. to her children, Lucy and Harry. The stories cover a broad range of subject matter and are unified by the conversation format and an emphasis on lessons learned. The lessons include vocabulary, history, physics and, as expected, morals. The story for the seventh evening is an account of the excavation of catacombs in Egypt. Hack's source seems to be *Narrative of a Journey in Egypt and the Country Beyond the Cataracts* (1816) by Thomas Legh, whom Mrs B. identifies as one of the travellers in her tale. Thus, like Atkins, Hack takes a book published for adults and repackages it for children, capitalising on the entertaining story but also seizing an opportunity to instruct. Also like Atkins, Hack sets the conversation in a domestic space. Mrs B. regales the children with nail-biting drama of mummies strewn about and inadequate air supply with near-fatal consequences, but all the drama is confined to the fireside. Mrs B. describes the catacombs:

> The walls were covered with paintings; and at the further end were two statues, dressed in very gay clothing, having on one side the figures of two boys, and on the other those of two girls. This was pleasant enough: but the whole of the chamber was strewed with pieces of cloth, with the legs, arms, and heads of mummies, which had been stripped of their curious wrappings by the Arabs and left scattered about in a disgusting manner.

'I should not have liked to be of that party, mamma,' Lucy replies, though she goes on to say she would quite like to see mummies intact.[41] The 'disgusting' scene Mrs B. presents is not especially disturbing to Lucy or to the reader since it is offered up in the safe space of the home.

It is worth noting that Atkins appears to have read Hack's *Winter Evenings* and even plagiarised at least one passage of dialogue. Of Egyptian theology, Hack's Lucy says, 'I am glad we were not alive then, or perhaps we might have believed such foolish things, and might have worshipped dogs and cats, and crocodiles too.'[42] Mrs B. responds: 'I dare say we should have been no wiser than our neighbours, and, indeed, I think we ought to be very thankful that we live in better times.'[43] Harry chimes in with a hymn from Isaac Watt. Atkins uses this dialogue word for word, the exchange taking place between Bernard and Mamma. However, while Atkins borrows Hack's dialogue, she chooses a different hymn. Bernard recites Taylor's 'A Child's Hymn of Praise'; Harry recites Watts's 'Praise for Birth and Education in a Christian Land'. Both hymns express the same sentiment, a sense of relief that Christianity makes so-called heathen faiths unnecessary.

Both Atkins and Hack use well-known hymns to assert Christian values over heathen ones, a strategy similar to that of Gosse and Chapman, who present the British Museum as illustrative of Bible passages. All four authors, along with Evans, frame the experience of ancient Egypt with a domestic setting and a Christian, English morality. The 'heathen' faith practised in ancient Egypt is overwritten by the Christian faith and its roots in Egypt as child characters, and presumably also child readers, learn about an alien time and place while the values of their own time and place are reinforced. The lives and cultural practices of those who lived and worshipped thousands of years earlier, the questionable and dangerous experiences of those who excavate the evidence of the ancient civilisation, and the archaeological material uncovered and displayed in Egypt and England are all packaged for children in the familiar wrappings of home.

Edwardian time-travellers to Egypt

The experiences of ancient Egypt considered thus far involve physical encounters in public spaces and didactic encounters in private spaces. This chapter will turn now to the lively fictional encounters depicted in Nesbit's *The Story of the Amulet*, in which the domestic subsumes the alien, just as the present subsumes the past.[44] The story begins with the children's rediscovery of the Psammead, the sand-fairy the children first encountered in Nesbit's 1902 novel *Five Children and It*. In *The Story of the Amulet*, the final of three books that feature Cyril, Robert, Anthea and Jane, the children are separated from the rest of their family. Their youngest sibling is with their mother, in Madeira for her health, and their father is working as a war correspondent in Manchuria. The four protagonists are left with their old nurse, who runs a boarding house in London. Though they enjoy the freedom of exploring London, from the start of the story, they are preoccupied with reuniting their family. Promising they will find an amulet that will give them their hearts' desire – the reassembly of their fragmented family – the Psammead directs the children to a shop near the British Museum, where they find one half of an Egyptian amulet. If whole, the amulet would grant their wish, but, while fractured – like their family – it performs a different magic. The Psammead explains: 'the half has the power to take you anywhere you like to look for the other half'.[45] The half-amulet transports the children to a variety of past times: along with prehistoric Britain, Babylon and Atlantis, they visit ancient Egypt, which is the source of the magic, a magic that weaves together archaeological artefacts and home.

In order to activate the amulet, the children must speak the name written on it, but the name is written in hieroglyphs, what Cyril calls 'pictures of chickens and snakes and things'.[46] Of course, they have no idea how to read the word on the charm, but they quickly realise they have at their disposal someone who is an expert at reading hieroglyphics. The attic room of the boarding house is occupied by a 'learned gentleman' who has 'a lot of stone images in his room', and the children decide to ask him for help with the amulet.[47] The learned gentleman, also known as Jimmy, is an archaeologist and proves to be a great resource not only in reading hieroglyphs but also in understanding ancient Egyptian culture. As mentioned above, Jimmy is loosely based on the eminent Egyptologist Ernest Wallis Budge of the British Museum. Though the personalities of the man and the character are quite different, the likeness in their expertise and influence makes for a meta-textual merging of the personal and the archaeological that echoes the book's central theme.

Nesbit first links archaeology with home in her description of Jimmy's rooms in the boarding house. When the children visit the archaeologist in the attic, they observe a conjunction of domestic space and museum space (Figure 2.1). On the table, the archaeologist's neglected dinner – a cold and congealing mutton chop – sits alongside 'queer-shaped stones, and books'.[48] There are glass cases against the wall 'with little strange things in them' and, behind the door, a mummy-case makes a possible pun.[49] The mummy may suggest the children's absent mother, although if it is a figure of motherhood, it is a stern and unforgiving one, for 'the face of [the mummy] seemed to look at them quite angrily'.[50] The amulet itself is characterised as a kind and loving mother. When the children speak the word of power inscribed on the artefact, it glows and speaks to them with a voice 'like the voice of your mother when you have been a long time away, and she meets you at the door when you get home'.[51] The amulet is a tyet. In *Egyptian Magic* (1899), Budge describes the tyet as having inscribed on it a 'word of power', just as Nesbit's fictional amulet has, and as being a symbol of the blood of Isis.[52] Isis is associated with fertility and motherhood, a connection Nesbit may allude to with the voice of the amulet.

The Story of the Amulet is a narrative of adventure, certainly, but the adventures themselves are always packaged in domesticity, as are each of the pasts the children visit: for example, their experience in prehistoric Britain involves uniting a child and her mother. As U. C. Knoepflmacher explains, 'the transhistorical voyages undertaken in [the novel] are prompted by the desire to recover the mother'.[53] Just as Atkins and Hack use tales of ancient Egypt told by mothers as vehicles for moral lessons, Nesbit uses archaeological adventure to promote the central importance of family. Jane persuades the others of the urgency of their quest, making their ultimate aim clear: 'Don't you think it's worth spending all [our pocket money], if there's even the chanciest chance of getting Father and Mother back safe?'[54] The purpose is not to have an exciting adventure, nor is it to learn history or even moral and religious values. The purpose is to bring the family together. In this way, Nesbit uses the past to tell a story about the present. Black explains how, at the end of *The Story of the Amulet*, readers see 'how every journey has been a cultural lesson – about other cultures but more profoundly about their own. The exotic has served ultimately to confirm the familiar.'[55] Even early in the novel, when the children

2.1 Illustration by H. R. Millar from E. Nesbit's *The Story of the Amulet* (London: T. Fisher Unwin, 1906), 'In the Middle of a Wall was a Mummy Case', showing a group of children looking at a mummy case in a room in an Edwardian house.
© Reproduced by kind permission of the Syndics of Cambridge University Library.

first find the amulet in the junk shop in London, it is tossed in with an array of domestic items: 'there was a dirty silver tray full of mother-of-pearl card counters, old seals, paste buckles, snuff boxes, and all sorts of little dingy odds and ends'.[56] At the end of the adventure, in the future which the children visit, the amulet is in another familiar setting: the British Museum.

When the children take their first journey to the past, they go to Egypt in 6000 BCE, what Jimmy later classifies as 'pre-dynastic Egypt'.[57] Their first impressions may be classified as geographic or scientific rather than archaeological. They recognise the Nile and see a crocodile and a hippopotamus. In just a few lines, Nesbit evokes the features of ancient Egypt with which her young readers are likely familiar. Yet, she quickly makes the scene even more familiar and non-threatening, for the hippopotamus turns out to be a girl:

> 'I believe a hippopotamus is going to happen to us,' said Jane – 'a very, very big one.'
> They had all turned to face the danger.
> 'Don't be silly little duffers,' said the Psammead in its friendly, informal way; 'it's not a river-horse. It's a human.'
> It was. It was a girl – of about Anthea's age. Her hair was short and fair, and though her skin was tanned by the sun, you could see that it would have been fair too if it had had a chance.[58]

Not only is the dangerous animal replaced by a girl, but the girl herself is described as looking quite English, with fair hair and would-be fair skin. Anthea makes the connection plain when she comforts the startled girl by saying, 'We are children – just like you.'[59]

After amiable initial encounters, first with the girl and then with the head of the village, the children find themselves in danger and must escape back to their proper time. The structure of the portal, the amulet enlarged into an archway, illustrates how present-day England and ancient Egypt are physically connected: 'The Amulet grew to a great arch. Out beyond it was the glaring Egyptian sky, the broken wall, the cruel, dark, big-nosed face with the red, wet knife in its gleaming teeth. Within the arch was the dull, faint, greeny-brown of London grass and trees.'[60] When the past is most alien and threatening, the children find the present framed within the amulet and return to the safety of home. It should be noted that, though the children are never seriously threatened in the present, Nesbit does not shy away from showing the threats of poverty in contemporary London. With her social agenda, most emphatic in the visit to the socialist utopia of future London, Nesbit makes a different and less comforting connection between past and present: she uses the social strife of the past to reveal similar struggles in the present. Thus, she at once domesticates the past and de-familiarises the present.

In *The Story of the Amulet*, journeys to the past illuminate the present, the present and the past co-exist at the site of the amulet, and material from the present is transported into the past. In *Portable Property*, John Plotz explains that he aims 'to explore why and how certain objects, artworks, and cultural practices came to serve as metonymic extensions of the home and family Victorians on the move had left behind'.[61] While travelling through time as well as space, the children deposit items from their London present into the past of ancient Egypt, thus making that alien place a fraction more familiar. Anthea wears a bangle – 'a half-penny trumpery thing'[62] – that she gives to the little Egyptian girl. Later, the children deliberately plan out what to take with them when they return to Egypt for a second visit:

> Soon the table was littered over with things which the children thought likely to interest the Ancient Egyptians. Anthea brought dolls, puzzle blocks, a wooden tea-service, a green leather case with *Necessaire* written on it in gold letters ... Cyril contributed lead soldiers, a cannon, a catapult, a tin-opener, a tie-clip, and a tennis ball, and a padlock – no key. Robert collected ... a penny Japanese pin-tray, a rubber stamp with his father's name and address on it, and a piece of putty.[63]

Later still, Cyril presents the broken bits of his Waterbury watch as an offering at an altar 'at the beginnings of belief'.[64] These familiar things, unmoored from their proper time, settle into the past as artefacts-to-be. Just as the relics displayed in museums become integrated into the London landscape, so the children's trumpery pocket things transport the Edwardian domestic to the remote past, a colonising gesture. Following Plotz, we can see that Anthea's bangle, Cyril's watch bits and Robert's putty bring home to the past; in each instance, depositing an artefact from the present and from home protects the children in part by extending the domestic from the present and from England into the past and into faraway places.

The novel's resolution involves a much more striking conjunction of ancient Egypt and contemporary England. Patrick Brantlinger does not mention Nesbit in *Rule of Darkness: British Literature and Imperialism, 1830–1914*, but he does observe, 'In numerous late Victorian and Edwardian stories ... occult phenomena follow characters from imperial settings home to Britain.'[65] The Egyptian priest Rekh-marā, also seeking the missing piece of the amulet, follows the children into present-day London. He appears, appropriately enough, in the middle of a magic show. The magician, Mr Devant, seizes the moment, proclaiming he's produced 'the Ancient Egyptian warranted genuine'.[66] Nesbit deposits Rekh-marā at a Maskelyne and Cooke show, a show that featured David Devant in the late 1800s and early 1900s and that ran at the Egyptian Hall from 1873 until the hall was demolished in 1904. Nesbit ensures her readers connect Rekh-marā to the Egyptian Hall, which had been torn down the year before, when the children struggle to find the show after the nurse mistakenly sends them to 'the Egyptian Hall, England's home of mystery'.[67] Nesbit bundles together the ancient past of Egypt and the quite recent past of the Egyptian Hall in a scene that emphatically places not only Egyptian magic but an actual ancient Egyptian in central London.

To resolve the problem of the Egyptian priest's presence in contemporary England, Nesbit concludes the novel with a fantastical, corporal packaging of the past. The children bring Rekh-marā home from the magic show and hide him in the boot room, yet another domestication of the exotic, until they finally find the missing half of the amulet. As soon as the charm is united, it grants the children's hearts' desire, as promised. They get word that their parents and baby brother will be arriving shortly, and the story's central problem – the fractured home – is resolved. However, Rekh-marā is still at large in 1906, and the children must tidy up this last loose end. At first, they propose the Egyptian can simply live out his days in contemporary London, but the Psammead explains this is not possible: 'nobody can continue to live in a land and in a time not appointed'.[68] Nesbit tests this rule with an earlier episode when the poor London street urchin Imogen is adopted by a loving mother in Roman Britain, but it is not clear in this instance which time is in fact Imogen's appointed time. The mother-of-the-past recognises the child and claims her as her own. When the learned gentleman asks if Imogen is truly this woman's child, the Psammead answers, 'Who knows? … each one fills the empty place in the other's heart. It is enough.'[69] Nesbit reprises this mode of making a family across time at the end of the novel when Rekh-marā is able to stay in the present through a sort of marriage with Jimmy.

The Psammead describes how the past can become one with the present: 'a soul may live [in another time], if in that other time and land there may be found a soul so akin to it as to offer it refuge, in the body of that land and time, that thus they two may be one soul in one body'.[70] Imogen and her mother do not share one body, but Rekh-marā and Jimmy do. Nesbit writes:

> [Their] eyes met, and were kind to each other, and promised each other many things … Rekh-marā quavered and shook, and as steel is drawn to a magnet he was drawn, under the arch of magic, nearer and nearer to the learned gentleman. And, as one drop of water mingles with another, when the window-glass is rain-wrinkled, as one quick-silver bead is drawn to another quick-silver bead, Rekh-marā, Divine Father of the Temple of Amen-Ra, was drawn into, slipped into, disappeared into, and was one with Jimmy, the good, the beloved, the learned gentleman.[71]

Thus, Egypt is brought not only into England and into the home, but into the very body of an Englishman. While this could be unsettling, Nesbit's

Biblical and archaeological pasts

language is filled with joy, and the union of Rekh-marā and Jimmy can be read as a happy personification of the absorption of ancient Egypt into England that runs throughout *The Story of the Amulet* and, indeed, throughout the long nineteenth century.

Conclusion: Mother Goose in hieroglyphics

I will conclude with a book that so thoroughly packages ancient Egypt in domestic wrappings that hieroglyphics are rewritten as a language of the nursery. In *Mother Goose in Hieroglyphics* (1849), key words in the familiar rhymes are replaced with pictures. For instance, in 'Little Jack Horner', a picture of a horn stands in for the syllable 'horn' and an ear of corn replaces the first part of the word 'corner' (see Figure 2.2).[72] Obviously, these are not actually Egyptian hieroglyphs, but the author takes advantage of the readers' familiarity with and interest in Egyptian writing. Replacing true hieroglyphs with these everyday images supplants the otherness of Egypt with the familiarity of home. The only explicit reference to Egypt in *Mother Goose in Hieroglyphics*

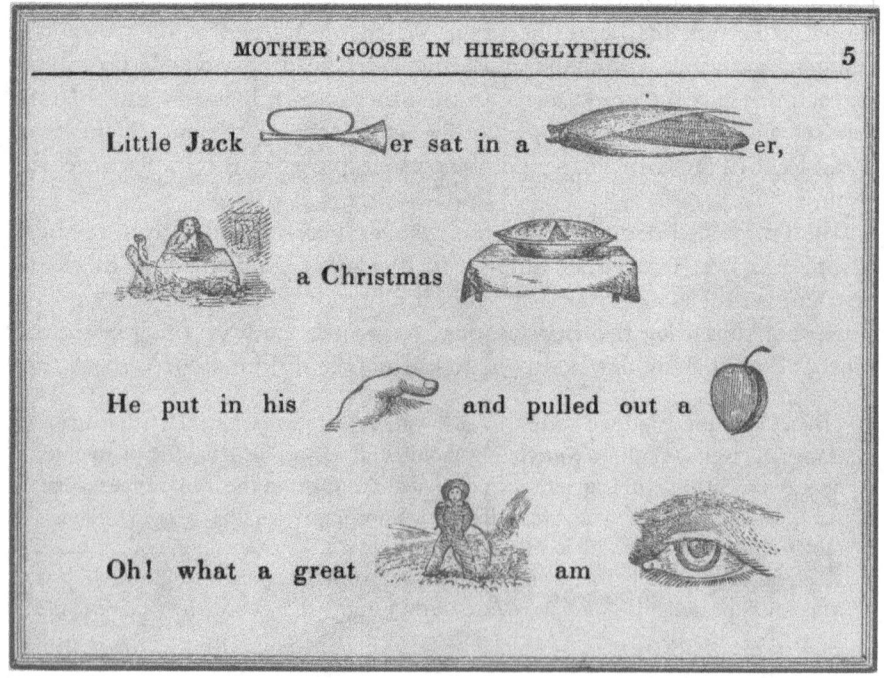

2.2 'Little Jack Horner' from *Mother Goose in Hieroglyphics* (Boston: Brown, Taggard & Chase, 1849), p. 5.

comes in the preface, in which the author exhorts the reader to purchase this book because for a sick or restless child what is wanted is 'a pretty book, written in pictures, as they wrote in Egypt a long while ago, when folks knew something, about the time when Mother Goose herself was a little gosling'.[73] The notion that Mother Goose might have originated in the time of the pharaohs is a colonising gesture, similar to those described by Plotz: like Anthea's bangle, Mother Goose is deposited, albeit in an off-hand sort of way, in the remote past of ancient Egypt. Thus, the past is made familiar just as the signs of the past – in this case hieroglyphics – are repackaged in the present. The domestic images shown in *Mother Goose in Hieroglyphics* are familiar, and the text itself is a nursery staple. Thus, it brings ancient Egypt home and thoroughly domesticates it.

Bringing Egypt home mitigates otherness: the mummy is demystified as it sits in a museum gallery (or an attic flat), Rekh-marā is subsumed within the body and soul of Jimmy, and Belzoni's adventures are replicated in the garden at home. Yet, these texts also reimagine England and the English home as places that include the foreign and the ancient. The geographically and temporally alien may be assimilated into the domestic, dominated by the present and by various notions of home, but the alien is there all the same. The presence of Egypt at home, in the Egyptian Hall or at the fireside, reveals that England contains within itself this remote past. Yet, just as the threat of Rekh-marā is contained within Jimmy, the alien past of ancient Egypt is carefully packaged in narratives that subordinate and domesticate antiquity.

Whether children read about artefacts or visit them in museums, whether they enjoy Nesbit's fantasy or learn from Atkins's lessons, in all the case studies examined here ancient Egypt is made accessible to a wide range of British children, those who live in London and have the means and opportunity to visit the British Museum, Egyptian Hall or Crystal Palace as well as those who enjoy these places only in the pages of books. Atkins, Hack and Evans depict children experiencing Egypt from home and through their narratives and offer such experiences to their readers. Nesbit and the unknown author of *Mother Goose in Hieroglyphics* entwine antiquity and domesticity and make ancient Egypt available in unexpected and captivating ways, highlighting how it is novel even as they go to great lengths to fold the foreign into the domestic. The variety of texts considered here reveals that bringing ancient Egypt into modern-day Britain was not only the project of writers of fantasy or those with a religious agenda; in multiple media, throughout the long nineteenth century, children encounter artefacts, stories and people from ancient Egypt and, time and again, they find that material woven into the fabric of home. On one level, this is a strategy to make the past accessible to young people, but on a deeper level, the pattern discussed here reveals yet another notch in Britain's imperial conquest. The British celebration of their might over Egypt extended even to the conquest of ancient Egypt, thoroughly domesticated and anglicised for children and the adults who accompany them on journeys through galleries and texts.

Notes

1. Anon., 'At the British Museum', p. 252.
2. *Ibid.*, p. 254.
3. *Ibid.*, p. 253.
4. *Ibid.*, p. 255.
5. Pascoe, *The Hummingbird Cabinet*, p. 111.
6. Writers took ancient Egypt as a compelling setting in works of historical fiction, such as G. A. Henty's *The Cat of Bubastes* (1889), and travel narratives, such as those of Richard Francis Burton, described journeys through Egypt. Many writers set Biblical stories in Egypt: *Rescued from Egypt* (1866) by the prolific A.L.O.E. and *Dr. Brewer's Guide to Scripture History*, referenced by Jane in Nesbit's *Story of the Amulet*, discussed below, are two examples.
7. Black, *On Exhibit*, p. 11.
8. *Ibid.*, p. 22.
9. *Ibid.*, p. 150.
10. Anon., 'At the British Museum', p. 252.
11. [Budge] and British Museum, *Guide to the Third and Fourth Egyptian Rooms*, p. 209.
12. Chapman, *First Visit*, n.p.
13. *Ibid.*, [p. 4].
14. Holy Bible, King James Version. Chapman, *First Visit*, [p. 4].
15. The Holy Bible. Chapman, *First Visit*, [p. 14].
16. *Ibid.*, [pp. 13–15].
17. Gosse, *Monuments of Ancient Egypt*, p. v.
18. *Ibid.*, p. 7.
19. *Ibid.*, p. 8.
20. Evans, *Sydenham Sinbad*, p. 7.
21. *Ibid.*, p. 131.
22. *Ibid.*, p. 15.
23. *Ibid.*, p. 17.
24. *Ibid.*, p. 19.
25. Altick, *Shows of London*, p. 236.
26. *Ibid.*, p. 245.
27. Pearce, 'Giovanni Battista Belzoni's exhibition', p. 112.
28. Quoted in Altick, *Shows of London*, p. 245.
29. *Ibid.*, p. 245.
30. *Ibid.*, pp. 245–246.
31. Black, *On Exhibit*, p. 150.
32. Lightman, *Victorian Popularizers of Science*, p. 129.
33. Myers, 'Science for Women and Children', p. 172.

34 Keene, 'Domestic science', p.19.
35 [Atkins], *Fruits of Enterprize*, pp. 231, 156, 114.
36 *Ibid.*, p. 163.
37 *Ibid.*, p. 89.
38 *Ibid.*, p. 161.
39 *Ibid.*, p. 278.
40 Pascoe, *Hummingbird Cabinet*, p. 123.
41 Hack, *Winter Evenings*, p. 65.
42 *Ibid.*, p. 69.
43 *Ibid.*
44 A related discussion of Nesbit's novel appears in Zimmerman, 'Excavating Children'.
45 Nesbit and Millar, *Story of the Amulet*, p. 32.
46 *Ibid.*, p. 33.
47 *Ibid.*, p. 33.
48 *Ibid.*, p. 35.
49 *Ibid.*
50 *Ibid.*, p. 36.
51 *Ibid.*, p. 44.
52 Budge, *Egyptian Magic*, p. 47.
53 Knoepflmacher, 'Of Babylands and Babylons', p. 315.
54 Nesbit, *Story of the Amulet*, p. 25.
55 Black, *On Exhibit*, p. 162.
56 Nesbit, *Story of the Amulet*, p. 26.
57 *Ibid.*, p. 85.
58 *Ibid.*, p. 56.
59 *Ibid.*, p. 58.
60 *Ibid.*, pp. 81–82.
61 Plotz, *Portable Property*, p. xiii.
62 Nesbit, *Story of the Amulet*, p. 58.
63 *Ibid.*, p. 203.
64 *Ibid.*, p. 283.
65 Brantlinger, *Rule of Darkness*, pp. 230–231.
66 Nesbit, *Story of the Amulet*, p. 272.
67 *Ibid.*, p. 270.
68 *Ibid.*, p. 288.
69 *Ibid.*, p. 190.
70 *Ibid.*, pp. 288–289.
71 *Ibid.*, pp. 289–290.
72 Anon., *Mother Goose in Hieroglyphics* (Boston: Brown, Taggard & Chase, 1849), p. 5.
73 *Ibid.*, p. 3.

References

Altick, R. D., *The Shows of London* (Cambridge: Harvard University Press, 1978).
Anon., 'At the British Museum', *All the Year Round* (14 August 1869), pp. 252–255.

Anon., *Mother Goose in Hieroglyphics* (Boston: Brown, Taggard & Chase, 1849).

[Atkins, S.], *Fruits of Enterprize Exhibited in the Travels of Belzoni in Egypt and Nubia; Interspersed with the Observations of a Mother to Her Children* (Boston: Munroe and Francis, 1824).

Black, B. J., *On Exhibit: Victorians and their Museums* (Charlottesville: University Press of Virginia, 2000).

Brantlinger, P., *Rule of Darkness: British Literature and Imperialism, 1830–1914* (Ithaca: Cornell University Press, 1988).

Budge, E. A. W., *Egyptian Magic* (Evanston: University Books, 1958).

[Budge, E. A. W.] and British Museum, *A Guide to the Third and Fourth Egyptian Rooms*, 2nd edn (London: Printed by Order of the Trustees, 1904).

Chapman, A. *The First Visit to the British Museum: Arranged for the Use of Young Gentlemen at Miss Chapman's Establishment* (Cresswell Park, Blackheath: Nisbet, 1849).

Evans, E., *Sydenham Sinbad: A Narrative of his Seven Journeys to Wonder-land* (London: Brown & Co., 1857).

Gosse, P. H., *The Monuments of Ancient Egypt: And their Relation to the Word of God* (London: Society for Promoting Christian Knowledge, 1847).

Hack, M., *Winter Evenings, or Tales of Travelers*, 3rd edn (London: Harvey and Darton, 1823).

The Holy Bible, King James Version, Cambridge Edition: 1769; King James Bible Online, 2017.

Keene, M., 'Domestic science: making chemistry your cup of tea', *Endeavor*, 32:1 (2008), 16–19.

Knoepflmacher, U. C., 'Of Babylands and Babylons: E. Nesbit and the reclamation of the fairy tale', *Tulsa Studies in Women's Literature*, 6:2 (1987), 299–325.

Lightman, B., *Victorian Popularizers of Science* (Chicago: University of Chicago Press, 2007).

Myers, G., 'Science for Women and Children: The Dialogue of Popular Science in the Nineteenth Century', in John Christie and Sally Shuttleworth (eds), *Nature Transfigured: Science and Literature, 1700–1900* (Manchester: Manchester University Press, 1989), pp. 171–200.

Nesbit E. and Millar, H. R., *The Story of the Amulet* (London, Puffin, 1996).

Nesbit E. and Millar, H. R., *The Story of the Amulet* (London: T. Fisher Unwin, 1906).

Pascoe, J., *The Hummingbird Cabinet: A Rare and Curious History of Romantic Collectors* (Ithaca: Cornell University Press, 2006).

Pearce, S. M., 'Giovanni Battista Belzoni's exhibition of the reconstructed tomb of Pharaoh Seti I in 1821', *Journal of the History of Collections*, 12:1 (2000), 109–125.

Plotz, J., *Portable Property: Victorian Culture on the Move* (Princeton: Princeton University Press, 2008).

Zimmerman, V., 'Excavating Children: Archaeological Imagination and Time Slip in the Early 1900's' in Eleanor Dobson and Gemma King (eds), *Excavating Modernity, Physical, Temporal and Psychological Stratification in Literature, 1900–1930* (New York: Routledge, 2018), pp. 63–82.

Part II

Classical pasts

3

Didactic heroes: masculinity, sexuality and exploration in the Argonaut story of Kingsley's *The Heroes*[1]

Helen Lovatt

Charles Kingsley transformed the Argonaut tradition for children with his version of the story in *The Heroes* (1856).[2] In Victorian Britain, one of the most popular Greek myths was that of Jason and the Argonauts, how they sailed from Iolchos through the Clashing Rocks and the Black Sea to Colchis, and with the help of Medeia (Medea) escaped with the Golden Fleece.[3] We can see this from performance traditions and burlesque: for instance, Planché's *The Golden Fleece: A Classical Extravaganza* (1845, Theatre Royal Haymarket), which burlesqued the 1845 *Antigone*.[4] The Argonaut myth was particularly flexible and multiplicitous: there was no canonical ancient version, since the first complete surviving epic (the *Argonautica* of Apollonius) was not written until the Hellenistic period, some time in the first half of the third century BCE. This was at least 500 years after the Homeric poems were thought to have been committed to writing; previously, they were part of an oral tradition. The story is made even more complex by the influence of Euripides' tragedy *Medea* on the tradition, a story in which Jason betrays Medeia for another princess, and she murders their children. Euripides' Jason is a rhetorically self-justifying politician who had an enormous influence on Jason's reputation as an untrustworthy lover. This chapter takes as its primary focus the representation of Jason, his masculinity and heroism in Kingsley's *The Heroes*.[5]

The Argonauts have long been felt to be suitable for children. The text which brought the medieval tradition to its climax, Raoul Lefèvre's *History of Jason*, was presented by its translator William Caxton to a child reader, the future king Edward V, then six years old. Nevertheless the Argonauts were not a standard part of Greek mythology for children before Kingsley.[6] In fact, theirs is a striking absence.[7] This may result from the fact that Apollonius'

Hellenistic epic poem was still not a canonical text, since its third-century BCE Greek was considered too hard for a school audience. Its ambivalence and complexity did not help: in contrast, Achilles in the *Iliad*, Odysseus in the *Odyssey*, and Aeneas in the *Aeneid* featured in canonical epics: essential educational texts for teaching both the ancient world and role models of masculinity. Nathaniel Hawthorne included the Golden Fleece in his *Tanglewood Tales* (1853), but it was the last story in his second book of Greek myths and finishes abruptly, rather dismissively, with the Argonauts simply leaving Colchis, avoiding Medeia's tragic heritage.

Kingsley reacts against both the medieval tradition, with its jousting, feasting and erotically suspect Jason, and Hawthorne's anachronistic, playful prose. At the same time Kingsley was writing, a burlesque on the London stage portrayed Medeia as 'the best of mothers with a brute of a husband'.[8] This called into question the masculinity and virtue of exemplary classical hero figures like Jason. A more complex representation of both Jason and Medeia was Franz Grillparzer's trilogy of plays *The Golden Fleece*, completed in 1821, which sets the Medeia myth in the context of the Phrixus and Argonaut stories and appears to have influenced both Hawthorne and Kingsley.[9] Kingsley's main aim seems to have been to recuperate Jason as well as re-classicising the story. Instead of following Hawthorne, or even Apollonius, he chose a rather surprising text on which to base his account, namely the *Orphic Argonautica*, a Greek hexameter poem probably written in the fifth century CE, which presents itself as a first-hand account by the mythical poet Orpheus. This text is still very little read and has as yet no established translation from Greek into English.[10] We might have expected instead Apollonius, Ovid or even the mythographical tradition, such as Apollodorus' *Bibliotheca* (which largely follows Apollonius).

Kingsley's *The Heroes*, with its reshaping of the *Orphic Argonautica* for juvenile audiences, provides a starting point from which to explore adaptations of the Argonaut story and the establishment of its place in Victorian childhood. The question of why Kingsley chose the *Orphic Argonautica* (*OA*) for his child audience is not easily answered, but this close intertextual relationship (in some parts, almost translation) gives us an opportunity to see where and how he adapted the story. This chapter also compares *The Heroes* with the earlier adaptation of the Argonaut story in Hawthorne's *Tanglewood Tales*. Kingsley was writing in response to Hawthorne, whose work he considered to be insufficiently authentic and serious.[11]

In addition, a useful perspective is given by comparison with a popular version of the Argonauts for adults by William Morris, poet, craftsman, designer and political activist. *The Life and Death of Jason* (1867), a seventeen-book mammoth narrative poem in rhyming couplets, was the poem which brought Morris literary success. Morris had studied Classics at Exeter College, Oxford, and, although his interests were primarily medieval, he went on to translate both the *Aeneid* (1876) and the *Odyssey* (1887). Morris was steeped in ancient epic but kept a medieval tone to the poem. He also undoubtedly knew, and probably knew well, the *History of Jason*, Caxton's translation of Lefèvre's French romance, since the editor of the 1913 edition for the Early English Text Society, John Munro, states that he 'had the advantage of William Morris's type-written copy of the Romance, a copy which, I believe, he had had prepared for his own press but never used'.[12] *The Life and Death of Jason* went through many editions and was influential on representations of the Argonaut myth for the next decades.[13]

A comparison of Morris with Kingsley's works for juvenile audiences allows us to draw out what is distinctive about nineteenth-century British versions of the Argonaut myth, and to explore the similarities and differences in the ways in which it was transmitted to children and adults. This chapter forms part of my wider project on the history of the Argonaut myth, which examines the interplay between myth and reception in the ways this particular story is used in different times and places.[14] It shows how Kingsley creates a much more authentically classical *Argonautica* than Hawthorne, while making Jason's morality, sexuality and masculinity appropriate for his nineteenth-century child audience.

The chapter will explore these versions thematically, looking first at the education of Jason, the figure of Cheiron (Chiron) the centaur, healer and educator of heroes, and the idea of a school for heroes. Kingsley also produced his own illustrations, one of which presents Jason with Cheiron and his students. How do Kingsley's illustrations interact with his text? Kingsley was a proponent of muscular Christianity.[15] How does he treat games and sport? One attraction of the *OA* is the figure of Orpheus, both priest and poet. How do Kingsley and Hawthorne handle ritual and religion? The importance of sexuality, both heterosexual and homosexual, is a challenge for nineteenth-century versions of the *Argonautica*, both those aimed at adults and at children.[16] The episode of the Lemnian women, in which the Argonauts repopulate the island of Lemnos after all the men were killed, is treated very differently by these texts, as is the story of Hylas, in which Heracles (Hercules) loses his boy lover, and the love of Jason and Medeia. Overall, these three texts produced in nineteenth-century Britain have an important influence on the tradition of the Argonaut story and make the Argonauts a standard part of children's culture for many years to come.[17]

Charles Kingsley's *The Heroes* (written in 1855 for publication in 1856) is one of the most influential children's accounts of Greek mythology from this period, as Sheila Murnaghan and Deborah Roberts have shown.[18] He dedicated it to his three children, Rose, Maurice and Mary. At this time he was living and working in the parish of Eversley in Hampshire and had already had significant literary success with *Westward, Ho!* (1855), about a young man (Amyas Leigh) who voyages to the New World with Francis Drake. His decision to write books for his children was a move away from politics and fame.[19] In 1863 *The Water-Babies* would guarantee him a lasting place in the canon of children's literature. He was an excellent classicist; he took a first-class degree in Classics from Cambridge, and his theological interests also had strong classical elements: he had recently written a novel about the early Christian philosopher *Hypatia* (1853), which was well received.[20] *The Heroes*, like *The Water-Babies*, was even more popular and has never gone out of print. It was written in response to Nathaniel Hawthorne's *Wonderbook* and the later *Tanglewood Tales*, the latter of which, as mentioned, includes a version of Jason and the Argonauts. Kingsley in his letters stated that he intended 'treating [the myths] in a somewhat more Classical fashion'.[21] Kingsley is also important in the study of nineteenth-century attitudes to masculinity.[22] The three stories chosen for *The Heroes* were those of Perseus, Jason and Theseus, a triptych of quest stories with a particular focus on initiation, kingship and challenged paternity. Kingsley's illustrations give us a further insight into his interpretation of the myth.

Kingsley had read widely in ancient material about the Argonaut myth, as we can see when he discusses alternative versions of the story, such as the return journey. However, he chose to make his primary model an unusual one:

> AND what happened next, my children, whether it be true or not, stands written in ancient songs, which you shall read for yourselves some day. And grand old songs they are, written in grand old rolling verse; and they call them the Songs of Orpheus, or the Orphics, to this day.[23]

This, of course, is the *Orphic Argonautica*, which – as described above – features the poet Orpheus as its primary narrator. A text of the *Argonautica of Orpheus*, as G. Hermann entitles it, was available in the Greek in 1805.[24] The prolegomena to this edition treats the date and authorship as unknown, leaving open the possibility of an early date, around the same period as the *Iliad* and *Odyssey*, or even older than them, since Orpheus was viewed in the ancient world as one of the earliest poet-heroes. Kingsley does not explicitly assert that Orpheus' authorship is genuine, but he treats the poem as the most authoritative version of the story, mostly giving this account priority wherever it covers the story in any detail. If it were taken to be an early poem, or even one arising from earlier oral traditions, then Kingsley could have felt it made his version more authentically classical. The *OA* does not cover the first section of the Argonaut story (Jason's education and his confrontation with Pelias). Kingsley takes this section predominantly from Pindar, *Pythian* 4 (a lyric poem written in 462 BCE, praising the victor in a chariot race by comparing his victory to that of the Argonauts), though he also shows awareness of alternative versions

Didactic heroes

from mythography.[25] For the story of Jason and Medeia, which the *OA* only summarises, and Pindar alludes to, Kingsley abridges the account of Apollonius Rhodius in his *Argonautica* (AR), book 3.[26] We can see the importance of the *OA* in Kingsley's narrative choices throughout: for instance, immediately after this reference to the Songs of Orpheus, the Argonauts swear an oath to Jason, administered by Orpheus, which corresponds in many details to the description in *OA* (gathering wood, slaying a bull, the heroes put their swords into the bull and drink bull's blood).[27] This vow is not in any other version, to my knowledge. Other distinctive elements include: a visit to Cheiron on Mount Pelion shortly after the Argonauts depart from Iolchos; Heracles' accidental killing of King Cyzicus in a night battle with six-armed giants on the island of Cyzicus; the portrayal of the Argonauts' arrival at the river Phasis (now called the Rioni, in modern Georgia), and their meeting with King Aietes (Aeetes) of Colchis, who is cleansing himself from a dream; the situation of the fleece and dragon, guarded behind triple bronze gates and seven-fold walls, and Orpheus' propitiation of spirits of the underworld in order to open the gates (although the ritual is carried out by Medeia in Kingsley's version and by Orpheus in the *OA*).

Kingsley does not always follow the *OA* in every detail: for instance, the *OA* gives us an idiosyncratic version of the Phineus episode, in which Phineus has blinded and exposed the children by his first marriage to the Boreads' sister. The sons of Boreas, Zetes and Calais, punish him by blinding him, and heal the children, while Boreas himself blows Phineus into the wilderness to die.[28] Kingsley softens this considerably, melding it with the better-known story from Apollonius in which the Boreads rescue Phineus from the Harpies. Phineus pleads for help but is taken to task by the Argonauts for imprisoning his wife Cleopatra and blinding their children. Zetes and Calais agree to rid him of the Harpies, but only on the condition that he swears to take back their sister. Jason heals the children and the Boreads leave the expedition for good to chase the Harpies.[29] This shows wide knowledge of the complex web of different versions and brings them together neatly into one more or less coherent whole.

Kingsley felt that authenticity was important in his education of his readers; we can see this in how he transliterates the Greek names. He often chooses the most authentic version in such a way as to defamiliarise them. Hawthorne, for instance, uses the name Aeëtes (the Latinised version), while Kingsley uses Aietes (a more accurate rendition of the Greek Αἰήτης); Hawthorne uses Medea and Chiron, while Kingsley uses Medeia and Cheiron. In a note after his preface to 'scholars', he refers to the book as a 'hasty *jeu d'esprit*' and apologises for inconsistency.[30] He claims to use 'plain Greek spelling' except where names are 'hopelessly Latinised', although he also worries about 'the sound of the word'. His anxieties about authenticity surface here, as he complains about 'our strange habit of introducing boys [*sic*] to the Greek myths, not in their original shape, but in a Roman disguise'. 'Plain' and 'original' suggest a desire for direct, unmediated contact with the Greeks, and the primacy of Greek culture as creating the myths, in contrast to Hawthorne's idea of myths as some essential property of wider cultures, both ancient and modern ('the immemorial birthright of mankind').[31] Kingsley's use of the *OA* seems to be part of his search for authenticity, and changes the balance of the Argonautic tradition, further decentring Apollonius' Hellenistic account as the most well-known ancient source. It might be expected that some versions would choose to follow Pindar or mythography (such as Apollodorus, or Bulfinch, or later Robert Graves in *The Greek Myths*), but the influence of children's literature, and Kingsley in particular, makes the *Orphic Argonautica* an equally powerful version.

We might think that Orpheus adds an element of poetic power and ritual competence that would appeal to Kingsley. But in fact, Kingsley seems to find the religious aspect of the text problematic, and significantly reduces the ritual actions of the Argonauts, particularly those of Jason. He may even have chosen the *OA* because it de-emphasises the central hero's ritual competence. In Apollonius, Jason's leadership revolves around his religious responsibilities and his successful communication with the gods.[32] In the *OA*, the main rituals are the sacrifice and oath before departure and the ritual to placate the goddess Artemis (or Hekate) in Colchis before they take the fleece. Neither are performed by Jason, but instead by Orpheus, who also purifies them of the death of Absyrtus (Apsyrtos) at Malea and finishes the poem with a sacrifice at Taenaron. Kingsley reduces the ritual activity still further, giving a full version only of the departure sacrifice and oath. For instance, he replaces the description of sacrifices to Rhea at Dindymum to atone for the killing of Cyzicus with funeral games, and the wedding night in Phaeacia is replaced with feasting and games, evoking *Odyssey* 8. Orpheus is still a prominent figure, but mainly for his singing rather than his religious activities.

If we compare *The Heroes* with Morris's adult version, we see that Morris associates complex ritual activity mainly with Medeia and her occult expertise, and also frequently includes inset songs, in various lyric metres, mainly performed by Orpheus. The fact that the *OA* places less emphasis on pagan ritual than Apollonius may be one of the features that attracted Kingsley, by allowing him to evade the defamiliarising effects of such practices, making the ancient world less distant for his young audience.[33] Later children's versions generally continue to avoid descriptions of ritual activity, while the adult novels of Graves and Treece (and to a certain extent Robert Holdstock) revel in their otherness.[34] The *OA* is significantly shorter than either Apollonius or Valerius Flaccus (an eight-book Latin epic from the first century CE), and this may have appealed to Kingsley. Further, the *OA* avoids episodes involving sexuality, especially de-emphasising Medeia. The other part which Kingsley chose to follow in detail is the return journey, which in the *OA* includes the far north. The expansiveness of the Argonauts' exploration may also have been a factor: this too is passed on to Morris, as I discuss below.

Masculinity and the erotic: women and sexuality

The Argonaut tradition has a great interest in women and sexuality, and the treatment of these elements of the story in Kingsley, Hawthorne and Morris show distinctive approaches in the Victorian period to Greek sexuality, and especially the difference between texts aimed at adults and at children. The classical and medieval Jason figures are dominated by their love affairs; while Odysseus and Aeneas encounter their fair share of beautiful, tempting women during the journeys of the *Odyssey* and the *Aeneid*, Jason is defined by his encounters with women, particularly Medeia, who often overshadows him in the tradition.

In the centuries before Kingsley, many versions of the Argonaut story gave even more prominence to themes of love and sexuality than Apollonius and Valerius. For instance, Maffeo Vegio's 1431 short Latin epic, the *Vellus Aureum*, forefronts events at Colchis with a primary focus on Medeia as she falls in love. In Raoul Lefèvre's 1460 romance, translated into English by Caxton in 1477, Jason first falls in love with a queen called Mirro, then is sent on the quest for the fleece, turns down Hypsipyle, but is nevertheless seduced by her, and is then enchanted by Medea in order that he should forget his first love. The vast majority of the plot revolves around affairs of the heart. Cavalli's 1649 opera *Giasone*, with a libretto by Cicognini, portrays Giasone as a love addict, torn between Medea and Isifile. In this respect, Morris stands firmly within this tradition, presenting the relationship of Jason and Medeia sympathetically and in a great deal of detail: how she falls in love with him, her anguish as she decides to help him, their joint subduing of the dragon, their betrayal of her brother Absyrtus, the long return journey and their purification by Circe, Medeia's revenge on Pelias and the events at Corinth in the final book. In contrast, the *OA* summarises Apollonius 3 (in which Medeia falls in love) in lines 858–886 (in twenty-eight lines, compared to the 1,407 lines of Apollonius) and resumes narrative proper at line 887 with Medeia leaving her father's palace – the point at which Apollonius starts his fourth book.

Kingsley, therefore, has a difficult choice: he is still closely following the *OA* as the Argonauts arrive at Colchis. In Apollonius the narrative shifts up to a divine level as Hera (Juno) and Athena scheme about how to help the Argonauts, and then to the perspective of Medeia. In the *OA* and in Kingsley, the primary focus is on Aietes, who has a foreboding dream about Medeia and goes to the river for purification. He takes both daughters, Medeia and her sister Chalciope, wife of Phrixus, to the river and they all encounter the Argonauts together. In both versions, Hera has particularly beautified Jason at this point: 'Among all of them, illustrious Jason stood out, for Hera honoured him exceedingly in every way, and gave him handsomeness and height and preternatural manliness.'[35] Kingsley's version here is essentially a translation of the *OA*: 'But Jason was noblest of all; for Hera, who loved him, gave him beauty and tallness and terrible manhood'.[36] The exchange with Aietes is the same, but when the *OA* enters summary mode, Kingsley moves to the point of view of Medeia's sister Chalciope. He keeps the narrative brief and has Medeia explain the perils and tasks to Jason, replicating the description of the extensive built defences of the fleece in the *OA*, which do not feature in previous texts, where it is simply in a grove with the dragon. However, Kingsley's Medeia comes across as young and uncertain, in comparison to Hawthorne's Medeia, who is wise and knowledgeable, like an adult compared to Jason. Hawthorne's Medeia already knows all about Jason, through her prophetic abilities, and has made her decision to help him in advance. She resembles the Medeia of Franz Grillparzer's 1821 *Golden Fleece* trilogy in her maturity, wisdom and independence from Aietes.

Kingsley mixes an abridged version of Apollonius with elements that echo Hawthorne to create his own version of the events of Apollonius 3. He minimises the erotic elements (both love and sexuality) of the relationship between Jason and Medeia: there is no mention of Eros shooting her with an arrow, and Medeia's primary emotion is pity, mixed with admiration. Chalciope emphasises Greek heroism and exceptionality: 'These men are not like our men; there is nothing which they cannot dare or do'.[37] Jason repeatedly refuses to give up his quest and go home,[38] as he frequently does in Grillparzer's play *The Argonauts*. Jason persuades Medeia to help him, only by asking and looking at her: 'I may yet win the golden fleece, if a wise maiden help bold men [...] He looked at Medeia cunningly and held her with his glittering eye ... Jason fell on his knees before her, and thanked her and kissed her hands; and she ... fled trembling'.[39] Even after she knows Aietes will kill her and goes to warn the Argonauts, she does not ask to go with them, and Jason offers that she 'shall be [his] queen'. All the heroes swear an oath: they 'vowed to her that she should be their queen'.[40] This vow obviously includes marriage to Jason, but the emphasis is on royal power and gratitude, rather than desire, or even love. Kingsley, therefore, emphasises Jason's masculinity and boldness, and de-emphasises the importance and explicitness of love and sexuality, while closely following ancient versions of the story.

The episode of the Lemnian women is an even stronger example of the way Kingsley sanitises the story for his Victorian child readers. This episode may be unfamiliar to those who have encountered the Argonaut myth through popular culture or children's literature, although it does feature in the 2000

TV mini-series *Jason and the Argonauts* (dir. Willing). In Apollonius and Valerius, the first port of call for the Argonauts was Lemnos, which was populated at that time by women alone, after the women had murdered their husbands and all their male relatives. They invite the Argonauts to stay and repopulate the island but are not unduly distressed when the men leave to continue their quest. The *OA* summarises this episode, as with Medeia's love: 'But why tell you a long and candid tale about these things – how much desire the Cyprian who rears Eros launched on the astonishing Lemnian women, to mingle with the Minyans in bed?'[41] Kingsley includes the preceding episode where the Argonauts visit Cheiron but cuts out Lemnos entirely: 'they came past Lemnos to the Hellespont'.[42]

Morris takes a different and more interesting tactic: he retains the story but keeps the Argonauts away.[43] A male survivor of the Lemnian massacre hails the ship from the shore and tells the story of the massacre in all its violent detail. This repeats the way Virgil and Ovid refuse to embroil Aeneas in a repeat of Odysseus' encounter with the man-eating cyclops, Polyphemus, by picking up a survivor called Achaemenides.[44] In Morris's tale, the violence of the Lemnian women is emphasised, and the survivor only escapes by throwing himself off a cliff, apparently mortally wounded, and hiding in a cave for a long period of time. The Argonauts are therefore prevented from facing the moral danger of sexual temptation and the literal danger of the murderous tendencies of the Lemnian women, while the sensational and exciting story is included and Jason can display his honour and kindness (and be like Aeneas) by taking on board the traumatised survivor. This also configures the Lemnian women as wholly monstrous, like the cyclops, and ensures that the story is told entirely from a male point of view. This is arguably a more misogynistic tactic than simply ignoring or bypassing the episode. It also exemplifies Morris's tendency to use motifs and patterns from elsewhere in the classical epic tradition.

Kingsley and Morris also treat the Hylas episode very differently. The relationship between Heracles and his young companion Hylas is clearly presented by Apollonius, as in Theocritus *Idyll* 13 and Propertius 1.20, as pederastic. Kingsley includes a brief version of the loss of Hylas and Heracles in Mysia, following the *OA*. While Heracles hunts, Hylas is stolen by water nymphs; when Heracles searches for him, distraught, the Argonauts depart to catch a fair wind, since they cannot find either of them. The *OA* clearly indicates the nymphs' sexual interest in Hylas, calling him a youth (κοῦρον),[45] although Heracles' anguish and loss is omitted, not ruling out, but not describing, his intense love for Hylas. Kingsley presents Hylas as a child: the nymphs 'came up to look at him and loved him, and carried him down under the lake to be their playfellow for ever happy and young'. However, he does bring back in some of the emotional intensity which the *OA* had suppressed: 'And Heracles sought for him in vain, shouting his name till all the mountains rang; but Hylas never heard him, far down under the sparkling lake.'[46]

Morris, in contrast, is much more interested in predatory females than male love.[47] The nymphs see Hylas' 'shapely body'[48] and enact a plan to ensnare him: they send one of their number to pretend to be a damsel in distress (a princess abandoned by her entourage on the way to her marriage). She lures him to the stream, kisses him and sends him to sleep with a song. Heracles searches for him because he has the loudest voice, and Hera inspires the Argonauts to leave, physically blowing them away so that they cannot return. This Hylas is definitely an adult, and there is no hint of a romantic relationship between him and Heracles. Morris therefore draws on Romance traditions of predatory, seductive and deceptive temptresses, like Hypsipyle and Medeia in Lefèvre, to increase the detail and depth of Hylas' seduction but completely removes all hint of a pederastic relationship. Graves is the first to resurrect a pederastic Heracles in *The Golden Fleece* (1944), where Heracles is brutal, mad, violent and excessive; and in Treece's 1961 novel *Jason*, Hylas is punished for his sexuality, hated by the Argonauts and chosen to be sacrificed by the predatory worshippers of the Mother goddess. Kingsley has therefore worked harder than Morris to occlude sexuality and to protect the unblemished masculinity of his heroes, but has found the *OA* to be a model sympathetic to his interests, which needs little adaptation, since it already glossed over or summarised the erotic aspects of the myth.

Greek myth, education and morality

Murnaghan and Roberts show how Hawthorne and Kingsley innovated in their approach to Greek myth as entertainment rather than reference material, by setting these two versions in the context of earlier works. They also analyse the paratexts of both – Hawthorne's framing narrative, with Eustace Bright telling stories to young children and his defence of this to Mr Pringle; Kingsley's preface and numerous in-text comments – to outline the authors' attitudes to history, myth, childhood and education. While Hawthorne is an essentialist who takes a cyclical view of history and works in a fundamentally American context, Kingsley prioritises a linear view of historical progress, with a British concern for empire and Anglican Protestantism. Hawthorne tends towards playful anachronism, as we can see with his presentation of Cheiron as a schoolmaster who is also a centaur. 'Just imagine the grave old gentleman clattering and stomping into the schoolroom ... I wonder what a blacksmith charged him for a set of iron shoes!'[49] This playfulness both familiarises and defamiliarises, by bringing the fantastic elements of Greek myth into stark and close contact with the everyday (horseshoes and blacksmiths), just as Rick Riordan has his Gorgons working in BargainMart as greeters.[50] In the same passage, Hawthorne toys with a rationalising interpretation, that Cheiron was a 'kind-hearted and merry old fellow' who liked to give rides on his back to the boys, and that later tales to these boys' grandchildren led to the idea of them having been taught by a centaur.[51] 'Little children, not quite understanding what is said to them, often get such absurd notions into their heads, you know.'[52] The imagined audience of *Tanglewood Tales* is, of course, a group of little children – and precocious, questioning children at that – so there is something doubly ironic in this aside, which clearly asks its fictional audience to reject it, while also treating them as if they are already patronising adults. Hawthorne often refers back to Cheiron as 'schoolmaster': both Pelias and Aietes treat Jason's references to him with irritation and grudging respect (Aietes calls him 'the four-footed pedant, his schoolmaster').[53] Hawthorne's framing narrative allows him to distance himself from the text of the stories, while also allowing him to anticipate and deflect potential critics through the figure of Mr Pringle. Ultimately, though, he is the author, and has chosen to handle myth in this way, so we are led to sympathise with Hawthorne's free adaptation when Eustace Bright declares that 'an old Greek' has 'no more exclusive right to them than a modern Yankee has. ... The ancient poets remodelled them at pleasure, and held them plastic in their hands; and why should they not be plastic in my hands as well?'[54]

In contrast, Kingsley treats Cheiron seriously as the Argonauts' master when they visit him, following the descriptions of the *OA* without irony: 'And the heroes wept when they left him, till their great hearts could weep no more; for he was kind and just and pious, and wiser than all beasts and men.'[55] Kingsley, too, is much more invested in the idea of school and schooling: Murnaghan and Roberts point out the nostalgia that characterises the visit to Cheiron.[56] While Hawthorne frequently refers back to Cheiron as a moral guarantor for Jason, Kingsley spends more time and space presenting the group of heroes learning together and relating to each other. In this way, Kingsley seems to have made popular the 'school for heroes' motif which has become so prominent in children's literature and culture in recent years.[57] For instance, 'Camp Half-Blood' in Rick Riordan's Percy Jackson series equates learning to be a demi-god with attending summer camp. In Kingsley's version, Aeson takes Jason to Cheiron's cave and himself holds back while the boy listens in fascination to Cheiron's music and singing and is welcomed into his school for heroes. The other pupils include Aeneas, Heracles, Peleus, Caeneus and Asclepius, and each is praised for their heroic achievements. This was one of the four moments in the story of the Argonauts that Kingsley chose to illustrate (Figure 3.1). The others were: Hera appearing to Jason on the bank of the Anauros; Jason's meeting with Medeia; and Jason taking hold of the fleece, as he climbs over the sleeping serpent, with Orpheus playing and Medeia advising. We can see Jason in these images growing from young child,

3.1 Illustration for *The Heroes*, first edition, by Charles Kingsley himself. From C. Kingsley, *The Heroes, or, Greek Fairy Tales for my Children* (Cambridge: Macmillan, 1856), p. 54.

to boy, overwhelmed by the authority of Hera, to young man, shyly but directly looking at Medeia, while she places her hand on his shoulder and looks modestly at the ground, to hero as he boldly grasps the fleece, wearing an impressive-looking helmet.

The fatherly and dignified centaur holds his lyre, eyes shut, in a narrative rapture, and is surrounded by his attentive pupils: the thoughtful Asclepius on the left holds herbs, a deer which has just been killed by another pupil (probably Heracles) lies at Cheiron's feet, while the youngest hero (perhaps Jason) rides on his back. Older children look after the younger, while the younger gaze admiringly at the older. Kingsley calls Jason a 'schoolfellow to the heroes' sons'.[58] The landscape around them is their key educational resource and at least two pupils hold weapons. The preponderance of physical activities in this education is offset by Cheiron holding his lyre; Kingsley deconstructs the opposition between song and sport to create a masculinity capacious enough for both story and physical strength.

In the next chapter Jason has grown up and insists on leaving Cheiron to try and take back his kingdom. This chapter, after the building of the *Argo*, contains a loose translation (or very close adaptation) of the visit to Cheiron in the *OA*, complete with the centaur lying 'with his huge limbs spread upon the rock', while Achilles plays to him, a song contest with Orpheus, and Cheiron beating his hooves on the ground 'for wonder at the magic song'.[59] By doubling this episode in the initial encounter between Aeson, Jason and Cheiron, which uses the image of Cheiron singing in his cave, Kingsley puts even more emphasis on Cheiron, poetry and education. The *OA*'s focus on its narrator and consequently on poetry and religion (Orpheus is a poet, priest and mystic) allowed Kingsley to connect literature, education and spirituality, while avoiding pagan ritual.

In contrast, William Morris paints a very different picture of Cheiron and Jason's meeting with him. Morris sets the meeting between Jason and Cheiron in woodland and presents Cheiron as a dignified old centaur, both man and horse grey with age, and a prophet who looks forward to Jason's heroism and troubles. Jason here is a young toddler, trying to grasp his servant's golden horn. Morris's poem was aimed at adults but he still devotes much of his first book to a presentation of Jason's education, with emphasis also on Cheiron's singing. His main change is the introduction of the goddess Hera at an earlier stage; vengeance against Pelias for allowing Neleus to kill Sidero on her altar is her motive, and she appears to Jason to send him into the world. Morris then presents the feasting and singing of Cheiron, not with the Argonauts but with Jason on his own, as the climactic scene of book 1.

Kingsley's preface reveals his attitudes to the Greeks in relation to childhood and education. Boys will learn Greek and girls will encounter classical culture in the world around them. On the one hand, he spells out explicitly the moral of his stories: 'Do right and God will help you.'[60] On the other, he expects children to go and research for themselves the locations of the various difficult Greek place names he uses: 'And if you are puzzled by the names of places in this book, you must take the maps and find them out. It will be a pleasanter way of learning geography than out of a dull lesson-book.'[61] There is a similar duality in his attitude to the Greeks: he emphasises their importance for every aspect of Western culture and his own closeness to them: 'Now, I love these old Hellens heartily; and I should be very ungrateful to them if I did not, considering all that they have taught me.'[62] But he also considers them to be like children in their primitive naivety:

> For nations begin at first by being children like you, though they are made up of grown men. They are children at first like you – men and women with children's hearts; frank, and affectionate, and full of trust, and teachable, and loving to see and learn all the wonders round them; and greedy also, too often, and passionate and silly, as children are.[63]

This dual attitude to his audience, both patronising and demanding, displays itself also in the way he tells the story of the Argonauts. He delights in the complexity of Greek myth and makes clear that there are variant traditions, but at the same time he offers his own authorised version which often does not signal which elements he has adapted and changed.

Games and play: muscular Christianity and Argonautic feats

A further example of Kingsley's focus on masculinity and the physical athleticism of heroism is his interest in sport and games. Although Hawthorne's tone is much more playful, Kingsley expands on games and competitiveness when they sometimes surface in the ancient narratives: for instance, the *OA* gives us a set of athletic games after the death of Cyzicus, which Kingsley reproduces.[64] For the feats of Jason at Colchis, Kingsley reverts to summarising Apollonius since the *OA*'s summary is so brief, and he brings out the athleticism and enthusiasm of Jason and the Argonauts: when Jason has applied Medeia's magic ointment to make him invulnerable and supernaturally strong, the Argonauts test its effectiveness. Kingsley presents this as a miniature set of athletic games:

> So they tried to bend his lance, but it stood like an iron bar; and Idas in spite hewed at it with his sword, but the blade flew to splinters in his face. Then they hurled their lances at his shield, but the spear-points turned like lead; and Caeneus tried to throw him, but he never stirred a foot; and Polydeuces struck him with his fist a blow which would have killed an ox, but Jason only smiled, and the heroes danced about him with delight; and he leapt, and ran, and shouted in the joy of that enormous strength, till the sun rose, and it was time to go and to claim Aietes' promise.[65]

In Apollonius Rhodius's *Argonautica*, the Argonauts test the weapons, and Idas in anger 'beat the end of the spear with his sword', but the other elements (spear-throwing, wrestling and boxing) are added by Kingsley. Apollonius' Argonauts give shouts of joy, and Jason is compared to a war-horse which leaps and prances and to lightning that darts down again and again from the clouds.[66] Kingsley has removed the epic similes to create a less distant and more self-reliant Jason. He has also removed any sense of the masculinity and heroism of Aietes, as antagonist. Apollonius has a long arming scene, which presents the magnificence, power and prowess of Aietes.[67] His predecessor, Pindar, our earliest substantial surviving Argonaut narrative, has even stronger parallels between Aietes and Jason: rather than explain the tasks that face Jason (to yoke the bronze-footed, fire-breathing bulls, plough the field of Ares and sow the dragon's teeth), Pindar's Aietes does it himself and then challenges Jason to repeat the task.[68] There is a much stronger polarisation in Kingsley between the masculinity of Jason and the cowardly tyranny of Aietes. Hawthorne goes even further in this polarity by not even allowing his Aietes to watch Jason's feats: in *Tanglewood Tales*, Jason yokes the bulls and defeats the sown men under the watchful gaze of Medeia alone and in the middle of the night.

The later tradition does not replicate this scene, but rather presents Jason spectacularly subduing the bulls and killing the earthborns with a large audience (for instance in the 2000 TV movie). Morris's Aietes is a respected king whose greatness is measured by his wealth – for instance, the banquet he offers to the Argonauts and the description of his banqueting hall.[69] In Morris, Medeia proves the efficacy of her potion by thrusting her own hand into a flame, like the Roman hero Scaevola.[70] Morris also does not dwell on the arming of Aietes or Jason, but instead describes the waking and dressing of Medeia on the morning of the contest.[71] It is no surprise that Kingsley, in *The Heroes*, works hard to build Jason's heroism, around the constraints imposed by his decision to follow the *OA*, in which the narrator Orpheus emphasises his own feats.

Returns and explorers: bringing the Argonauts home

There are many different ways that Kingsley could bring the Argonauts home, but both he and Morris choose routes that go into the far north, passing through the English Channel and evoking a strong connection with the geographical identity of their readers, young and old. Both Kingsley and Morris represent the Argonauts as explorers and flirt with the idea of them coming home to Britain.[72] The ancient versions of the *Argonautica* take various different routes: back through the now stationary Clashing Rocks, as in Sophocles or Herodorus; up the Danube, and down another river to the Adriatic or the South of France, as in Apollonius; even into the far south, through Oceanus, the circling sea, as in Hesiod's *Catalogue of Women*.[73] However, Kingsley follows a similar route to the *OA*, which is also the most expansive and impressive route: up into the far north, over the frozen sea, back down the Spanish coast and into the Mediterranean via the Pillars of Hercules. Kingsley emphasises the variety of different possible sources for the return journey, but explicitly chooses that of the *OA*:

> Whither they went I cannot tell, nor how they came to Circe's isle. Some say that they went to the westward, and up the Ister stream, and so came into the Adriatic, dragging their ship over the snowy Alps. And others say that they went southward ... But all these are but dreams and fables, and dim hints of unknown lands. But all say that they came to a place where they had to drag their ship across the land nine days with ropes and rollers, till they came into an unknown sea. And the best of all the old songs tells us how they went away toward the North.[74]

Kingsley emphasises the fragility of our knowledge of myth and ancient history: he 'cannot tell'; 'some say' one thing, 'others' another. The reference to our distance from the past in the idea of 'dreams and fables', 'dim hints of unknown lands', suggests an analogy between physical and temporal distance. He equates the mystical experience of a half-remembered dream to the epistemological uncertainty that inevitably arises when dealing with a myth that is millennia old. It is unusual for a version aimed at child readers to be so explicit about the difficulties and uncertainties of working with myth. Ultimately, however, Kingsley offers his own guidance and preference by calling the *OA* 'the best of all old songs', not a description that any of its current readers would be likely to adopt. Kingsley goes on to describe in some detail all the different places mentioned in the *OA*'s return journey, with their outlandish tribes, making suggestions in brief footnotes about how these names might be interpreted. Kingsley interprets the island of Ierne ('νήσοισιν Ἰερνίσιν', 'νῆσον ... Ἰερνίδα')[75] as Britain, mentioned by the *Argo*'s prophetic branch as a place to be avoided, and from which they are blown by a terrible storm out into the ocean (presumably the Atlantic).[76]

Morris spends three books describing the journey north and finally west to the ocean and back into the Mediterranean past the Pillars of Hercules. He describes sailing past the southern coast of Britain for four days with two mentions of white cliffs,[77] and the changing landscape from white cliffs to meadows, to red and grey cliffs. They encounter various native tribes, who are for the most part represented as primitive and unable to communicate. Medeia is their guide since she has built up knowledge of the northern peoples through contact at Colchis. In contrast, Hawthorne ceases his narrative at the moment of departure from Colchis.

The northern Odyssey of the *OA*, Kingsley and Morris is fairly idiosyncratic: it does not feature in any of the major twentieth-century versions (e.g. Graves; Treece; or any of the films).[78] However, there may be echoes of it in the fantasy trilogy by Robert Holdstock (*The Merlin Codex*), which begins with the *Argo* submerged in a Finnish lake and spends considerable time in Iron Age Britain. The effect of this expansion of the return voyage is to make the Argonauts much more impressive explorers and to emphasise their imperial, colonial credentials. British readers are brought into the story as the Greek heroes touch on their own homeland. Britain is a peripheral, mysterious and potentially dangerous place, as represented by the *OA*. The Argonauts hardly control their movements in the far north and certainly do not conquer or trade effectively. Kingsley, in fact, follows the *OA* very closely here, and the *OA* itself may well be influenced by Valerius Flaccus, whose proem talks about Vespasian's circumnavigation of Britain as a feat of Roman imperialism.[79] Kingsley's Argonauts, though, face immeasurable dangers and immense distances and stay strong in the face of difficulties. This sets up the pioneer and explorer as an ideal of masculinity.

Kingsley also brings in Britain erroneously to his account of Cyzicus, when he claims that the young king tragically killed at night by the Argonauts was the son of Aeneas, rather than that of an unrelated king with the similar-sounding name of Aeneus, as in the *OA* (Αἰνῆος φίλος υἱος, 'the dear son of Aeneus').[80]

> And there they met with Cyzicus, ruling in Asia over the Dolions, who the songs say was the son of Aeneas, of whom you will hear many a tale someday. For Homer tells us how he fought at Troy, and Virgil how he sailed away and founded Rome; and men believed until late years that from him sprang our old British kings.[81]

The idea of British descent from the Trojan Brutus had been a popular story since the twelfth-century chronicler Geoffrey of Monmouth; Kingsley is careful not to endorse it as authentic, but by including it makes a claim for British inheritance of Greek and Roman heroism. This aside shows Kingsley making an effort to connect with his readers through their education, or their likely future education, and to link that with their national identity.

Conclusion

Kingsley's rich and complex version of the Argonaut myth shows awareness of many different ancient traditions but is fundamentally shaped by its reliance on the *Orphic Argonautica*. Kingsley takes a very different approach to myth and the past from Hawthorne and inspires William Morris, although some elements of his version do not transfer effectively on to this version for adults. The difference between target audiences of adults and children is less crucial in many respects than one would expect, although Morris's version is noticeably more sexualised, with a strong interest in *femmes fatales*. Kingsley and Morris are both expansive in their portrayal of space and its conquest, while all three nineteenth-century versions recuperate Jason. Kingsley is distinctive for repeatedly warning Jason and offering him chances to go back: when he is warned about Pelias before encountering him, 'Jason laughed a great laugh, like a war-horse in his pride.'[82] Pelias is impressed despite himself with Jason's willingness to undertake difficulty and danger. He observes: 'One thing at least I know, that he will go, and that gladly; for he has a hero's heart within him, loving glory and scorning to break the word he has given.'[83] When Jason accepts the quest, 'Then Pelias looked at him and almost loved him in the midst of all his hate.'[84] When Jason meets with Medeia and her sister Chalciope, they both warn him to go home:

> and when Chalciope saw him she wept, and took his hands, and cried, 'O cousin of my beloved, go home before you die!' 'It would be base to go home now, fair princess, and to have sailed all these seas in vain.' Then both the princesses besought him; but Jason said, 'It is too late.'[85]

In the following lines, Medeia explains the barriers and tasks that stand in his way, but Jason insists on attempting the trial: first he replies: 'unjustly shall I die in my youth, for I will attempt it ere another sun be set'.[86] Then at her description of snake and walls, he replies:

> No wall so high but it may be climbed at last, and no wood so thick but it may be crawled through; no serpent so wary but he may be charmed, or witch-queen so fierce but spells may soothe her; and I may yet win the golden fleece, if a wise maiden help bold men.[87]

The emphasis is strongly on Jason's determination, and in this respect Kingsley seems to have drawn on the 1821 drama of Franz Grillparzer.[88] Only after they have acquired the fleece does Kingsley displace agency onto Medeia, who is wholly responsible for killing her brother Absyrtus: she 'laid a cruel and cunning plot', and 'all the heroes shuddered ... yet they did not punish that dark witch-woman'.[89] In his final section, 'What was the end of the Heroes', Kingsley acknowledges that 'the old songs end it sadly' and sums up his overall interpretation: 'Jason had taken a wicked wife and he had to bear his burden to the last'.[90] Yet the Argonauts are also towering figures, greater than generations to come: 'And in time the heroes died, all but Nestor, the silver-tongued old man; and left behind them valiant sons, but not so great as they had been. Yet their fame, too, lives till this day, for they fought at the ten years' siege of Troy'. He looks to the Trojan War and the return of Odysseus as a 'sweet

Didactic heroes

story' and moves on to the tale of Theseus as 'a more cheerful one'.[91] Kingsley preserves the problems of ancient heroism.

Although Kingsley puts great emphasis on learning, on the future education of his readers, and on the Greeks' ability themselves to learn, there is a limit to learning that cannot change fundamental moral character, in his view. In the end, he is not comfortable smoothing over the contradictions and complexities of the ancient traditions, and he acknowledges that the achievement of great deeds can come at the price of moral integrity. In this, his version is more challenging than that of Hawthorne, or that of Morris, whose Medeia is much more sympathetic. The choice to follow the *Orphic Argonautica* must be, in its way, a different gesture of authenticity. It allows Kingsley to recuperate Jason, without alienating his young readers with too much Greek ritual, to emphasise the power of poetry without losing sight of athleticism and heroism, and to connect with both the ancient world and contemporary Victorian ideas of sexual morality, masculinity and imperialism.

Notes

1 Acknowledgements: Thank you to the editors for inviting me to the conference which inspired this chapter, and for their many valuable and thoughtful contributions to the writing process, and their patience as my thoughts developed.
2 Charles Kingsley and Nathaniel Hawthorne are key texts in the portrayal of Greek myth for children, starting a powerful tradition of Greek myth as leisure reading: on them and their precursors, see Murnaghan and Roberts, *Childhood and the Classics*, p. 11–46, with a subsequent chapter on the reception of Hawthorne and Kingsley (pp. 47–80).
3 Kingsley generally uses Greek names, so this chapter follows his choices throughout, except in direct quotations where the authors followed different conventions.
4 On Planché's burlesque, see Macintosh, 'Medea Transposed', pp. 81–93.
5 For an exploration of how images of masculinity and heroism from the past are negotiated in this period, see Gribling, *The Image of Edward the Black Prince*.
6 Lefèvre's romance, celebrating the Order of the Golden Fleece, founded by Philip the Good of Burgundy, was one of the first books printed in England by Caxton. It was widely read and reflected the various medieval versions preserved in works of the Vatican mythographers and other authors, such as Joseph of Exeter, Boccacio and Chaucer. See Dominguez, *Medieval Argonautica*. Cavalli's opera *Giasone* (1649) presents a similar Jason, defined by his erotic entanglements. These texts mainly draw on Latin traditions, such as Ovid *Heroides* 6 and 12, *Metamorphoses* 7, Seneca *Medea* and the prose romance of Dares Phrygius. The works of neither Valerius Flaccus, which was only rediscovered in the early fifteenth century, nor Apollonius, which was translated into Latin in 1550 by Hartung, and into English prose by Edward Burnaby Green in 1780, but otherwise only accessible to those who read

Greek, were central to the medieval and early modern tradition. On the reception of Valerius, see Zissos, 'Reception of Valerius Flaccus' Argonautica'.

7   See for instance *Wallis's New Game of Universal History and Chronology* (in the Introduction to this book), in which the boats mentioned are Noah's Ark, the ship of Danaüs and the ship which Aeneas took to Italy.
8   Robert Brough, *Medea: or the best of mothers with a brute of a husband* (1856), which parodied Adelaide Ristori's performances as Medeia in the same period. On Brough, see Monrós-Gaspar, *Victorian Classical Burlesques*.
9   Kingsley, for instance, adopts the motif of Medeia's repeated attempts to stop Jason taking the fleece, which are important in Grillparzer. Hawthorne's Medeia, like Grillparzer's, is independent of her father, elusive, wise and powerful. Grillparzer's Jason is daring, emotional and dramatic, declaring himself madly in love with Medeia after only briefly catching a glimpse of her, but also selfish, stubborn and dismissive, ignoring her attempts to refuse him and prevent the tragedy to come. Grillparzer was inspired by a desire to rehabilitate Medeia, especially after reading Apollonius and Valerius Flaccus.
10 The final 300 lines were translated into English by William Preston in 1803. Vian's Budé edition (Vian, *Les Argonautiques Orphiques*) provides a translation into French and some notes; Colavito's translation (Colavito, *The Orphic Argonautica*) is primarily taken from the Latin translation of Johann Mattias Gesner of 1764, although it does refer to Vian and translations in other languages, such as that of Luciano Migotto in Italian (1994). There is also an idiosyncratic but lively translation in a PhD thesis: Inman, *Orpheus' Argonautica*. I took part in a reading group at the University of Nottingham, from which my colleague Oliver Thomas produced a working translation of the *OA*, and I am very grateful to him for sharing it with me.
11 'An early biographer claims that Kingsley found Hawthorne's works "distressingly vulgar" and it seems likely he was put off by their irreverent treatment of classical material', Murnaghan and Roberts, *Childhood and the Classics*, p. 25, citing Thorp, *Charles Kingsley*, p. 170.
12 Munro, *History of Jason*, p. vii.
13 The sumptuously decorative visuality of Morris's poem is reflected in artistic representations, such as Evelyn De Morgan's painting *Medea* (1889).
14 Lovatt, *In Search of Jason and the Argonauts*.
15 On muscular Christianity, see two chapters featuring Kingsley: Fasick, 'Charles Kingsley's Scientific Treatment of Gender' and Srebrnik, 'The Re-subjection of "Lucan Malet"'.
16 Sexuality in Apollonius: surprisingly little, but a starting point is Skinner, *Sexuality in Greek and Roman Culture*, pp. 238–241. Hunter, *Argonautica of Apollonius*, pp. 46–74, treats love, with some focus on sexuality. On Victorian sexuality and same-sex romantic friendships see Oulton, *Romantic Friendship in Victorian Literature*. On the Victorians and Greek culture generally: Jenkyns, *Victorians and Ancient Greece*; Goldhill, *Victorian Culture and Antiquity*, especially chapter 7, 'Only Connect', which makes Kingsley one of its main subjects. On Greek culture and homosexuality in the Victorian period, see Dowling, *Hellenism and Homosexuality* and Prins, 'Greek Maenads, Victorian Spinsters'.

17 The 1963 film *Jason and the Argonauts* (dir. Don Chaffey) was squarely aimed at a family audience. An interesting example from earlier in the twentieth century is the *Argonaut Club*, a radio programme, first broadcast in 1933, on ABC Radio in Melbourne, Australia, which ran in various formats until 1972.
18 On Kingsley's life and the context of *The Heroes*, see Klaver, *Apostle of the Flesh*. Murnaghan and Roberts, *Childhood and the Classics*, devote two chapters to Hawthorne and Kingsley's Greek myths, their reception and illustration (pp. 11–80). They clearly show the influence and importance of both *The Heroes* and *Tanglewood Tales*.
19 Klaver, *Apostle of the Flesh*, p. 409.
20 On *Hypatia* in the context of Victorian masculinity and receptions of Rome, see Eastlake, *Ancient Rome and Victorian Masculinity*, pp. 107–109.
21 Klaver, *Apostle of the Flesh*, p. 410, citing a letter from Kingsley to Ticknor and Fields, 15 October 1855.
22 See, for instance Adams, *Dandies and Desert Saints*.
23 Kingsley, *The Heroes*, p. 72.
24 Hermann, *Orphica*.
25 A lively translation of Pindar is Nisetich, *Pindar's Victory Songs*, and Braswell, *Commentary on the Fourth Pythian Ode* is a detailed discussion.
26 Apollonius Rhodius' Hellenistic epic is the first surviving full account of the myth, and also has a rich ancient scholarly tradition that tells us a great deal about the myth in the ancient world. A readable translation is Green, *Argonautika*, and a good general study is Hunter, *Argonautica*.
27 *OA*, 305–328.
28 *Ibid.*, 670–690.
29 Kingsley, *The Heroes*, pp. 79–80.
30 *Ibid.*, p. xvix.
31 Hawthorne, *Wonder Book*, p. 171.
32 Mori, *Politics of Apollonius Rhodius' Argonautica*, pp. 140–186. For the text, see Apollonius Rhodius, *Argonautika*. Jason performs rituals or plays a central role in them at 1.406–436; 1.1133; 2.490–495; 2.1271–1275; 3.1191–1224; 4.1305–1336; 4.1593–1602.
33 The author's preface to *The Heroes* gives the book an explicitly Christian message. Kingsley presents it like a letter to his child readers ('My dear Children', p. xi) and ends with a Christian moral: 'Do right and God will help you', (p. xviii). The Greeks come second only to the Bible as a source of knowledge (p. xii), and Kingsley considers them 'like brothers'; they learn from everyone, but especially from God: 'For you must not fancy, children, that because these old Greeks were heathens, therefore God did not care for them.' He teaches his child readers about Greek religion in the context of the Greeks' failure to adopt monotheistic philosophies (they 'loved their idols and their wicked idol feasts until they all came to ruin', p. xvi). Nevertheless, in this narrative of Greek history, the archaic Greeks of the myths in *The Heroes* are pre-lapsarian: 'at the time of which this little book speaks, they had not fallen as low as that' (p. xvi). Throughout the preface, we can see the double way in which Kingsley both assimilates and distances himself and

his readers from the Greeks, and the same doubleness is at work in the narrative, where he uses complex terminology and difficult names, but avoids portraying alienating ritual.

34 Graves, *Golden Fleece*; Treece, *Jason*; Holdstock's *Merlin Codex* series, begins with *Celtika* and continues in *The Iron Grail* and *The Broken Kings*.
35 Kingsley, *The Heroes*, pp. 84–85.
36 *OA* 807–808. All translations from *OA* are from Thomas.
37 Kingsley, *The Heroes*, p. 86.
38 *Ibid.*, pp. 87, 88, 93.
39 *Ibid.*, pp. 88–89.
40 *Ibid.*, p. 93.
41 The episode is at *OA*, 471–489; the quote is from *OA*, 476–478.
42 Kingsley, *The Heroes*, p. 76.
43 Morris, *Life and Death*, 4.210–359.
44 On this episode and its poetics, see Hinds, *Allusion and Intertext*, pp. 111–112.
45 *OA*, 647.
46 Kingsley, *The Heroes*, p. 78.
47 The same tendency is visible in the painting of the scene by J. W. Waterhouse *Hylas and the Nymphs* (1896), which recently aroused controversy for its portrayal of multiple, naked, predatory, and very similar, water nymphs; Manchester Art Gallery decided to remove it from the walls. See, for instance, the editorial from the *Guardian*, 'The *Guardian* view on Hylas and the Nymphs: not censorship'. On Waterhouse in context, see Goldhill, 'The art of reception'.
48 Morris, *Life and Death*, 4.397.
49 Hawthorne, *Tanglewood*, p. 202.
50 Riordan, *Heroes of Olympus*, p. 5.
51 Hawthorne, *Tanglewood*, p. 201.
52 *Ibid.*, p. 202.
53 *Ibid.*, p. 212; p. 231.
54 *Ibid.*, p. 171.
55 Kingsley, *The Heroes*, p. 75.
56 Murnaghan and Roberts, *Childhood and the Classics*, p. 39.
57 There was an Accademia degli Argonauti in eighteenth-century Bologna, run by the Jesuits: see the altar-piece from 1710, with the comments of Berselli, 'Saint Francis Xavier Recommending the Argonauts to the Virgin'. Periodicals also featured the motif, for instance, Colby, 'Old Chiron and his school'.
58 Kingsley, *The Heroes*, p. 57.
59 *Ibid.*, pp. 74–75.
60 *Ibid.*, p. xviii.
61 *Ibid.*, p. xiii.
62 *Ibid.*
63 *Ibid.*
64 *OA*, 575–593; Kingsley, *The Heroes*, p. 77.
65 *Ibid.*, p. 89.
66 AR, 3.1248–1251, 1253, 1254–1255, 1259–1261, 1265–1267.

Didactic heroes

67 *Ibid.*, 3.1225–1245.
68 Pindar, *Pythian*, 4.224–232.
69 Morris, *Life and Death*, 6.467–505.
70 *Ibid.*, 7.361–364.
71 *Ibid.*, 8.1–8.
72 On empire and children's literature of the late nineteenth and early twentieth century, see Kutzer, *Empire's Children*. Adventure stories during the nineteenth century also construct both masculinity and otherness in geography, as Phillips, *Mapping Men and Empire*, shows. The temptation to connect the Argonauts with British identity is not specific to Victorian or children's literature: Robert Holdstock, with his mash-up of Argonauts and Arthurian legend, Celts and Greeks, creates a different version of multi-cultural, multi-temporal identity for adult fantasy readers of the early 2000s.
73 Hesiod, *Catalogue of Women*, fragment 241 in Merkelbach and West, *Fragmenta Hesiodea*. For these and for all other aspects of the Argonauts in early Greek myth, see Gantz, *Early Greek Myth*: p. 362 on returns; on the whole story pp. 340–373.
74 Kingsley, *The Heroes*, p. 99.
75 *OA*, 1166, 1181.
76 Kingsley, *The Heroes*, p. 101.
77 Morris, *Life and Death*, 12.292, 297.
78 See notes 17 and 34.
79 Valerius Flaccus, *Argonautica*, 1.7–9.
80 *OA*, 503.
81 Kingsley, *The Heroes*, p. 76.
82 *Ibid.*, p. 62.
83 *Ibid.*, p. 65.
84 *Ibid.*, p. 66.
85 *Ibid.*, p. 87.
86 *Ibid.*, p. 88.
87 *Ibid.*, p. 88.
88 In Act 3 of Grillparzer's *The Argonauts*, Medea repeatedly warns Jason and tries to stop him (1416–1427, 1491–1506), including by attempting suicide with Jason's sword.
89 Kingsley, *The Heroes*, p. 97.
90 *Ibid.*, p. 123.
91 *Ibid.*, p. 125.

References

Adams, J. E., *Dandies and Desert Saints: Styles of Victorian Masculinity* (Ithaca and London: Cornell University Press, 1995).
Apollonius Rhodius, *The Argonautika by Apollonios Rhodius*, trans., with introduction, commentary, and glossary, by Peter Green (Berkeley and London: University of California Press, 1997).

Berselli, Elisabetta, 'Saint Francis Xavier recommending the Argonauts to the Virgin', in Museum With No Frontiers, *Discover Baroque Art*, 2019, at www.discoverbaroqueart.org/database_item.php?id=object;BAR;it;Mus12;26;en.

Braswell, B. K., *A Commentary on the Fourth Pythian Ode of Pindar* (Berlin: de Gruyter, 1988).

Colavito, J., *The Orphic Argonautica: An English Translation* (Albany: Jason Colavito, 2011).

Colby, F. M., 'Old Chiron and his school', *Young Folks* (14 June 1884), p. 183.

Dominguez, F. A., *The Medieval Argonautica* (Potomac: Porrua Turanzas, 1979).

Dowling, L. C., *Hellenism and Homosexuality in Victorian Oxford* (Ithaca and London: Cornell University Press, 1996).

Eastlake, L., *Ancient Rome and Victorian Masculinity* (Oxford: Oxford University Press, 2019).

Fasick, L., 'Charles Kingsley's Scientific Treatment of Gender', in D. E. Hall (ed.), *Muscular Christianity: Embodying the Victorian Age* (Cambridge: Cambridge University Press, 1994), pp. 91–113.

Gantz, T., *Early Greek Myth: A Guide to Literary and Artistic Sources* (Baltimore and London: Johns Hopkins University Press, 1993).

Goldhill, S., 'The art of reception: J.W. Waterhouse and the painting of desire in Victorian Britain', *Ramus*, 36 (2017), 143–186.

Goldhill, S., *Victorian Culture and Antiquity: Art, Opera, Fiction and the Proclamation of Modernity* (Princeton: Princeton University Press, 2011).

Graves, R., *The Golden Fleece* (London: Cassell, 1994).

Green, P., *The Argonautika* (Berkeley: University of California Press, 1997).

Gribling, B., *The Image of Edward the Black Prince in Georgian and Victorian England: Negotiating the Late Medieval Past* (Woodbridge: Royal Historical Society, 2017).

Guardian, 'The *Guardian* view on Hylas and the Nymphs: not censorship', *Guardian* (7 February 2018).

Hawthorn, N., *Tanglewood Tales, for Boys and Girls: Being a Second Wonder-Book* (London: Chapman and Hall, 1853).

Hawthorne, N., *Wonder Book* (Boston: Ticknor and Fields, 1855), originally published 1851.

Hermann, G., *Orphica* (Leipzig: C Fritsch, 1805).

Hinds, S., *Allusion and Intertext: Dynamics of Appropriation in Roman Poetry* (Cambridge: Cambridge University Press, 1998).

Holdstock, R., *Celtika* (London: Simon and Schuster, 2001).

Holdstock, R., *The Broken Kings* (London: Simon and Schuster, 2006).

Holdstock, R., *The Iron Grail* (London: Simon and Schuster, 2002).

Hunter, R. L., *The Argonautica of Apollonius: Literary Studies* (Cambridge: Cambridge University Press, 1993).

Inman, J. A., 'Orpheus' Argonautica: Language, Tradition, Allusion and Translation' (dissertation, University of Texas at Austin, 2014).

Jenkyns, R., *The Victorians and Ancient Greece* (Oxford: Oxford University Press, 1980).

Kingsley, C., *The Heroes, or, Greek Fairy Tales for my Children* (Cambridge: Macmillan, 1856).

Klaver, J. M. I., *The Apostle of the Flesh: A Critical Life of Charles Kingsley* (Leiden and Boston: Brill, 2006).
Kutzer, M. D., E*mpire's Children: Empire and Imperialism in Classic British Children's Books* (New York and London: Garland, 2000).
Lovatt, H. V., *In Search of Jason and the Argonauts* (London: Bloomsbury, 2021).
Macintosh, F., 'Medea Transposed: Burlesque and Gender on the Mid-Victorian Stage', in E. Hall, F. Macintosh and O. Taplin (eds), *Medea in Performance: 1500–2000* (Oxford: Oxford University Press, 2000), pp. 75–99.
Monrós-Gaspar, L., *Victorian Classical Burlesques: A Critical Anthology* (London: Bloomsbury, 2015).
Mori, A., *The Politics of Apollonius Rhodius' Argonautica* (Cambridge: Cambridge University Press, 2008).
Morris, W., *The Life and Death of Jason* (Kelmscott: Kelmscott Press, 1867).
Munro, J. (ed.), *The History of Jason: Translated from the French of Raoul Le Fevre by William Caxton c. 1477* (London: Early English Text Society and Kegan Paul, Trench, Trubner, 1913).
Murnaghan, S. and Roberts, D. H., *Childhood and the Classics: Britain and America, 1850–1965* (Oxford: Oxford University Press, 2018).
Nisetich, F. J., *Pindar's Victory Songs* (Baltimore and London: Johns Hopkins University Press, 1980).
Oulton, C. W. de la L., *Romantic Friendship in Victorian Literature* (London: Routledge, 2007).
Phillips, R., *Mapping Men and Empire: A Geography of Adventure* (London and New York: Routledge, 1997).
Prins, Y., 'Greek Maenads, Victorian Spinsters', in R Dellamora (ed.), *Victorian Sexual Dissidence* (Chicago and London: University of Chicago Press, 1999), pp. 43–82.
Riordan, R., *Heroes of Olympus: The Son of Neptune* (London: Puffin, 2017).
Skinner, M., *Sexuality in Greek and Roman Culture* (Oxford: Blackwell, 2005).
Srebrnik, P., 'The Re-subjection of "Lucan Malet": Charles Kingsley's Daughter and the Response to Muscular Christianity', in D. E. Hall (ed.), *Muscular Christianity: Embodying the Victorian Age* (Cambridge: Cambridge University Press, 1994), pp. 194–214.
Thorp, M. F., *Charles Kingsley: 1819–1875* (Princeton: Princeton University Press, 1937).
Treece, H., *Jason* (London: Random House, 1961).
Vian, F., *Les Argonautiques Orphiques* (Paris: Les Belles Lettres/Budé, 1987).
Zissos, A., 'Reception of Valerius Flaccus' Argonautica', *International Journal of the Classical Tradition*, 13 (2006), 165–185.

4

'Fun from the Classics': puzzling antiquity in *The Boy's Own Paper*

Rachel Bryant Davies

It is a scene which would have been familiar to many readers of the newly established *Boy's Own Paper* (*BOP*): a classroom full of boys facing the schoolmaster, in cap and gown, quizzing them over their homework. In the case of one fictional Latin class in October 1879, however, an unexpected response 'quite took the wind out the sails' of a novice teacher's 'grammatical discourse'. On being asked to explain the grammatical case of a noun, one hapless pupil asserted that the ablative case existed '[t]o make it more difficult for us'. This unexpected answer, or 'little accident', was just one incident in the fictional lesson, but held a prominent place in the first chapter of 'The amateur dominie', a five-part serialisation by a prolific contributor of school stories.[1] Published in the first year of *BOP*'s long life, this school story would inspire a succession of reflections, puzzles, contributions and cartoons which set out to prove instead that 'nothing is so terrible but it has its humorous side, and most boys manage to get some fun or other out of the classics'.[2] In response to readers' feedback, this group of articles, mostly by a contributor known as 'Odd Fellow', would continually revisit the idea of 'Classical fun' during the 1880s and 1890s.[3]

Such interactive journalism, exploring the changing perceptions of classical education, alongside fictional depiction of elite schooling and readers' engagement with classically themed submissions, became a powerful example of the fine balance between Victorian pedagogy and entertainment, as well as the inextricable entanglement of adults' and children's consumerism. 'Fun from the Classics', as the first article in Odd Fellow's series was entitled, both reinforced and poked fun at stereotypically formalised pedagogy. Even as the privileged status of Classics in educational curricula was beginning to be challenged by science and modern language lessons, juvenile periodicals increasingly emphasised amusement over instruction.[4] This is evident from a comparison of *BOP*'s riddles and stories with articles in the separate, earlier *Boy's Own Magazine* which in the 1850s had published 'Hints to candidates preparing for the University Certificate', including detailed advice on grammatical revision and practice questions.[5] Educational commissions in the 1860s revealed a decline in 'farcical' rote-learning of Latin, while 'industrial utilitarianism' replaced ancient Greek lessons.[6] As Murnaghan and Roberts have shown, however, although pleasure reading was 'variously and inescapably bound up with education', the decline of Classics in school curricula was not mirrored in the popularity of fiction inspired by the Classics.[7]

A range of article formats created or reinforced more direct, interactive relationships with antiquity.[8] The school stories, multilingual puns and cartoons which explained 'the advantages of a classical education' in *BOP* sat alongside serialised mythologies in *Young Folks* and puzzles in *Little Wide-Awake* and *St Nicholas*, as well as *Atalanta*'s promotion to girls of the Cambridge Classical Tripos at Girton. In particular, the content, presentation and analysis of puzzle-pages, often the readers' favourite section,[9] enables us to track what readers were expected to know, learn, research – and enjoy.

'Puzzle mania', the title of a lengthy discussion in Dickens's periodical *All the Year Round*, was a recognised phenomenon in the 1870s and 1880s.[10] The 'proliferation of printed puzzles that marked the second half of the nineteenth century' varied wildly in format, encompassing all sorts of word-games, conundrums and visual teasers.[11] Although this 'puzzle culture', as Dehn Gilmore terms it, has largely been overlooked, it claims 'a prominent place in periodical literature of the nineteenth century'.[12] As Greg Hecimovich points out, this is largely because: 'The serial format provided the perfect forum for these games. Contributors posed riddles to be solved by the next issue, and subscribers competed to be the first to guess the answer. Significantly, the answer to one serial riddle frequently became the source and text for the next.'[13] As this pattern of reciprocity and repetitiveness suggests, such interactive contests are important sources for unpacking the circulation of different sorts of knowledge and the relationship between pedagogy and play since, as Sara Lindey demonstrates, 'story papers were important places of self-education for nineteenth-century boys'.[14]

Unprecedented numbers of readers experienced these classical encounters. The relative cheapness of this new print media generated mass audiences: as Kelly Boyd claims, 'the total circulation of the boys' story papers was well over a million a week, making them one of the most widely consumed forms of entertainment in late Victorian Britain'.[15] Affordable pricing and interactive content, such as the puzzles and other competitions, reveal that readers were not only socially varied but actively participating in a 'community of reader/writers'.[16] Within this newly proliferating and accessible format, classical antiquity became a powerful example of the fine balance between Victorian pedagogy and entertainment, as well as the inextricable entanglement of adults' and children's consumerism.

BOP's set of articles on 'Classical fun' illuminates these enjoyable everyday encounters with classical antiquity. Starting from an analysis of some rather academic forerunners of the types of puzzle familiar from other children's periodicals, it celebrates the links of this subject matter with the classroom, while opening a window onto lively, more informal, encounters with classical antiquity. What makes this such an interesting case study, however, is the overwhelming level of contributions and correspondence from both child and adult readers, and the topic's striking longevity: offerings with very similar titles span thirteen years. This combination of factors enables analysis of the shifting relationships between readers' requisite or provided knowledge and the educative and commercial priorities of children's periodicals.

I will examine this rather self-conscious sample from *BOP* in light of a representative selection of earlier puzzles from other titles such as *Beeton's Boy's Own* and *Boys of England*. Together, these titles represent the middle to upper end of the children's periodicals market in the last third of the nineteenth century. 'Puzzles' come in many guises – anagrams, cartoons, quizzes and so on – but each variation shares the ability to turn the content of grammar lessons (most commonly presented as deadly dull) into amusing leisure pastimes, comradely reminiscences and family teasing. As an article on ancient jokes in *BOP* recognised when exhorting readers to 'be thankful … there are now countless writers who make the edification and amusement of boys their chief employment', this burgeoning variety and availability of the Victorian press enabled some of children's most sustained encounters with the past.[17] Greco-Roman antiquity was particularly targeted by these periodicals for unconventional reinvention; here, I will consider how they embody the active circulation, acquisition and consumption of knowledge. In unpacking these competing Greco-Roman heritages I will focus on how puzzles promoted the cultural and political work of classical antiquity while encouraging less constrained, more playful, relationships with the past.

'Boys, old and young': contributors, players and readers of puzzles in children's periodicals

It is striking that, although the series of 'Fun from the Classics' articles began almost three years after the publication of 'The amateur dominie', it opened with Odd Fellow's recollection of 'reading in one of the stories which have appeared in our universally popular *Boy's Own Paper*', which must refer to this tale.[18] From the very outset, this reminiscence constructs a shared community of 'boys, old and young' which mimics, or even substitutes for, the shared community of school alumni.[19] As Boyd points out, while 'in the Victorian period, elite boys were the imagined readership of boys' story papers', authors also 'extracted the most attractive elements of public-school life and reshaped them into an imaginative landscape for working-class boys'.[20] These classical stories and articles are particularly significant since *BOP* was celebrated by contemporary observers as 'the only first class magazine which has forced its way into the slums as well as the best homes'.[21]

It is perhaps surprising, then, that the author self-consciously claims to be celebrating school memories that were often presented as among the least popular, if not downright traumatic in his opinion; but he emphasises the retrospective comic potential (of the less physically traumatic punishments, at least – he does not refer here to corporal punishment). The pseudonym 'Odd Fellow' was perhaps adopted by a staff-writer for this series: although an active contributor to *BOP* from 1882 to 1883, he emerges in 1881 with several columns entitled 'Odd bits by an odd fellow' – compilations to fill up odd gaps – and finished with an article in 1885 that teases readers: 'some of you must think the Odd Fellow no longer exists'.[22]

Throughout his articles, Odd Fellow both draws on and creates a shared knowledge of the key role played by Latin and Greek in British public-school and grammar-school life: his second column, for examples, holds Ulysses up as a manly example of weeping in adverse situations (although it is noted that boys usually refrain from weeping when caned).[23] He sets about this by establishing a shared camaraderie of fellow sufferers: Heine's comments that '[t]he Romans certainly could never have had sufficient spare time for the conquest of the world if they had been first compelled to *learn* Latin' and that '[t]he monks in the middle ages were not so far wrong when they asserted that Greek was an invention of the evil one' establish sympathy with current and recent victims.[24] Meanwhile, a verse by W. S. Gilbert recalled 'the horrible ghosts that schooldays scared' with an accompanying sketch of the poet chased by an embodied copy of Caesar's *Gallic Wars*.[25] This ballad, originally published in the periodical *Fun*, which was known as 'the poor man's *Punch*', sets the more playful mood for the rest of the article.

After several examples of comic mistranslations drawn from elite institutions such as Westminster School, just as telling is the author's suggestion that boys could use his article to make fun of their sisters for not knowing Latin. He suggests readers 'ask your sister to read the above and you will have the chance of a laugh at her if she fails to make the third line scan'.[26] The verse in question, attributed to 'Dr. Porson', an eighteenth-century Regius Professor of Greek at Cambridge, is 'supposed to be spoken by a man drawn for the militia':

Ego numquam audivi [I have never heard] such terrible news,
At this present *tempus* [time] my senses confuse;

I am drawn for a *miles* [soldier] – I must go *cum marte* [with Mars (god of War)]
And, *concinnus esse* [being ready], engage Bonaparte.

These verse riddles are bilingual puns which rely on the reader synthesising both languages. Odd Fellow explains that they are 'known technically as Macaronics'; otherwise called cod- or dog-Latin. Here, he was expecting that most girls, without a Latin schooling, would mistake *mīles*, soldier, pronounced with two syllables, for the English word, 'miles'.[27] This recommended prank suggests that girls did come into contact with the content of *BOP*, even if sometimes inadvertently. By 1890, an article about a Greek word *pompholugopaphlasma* (an Aristophanic word for sound made by rock crashing into water) would claim that 'girls read this magazine quite as much as boys do',[28] but Odd Fellow had firmly marked the *BOP* of his era as an ideally male space. In contrast, as we shall see, more unisex titles such as the American monthly *St Nicholas* praised girls for their 'patient ingenuity' in solving classical puzzles, and there are many common girls' names listed as prize-winners in this month's list alone.[29]

Since *BOP*, and Odd Fellow's article, was explicitly aimed at boys, it is all the more notable that Odd Fellow does not explain the differing pronunciations of 'miles', nor the 'easy process' whereby the Greek script 'conceals the nursery rhyme "Little Baby Bunting, Daddy's gone a hunting"', is transliteration: each individual letter is changed from Latin script to Greek script, rather than each word or phrase being translated. This expectation of Latin linguistic skill, and possible familiarity with the Greek alphabet, is an example of its perceived mission to 'bring the ethos of the public schools to the elementary schools'.[30] Although *BOP*'s price-tag of a penny per week made it 'more accessible financially to working class children',[31] Odd Fellow appears to be assuming he has middle- and upper-class readers 'brave enough to read an article with so much Latin in it'. This impression is further reinforced towards the end of this first article; segueing from comic cod-Latin macaronics into Greek transliterations of nursery rhymes, Odd Fellow admits that he sometime 'receive[s] a postcard inscribed in Greek characters, which effectively protects it from the eyes of the servants'.[32]

Even if Odd Fellow were not immediately aware of a wider range of *BOP* readers, he would become aware, through subsequent correspondence, of the mix of adult and child readers, as well as those who had not learned Latin. While such periodicals were ostensibly marketed for children, they also needed to appeal to the adults whose money would usually have purchased the periodicals. Diversity, both in age and social range, is also implied in the fictional Latin class which inspired the series, since it is narrated by the eponymous 'Amateur dominie'. This choice perhaps echoes the author's own experiences in schools, but certainly suggests the expectation of adult readers, such as the 'old boy who says his "hair is getting very thin on the top"'. This story also characterised a wider social range of boys than suggested by Odd Fellow's comment about servants. The form taught by the protagonist includes 'Some couple of dozen boys of all sizes, and apparently from various classes of society', and it is pointed out that the head of the class wears 'much-patched knickerbockers'.[33]

Despite initial appearances, then, classical puzzles tell an important part of the story of how privileged knowledge reached more participants – especially children – than ever before, in new and more enticing formats. In the second half of the nineteenth century, the developing print media was exploited by a wide range of titles which explicitly aimed at providing edifying reading matter and activities: *BOP*, for example, was first published by the Religious Tract Society in 1879 with the twin purpose of instilling literacy and morality. Their renegotiation of classical education into enjoyable puzzles highlights the nexus they embody between accessibility, interaction and relevance – all issues explicitly acknowledged by these publications, which aimed to balance pedagogy and play. This dual intent is encapsulated in subtitles, for example: 'an illustrated journal of fact, fiction, history and adventure' (*Beeton's Boy's Own*) or 'a magazine of sport, sensation, fun and instruction' (*Boys of England*).

Examples of puzzles to be discussed often relied on extensive and detailed classical knowledge – but were found in periodicals ranging from a penny weekly to sixpence monthly. This new accessibility has been studied in relation to Shakespeare, fairy tales and scientific knowledge.[34] But Classics occupies a particularly delicate position: linguistic skill was an elite marker, yet fierce debates raged over the relevance of classical education even as the Education Act of 1870 promised universal literacy and numeracy. Moreover, before exhibitions of unearthed antiquities prompted wild excitement in Victorian Britain, classical mythology had already long been the staple of popular entertainment, from street shows (William Hogarth's 1773 painting of Southwark Fair gives centre-stage to a booth showing the siege of Troy) and chapbooks (e.g. 'History of the Destruction of Troy', Glasgow, 1799), to circuses such as Astley's Amphitheatre and marionette shows in Regency pleasure gardens.[35]

Puzzles in children's periodicals are crucial in assessing the sorts of relationships with the past experienced by these new, vast, readerships. Periodicals reached more consumers across a geographically wider region (often across the anglophone world): sales of *BOP* could number as many as 500,000 while the other titles discussed regularly achieved 40,000 a month (*Beeton's Boy's Own* in 1862) or 250,000 a week (*Boys of England* in the 1870s).[36] Moreover, in encouraging reader participation, puzzles embody active consumption (although we must remember that published contributions were possibly encouraged and certainly selected and edited by adults). While weeklies or monthlies seem more ephemeral than expensive books and board games, they could be bound for posterity; subscriptions could also cement longer relationships with a title. As we shall see, it was the interaction promoted by the puzzles themselves which seems to have been an extremely effective way to ensure repeat purchases.

'Boys seem to take more interest in Greek and Latin than I thought possible': reader enthusiasm

Odd Fellow was overwhelmed by the response to his articles, opening his second offering of the series with not a little surprise that '[m]y previous paper seems to have interested a good many boys, old and young, to judge from letters I have received in reference to it' and noting the following year that 'boys seem to take more interest in Greek and Latin than I thought possible'.[37] He proceeded to quote their offerings liberally, probably to gratify as many correspondents as possible: a typical strategy to promote circulation. His series reveals the sheer number of unsolicited submissions that articles could inspire. One of the best is this macaronic dinner invitation sent by an 'Old Boy' from New York's Medical Club.[38] Like the joke by which sisters could be confused, this largely relied on homophones: after the heading, 'Sciens, Socialite, Sobriete' ('Science! Sociality! Sobriety!' or, in translation, 'Learned ones: be merry, be sober!), the joke lies in concealing the English message by using Latin, or apparently Latin, words as code, rather than in any Latin meaning:

> Doctores! Ducum nex mundi nitu Panes: triticum at ait. Expecto meta fumen tu te and eta beta pi. Super attento uno Dux, hamor clam pati, sum parates, homine, ices, jam, etc. Sideror Hoc.[39]

> [Doctors! Do come next Monday night to Paines': try to come at eight. Expect to meet a few men to tea and eat a bit o' pie. Supper at ten to one of ducks, ham or clam pate, some pear tarts or many, ices, jam, etc. Cider or hock.]

The most effective way to encourage mass repeat custom, however, was through competitions. Almost all periodicals had letters and puzzle pages; more expensive ones ran essay, poetry and drama competitions. Many periodicals offered prizes to encourage readers to compete in their puzzle pages; some were offered by other readers, as in *Routledge's Magazine for Boys* in 1867.[40] Even more commercially savvy was to encourage readers to submit their own puzzles: free copy which also encouraged repeat purchases as expectant authors hoped to see their composition, and name, in print. *Boys of England* had so many hopeful contributors that – presumably following complaints from disappointed readers – they resorted to posting the following 'Notice to our contributors':

> To save contributors the trouble of writing respecting the non-insertion of their puzzles, we shall, in future, adopt the plan of naming the month during which

those under consideration were received. The full list of 'Accepted' and 'Declined' is a portion of those received during the month of December 1867.

The numbers suggest how eager readers were to submit. This 'portion' of just one month's offerings comprises thirty-six submissions, of which eighteen were accepted, two honourably mentioned, and sixteen were declined.[41]

The extent of such interactions was also emphasised by the regular publication of rules. Routledge's published 'Regulations to be observed by solvers of our puzzles' does not shy away from the commercial aspect of such competitions and submissions. Like *Boys of England*, they struggled with readers' enthusiasm: No. 12 made clear that 'we have so many [submitted puzzles] on hand that we must request our friends not to send any more'. The same regulation also makes clear that these were accepted as free copy only ('We do receive Puzzles from our subscribers, but do not pay for them.') and dealt with what was apparently a pressing practical issue for readers: 'The insertion of these does not disqualify authors from our competition.' Despite calling readers 'our friends', the periodical kept a strictly commercial focus: they refused to pay postage (No. 7) and No. 14 explains that purchase was definitely necessary: the inclusion of a 'letter or sign which we print every month' ensured that 'only those who buy the Magazine may compete'.[42]

Other vital commercial issues were raised in the instructions for submissions: when *Beeton's Boy's Own* advertised the Essayists' Association prize topics (the siege of Troy), the organisers recognised the power of their consumers in authorising a potential change to the format of the competition, 'provided a sufficient number address us on the subject'.[43] Rather more pressingly for entrants, and another reminder of the financial precarity of many periodicals, they also apologised for the smallness of the prizes 'due to paying this month for our prospectuses' and promised 'next month shall see an improvement'.[44] The next topic was very similar: the friendship of Achilles and Patroclus. This continuity reflects the centrality of Homer's *Iliad* in school curricula as well as popular culture (particularly following Schliemann's excavations at Hisarlik from 1871) and guaranteed a large number of entries, since the publishers were forced to decree that 'only such contributions as possess real merit will be accepted for insertion'.[45]

Certainly, an open comic script competition in *Routledge's Every Boy's Annual* in 1871 yielded two Trojan comedies among the six titles singled out for praise. Since they condense classical epic into a mini-drama in the style of the burlesques which had dominated Britain's theatrical scene for much of the century, it is not surprising both were criticised for too many characters, although their subtitles, 'The difficulties of Paris' and 'The Trojan wanderers', sound more exciting than the rather clichéd winning prize poem from *Beeton's* competition.[46]

These sorts of judges' reports are extremely revealing. Such feedback could be harsh: comments on contributed 'Crackers for the ingenious' in *Boys of England* included 'not up to the mark' or 'confused' (although of course this does not necessarily correlate to the author's education).[47] Again, these comments imply that the editors had plenty of contributions from which to choose. Other reports emphasised the educational benefits of participation. In 1876, one such report devoted a long article to analysing, explaining and praising entries. This was American monthly *St Nicholas*, whose prize-winners' addresses included England and Scotland as well as the USA and Canada. Its judges acknowledged that 'The Pilot Puzzle has required a good deal of patient ingenuity' and 'considerable research' in 'public libraries' as well as among 'parents and friends'. In particular, they singled out a 'little girl' who asked her father's friend for information about a Greek word (the translation for 'broad' – '*platon*'), which led her to the name of the philosopher Plato (the periodical does not explain that it was supposedly his wrestling coach who bestowed this nickname to describe Plato's shoulders).[48]

This report is significant, then, not only for revealing the geographic dispersal and mixed gender of its competitors, but also for the prominence it placed on the acquisition through 'many days' hard work', rather than simply prior possession, of the knowledge needed to solve the puzzles.[49] Because *St Nicholas* celebrated its young competitors' efforts and made clear that they were not expected just to know already how to identify the historical 'greats' whose biographies they were asked to provide: its puzzle was educative as well as presumably, enjoyable. When adult relatives were often the buyers and palatable instruction was the periodicals' selling-point, such claims of publishing educative and informative items created an especially dynamic process of rehearsing, performing or providing the requisite knowledge.

'Classics … is not defunct yet': the requisite knowledge of contributors and readers

The crucial question of what readers needed to know to appreciate riddles, participate in competitions and solve puzzle was – eventually – pinpointed by Odd Fellow. It is likely that readers brought this issue to his attention: the first 'Fun from the Classics' was full of untranslated Latin and cryptic hints at jokes contained therein but his second article, three months later, was much more accessible. Pleased that 'My previous paper seems to have interested a good many boys', he proceeded to publish select submissions. These include lines from verse compositions (ideally with as few long words as possible to make up the required number of syllables) and grammatical puzzles which play on the ambiguities of homographs (words with different meanings despite the same spellings) and rely on knowledge of inflected endings. In addition to providing some translations, he does explain that palindromes are 'lines which read the same forward and backwards' and offers 'A good way to remember the different feet' [metrical unit]. Most striking, however, is the end of the article, where he acknowledges, 'Many boys nowadays do not learn Latin, so for their consolation I append a couple of French puzzles.' Although he does not supply translations, he does include instructions on how to solve these tongue-twisters ('They should be read very quickly').[50]

Another four months later, in March 1883, he addressed this issue explicitly, having received, and published, still more comments and contributions. It is amusing that here – one of the few collections of puzzles where the classical is clearly delineated from other historical periods – his surprise that 'Really, boys seem to take more interest in Greek and Latin than I thought possible' is emphasised by a decorated capital letter (Figure 4.1) with a boy peeping through. The real surprise is that this boy wears medieval armour reminiscent of illustrations in the medieval-themed adventure novels for boys which were popular in the late nineteenth century.[51] This elite symbol was most likely the result of thrifty repurposing by the *BOP* typesetters since other decorated initials in this series show a medieval queen and the moon. Nonetheless, it represents the fluidity, and even the dangerous interchangeability, between the competing claims of different histories – all the more ironic since this contributor stakes a particular claim for the importance, and popularity, of classical education. Odd Fellow's surprise, however, had arisen not from this merging together of different pasts, but from debates over the alternatives to the classical curriculum which were becoming available in some schools and had led him to believe that interest in antiquity was declining. Odd Fellow's post-bag full of reader contributions, however, proves the experts wrong:

> If we are to believe what certain educationalists tell us, the study of the classics is rapidly dying out at school. Well, it may be so, but at any rate it is not defunct yet, for no one can find any pleasure in deciphering a macaronic or construing a puzzle who has not made some acquaintance with ancient authors. And that there are some who have found amusement in these papers I have reason to know.[52]

What proves to Odd Fellow that 'classics ... is not defunct yet', is his justifiable conviction that his readers would not have submitted their own examples had they not possessed the requisite linguistic skills. Cementing the ongoing relationship with schooling, he proceeds to print further submissions, including the perennially popular incorrect exam translations.

Despite one subsequent submission of the doctors' invitation, it is interesting that *BOP* then took a break from variations of 'Classical fun'. It was not until six years later, in October 1888, that an article by 'Philip Kent BA' entitled 'Some queer translations' took up Odd Fellow's mantle. Kent also emphasised comic mistaken translations as a universal schoolboy experience but was rather

STILL MORE FUN FROM THE CLASSICS.

BY THE ODD FELLOW.

REALLY, boys seem to take more interest in Greek and Latin than I thought possible. If we are to believe what certain educationists tell us, the study of the classics is rapidly dying out at school. Well, it may be so, but at any rate it is not defunct yet, for no one can find any pleasure in deciphering a macaronic or construing a puzzle who has not made some acquaintance with ancient authors. And that there are some who have found amusement in these papers I have reason to know.

4.1 An initial capital letter using a medieval boy-knight to illustrate an article about the popularity of Latin, Greek and classical antiquity: 'Odd Fellow', 'Still more fun from the Classics', *Boy's Own Paper* (17 March 1883), p. 398.

more inclusive. He carefully explained 'their principal source' as 'the identity or close similarity between a foreign word and an English one' and, vitally, worked out his examples. This article also included French samples, but without singling out those readers who might only understand those.[53]

This problem of potentially lacking knowledge was cunningly circumvented in *Beeton's Boy's Own* by some double acrostics which used English poetry. These puzzles offered quotes as clues; the initial and final letters of each answer form hidden words, usually names. One used lines from Tennyson's 'Ilion, Ilion' to elicit that city's name (an alternative for Troy), which in turn formed the third letter in the answers: Guinevere and Lancelot. Over the page in the same issue, another used Pope's translation of the *Iliad* to prompt the answers: Achilles and Menelaus.[54] Here, knowledge of English literature and translations worked with the classical to enable as many as possible of the title's 40,000 subscribers to participate.[55] The overall clue for Achilles, 'Thetis' god-like son', was not too difficult, although the length of Menelaus' clue makes it appear more obscure: 'Soon to thy cost the field would make thee know/Thou keep'st the consort of a braver foe.' The individual clues for the eight component letters required more in-depth knowledge, however: the second, for example, reads: 'The shaded tomb of Alphytus stood'. This quotation from *Iliad* 2.732 in Pope's translation was presumably intended as a simple clue since the answer, Cyllene, was in the previous line. However, it relies on the assumption that the puzzler had read and remembered the 'catalogue of ships', and in any case would have been more recognisable if *Beeton's* had spelled the name correctly, as Æpytus.[56]

Unsurprisingly, many puzzles revolved around such educational and cultural staples, but many clues and answers are obscure names, often from contemporary reference books (which, however, in the pre-digitisation era required the puzzle-solver to have read and remembered, rather than search, the content). But when specifically classical knowledge was required, where could this come from, if not directly from an elite classroom, such as that evoked in 'The amateur dominie'? As we have seen, periodicals mimicked such classrooms: Odd Fellow's series began by taking up the challenge to transform such intense dislike.

Elsewhere in *BOP*, one of its very first issues featured a poem entitled 'Oratio obliqua: a legend of the Latin grammar', which 'relates/Of one poor boy the tragic fate' who asked 'what's the good of those/Disgusting bits of Latin prose'.[57] In subsequent years, *BOP* would feature many more fictional boys struggling with classical syntax. Some, such as an episode in 'On special service: a naval story', included a Latin lesson embedded in a wider narrative (the youthful hero's many grammatical mistakes indicate his excitement over attaining a cadetship).[58]

Others centred around the classical encounter. An especially informative – and rather disingenuously entitled – *BOP* story, 'The strange adventure of a small boy' concentrated on a tiresome preparation session.[59] Like the victim of the 'grim vision' of the 'Oratio obliqua', this protagonist made the mistake of describing Latin syntax as 'beastly rot'. In revenge, the anthropomorphic cases of the nouns, 'clad in the toga of the ancient Romans', spirit him away while he sleeps at his desk, and charge him with neglect and insolence. Throughout the process, the cases enact their attributes and functions; for example, the archaic and rarely used locative form, which designated 'place where', is described as 'a poor little wretched object, with only one arm and one leg' who claims, 'I can tell you where you live.'[60]

In addition to these linguistic lessons, mythological stories and articles were often informative. One of the most recurrent topics across all types of article was Homer's *Iliad*, which was retold in several other periodicals concurrently with *BOP*'s enthusiasm for 'Classical fun': *Chatterbox* (also singled out by Alec Ellis as financially accessible to working-class children and considered a lower-middle class staple by Marjory Lang) ran a twenty-one-part series retelling the *Iliad* throughout 1882, while *Young Folks* featured a highly fictionalised version, 'Achilles, the young hero of Thessaly', in thirty-three chapters between March and June 1885.[61] While the school stories performed or rehearsed the acquisition of classical knowledge, fictional retellings also provided or reinforced much of the knowledge necessary to solve the puzzles.

'Books to bother the English': familiarising or distancing the past through classical puzzles

Despite the frequency of such retellings and informative articles since the mid-nineteenth century, and despite the positive response to Odd Fellow's linguistic articles in the 1880s, it is hard to escape the conclusion that the editor became increasingly conscious of readers' changing exposure to Classics. Odd Fellow had himself addressed this market-led mentality in his article on 'what the ancients deemed fun'. He begins his potted history of 'Greek wit' and 'Roman fun' by rejoicing that 'fortunately the idea of what constitutes fun has changed since then, and now none but the most cruel-minded take delight in the misfortunes of others'. It is perhaps a little ironic that after offering plenty of opportunistic moralising (Martial's epigrams, for example, prompt the comment that 'Good-natured wit attracts, ill-natured repels'), he condemns the entire nineteen surviving books of Aulus Gellius' *Attic Nights* (an ancient miscellany), and possibly everything else just discussed, as 'wearisome productions'. Instead, he exhorted his readers to 'be thankful that we are better off; that ... there are now countless writers who make the edification and amusement of boys their chief employment'.[62]

Odd Fellow's description of contributors as full-time journalists suggests that this pseudonym may disguise one of *BOP*'s staff writers. In any case, this

'Fun from the Classics': puzzling antiquity

4.2 Cartoon of anachronistic classical figures: Anon., 'Fun from the Classics', *Boy's Own Paper* (11 March 1893), p. 38.

comment aptly encapsulates the ultimate, commercial, purpose of these classical puzzles. It is certainly noticeable that the latest *BOP* articles which resurrect the idea of 'Classical fun' are two sets of visual jokes. In March 1893, three statues were updated to reflect an interesting trio of modern leisure activities: theatre, cricket and curling, from left to right (Figure 4.2).[63] This cartoon was the entire item, with no explanation beyond the brief labels.

The leftmost figure strikes a dramatic attitude. He is depicted in the standard pose of orators and politicians, wearing tunic and toga and holding a scroll. Marc Antony is clearly signalled with his Latin name, Marcus Antonius, as well as a quote (unattributed) from his famous speech beginning 'Friends, Romans, Countrymen' from Shakespeare's *Julius Caesar*.[64] In the middle is Publius Decius Mus, one of the Roman consuls in 340 BCE, an example of outstanding bravery in battle. Relatively obscure now, his doings as narrated in Livy's *History of Rome* were related in Smith's *Dictionary of Greek and Roman Biography and Mythology*.[65] His name is not only provided but familiarised, through the addition of an honorific 'Esq.'.

While Marc Antony is (de)familiarised through his newly appropriate undertaker's top hat with mourning veil, Decius' armour is transformed into cricket kit, with his bat substituting for a sword, and shin-guards for greaves. On the right is what the cartoonist claims to be a transformation of a famous Greek athlete, discovered in Roman copies of the original Greek bronzes (of which only descriptions survive). In a cunning switch, he holds curling stone and broom. Overall, this statue comically emphasises the otherness which the familiar names and clear signage of Marc Antony and Decius elided. A clue is inscribed onto the athlete's plinth in Greek script. Once translated, this reinforces the comical substitution of the curling stone: 'the spinning (curling) discus-thrower'. However, the statue's upright posture, one arm straight and holding the discus while the other bends at the elbow is more reminiscent of the *discophoros* (discus-bearer) after Polyclitus, rather than the crouched, running *discobolos* pose attributed to Myron.[66] Roman copies of both statues are in the British Museum's Townley Collection but were probably conflated because the discus- (or quoits-) thrower was better known: it was displayed at the Crystal Palace, was described to a correspondent by *Young Folks' Paper* in 1883 and would be recommended in *BOP* as a model for school sports in 1895.[67]

The next set of mythological cartoons, from 1895, take the anachronisms even further (Figure 4.3) and demonstrates the increased necessity for more obvious anachronisms and the use of captions. Here, English captions signal characters and episode. At the top, Diana bathes in a bathroom, rather than a forest, with the hunter Actaeon clutching a shotgun (in the myth he was accompanied by hunting-dogs who would tear him apart as punishment for seeing Diana bathe). In the middle cartoon, Orpheus clutches a violin instead of Apollo's lyre; it also appears that Eurydice's entrance to the underworld is through a hole on one of the new golf-courses. Finally, the bottom cartoon shows Heracles shooting the Stymphalian birds, his sixth labour, with a cannon instead of arrows.[68]

Anachronisms emphasise the familiarity of past even as their comedy lies in awareness of its incongruous otherness, wherein lies the riddle of a puzzle prior to its solution. This sort of visual joke is familiar from classical burlesques in the theatre, where popular scientific acts such as Jenny, 'The Talking Fish', could supplant the goddess Venus in the *Aeneid*, or Charles Kean's Shakespearean productions were reprised by Homeric characters.[69]

Visual anachronisms were, perhaps, easier to convey than linguistic puzzles, but anachronistic, or transhistorical comparisons regularly featured in verbal riddles. One double acrostic which would form 'the name of a celebrated hero of modern history' and 'a hero in ancient history' came out as Garibaldi and Alexander. This submission, by 'Una', is an interesting comparison in light of their respective political impacts: Garibaldi as nationalist unifier of Italy, and Alexander as the unifier of Greece and creator of a vast empire. It is hard to know how many readers would have solved this before the official answers were published, though. One clue – 'a distinguished hero at the siege of Troy' – was seriously misleading: the official answer was given as Iapyx without any explanation that he is only named once in *Aeneid* 12 as Aeneas' surgeon. For readers more used to seeing major players such as Achilles and

'Fun from the Classics': puzzling antiquity

4.3 Comically updated cartoons: Anon., 'Fun from the Classics', *Boy's Own Paper* (13 April 1895), p. 448.

Hector as clues, this is really nasty even if he did feature in Smith's *Classical Dictionary*. This, and the range of clues (including the grammatical: 'An article' – 'an') suggests that the overall acrostic answer (Garibaldi and Alexander) was important enough to the submitter, presumably by a child reader, that it was worth (in a pre-digital era) combing the *Dictionary* for words composed of suitable letters.[70]

Similarly intriguing parallels are raised by the same paper's 'Historical mental pictures': which gave brief vignettes to identify characters. One strikingly juxtaposed Spartacus' slave revolts, Henry III's coronation and the Duke of Suffolk's beheading (in Henry VI's reign): all linked by political revolt.[71] In a slightly simpler way, the same *Beeton's* issue that used Tennyson and Pope's poetry in acrostics further juxtaposed the historical Anne Neville ('Edward's widow, Richard's wife') next to Diana, goddess of Ephesians (classical but also biblical, from Acts of the Apostles).[72] Classical figures, while important, were but one facet of such puzzles: the juxtaposition of chronologically discrete episodes submerged them into wider national or Christian narratives.

Such comparisons between ancient and modern were common enough to be mimicked by readers. One submitted example, in *Boys of England*, was rather easier. This was a cheaper publication, at a penny a week, and had its 'greatest following among lower-middle-class and working-class adolescents' although, as Kristen Drotner explains, the fact that most 'conscientious parents' banned it simply increased its appeal for middle-class boys.[73] In line with this profile, it had a much lower classical content, as is immediately evident: 'An interjection; a mountain near Troy; a small table; a kind of dog. The initials read downwards will give the name of a great statesman; and the finals read downwards will give the name of a great engineer. W. Dickinson.'[74] The official answers were 'pshaw', Ida (one of the most recurrent clues which would have been familiar from the stories and articles), tablet and Talbot-hound. The statesman turns out to be (William) Pitt and the engineer (James) Watt. This simple example illustrates the reciprocity between ancient and modern which underpinned many such puzzles.

Such embeddedness, alongside frequent recourse to the same suspects, such as the *Iliad*, emphasised the familiarity of classical antiquity – at the same time as the sheer difficulty of other clues could highlight its otherness. Both sorts of puzzles co-existed quite happily: in the same year, *St Nicholas* offered what was essentially an Iliadic word search as well as a tricky double acrostic. The former 'Classical puzzle', a submission, asked readers to 'Take a letter from each of the following names, and find a famous Greek hero' (letters bolded below: my emphasis).

1. Ajax 2. He**c**tor 3. Anch**i**ses 4. Priam 5. Ulysses 6 Alexander 7. Homer 8. Aeneas. G. and T.[75]

Achilles, the answer comprised from the letters bolded above, must have been easy to spot since his name is a glaring omission from these clues which comprise, in order: 1. another of the most famous Greek warriors (and protagonist of a tragedy by Sophocles); 2. the Trojan prince who led the army and was killed by Achilles; 3. Aeneas' father; 4. the King of Troy; 5. the Greek warrior and eponymous hero of Homer's Odyssey; 6. the Trojan prince who judged the contest of the Golden Apple, also known as Paris; 7. the bard credited with the oral poems about these heroes; and 8. Aeneas, who led the Trojan refugees to Italy and the eponymous hero of Virgil's epic poem, *The Aeneid*.

The latter example, a 'Classical double acrostic', also has straightforward ultimate answers: Virgil and *Aeneid*. However, official answers revealed extremely obscure names as components: V-irgini-A; I-rene-E; R-hiutho-N; G-lauc-E; I-nfer-I; L-ycome-D.[76] It is no surprise that the lists of successful answers reflects this difficulty: whereas 125 readers sent the answer 'Achilles', only about twenty-five (many with the same names and pseudonyms) answered the double acrostic.[77] Such difficulties emphasise the extent to which supposedly familiar classical knowledge could actually be experienced as irrelevant, distant or unintelligible.

'The Greeks and Romans were actual people': pedagogical play, imaginative interaction and moral didacticism

The *Boy's Own* series had started from the difficulty of understanding the classical past. Hope's fictional teacher, the 'amateur dominie', had grappled with idea that his pupil seemed to 'imagine that all the forms, principles, and literature of the Roman language had come into existence for no other end than to serve as a toilsome treadmill for him'.[78] Odd Fellow pragmatically concluded that '[t]his reply illustrates the attitude of mind of many a youngster' since '[b]oys fail to grasp the notion that the Greeks and Romans were actual people who spoke Greek or Latin' and 'only conceive them as beings who composed books to bother the English'.[79]

Such exasperation was, ironically, a result of the ubiquity of rote-learning Latin and Greek in elite classrooms. Over-familiarity within strictly pedagogical contexts created imaginative distance from the authors and events studied. Odd Fellow perceived a challenge to bridge this gap through transforming classical reminiscences into a fun, shared experience of initiation into manliness. Acknowledging linguistic failures and celebrating the puzzling nature of the past made it accessible. In a jokes column which appeared later in 1882, for example, one (now-familiar) wisecrack by 'the last boy in the form' proposes 'a theory about the dead languages ... I think they were killed by being studied too hard'.[80]

Odd Fellow's other three major articles in *BOP* combined his obvious love of humour with the mixture of pedagogy and reminiscence that had been so successful in the 'Fun from Classics' series. The first, from February 1883, printed in full the Lord's Prayer in Latin and Greek (for boys who had not previously seen it but were studying those languages), plus meal-time graces, in Latin, as said at Westminster and Eton Colleges in the eighteenth century. Not long after, the second and third, on corporal punishment and its alternatives, presented a much greater challenge to his humorous approach, as implied in the titles, 'A ticklish subject' and 'Boy-baiting'.[81] Here, he condemns cruelty but also mentions stories of escape, with comic intent. It is striking that alongside his anecdotes from Westminster, Eton, Marlborough and Harrow, he not only draws on classical models such as Spartan boys, but quotes verses to show that '[t]he rod, and the woes resulting from its uses, have exercised the pen of many poets'.[82] These subsequent articles, however, do not seem to have inspired replies worthy of publication: clearly it was the experience of puzzling over Latin which resonated most powerfully with readers of *BOP*.

The sheer extent of these everyday imaginative interactions with the classical past is significant in light of contemporary socio-political connotations of classical education. Hope's story enters this minefield. His idealistic teacher, frustrated with contemporary education, considers the 'Delectus', or anthology, could be 'in itself a liberal education' and complains that, instead, 'this fine book should serve only as the gerund-grinding hurdy-gurdy of wooden-witted pedagogues'. The narrative details exactly this painstaking, and mistaken, process of translation and grammatical analysis, on which the fictional class insist their new teacher test them, before they speedily become frustrated. A proverb from Phaedrus' fable of the pilot and the sailors ('in prosperity, be cautious; in adversity, be hopeful) is the featured sentence, common from the major translation textbooks: its philosophic acceptance of the mingling of sorrow and joy suggests an ironic comment on the reversed roles of teacher and pupils in the school story, and on the school story's combination of education and leisure.[83]

The dissident implications of this story are entirely glossed over by Odd Fellow but he was strangely defensive of his title, 'More fun out the Classics': 'some of you may say that none of the above are *in* the classics', but 'if they are not *in* them they must be *out* of them' [my emphasis].[84] This justification suggests that some readers criticised his project. Yet, as we have seen, the articles moved beyond collation and analysis, to informative and educative. Together with the repeated exploitation of ancient material as fodder for acquiring modern, often scientific, prizes, these classical puzzles and riddles demonstrate one aspect of how classical antiquity became a prime example of balancing the entertaining and informative, moral and religious for Victorian child consumers.

'Fun from the Classics': puzzling antiquity

Alexander Kinglake would compare his 'reverence' and 'love' for the *Iliad* with 'an old woman deeply trustful sit[ting] reading her Bible'. 'It was not the recollection of school, nor college learning' he maintained, 'but the rapturous and earnest reading of my childhood which made me bend forward so longingly to the plains of Troy' during the journey he recounts in *Eothen*.[85] These periodicals foster that imaginative engagement for less elite families. These classical puzzles and riddles, in *BOP* and similar titles, reveal the commercialisation of classical knowledge as experienced by a mass readership of active participants. The proliferation and availability of print media from the latter half of the nineteenth century enabled more children than ever before to engage with stories. While children had increasingly been targeted as consumers of toys, books and games through the century, periodicals – often sponsored by religious education societies – brought a more interactive, reciprocal relationship between readers, who became researchers, puzzlers and contributors. The classical articles show the importance of these new cross-class audiences enabled by ephemeral media in understanding how knowledge which embodied the elite, and was most often associated with boys' schooldays, worked throughout society.

This commercialisation of educative interaction, which successfully balanced pedagogy and play, promoted sales and ensured repeat custom. Commercialisation of knowledge is inherent in prize puzzles, which aimed to encourage repeat custom, but is also starkly evident in concern over whether readers understood published content. The puzzles themselves, which open up potentially competing interpretations only to close them down with a correct answer, exemplify complex relationships between assuming and disseminating knowledge which is linked to wider cultural debates regarding who should have access to that knowledge. Nor do these puzzles enable us to track what aspects of Classics were expected to be known, but their juxtapositions show that Classics as 'cultural glue' was deeply entangled with – and even underpinned – other forms of knowledge.

This sort of playfulness engaged with different pasts but often privileged antiquity: which as a quintessential school subject highlights how children's commercial encounters with Classics balanced education and leisure. It is the delightful paradox of these puzzles, riddles and conundrums, whether in prize contests, articles or stories, that they both commiserate with readers and celebrate classical knowledge. Stories both nostalgically recall, or vicariously create, memories of puzzling over various aspects of antiquity. In presenting readers with fresh puzzles, competitions both enabled participants to relive their schooldays more successfully than in the stories and afforded the opportunity for autodidacts to gain the requisite knowledge through research or studying the official answers.

Periodicals to some extent bucked the decline of classical domination in the school curriculum but trod a tricky tightrope: while, for some, the school stories and didactic content could partially replace formal lessons, the articles needed to be sufficiently accessible for *BOP*'s wide readership. Both Odd Fellow's surprise at his full post-bag, and the phasing in of visual anachronisms under the same title as the earlier grammatical riddles, shed light on the increasingly problematic dynamic of classical education as elite status marker in the late nineteenth and early twentieth centuries.

Playing with or puzzling over the classical past turned a grim pedagogical chore into comedy (for some readers – although this is not Odd Fellow's intention – the transformation may have been from mysterious enigma into a subversive mockery). Although puzzles drew on many historical periods, the propensity of school stories to feature Latin, and for adventure stories to draw on Greek myth or ancient history, explains the recurrence of classical puzzles. Arguably, Odd Fellow's series, which tackled head-on the triangulation between fictional school stories, elite public-school reminiscences and didactic leisure competitions could only work with Latin and Greek. It is surely no coincidence that a later *BOP* story, 'Some school grins', included the teacher suggesting that a macaronic-style translation should be sent to *Punch*;[86] this ironically reverses the experience of the puzzled pupil in 'The amateur dominie', who, on offering up his fateful analysis of the Latin ablative as a deliberately enigmatic affront, spoke 'not with any great confidence, but as one offering a guess at the solution of some profound mystery'.[87]

Notes

1 Hope, 'Amateur dominie'. The author, whom *BOP* advertised as well-known, was not only a prolific contributor of school stories but also wrote books such as *Romance and Legend of Chivalry; Treasury of Classical Mythology; Classical Mythology: Myths and Legends; The Illustrated Guide to Classical Mythology; Classical Legends*. 'Amateur dominie' was published in five instalments between 4 October 1879 and 1 November 1879, all illustrated by D. H. Friston.

2 'Odd Fellow', 'Fun from the Classics'.

3 This was the title given to a series of articles by 'Odd Fellow' in *BOP*, 'Fun from the Classics' (19 August 1882); 'More fun out of the Classics' (4 November 1882), 'Classical fun' (25 November 1882), 'Still more fun from the Classics' (17 March 1883) and some published anonymously in *BOP*: 'More "Fun from the Classics"' (25 November 1882), 'Fun from the Classics' (11 March 1893), 'Fun from the Classics' (13 April 1895).

4 Dixon, 'From instruction to amusement', p. 66.

5 Anon., 'Hints to candidates'; Anon., 'Hints to candidates preparing for the University Certificate'.

6 Clarke, *Classical Education*. Oxford and Cambridge dropped compulsory Greek in 1920, and Latin in 1960: see Stray, *Classics Transformed*, pp. 265–270.

7 Murnaghan and Roberts, *Childhood and the Classics*, p. 2.
8 On boy's periodicals, see: Boyd, *Manliness*; Cox, *Take a Cold Tub, Sir!*; Kirkpatrick, *From the Penny Dreadful*. On classical education in nineteenth-century Britain, see Clarke, *Classical Education* and Stray, *Classics Transformed*; on classical culture in Victorian Britain see Bryant Davies, *Troy, Carthage and the Victorians*; Goldhill, *Victorian Culture and Classical Antiquity*; Jenkyns, *The Victorians and Ancient Greece*; Richardson, *Classical Victorians*; Turner, *Greek Heritage in Victorian Britain*; Vance, *Victorians and Ancient Rome*.
9 Hecimovich, *Puzzling*, p. 80.
10 [Dickens], 'The "puzzle" mania'.
11 Gilmore, '"These verbal puzzles"', p. 298.
12 Hecimovich, *Puzzling*, p. 79.
13 *Ibid*.
14 S. Lindey, 'Boys write back'. On periodicals as correspondence societies, see Walton, '"Spinning the webs"'.
15 Boyd, *Manliness*, pp. 49–50.
16 Lindey, 'Boys write back', p. 73.
17 'Odd Fellow', 'Classical fun'.
18 'Odd Fellow', 'Fun from the Classics'.
19 'Odd Fellow', 'More fun out of the Classics'; this was a common phrase in *BOP*, recurring in Malan, 'Pompholugopaphlasma' and forming the subtitle of a serial, 'Uncle Towser: a story for boys young and old' also by Malan in *BOP* (5 October 1889–8 March 1890).
20 Boyd, *Manliness*, pp. 14, 16.
21 Salmon, *Juvenile Literature as it Is* (1888), p. 184, quoted in Lang, 'Childhood's champions', p. 28.
22 'Odd Fellow', 'Odd bits', and 'Odd Fellow', 'Boy-baiting'.
23 'Odd Fellow', 'Odd bits'.
24 'Odd Fellow', 'Fun from the Classics', quoting Heine (*Ideen: Das Buch Le Grand*, chapter 7).
25 'Our depressed contributor' [W. S. Gilbert], 'Haunted', *Fun* (24 March 1866), p. 12.
26 'Odd Fellow', 'Fun from the Classics'.
27 *Ibid*.
28 Malan, 'Pompholugopaphlasma'.
29 [Deane], 'The riddle-box: answer to "the race of the pilots"'.
30 Avery, *Childhood's Pattern*, p. 194.
31 Ellis, 'Recreational reading', p. 187.
32 'Odd Fellow', 'Fun from the Classics'.
33 Hope, 'Amateur dominie', p. 7.
34 Dixon, 'Children's magazines and science'; Onion, 'Writing a "wonderland"'; Prince, *Shakespeare in the Victorian Periodicals*; Prince, 'Shakespeare in the Victorian Children's Periodicals'; Sumpter, *Victorian Press*.
35 See further Bryant Davies, *Troy, Carthage and the Victorians*, pp. 125–202.
36 See North, *Waterloo Directory*, 2: 412, 411, 404.

37 'Odd Fellow', 'More fun out of the Classics'; 'Odd Fellow', 'Still more fun from the Classics'.
38 Anon., 'More "Fun from the Classics"'.
39 *Ibid.* This was also published in *Harper's New Monthly Magazine* ('Editor's drawer', December 1867, p. 134) and the *Advocate* (Harvard University magazine), (22 May 1868), pp. 92–93, as well as recurring in various medical periodicals. 'Latin rampant. Vide [see] the recent squib of a Dr Payne …'. Differences: 'one', not 'uno'. Emending 'parates' (sometimes spelled 'paratis') to 'partartes' (pear tarts) makes more sense for dessert.
40 Anon., 'Regulations'.
41 Anon., 'Crackers for the ingenious'.
42 Anon., 'Regulations'.
43 [Beaufort], 'Essayists' Association'.
44 *Ibid.*
45 Henderson, 'The Siege of Troy (Extract)'.
46 Anon., 'Original burlesque'; Anon., 'Essayist's Association'.
47 Anon., 'Crackers for the ingenious'.
48 [Deane], 'The riddle box: answer to "race of the pilots"', p. 341.
49 *Ibid.* A British address is given for the fifth prize-winner: G. W. S. Howson, of Yorkshire, England. Mention is also made of a wittily incorrect answer suspected to be 'from rather an old "boy"' which 'quite upset the gravity of the judges'.
50 'Odd Fellow', 'More fun out of the Classics'.
51 'Odd Fellow', 'Still more fun from the Classics'.
52 *Ibid.* An example of his 'post-bag' is the submitted set of comically incorrect translations ('An Old Boy', 'Our note book') described as 'having currency in the legends of Scottish schools'.
53 Kent, 'Some queer translations'.
54 Anon., 'Puzzle pages', pp. 502–503.
55 Boyd, *Manliness*, p. 29.
56 Anon, 'Puzzle pages', p. 502.
57 Macdowell, 'Oratio obliqua'. This is the grammatical construction known as 'indirect speech'; here, the name is used for the boy's mysterious fatal disease. Compare the comical quasi-scientific terms discussed by Keene in Chapter 1.
58 Stables, 'On special service'.
59 The preparation class, or homework session, clearly marks this as an elite boarding school.
60 Care, 'The strange adventure'.
61 Ellis, 'Recreational reading', p. 187; Lang, 'Childhood's champions', p. 25.
62 'Odd Fellow', 'Classical fun'.
63 Anon., 'Fun from the Classics', 1893.
64 'I come to bury Caesar, not to praise him': Shakespeare, *Julius Caesar*, Act 3, Scene 2.
65 Livy, *Ab Urbe Condita* 8.9–10; Smith, *Dictionary*, p. 1123.
66 Examples of both are in the British Museum's Townley Collection: Museum ID 1805,0703.43 and 1882,0422.1.

67 Anon. 'Our letter box'; Alexander, 'Some new games for boys'.
68 Anon., 'Fun from the Classics', 1895.
69 See further Bryant Davies, *Troy, Carthage and the Victorians*, pp. 249–252, 260, 238.
70 'Una', 'Double acrostic enigma'; 'Una', 'Answer: double acrostic enigma'.
71 M. E. R., 'Historical mental picture'; M. E. R., 'Answers to our March puzzles'.
72 Anon., 'Puzzle pages', p. 502.
73 Drotner, *English Children and their Magazines*, pp. 76, 129.
74 Anon., 'Crackers for the ingenious'.
75 'G. and T.', 'The riddle-box'; Deane, 'The riddle-box: answers to puzzles in March number'.
76 Sedgwick, 'The riddle-box'; Deane, 'The riddle-box: answers to puzzles in December number'.
77 Answers received before the 18th of both subsequent months: *ibid*.
78 Hope, 'Amateur dominie', p. 7.
79 'Odd Fellow', 'Fun from the Classics'.
80 'Odd Fellow', 'A column of comicalities'.
81 'Odd Fellow', 'Boy-baiting'.
82 'Odd Fellow', 'A ticklish subject'.
83 Hope, 'Amateur dominie', p. 7. This proverb appears in many contemporary textbooks; the most famous was the *Delectus* by Richard Valpy (1785), long-standing headmaster of Reading Grammar School, which was frequently revised, e.g. Leary, *Valpy's Latin Delectus*, p. 18. Translated as 'Meet ill with hope and good with fear', it is also linked with Aesop in 'Marmaduke Park', *Aesop in Rhyme*, p. 134.
84 'Odd Fellow', 'More fun out of the Classics'.
85 Kinglake, *Eothen*, pp. 56–58.
86 Hervey, 'Some school grins'.
87 Hope, 'Amateur dominie', p. 7.

References

Alexander, A., 'Some new games for boys', *Boy's Own Paper* (22 June 1895), p. 599.
'An Old Boy', 'Our note book: classical fun', *Boy's Own Paper* (12 May 1883), p. 516.
Anon., 'Crackers for the ingenious', *Boys of England* (10 April 1868), p. 335.
Anon., 'Fun from the Classics', *Boy's Own Paper* (11 March 1893), p. 38.
Anon., 'Fun from the Classics', *Boy's Own Paper* (13 April 1895), p. 448.
Anon., 'Hints to candidates', *Boy's Own Magazine* (1 March 1858), p. 83.
Anon., 'Hints to candidates preparing for the University Certificate', *Boy's Own Magazine* (1 April 1858), p. 123.
Anon., 'More "fun from the Classics"', *Boy's Own Paper* (25 November 1882), p. 127.
Anon., 'Original burlesque', *Routledge's Every Boy's Annual* (1 January 1871), p. 64.
Anon. 'Our letter box', *Young Folks Paper: Literary Olympic and Tournament* (7 July 1888), p. 16.
Anon., 'Puzzle pages' [double acrostics], *Beeton's Boy's Own* (1 September 1869), pp. 501–504.

Anon., 'Regulations to be observed by the solvers of our puzzles', *Routledge's Magazine for Boys* (1 March 1867), p. 6.

Avery, Gillian, *Childhood's Pattern: A Study of the Heroes and Heroines of Children's Fiction 1770–1950* (London: Hodder and Stoughton, 1975).

[Honourable Secretary], 'Beaufort, W. W. S., Essayists' Association (October Report)', *Beeton's Boy's Own Magazine* (November 1870), unpaginated.

Boyd, Kelly, *Manliness and the Boys' Story Paper in Britain: A Cultural History, 1855–1940* (Basingstoke: Palgrave Macmillan, 2002).

Bryant Davies, Rachel, *Troy, Carthage and the Victorians: The Drama of Classical Ruins in the Nineteenth-Century Imagination* (Cambridge: Cambridge University Press, 2018).

Care, Andrew, 'The strange adventure of a small boy', *Boy's Own Paper* (1 September 1894), p. 753–755.

Clarke, M. L., *Classical Education in Britain 1500–1900* (Cambridge: Cambridge University Press, 1959).

Cox, Jack, *Take a Cold Tub, Sir! The Story of the Boy's Own Paper* (Guildford: Lutterworth Press, 1892).

[Deane, Cyril], 'The riddle-box: answer to prize-puzzle, "the race of the pilots" in December number of *St Nicholas*', *St Nicholas* (1 March 1876), pp. 341–344.

Deane, Cyril, 'The riddle-box: answers to puzzles in March number' (classical double acrostic), *St Nicholas* (1 April 1876), p. 408.

Deane, Cyril, 'The riddle-box: answers to puzzles in December number' (classical puzzle), *St Nicholas* (1 January 1877), p. 230.

[Dickens, Charles], 'The "puzzle" mania', *All the Year Round*, 24:578 (1879), 114–116.

Dixon, Diana, 'Children's magazines and science in the nineteenth century', *Victorian Periodicals Review*, 34:3 (2001), 228–238.

Dixon, Diana, 'From instruction to amusement: attitudes of authority in children's periodicals before 1914', *Victorian Periodicals Review*, 19:2 (1896), 63–66.

Drotner, Kristen, *English Children and their Magazines, 1751–1945* (New Haven: Yale University Press, 1988).

Ellis, Alec, 'Influences on the availability of recreational reading for Victorian working class children', *Journal of Librarianship and Information Science*, 8:3 (1976), 185–195.

'G. and T.', 'The riddle-box: classical puzzle', *St Nicholas* (1 March 1876), p. 341.

Gilmore, Dehn, '"These verbal puzzles": Wilkie Collins, newspaper enigmas, and the Victorian reader as solver', *Victorian Literature and Culture*, 44 (2016), 297–314.

Goldhill, Simon, *Victorian Culture and Classical Antiquity: Art, Opera, Fiction, and the Proclamation of Modernity* (Princeton: Princeton University Press, 2011).

Hecimovich, Greg A., *Puzzling the Reader: Riddles in Nineteenth-century British Literature* (Bern: Peter Lang, 2008).

Henderson, F. R., 'The Siege of Troy (extract)', *Beeton's Boy's Own Magazine* (November 1870), unpaginated.

Hervey, H., 'Some school grins', *Boy's Own Paper* (23 December 1899), p. 187.

Hope, Ascott R., 'The amateur dominie', *Boy's Own Paper* (4 October 1879), pp. 6–8.

Jenkyns, Richard, *The Victorians and Ancient Greece* (Oxford: Blackwell, 1980).

Kent, Philip, 'Some queer translations', *Boy's Own Paper* (13 October 1888), p. 30.

Kinglake, Alexander, *Eothen: Traces of Travel Brought Home from the East* (London: John Olliver, 1844).
Kirkpatrick, Robert, *From the Penny Dreadful to the Ha'penny Dreadfuller: A Bibliographical History of the British Boys' Periodical, 1762–1950* (London: British Library, 2013).
Lang, Marjory, 'Childhood's champions: mid-Victorian children's periodicals and the critics', *Victorian Periodicals Review*, 13:1/2 (1980), 17–31.
Leary, Lindsay T. H. (ed.), *Valpy's Latin Delectus* (London: William Tegg, 1867).
Lindey, S., 'Boys write back: self-education and periodical authorship in late-nineteenth-century story papers', *American Periodicals*, 21:1 (2011), 72–88.
Macdowell, H., 'Oratio obliqua: a legend of the Latin grammar', *Boy's Own Paper* (28 June 1879), p. 381.
Malan, Rev. A. N., 'Pompholugopaphlasma', *Boy's Own Paper* (1 November 1890), p. 73.
'Marmaduke Park' (ed.), *Aesop in Rhyme, or, Old Friends in a New Dress* (Philadelphia: C. G. Henderson & Co., 1855).
M.E.R., 'Answers to our March puzzles', *Merry and Wise* (1 April 1871), p. 235.
M.E.R., 'Historical mental picture', *Merry and Wise* (1 March 1871), p. 185.
Murnaghan, Sheila and Roberts, Deborah H., *Childhood and the Classics: Britain and America, 1850–1965* (Oxford: Oxford University Press, 2018).
North, J. S. (ed.), *Waterloo Directory of English Newspapers and Periodicals, 1800–1900* (Waterloo, Ontario: North Waterloo Academic Press, 1997) 50 vols.
'Odd Fellow', 'A column of comicalities', *Boy's Own Paper* (23 December 1882), p. 208.
'Odd Fellow', 'A ticklish subject', *Boy's Own Paper* (30 June 1883), p. 638.
'Odd Fellow', 'Boy-baiting', *Boy's Own Paper* (14 March 1885), p. 375.
'Odd Fellow', 'Classical fun', *Boy's Own Paper* (25 November 1882), p. 122.
'Odd Fellow', 'Fun from the Classics', *Boy's Own Paper* (19 August 1882), p. 751.
'Odd Fellow', 'More fun out of the Classics', *Boy's Own Paper* (4 November 1882), p. 70.
'Odd Fellow', 'Odd bits by an odd fellow', *Boy's Own Paper* (5 March 1881), p. 375.
'Odd Fellow', 'School graces etc', *Boy's Own Paper* (10 February 1883), p. 3.
'Odd Fellow', 'Still more fun from the Classics', *Boy's Own Paper* (17 March 1883), pp. 398–399.
Onion, Rebecca, 'Writing a "wonderland" of science: child-authored periodicals at the Brooklyn Children's Museum, 1936–1946', *American Periodicals*, 23:1 (2013), 1–21.
'Our Depressed Contributor' [W. S. Gilbert], 'Haunted', Fun (24 March 1866), p. 12.
Prince, Kathryn, 'Shakespeare in the Victorian Children's Periodicals', in K. Chedgzoy, S. Greenhalgh and R. Shaughnessy (eds), *Shakespeare and Childhood* (Cambridge: Cambridge University Press, 2007), pp. 153–168.
Prince, Kathryn, *Shakespeare in the Victorian Periodicals* (London: Routledge, 2011).
Richardson, Edmund, *Classical Victorians: Scholars, Scoundrels and Generals in Pursuit of Antiquity* (Cambridge: Cambridge University Press, 2013).
Sedgwick, 'The riddle-box: classical double acrostic', *St Nicholas* (1 December 1876), p. 151.
Smith, William, *Dictionary of Greek and Roman Antiquities* (London: Taylor and Walton, 1842).
Stables, Gordon, 'On special service: a naval story', *Boy's Own Paper* (18 April 1885), p. 457.

Stray, Christopher, *Classics Transformed: Schools, Universities, and Society in England, 1830–1960* (Oxford: Clarendon Press, 1998).
Sumpter, Caroline, *The Victorian Press and the Fairy Tale* (Basingstoke: Palgrave Macmillan, 2008).
Turner, Frank, *The Greek Heritage in Victorian Britain* (New Haven: Yale University Press, 1981).
'Una', 'Answer: double acrostic enigma', submitted to M.A.M, 'Our puzzle department', *Merry and Wise* (1 May 1868), p. 276.
'Una', 'Double acrostic enigma', submitted to M.A.M, 'Our puzzle department', *Merry and Wise* (1 April 1868), p. 218.
Vance, Norman, *The Victorians and Ancient Rome* (Oxford: Blackwell, 1997).
Walton, S., '"Spinning the webs": education and distance learning through Charlotte Yonge's *Monthly Packet*', *Victorian Periodicals Review*, 49: 2 (2016), 278–304.

Part III

Medieval and early modern pasts

5

Youthful consumption and conservative visions: Robin Hood and Wat Tyler in late Victorian penny periodicals

Stephen Basdeo

Since his first appearance in a Yorkshire Assize roll in 1225, the story of the outlaw Robin Hood, who is said to have stolen from the rich to give to the poor, has stood for truth, justice and resistance to oppression.[1] Second only to Robin Hood among medieval heroes is Wat Tyler who, along with Jack Straw and John Ball, heroically led an army of up to 50,000 to London in the summer of 1381 to demand an end to the poll tax, the abolition of serfdom and the freedom for all men to buy and sell in the marketplace.[2]

As the centuries wore on, stories of the lives and deeds of Robin Hood and Wat Tyler were continually adapted in literary works in order to serve a variety of political agendas. While stories about the two men originally represented a challenge to local and kingly authority, their post-medieval stories followed different ideological trajectories: Robin Hood was gradually 'gentrified', according to Stephen Knight, while Wat Tyler became an inspirational symbol for radicals and revolutionaries, from the English Revolution down to the Chartist period.

Much has been written on portrayals of Robin Hood and Wat Tyler in the earlier part of the nineteenth century. Both men's stories were retold in expensive literary works which presented a conservative view of the medieval past, which corroborates Clare A. Simmons's assertion that, after c. 1830, medievalism became conservative and expensive.[3] However, this chapter analyses portrayals of Robin Hood and Wat Tyler in boys' magazines and penny dreadfuls which invite a more nuanced reading. As this chapter argues, medievalism could be cheap and conservative, and both men's stories even appeared in respectable boys' penny magazines, but they were often received as subversive by reviewers. The lines between respectable cheap reading matter and controversial penny dreadful were often blurred and the former came in for censure just as much as the latter. The ideological position of the actual stories rarely mattered to reviewers when judging the respectability of the text.

Robin Hood

Shortly before the beginning of the Victorian era, in the *Quarterly Review* in 1832, Robert Southey, an author who wrote about both Wat Tyler and Robin Hood,[4] defined conservatism as an ideology that was supportive of the Protestant ascendancy, being patriotic, having a paternalistic attitude to the poor, a respect for hierarchy and favouring gradual political reform over violent revolution.[5] A definition of conservatism from a man such as Southey is useful because he famously became a staunch conservative after having abandoned the radical ideology of his youth and was, therefore, familiar with debates from across the political spectrum. A similar conservative ideology is conveyed in George Emmett's *Robin Hood and the Archers of Merrie Sherwood* (1868–1869), which was sold in monthly penny parts. In contrast, Pierce Egan the Younger's earlier *Robin Hood and Little John* (1838–1840), which Emmett drew heavily upon, depicted Sherwood Forest as a democratic space in which Robin has to be elected by his fellow outlaws as their leader.[6] The forest community of Sherwood in Emmett's tale, however, is separated into classes and is a mirror of Victorian social strata, divided as it is into masters and servants. Robin Hood is the Earl of Huntingdon and Little John is his servant, whom Robin disciplines frequently and in a condescending manner, as the following typical exchange indicates:

> 'Thou wilt keep that prating tongue o' thine quiet,' said Robin ...
>
> 'I am quiet, good master,' said John hastily, – 'as quiet as a chauntry of monks when the superior is away. Body o'me, I would sooner be cooped up with forty devils than one sleek monk. Quiet, by Saint Hubert! I'll not speak for seven long days!'[7]

In every late Victorian Robin Hood story, the outlaw is always the Earl of Huntingdon and there is little need to go into the undemocratic and hierarchical depiction of Sherwood Forest in each text. (It should be said, however, that Robin Hood does treat his men with more respect in other stories.) In Emmett's tale, ranked below Earl Robin are his yeomen, Little John and Will Scarlet. Finally, at the bottom of Sherwood society are a number of rank-and-file men who are assigned no special social status.

Thus, the message from these Robin Hood penny dreadfuls was clear: because a hero such as Robin Hood keeps existing social hierarchies in place in Sherwood Forest, so too should hierarchies be respected. This did not, however, preclude Robin and his men being kind to the poor. The most famous trope to emerge from the post-medieval Robin Hood tradition is that he stole from the rich and gave to the poor: a tradition that started in John Major's *Historia Maioris Britanniae* (1521), which states that Robin Hood 'would allow no woman to suffer injustice, nor would he spoil the poor, but rather enriched them from the plunder taken from the abbots. The robberies of this man I condemn, but of all robbers he was the humanest and the chief.'[8] While for the most part, Robin Hood penny dreadfuls are not overtly religious, his activities in supplying the wants of the poor with plundered booty are presented often as an extension of Christian charity.

Furthermore, there is no hint that the Robin Hood of penny dreadfuls wishes to overturn the existing hierarchy or even fight for political rights for the poor. He is charitable to them, but that is all. His usual enemies in every penny dreadful are Prince John and invariably either members of the Knights Templar, which is an obvious hangover from Scott's *Ivanhoe* (1819), or the Sheriff of Nottingham's henchmen. Other enemies include characters from the usual repertoire of villains from the Robin Hood canon such as Guy of Gisborne. A story of Robin's rivalry with Gisborne was serialised in *Boys of England* in 1887 and it features a rather gruesome image of Robin decapitating Guy.[9] While *Boys of England* is not immediately identifiable as a Victorian penny dreadful to modern scholars – often being thought of as one of the more 'wholesome' magazines available – it frequently received similar criticisms to those levelled at the more salacious periodicals, and in court records was often included in the list of 'dangerous' magazines, a point also raised by John Springhall.[10] And there was, of course, Robin Hood's arch-enemy, the Sheriff of Nottingham. All of the villains usually act under the direction of Prince John. When Robin Hood stories are set against the backdrop of the 1190s, they are inherently conservative. Robin is usually outlawed because he has stayed loyal to King Richard and has refused to side with John in attempting to seize his throne. As Stephen Knight argues, therefore, in such settings Robin Hood becomes nothing less than an upholder of the true political order.[11]

Above all, Robin Hood's loyalty to the king means that, more often than not, he was depicted as a deeply patriotic and nationalist figure and held up as an example of the superiority of the Anglo-Saxon 'race'. It was easy for late Victorian writers to superimpose late Victorian Anglo-Saxonism on to the story of Robin Hood: Walter Scott had, of course, initiated the trope of the outlaw's Anglo-Saxon heritage in *Ivanhoe*. Scott's vision of medieval English society as being divided into two races, Saxon and Norman, was racialist; social, cultural and linguistic differences existed between the Normans and the Saxons, yet there was no sense in *Ivanhoe* that those of

Saxon heritage were biologically superior to other races. In fact, in *Ivanhoe*, Scott argues that the English nation will be at its best when Normans and Saxons put aside their differences and work together for the good of the nation.

However, in late Victorian stories, there was a glorification of Anglo-Saxon heritage. Readers of the *Boy's Own Magazine* were counselled to seek out medieval and early modern Robin Hood ballads because 'if the study of Latin is likely to make a scholar expert in the use of polished language, the study of old English ballads is highly conducive to the acquisition of that best of all English – strong, simple Saxon-English'.[12] Robin Hood ballads were reprinted in numerous books in the late Victorian period; reprints of Joseph Ritson's *Robin Hood: A Collection of all the Ancient Poems, Songs, and Ballads* (1795) appeared in 1820, 1823, 1860 and in 1884. Other late Victorian editors sought to emulate Ritson's work in a number of cheap collections of Robin Hood ballads as well, and some were even reprinted in boys' magazines. In reality, early Robin Hood poems are not written in Old English but in Middle English, and there is very little that is Saxon about them. In Will Williams's 'Bold Robin Hood and his merry, merry men', which appeared in the supposedly respectable penny magazine *Our Young Folks* in 1873, the Saxon Robin Hood is 'the bold and dauntless hero – the hero of a valiant thousand deeds'.[13] While he is outlawed due to the machinations of Prince John and his henchmen, he remains unwaveringly loyal to the king, and at the close of the story the reader is told that 'Robin Hood was a true patriot, as his career, so often portrayed, shows – a great-hearted man in an age when great-hearted men were few.'[14] Cultivating an admiration for the allegedly Saxon Robin Hood, as well as an interest in studying Middle English and early modern texts would, in the opinion of late Victorian penny authors, inculcate a love of their country and pride in it.

Wat Tyler

In contrast to Robin Hood, it was difficult for late Victorian children's fiction writers to imbue Wat Tyler with a conservative ideology. The historical Tyler was, after all, a man who led a crowd of discontented people to demand redress from the king. His comrade, John Ball, uttered the famous lines yearning for equality, asking 'Whan Adam dalf, and Eve span, Wo was thanne a gentilman?' [When Adam delved and Eve span, who was then the gentleman?].[15] As far as the political leanings of penny dreadful Wat Tyler stories are concerned, only a few are avowedly radical or contain anti-establishment sentiments. A story entitled 'The death of Wat Tyler', which appeared in the *Boys' Comic Journal* in 1892, told the story of Tyler's death at Walworth's hand and the subsequent revocation of the royal charters by Richard II, before counselling its readers to 'put not your faith in princes'.[16] The anonymous author followed up this injunction by saying,

> [After the revolt] all pardons were revoked by parliament, the people ground again under the yoke of slavery, and hundreds of men who expected to hear no more of the rebellion were dragged from their homes and executed. Right or wrong, Wat Tyler set a seal on the liberties of the people. Doubtless, he was a ruffian, but in those days the arrogance and cruelty of the nobility manufactured ruffians wholesale.[17]

This passage justifies the historical Wat Tyler's actions, as well as those of the crowd, to those reading it. He is still a 'ruffian', however, which puts him on a par with the newly identified 'hooligan' of the late nineteenth century. Most of the Wat Tyler stories considered here, though, present his actions in an extremely negative light, or disavow them completely. An effort is made in these stories to neuter any subversive elements that may be present in its retelling of Wat Tyler's life story.

In *The Sword of Freedom; or, The Boyhood Days of Jack Straw* (c. 1870) the eponymous rebel is actually the son of a nobleman, as many heroes of Victorian fiction turn out to be. The novel is similar to a Robin Hood novel: having been outlawed for a petty misdemeanour, Straw, and some of his associates, flee to the forest and begin living the life of outlaws. Jack Straw and his comrades are in fact indistinguishable from contemporary depictions of Robin Hood which accompanied this serial's first two issues; they are dressed in the same types of outfits – feathered hats and tunics – and the background in the opening numbers of both *The Sword of Freedom* and George Emmett's *Robin Hood* is a forest (see Figures 5.1 and 5.2). Judging by its appearance, the author and publisher clearly meant for *The Sword of Freedom* to be received as a Robin Hood story to draw on the popularity of such tales published in a variety of outlets. Straw's moral compass is similar to that of Robin Hood's, for Straw and his men are unwaveringly loyal to King Edward III in spite of being an outlaw. At one point in the novel, Edward's courtiers conspire against him to overthrow him by imprisoning him in the Tower of London and hiring assassins to murder him. Jack Straw learns of the plot and offers his services for the task. However, because he is loyal to the king, Jack betrays the traitors by saving the king's life instead of killing him in the tower. The king immediately wishes to grant Jack a reward. Jack does not ask for any favours himself, however, but says,

> I would ask you, Sire, to dissolve the infamous yearly tax upon their persons; to give them liberty of speech; to let every man hire his ground at State valuation, and not at the price nobles put upon it – for, by doing so, they crush the loyal and honest man and often make him a rebel and a thief … the serfs are more to you than your nobles – and for this reason, Sire: they are the builders-up of

the fortunes of the nobles; they are the men who, when the peace of the country is threatened by foreigners, fly to arms; and, on the battlefield, they prove that they have as much, and more, courage than those who tread upon them with iron heels, and contemptuously call them slaves and hounds.[18]

True to his word, and completely out of keeping with the historical record, the king in this story complies with young Jack's request. The reason why a man such as Jack Straw, who is so unwaveringly loyal to the monarch, would then go on to associate with rebels like Wat Tyler and John Ball and take a leading role in the Peasants' Revolt, is not explained until the end of the novel. It is revealed that in 1381, Jack Straw is an old man who, by virtue of his service to the king, has inherited vast estates. He is admired by the people at large and known as 'the Friend of the People'. He then dies peacefully in his bed just before the revolt and exclaims: 'the name under which, for so long I fought, is, to all of us, dead; let us hope and trust that he who, for his own purpose, is pleased to revive it, will keep from disgrace the name of Jack Straw'.[19] Unfortunately for this fictional Jack Straw, it transpires that a disreputable fellow assumed his name afterwards. It was the imposter who would go on to associate with Tyler and the mob in the rebellion. It is unlikely that the honourable, patriotic, and ultimately fictional, Jack Straw of *The Sword of Freedom* would have approved of the actions of the historical Jack Straw, who was executed in 1381 and whose head was placed atop London Bridge to serve as a warning for other would-be rebels.

Some writers simply ignored the revolt. A story entitled 'Wat Tyler; or, The King and the Apprentice' appeared in the *Young Englishman* in 1867 over thirty-five issues. This was one of the longer serials to have appeared in the columns of this magazine, which is perhaps an indication of the serial's popularity. It depicts the eponymous young rebel as the son of a working-class family. Known as 'the honest Wat Tyler', he is a good-natured but headstrong young lad who wants nothing more than to please his parents by making his way in the world through learning a trade.[20] He is sent by his parents to be an apprentice blacksmith under the stewardship of his uncle, Dick (who, for a medieval man, lives a curiously Victorian lifestyle). Wat tires of this life and becomes an outlaw for a short time. However, he is pardoned by King Edward III and eventually marries the daughter of a nobleman, who bears him a son. Not a single word is said in reference to the revolt, and the publishers were merely using Wat Tyler to present a generic medieval story of a lad becoming an outlaw before reforming himself and making his way in the world.

There is definitely a focus upon young characters in other stories which was likely intended to have greater appeal for younger readers. For example, 'Gentle deeds; or, serfdom to knighthood', which was serialised in *Our Young Folks Paper* in May 1886, follows the adventures of a village boy called Simon

ROBIN HOOD
AND THE ARCHERS OF MERRIE SHERWOOD.
BY GEORGE EMMETT,

Author of "Tom Wildrake's Schooldays," "For Valour," and "Midshipman Tom," "Captain Jack," Etc., Etc.

MUCH, THE MILLER'S SON, RELATES HIS STORY.

"Come, listen to me, ye gentlemen,
That be of freeborn blood,
I shall tell you of a good yeoman,
His name was Robin Hood."
OLD BALLAD.

No memory in the world ever produced a hero whose memory has lived through so many years as that of Sherwood's forester—bold Robin Hood.

Much has been written about his doings, but among the many versions there has been but a slight sprinkling of the true life of this remarkable outlaw.

Endeared to the youth of England by the old songs, quotations, games, and proverbs which a few centuries since were made to his remembrance, it is surprising that the modern versions of his life, except in one or

5.1 First number of George Emmett's *Robin Hood*, p. 1.

5.2 *The Sword of Freedom; or, The Boyhood Days of Jack Straw*, c. 1870, issue 2, p. 2.

who meets an outlaw named Wat Tyler and his band called 'the men in green'. They are not benevolent outlaws of the Robin Hood variety but, rather, are depicted as brutal cut-throats (this is a very similar plot point to that which appears in William Harrison Ainsworth's 1874 Wat Tyler novel entitled *Merry England; or, Nobles and Serfs*, in which Tyler and his band are cut-throat outlaws). Tyler appears only briefly in this serial, however, and the story, as its title suggests, follows young Simon's rise through society to serve the Black Prince and become a knight. Service to the nation is evidently presented as a means of social mobility.

There were, of course, some conservative and expensive portrayals of Robin Hood and Wat Tyler presented to children. G. A. Henty perhaps drew inspiration from this obscure serial when he wrote *A March on London* (1896), which retells the story of the 1381 rebellion. In this story, a young village boy named Albert is offered the opportunity to serve in the Hundred Years' War (1337–1453). Albert and his father, Edgar, travel to London, not as part of the revolt but to sort out some family affairs. His father has little admiration or sympathy with the rebels:

> 'Is there any chance of trouble in the city, father?' Albert asked.
>
> 'I know not, lad. The better class of citizens are assuredly opposed to those who make these troubles ... Would that Lancaster was here with a thousand or so of men-at-arms,' [Edgar] went on, gloomily; 'there is no one at the Court who can take command.'[21]

Edgar takes Albert into Kent where a chance meeting with Wat Tyler occurs. The father proves to be a formidable political debater:

> 'You are the son of the man at St. Alwyth,' [said Wat Tyler]. 'I have seen you in the streets before. What think you of what we are doing? I have heard of you attending meetings there.'
>
> 'I think that you have been cruelly wronged,' Edgar answered, quietly, 'and that the four points that you demand are just and right. I wish you good fortune in obtaining them, and I trust that it will be done peacefully and without opposition.'
>
> 'Whether peacefully or not, we are determined that they shall be obtained. If it be needful, we will burn down London and kill every man of rank who falls into our hands, and force our way into the king's presence. We will have justice!'
>
> 'If you do so you will be wrong,' Edgar said, calmly; 'and moreover, instead of benefiting your cause you will damage it ... you would set the nobles throughout the land against you, you would defeat your own good objects, and would in the end bring destruction upon yourselves; so that instead of bettering your position you would be worse than before.'[22]

Even though there is very little difference in terms of plot and political ideology between Henty's story and *Our Young Folk's Paper* and some of the other Wat Tyler penny serials mentioned above, it was Henty's tale which drew praise from the conservative press.[23] Henty's book would have cost a purchaser a total of 6 shillings when first published.[24] In 1898, according to one report from 1905, the average urban labourer earned 16s 9d per week, with a higher average rate of 22s 2d per week being recorded in northern industrial towns.[25] This is more than two days' work for a single volume; historical romances by the likes of Henty are unlikely to have been purchased by working-class labourers even on the higher end of the average income. Of course, Henty's brand of conservative medievalism, as displayed not only in *A March on London*, but also in his *A Knight of the White Cross*, as well as conservative tales by other writers, such as Edward Gilliatt's *In Lincoln Green* (1897) and Escot Lynn's *When Lionheart was King* (1908), were sometimes available for free for working-class children.[26] During the late-Victorian and Edwardian eras, many of these books were given out as school or Sunday School prizes: historical tales were especially popular choices for prize-givers.[27] Not all prize books were fiction, however: for example, books such as Henry Newbolt's *Froissart in Britain* (1902) and M. Edgar's *The Boys' Froissart* (1912), which were abridged and translated editions of Froissart's chronicles and preserved his disdain for the rebels, were also awarded as prizes. Each book would probably have been too expensive for average labourers to purchase outright for one of their children: Newbolt's book sold for 2s 6d,[28] and, depending upon the binding used, prices for the latter ranged from 5 shillings for a cloth-bound edition to 10s 6d for velvet Persian yapp binding.[29] As far as portrayals of Robin Hood and Wat Tyler go, not only were there conservative and cheap medievalist tales but also conservative and expensive medieval novels which were often awarded free of charge.

Readers' reception of Robin Hood and Wat Tyler

Thus far, as we have seen, there was little that was controversial in the actual text of these penny dreadfuls. The *texts* of the Robin Hood stories are conservative, stressing the values of patriotism, the superiority of the Anglo-Saxon 'race', a paternalist attitude towards those who are less fortunate, and loyalty to the political and social order. Wat Tyler penny dreadfuls – with one exception, that of *The Sword of Freedom* – depict him more often than not as a brute, and they usually condemn his actions in the revolt. This perhaps suggests that the name of Jack Straw was not as famous in the annals of Victorian popular history, and that his story was more easily moulded to suit a conservative agenda. Yet reviewers did not read these periodicals as conservative but viewed them as subversive, and as providing an addictive entry point into a life of crime. John Springhall argues that penny dreadfuls, particularly those which recounted stories of historical thieves such as Jack Sheppard (1702–1724) and Dick Turpin (1705–1739), or fictional ones such as *The Wild Boys of London* (c. 1866), were a scapegoat for late Victorian fears surrounding the rise of juvenile crime.[30] Such anxieties seemed to be confirmed when juvenile delinquents, standing before magistrates in the dock, confessed that their crimes were due to the fact that they had been led into their evil course of life through reading such literature. For example, Stephen Easton, an eighteen-year-old burglar, said at his trial that 'it was all owing to reading books – the *Boys of England, Young Men of Great Britain*, and others'.[31] It will be noted in that passage that even the supposedly respectable penny papers attracted censure and that what was needed, so some commentators thought, was a wholesale reform of working-class children's reading matter. This reformation was viewed as especially urgent since the implementation of the Education Act (1870), which made it compulsory for all children to receive schooling in the basics of the 'three Rs'. The problem and the solution were made clear in a pamphlet written by Charlotte Yonge in *What Books to Lend and What Books to Give* (1877):

> Wholesome and amusing literature has become almost a necessity among the appliances of parish work. The power of reading leads, in most cases, to the craving for books. If good not be provided, evil will only too easily be found … If the boy is not to betake himself to 'Jack Sheppard' literature, he must be beguiled by wholesome adventure. If the girl is not to study the 'penny dreadful,' her notions must be refined by the tale of high romance or pure pathos.[32]

There is no doubt that Henty's Wat Tyler story would have fallen into the category of one of Yonge's approved books. The controversy surrounding stories of Jack Sheppard stemmed from the moral panic over William Harrison Ainsworth's eponymous novel published in 1839, which allegedly inspired the valet Benjamin Courvoisier to murder his master Lord William Russell. Ainsworth's novel led to a proliferation of cheap Jack Sheppard novels throughout the century.[33]

The young offenders cited the names of magazines rather than individual stories' titles and rarely mentioned Robin Hood by name. Only occasionally did moralists in the press connect stories specifically about Robin Hood and Little John to contemporary tales of crime:

> Talk of Robin Hood and Little John, and their dingy imitators in this metropolis described by Dickens and Ainsworth … The same man passes from one form into another – developing, according to the changes in society, from a forester to a mountaineer, thence to a highwayman, thence to an instructor of pickpockets and the receiver of their day's work in St. Giles.[34]

Young readers themselves on occasion often connected Robin Hood with more dubious types of criminals such as Sheppard and Turpin. For example, when recalling his childhood in the 1870s, a Calvinist minister from South Wales who grew up in a working-class household revealed, 'Robin Hood was our patron saint or ideal. We sincerely believed in robbing the rich to help the poor ... Our real heroes were robbers like Jack Sheppard, Dick Turpin, and Charles Peace, whose "Penny dreadful" biographies we knew by heart.'[35] This minister evidently recalled his youthful readings of such tales with fondness, and of course some contemporary commentators had a more balanced assessment of penny dreadfuls. Arthur Quiller-Couch, in an essay entitled *The Poor Little Penny Dreadful* (1896), remarked that often penny dreadfuls 'were even rather ostentatiously on the side of virtue. As for the bloodshed in them, it was comparable to that in many of the five-shilling adventure stories at that time read so eagerly by boys of the middle and upper classes.'[36] The fact that Victorian moralists never bothered actually to read the stories that they were condemning explains why Robin Hood and Wat Tyler rarely appeared by name; instead the magazines as a whole, the publishers of the stories, were condemned.

Conclusion

Further studies are needed on the affordability of medievalism in the late Victorian period to clarify intent and audience. Paradoxically it was usually radical appropriations of the medieval past that were expensive. At the same time as these more conservative visions circulated in the penny dreadfuls they competed with socialist appropriations and interpretations of the period in the latter half of the nineteenth century. One of the first socialist historiographical works was Charles Edmund Maurice's *Lives of English Popular Leaders in the Middle Ages: Tyler, Ball, and Oldcastle* (1875), which would have set a would-be reader back 7s 6d.[37] William Morris's *A Dream of John Ball* (1888), in which a time-traveller goes back to 1381 and meets John Ball, cost 4s. 6d. upon its first publication.[38] The Kelmscott edition of this text, as one would expect, was even more expensive, retailing at £1 10s.[39] As a movement that is ostensibly about bettering the condition of the working classes, it is curious to see that Morris's influential socialist texts were among the most expensive that people could buy. This should not surprise many scholars who work on late Victorian socialism, for it was a 'very middle-class affair' at this point.[40] In fairness to Morris, however, his and E. Belfort Bax's 'Socialism from the root up', which provides a history of medieval socialism, could be had for a penny in *Commonweal*, and an earlier version of *A Dream of John Ball* was circulated in the same magazine in 1886. Nevertheless, it would surely have made more sense for socialists to target the cheaper end of the literary market – but they did not, which allowed conservative portrayals of the medieval past to dominate the marketplace.

Cheap and conservative accounts of Robin Hood and Wat Tyler during the late Victorian period did indeed dominate the lower end of the literary marketplace. Authors strove to give a respectable slant to their stories; Sherwood Forest society in the penny novels discussed here is decidedly undemocratic, in contrast to earlier Robin Hood works by the likes of Pierce Egan the Younger; Wat Tyler is rarely the hero of the story, as such, but depicted as a ruffian or, in other cases, he is a hero but the revolt is simply ignored by authors. In spite of these authors' 'conservatising' efforts, reviewers did not read their stories as conservative but regarded them as dangerous and potentially subversive. There was a tension between the ideology of the text and its reception, and if scholars are to gain a more comprehensive understanding of such texts then this needs to be taken into account. It did not matter, furthermore, whether the stories were published in so-called penny dreadful magazines or in the more respectable periodicals; if they were cited by a juvenile criminal in the dock in front of a judge then they were dangerous and there was no division in contemporaries' minds between so-called 'Jack Sheppard' literature and the likes of the *Boys of England*. This shows that the division between respectable reading matter and dangerous literature has been stated more frequently and forcefully by modern scholars than it ever was by the Victorians themselves.

Notes

1 These sources were originally discussed, and a similar argument made, in my thesis: Basdeo, 'The Changing Faces', ch. 5. For general discussions of Robin Hood in Victorian penny literature see Carpenter, 'Robin Hood in Boy's Weeklies to 1914', pp. 47–68 and Basdeo, 'Radical Medievalism', pp. 48–64. These are both works whose findings have informed the chapter presented here, as has the work of Barczewski, *Myth and National Identity*. For a discussion of the 'gentrification' of the Robin Hood legend see Knight, *Reading Robin Hood* and Knight, *Robin Hood: A Complete Study*.
2 Unfortunately for Tyler, William Walworth killed him after the former was rude to the king during a meeting between Tyler and the king at Smithfield. John Ball and Jack Straw were also later executed on the king's orders. For an overview of the historical sources relating the events of 1381 see Dobson, *The Peasants' Revolt of 1381*.
3 Simmons, *Popular Medievalism*, p. 191.
4 The following texts were written by Robert Southey: 'Harold; or, The Castle of Morford'; *Wat Tyler*. See also Robert and Caroline Southey, *Robin Hood*.

5 Eastwood, 'Robert Southey'.
6 Egan, *Robin Hood and Little John*, 1851, p. 158. The depiction of Robin Hood as an elected leader also occurs in the anonymous *Little John and Will Scarlet*.
7 Emmett, *Robin Hood*, p. 42.
8 Major, 'Historia Maioris Britanniae'.
9 Anon., 'Robin Hood and Guy of Gisborne'.
10 Springhall, 'Healthy Papers for Manly Boys', p. 108.
11 Knight, *Robin Hood: A Mythic Biography*, p. 63.
12 Anon., 'A ballad of Robin Hood'.
13 Williams, 'Bold Robin Hood', 1873, p. 617. The magazine in question changed its name several times. Titles included *Our Young Folks*, *Our Young Folks Paper*, *Our Young Folk's Paper*, *Our Young Folks' Weekly Budget*. This accounts for the inconsistency in later records.
14 Williams, 'Bold Robin Hood', 1874, p. 108.
15 Ball, 'John Ball's Sermon Theme'.
16 Anon., 'The death of Wat Tyler'.
17 *Ibid.*
18 Lambe, *The Sword of Freedom*, pp. 148–149.
19 *Ibid.*, p. 185.
20 Anon., 'Wat Tyler; or, the king and the apprentice', p. 338.
21 Henty, *A March on London*, pp. 64–65.
22 *Ibid.*, pp. 54–55.
23 Anon., 'A march on London'.
24 Henty, *A March on London*, p. ii.
25 Anon., ['Book advertisement'], 1905.
26 For a discussion of Henty's Wat Tyler novel and its relation to those Wat Tyler novels which came before see Basdeo, *The Life and Legend of a Rebel Leader: Wat Tyler*, ch. 5.
27 Simon Goldhill, *Victorian Culture and Classical Antiquity*, p. 229.
28 Anon., ['Book advertisement'], 1902, p. 7.
29 'Yapped' means that the leather covers overlap the text block, thereby preserving the gilded page edges from the elements, and this style of binding was common in nineteenth-century Bibles.
30 Springhall, '"Pernicious reading"?'.
31 Anon., 'A boy burglar'.
32 Yonge, *What Books to Lend*, pp. 5–6.
33 E.g. Anon., *Jack Sheppard: His Real Life and Exploits*; Anon., *Jack Sheppard; or, London in the Last Century*; Anon., *Jack Sheppard the House-Breaker*.
34 Anon., 'Talk of Robin Hood and Little John'.
35 Rose, *Intellectual Life of the British Working Classes*, p. 368. Original reference: Howard, *Winding Lanes*, pp. 27–30.
36 Quiller-Couch, *Adventures in Criticism*, cited in Kirkpatrick, *Wild Boys in the Dock*, p. 28.
37 Maurice, *Lives of English Popular Leaders*, p. 2.
38 Anon., 'Advertisement', p. 710.

39 Anon., 'Book sales for 1893', p. 17. For more information on the history of the Kelmscott Press, see: Peterson, *Kelmscott Press*.
40 Bevir, *Making of British Socialism*, p. 37.

References

Ainsworth, William Harrison, *Jack Sheppard*, 3 vols (London: Bentley, 1839).
Ainsworth, William Harrison, *Merry England; or, Nobles and Serfs*, 3 vols (London: Tinsley, 1874).
Anon., 'A ballad of Robin Hood', *Boy's Own Magazine* (1 January 1855), p. 25.
Anon., 'A boy burglar', *Reynolds's Newspaper* (28 October 1877), p. 6.
Anon., 'Advertisement', *Athenaeum* (24 November 1888), p. 710.
Anon., 'A march on London', *Spectator* (6 November 1887), p. 9.
Anon., ['Book advertisement'], *Spectator* (1 November 1902), p. 7.
Anon., ['Book advertisement'], *Spectator* (25 February 1905), p. 8.
Anon., 'Book sales for 1893', *Athenaeum* (6 January 1894), pp. 16–17.
Anon., *Jack Sheppard: His Real Life and Exploits* (London: C. Fox, [n. d.]).
Anon., *Jack Sheppard; or, London in the Last Century* (London: G. Mansell, 1845).
Anon., *Jack Sheppard the House-Breaker* (London: Glover, 1840).
Anon., *Little John and Will Scarlet* (London: H. Vickers, 1865).
Anon., 'Robin Hood and Guy of Gisborne', Boys of England (4 March 1887), p. 92.
Anon., 'Talk of Robin Hood and Little John', *The Times* (22 June 1855), p. 6.
Anon., 'The death of Wat Tyler', *Boys' Comic Journal*, 19: 474 (1892), p. 190.
Anon., 'Wat Tyler; or, the king and the apprentice', *Young Englishman's Journal*, 22 (1867), pp. 337–338.
Ball, John, 'John Ball's Sermon Theme', in James M. Dean (ed.), *Medieval English Political Writings* (Kalamazoo: Medieval Institute Publications, 1996), https://d.lib.rochester.edu/teams/text/dean-medieval-english-political-writings-john-balls-sermon-theme.
Barczewski, Stephanie, *Myth and National Identity in Nineteenth-Century Britain: The Legends of King Arthur and Robin Hood* (Oxford: Oxford University Press, 2000).
Basdeo, Stephen, 'Radical Medievalism: Pierce Egan's Robin Hood, Wat Tyler, and Adam Bell', in Stephen Basdeo and Lauren Padgett (eds), *Imagining the Victorians* (Leeds: Leeds Working Papers in Victorian Studies, 2016), pp. 48–64.
Basdeo, Stephen, 'The Changing Faces of Robin Hood, c. 1700–c.1900: Rethinking Gentrification in the Post-Medieval Tradition' (PhD dissertation, University of Leeds, 2017).
Basdeo, Stephen, *The Life and Legend of a Rebel Leader: Wat Tyler* (Barnsley: Pen and Sword, 2018).
Bevir, Mark, *The Making of British Socialism* (Princeton: Princeton University Press, 2011).
Carpenter, Kevin, 'Robin Hood in Boy's Weeklies to 1914', in Julia Briggs, Dennis Butts amd Matthew Orville Grenby (eds), *Popular Children's Literature in Britain* (Aldershot: Ashgate, 2008), pp. 47–68.
Dobson, R. B. (ed.), *The Peasants' Revolt of 1381* (London: Macmillan, 1970).
Eastwood, David, 'Robert Southey and the intellectual origins of romantic conservatism', *English Historical Review*, 104:411 (1989), 308–331.

Edgar, M. (ed.), *The Boys' Froissart* (London: Harrap, 1912).
Egan, Pierce, *Robin Hood and Little John; or, The Merry Men of Sherwood Forest* (London: W. S. Johnson, 1851).
Emmett, George, *Robin Hood and the Archers of Merrie Sherwood* (London: Hogarth House, [n. d.]).
Goldhill, Simon, *Victorian Culture and Classical Antiquity: Art, Opera, Fiction, and the Proclamation of Modernity* (Princeton: Princeton University Press, 2011).
Henty, G. A., *A March on London: Being a Story of Wat Tyler's Insurrection* (London: Blackie, 1898).
Howard, J. H., *Winding Lanes* (Caernarvon: Calvinist Methodist Printing Works, 1938).
Kirkpatrick, Robert, *Bullies, Beaks and Flannelled Fools: An Annotated Bibliography of Boys' School Fiction, 1742–1990* (London: Privately Printed by Robert J. Kirkpatrick, 1990).
Kirkpatrick, Robert, *From the Penny Dreadful to the Ha'penny Dreadfuller: A Bibliographical History of the British Boys' Periodical 1762–1950* (London: British Library, 2012).
Kirkpatrick, Robert, *Wild Boys in the Dock: Victorian Juvenile Literature and Juvenile Crime*, Children's Books History Society Occasional Paper 11 (London: Children's Books History Society, 2013).
Knight, Stephen, *Reading Robin Hood: Content, Form and Reception in the Outlaw Myth* (Manchester: Manchester University Press, 2015).
Knight, Stephen, *Robin Hood: A Complete Study of the English Outlaw* (Oxford: Blackwell, 1994).
Knight, Stephen, *Robin Hood: A Mythic Biography* (Ithaca: Cornell University Press, 2003).
Lambe, R. J., *The Sword of Freedom; or, The Boyhood Days of Jack Straw* (London: Boys of England Office, [n. d.]).
Major, John, 'Historia Maioris Britanniae', in Stephen Knight and Thomas Ohlgren (eds), *Robin Hood and Other Outlaw Tales* (Kalamazoo: Medieval Institute Publications, 1997).
Maurice, Charles Edmund, *Lives of English Popular Leaders in the Middle Ages: Tyler, Ball, and Oldcastle* (London: Henry S. King, 1875).
Peterson, W. S., *The Kelmscott Press: A History of William Morris's Typographical Adventure* (Oxford: Oxford University Press, 1991).
Quiller-Couch, Arthur, *Adventures in Criticism* (London: Cassell, 1896).
Rose, Jonathan, *The Intellectual Life of the British Working Classes* (New Haven: Yale University Press, 2001).
Simmons, Clare A., *Popular Medievalism in Romantic-Era Britain* (Basingstoke: Palgrave, 2011).
Southey, Robert, 'Harold; or, The Castle of Morford', Bodleian MS Eng. Misc. e. 21.
Southey, Robert, *Wat Tyler: A Dramatic Poem* (London: W. Hone, 1817).
Southey, Robert and Southey, Caroline, *Robin Hood: A Fragment* (London: William Blackwood and Sons, 1847).
Springhall, John, 'Healthy Papers for Manly Boys: Imperialism and Race in the Harmsworths' Halfpenny Boys' Papers of the 1890s and 1900s', in Jeffrey Richards

(ed.), *Imperialism and Juvenile Literature* (Manchester: Manchester University Press, 1989), pp. 144–172.

Springhall, John, '"Pernicious reading"? "The Penny Dreadful" as scapegoat for late-Victorian juvenile crime', *Victorian Periodicals Review*, 27:4 (1994), 326–349.

Williams, Will, 'Bold Robin Hood and his merry, merry men', *Our Young Folks' Weekly Budget of Tales, News, Sketches, Fun, Puzzles, Riddles* (6 December 1873), p. 617 and (14 February 1874), p. 108.

Yonge, Charlotte, *What Books to Lend and What to Give* (London: [n. p.], [n. d.]).

6

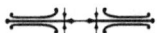

A tale of two ladies? Stuart women as role models for Victorian and Edwardian girls and young women

Rosemary Mitchell

As scholars such as Rohan Maitzen and Alison Booth have argued, historical women were habitually used as gender role models for Victorian and Edwardian girls and young women, frequently in the attempt to promote domestic ideology and 'traditional' gender roles to middle-class audiences.[1] To date, scholarship has tended to focus most emphatically on the representation of Tudor women such as Lady Jane Grey, Elizabeth I and Mary Queen of Scots.[2] This chapter will explore how Stuart women were appropriated to this purpose, using biographies, individual and collective, and articles from magazines and periodicals, often exclusively aimed at girls and young women, as the key primary sources. While figures such as Lady Rachel Russell, Lucy Hutchinson and Lady Arabella Stuart were easily appropriated, other Stuart women proved less adaptable as exemplary role models. These included the French-born queen, Henrietta Maria, often seen as exercising a malign political and religious influence over her husband. Through a comparison of Victorian and Edwardian reinventions of Henrietta Maria, wife of Charles I, and Rachel Russell, wife of William Russell, one of the alleged Rye House plotters, this study will highlight the tensions – arising from their religious allegiances, political participation and national identities – which underpinned representations of these two Stuart women as domestic role models.[3]

A comparative study of the two women, therefore, clearly illustrates the process of exemplification and its problems. While Russell was easily represented as a role model, appearing repeatedly in this guise in collective biographies, Henrietta Maria resisted exemplification, appearing largely as a subject of more extensive and 'serious' biographies instead. Writing the lives of both these women raised issues about their political agency, while their religious identities and their nationalities also affected their perceived suitability as potential role models for girls and young women. While Rachel Russell's level of political involvement, companionate but conventional marriage and deep Anglican piety were deemed admirable, Henrietta Maria's reputation for exercising too much influence over her husband and her devout Catholicism made her a problematic figure. Russell's half-French blood presented no problem in terms of her exemplification (her ancestry was Huguenot Protestant), but Henrietta Maria was perceived as far too French, both temperamentally and politically. In periodicals and magazines aimed at girls and young women, both women often appear in more cursory, diverse and even playful contexts, demonstrating the increasingly blurred boundary between consumer and leisure cultures and more didactic forms of historical education – but they generally retain the reputations reflected in the more formal biographical genres. So, despite the recreational character, and often random and episodic appearance, of items representing these two Stuart women in periodicals and magazines, they served to reinforce the suitability of Russell as a role model – and to demonstrate the difficulty of enlisting Henrietta Maria as an exemplar.

Mid-century Henrietta Maria: attempted exemplification in Strickland's *Lives* and Everett Green's *Letters*

Elizabeth Strickland's biography of Henrietta Maria, which appeared in volume 8 of the *Lives of the Queens of England* (1840–1848), is a necessary point of departure for this study.[4] The *Lives of the Queens* – which was widely read by both middle-class and upper-class men and women of all ages, but may have had a particular appeal for young women in their later teenage years – offered the only full-length English life of the queen available in the early Victorian period. It was, therefore, no doubt, a key influence on her Victorian representation, shaping – either directly or indirectly – the collective biographies and periodical accounts which will be considered later in this chapter. The attempted exemplification of Henrietta Maria in this biography, and in Mary Anne Everett Green's significant text, *Letters of Queen Henrietta Maria* (1857), illuminates the difficulties in appropriating the queen as a role model for girls and young women.

Strickland presented a decidedly Tory and pro-royalist version of the Civil War which represented Charles I as a martyr, and Cromwell and his associates as a 'regicide junta', bent on the repression of the people and the despoliation of the Church.[5] She was anxious to exonerate Henrietta Maria from the charges against her in pro-Commonwealth Whig narratives of the Civil War: as Mary Spongberg's excellent article on Strickland's biography of the queen suggests, this 'sympathetic representation of Henrietta Maria can be read ... [as] an alternate feminine historiography of Britain, which contrary to the Whig tradition retained a sympathy for things French, Catholic, and Stuart'.[6] Therefore, Spongberg suggests, we should see Agnes and Elizabeth Strickland as serious historians offering a challenge to existing national historiography and distinguish their work from more populist anthologies of women's lives. 'The identification of royal lives [such as these] with collective female biography genders the texts in ways which diminishes their historicity', she argues.[7]

While Spongberg is right to suggest that the Strickland sisters and similar women writers of royal biography, such as Everett Green,[8] are serious writers of political history, I would argue that the Strickland sisters still attempted to contribute to the project of exemplification for their female readers. If Elizabeth Strickland's biography of Henrietta Maria did not succeed in presenting her as an exemplary figure, it was not simply because of her biographer's ambition to construct a Tory political historiography. It was also because the queen was a highly problematic subject for such exemplification. As Spongberg demonstrates, Henrietta Maria had received a poor historiographical press in the seventeenth and eighteenth centuries, from writers as diverse as Gilbert Burnett (1643–1715) and Catherine Macaulay (1731–1791).[9] Certainly, the Victorian celebration of Charles I as a good family man allowed Strickland to highlight the romantic devotion of husband and wife, presenting Henrietta Maria as a dedicated wife and a fond mother. But the result of Strickland's emphasis on the queen's exemplary domestic virtues, combined with her attempt to exonerate her from the charges of being too French, too Catholic, and too prone to absolutism, is a somewhat uneasy narrative. In Spongberg's words, 'Henrietta Maria resists … easy categorisation [as a "good" or "bad" queen], being both a model of wifely virtue and a serious political liability'.[10]

While acknowledging some early difficulties, Strickland paints the picture of a happy marriage: 'An increasing and lovely family cemented their conjugal union. Henrietta was a fond mother, and devoted much of her time to her nursery.'[11] Strickland also manages to defuse the threat potentially posed by Henrietta Maria's French style, which for a British readership might suggest the triumph of sensuality over virtue: she stresses that the taste of both queen and king for 'elegant amusements' adds to the refinement of the court. She combines her praise for *both* the domestic virtues *and* the cultural sophistication of the royal couple by a laudatory description of Anthony Van Dyck's portrait of the pair, with their two eldest sons, a vignette version of which appears significantly on the title page of Strickland's volume (Figure 6.1).[12]

Strickland also deals robustly with the charges of political interference which had bedevilled the queen's reputation, as Spongberg notes.[13] Strickland exonerates Henrietta Maria of the charge of imploring Charles I to consent to the execution of his loyal servant, the Earl of Strafford, in order to save herself and her children, commenting that 'Henrietta's faults arose, not from want of

6.1 Queen Henrietta Maria with Charles I and sons, after Anthony Van Dyck, from Agnes and Elizabeth Strickland, *The Lives of the Queens of England* (London: Colburn and Co. 1845–1848), VIII, title page.

courage, but from loquacious communication'.[14] This is demonstrated when she communicates the king's intention to arrest five radical parliamentarians to Lady Carlisle, a political spy for the king's opponents whose prompt message allows the five 'birds' to escape.[15] Strickland is keen to stress Henrietta Maria's more effective political activities, too – such as her success in securing loans for the royalist cause from the Dutch Republic and from loyalist English gentry, and in rallying troops in Yorkshire.[16] Her courage in moments when her life is threatened is also dwelt on, as too her deep and genuine grief on the execution of her husband.[17] However, Strickland is unable to clear the queen of the charge of *religious* interference: Henrietta Maria's vain attempt to persuade her younger sons to adopt her religion, which leads to the persecution of Henry of Gloucester, is 'decidedly the worst action queen Henrietta ever committed'.[18] While she moderates her criticism of Henrietta Maria's Roman Catholicism quite radically in comparison with earlier historians, Strickland nevertheless admits that 'The narrow bigotry in which she had been reared marred the popularity which must infallibly attended this fine disposition.'[19]

Mary Anne Everett Green's *Letters of Queen Henrietta Maria* (1857) offered an apparently more detached perspective on the queen than Strickland's biography. Although it was an anthology of sources with 'extremely slight' editorial comments, it gives a surprisingly sympathetic impression of 'one of our most talented and unfortunate queens'.[20] Everett Green is particularly uncritical of the queen's religious activities (although she does not endorse Roman Catholicism itself), excusing her resolve to further the interests of English Catholics and to bring up her children as Catholic: 'Blame does not attach to her for her strenuous adherence to that which she firmly believed to be right.'[21] An account of the queen's foundation of the convent at Chaillot is included,[22] but not – notably – any reference to the queen's attempt to convert her son Henry to Catholicism.[23]

Like Strickland, Everett Green presents Henrietta Maria and Charles as the model of a happy couple, commenting that their letters to Marie de' Medici 'present a pleasing picture of the domestic union of the pair'.[24] However, Everett Green's queen becomes an increasingly influential public figure – and this is viewed, unexpectedly, as a positive feature of her marriage. Everett Green's attempt at exemplification, therefore, seems to aim to cast Henrietta Maria as a heroic woman, a latter-day Joan of Arc, rather than a model of domesticity. She makes a point of including letters which, in her opinion, demonstrate that the queen 'was the real, though not the nominal head' of government during the king's absence in Scotland in 1641.[25] A further series of letters from the early stages of the Civil War is prefaced with the comment: 'In strength and firmness of mind, the daughter of Henri Quatre far surpassed her husband, and the letters clearly show how earnestly she endeavoured to support the vacillating mind of the king, and to lead him to adopt vigorous and decisive measures.'[26]

What increasingly emerges from her editorial comments is the picture of a heroic woman, decidedly more admirable than either her husband or his male advisers. The queen's 'all but omnipotent' influence on the king is essentially justified in Everett Green's opinion, given his own lack of moral resolution.[27] If Strickland's attempt to make Henrietta Maria into an exemplary domestic figure is compromised by the queen's sometimes unfortunate attempts at religious and political interference, Everett Green's is wrecked, paradoxically, by Henrietta Maria's *failure* to influence her husband. Strickland's queen falls short of the ideal of the domestic icon, while Green's is a frustrated military heroine.[28]

Mid-century Rachel Russell: exemplification through the influence of the *Letters* and Guizot's *Married Life*

By contrast with Henrietta Maria, whose pre-Victorian historical reputation was highly problematic, Rachel Russell had always enjoyed a positive press – and this was sustained in the early-nineteenth-century accounts of her life which would have both been read by (middle-class) girls and young women, and have shaped the representation of Russell in collective biographies and periodicals and magazines more specifically aimed at a juvenile audience. As Amy Culley points out in her illuminating study of Russell's representation by women writers between 1770 and 1840, she was 'traditionally celebrated for her symbolic political value as a model of wifely devotion, piety and maternal duty'.[29] Unlike Henrietta Maria, Russell was praised in Gilbert Burnet's *History of His Own Time* (1724–1734), but – as Culley suggests – the key primary source shaping the positive representation of Rachel Russell was *The Letters of Lady Rachel Russell* (1773), originally transcribed by Thomas Sellwood.[30] The *Letters* were intended as an apologia for the political actions of William Russell, in which Rachel appears as the 'exemplary wife and widow', a model for other women; subsequent extracts from the *Letters* were often selected to reflect her domestic virtues and her piety, downplaying the evidence in her correspondence of public engagement and estate management, as well as of her 'endurance and survival'.[31] Nevertheless, Culley argues, the *Letters* 'inspired various readings of her life and complicated her straightforward association with exemplary womanhood'.[32] She explores some accounts which offer diverse and ambivalent representations of their subject: Catharine Macaulay, in her *History of England from the Accession of James I to the Revolution* (1763–1783), 'effectively combines maternal and family duty with classical heroism', marginalising her piety,[33] while Mary Berry's *Some Account of the Life of Rachael Lady Wriothesley Lady Russell* (1819) combined a picture of an idyllic marriage with a recognition of Russell's activities in her widowhood, including her 'political interests'.[34] However, Culley concludes that by the mid-century biographies increasingly foregrounded Russell's domestic virtues: her role as exemplary and pious wife, mother, and widow.[35] This insight certainly seems confirmed by the texts produced after 1850.

Another key text in the mid- to late century development of Rachel Russell's reputation was *The Married Life of Rachel Lady Russell* (1855). This translation of a lengthy essay by the French politician and historian, François Guizot, was published by the librarian at Woburn Abbey, John Martin.[36] With the numerous editions available of Rachel Russell's letters, it was a major influence on the many accounts of her life, often in collective biographies of exemplary women intended for a readership of girls and young women. As the title suggests, the emphasis was firmly on Russell as model of domestic virtue, and specifically as a devoted wife: 'love in the household of a Christian nobleman' is Guizot's theme. Despite the obvious political sympathies which – as a committed liberal – he believed that he shared with the Russells, retreat from public life is often the burden of the essay.[37]

Guizot presents the Russells' marriage as an ideal: he stresses their 'natural and intimate sympathy' as the real cause of their union, highlighting the 'Paradise regained' which it represents.[38] Rachel testifies her devotion as a wife by 'entering into all his concerns, his tastes', and combining 'Christian and human sentiments, piety and love'.[39] In terms of political involvement, the suggestion is that, although she is, like her husband, 'patriotically interested in the fate of her country', her 'more discriminating judgement' leads her to urge him (unsuccessfully) to keep a low profile.[40] Guizot's account of the political events involving William Russell is deliberately brief, and when he is arrested, the historian announces: 'I have no intention of relating here this memorable and celebrated trial. It is solely the private life of Lord and Lady Russell, their personal relations and mutual sentiments, in their sorrowful as in their bright days.'[41] He gives a touching account of their final meeting,[42] and of how Lady Rachel feels her grief and spends 'forty years of widowhood [belonging] exclusively to the memory of her adored husband'.[43] There is much stress on her reliance on spiritual consolation,[44] but also on the fact that 'her life was active', devoted to the education of her children and the management of her household.[45] When the 1688 Revolution brings her and her party 'suddenly to triumph', 'she neither quitted her house nor put off her mourning', rarely attending court or social events.[46] In her old age, it is 'religion, its anxieties, its duties, its exercises [which became] her study and her habitual practice'.[47]

Collective biographies: the exemplary wife and the absent queen

A comparative exploration of the representation of both women in the collective biographies produced in the late nineteenth century reflects their respective mid-century reputations. Alison Booth's pioneering work has demonstrated how substantial and influential a literary genre this was, and she stresses the extent to which female collective biography was a form of 'self-help history', intended to teach its (female) readership, probably largely but not exclusively middle class and often juvenile, 'how to make it as a woman'.[48] Most mid-century collections, she suggests, promoted 'conventional standards of female domestic virtue', but often struggled with the fact that 'the aims of forming (feminine) subjects' conflicted with 'the aims of historiography'.[49] Booth's online collaborative 'Collective Biographies of Women' project shows how often Rachel Russell features in such collective projects of exemplification – and equally, how infrequently Henrietta Maria makes an appearance, for that very reason. While Russell – who is one of Booth's 'Featured Subjects' – appears in at least twenty-six such volumes, Henrietta Maria appears in only four.[50] And while Russell was clearly seen by the writers of such collective biographies as an ideal subject for exemplification, the authors of the volumes in which Henrietta Maria was included highlighted the principle of selection on grounds of historical significance: they were clearly not attempting to showcase role models for girls and young women.

Such is the frequency of Russell's inclusion that it is only possible to examine four examples of these volumes. Emily Freire Owen's *The Heroines of Domestic Life* (1861) begins with a preface stating that, although a woman's virtues might make her part of the historical record, they can (and should) remain 'essentially domestic', as 'association with aspects of severer duty, is apt to give a masculine hardness to the minds and manners, inauspicious to feminine delicacy'.[51] Anxious to offer 'pure models of excellence' to her readers, she devotes this series: 'to the illustration of the domestic virtues ... courage, conjugal and filial piety, philanthropy and self-culture [...in order to] teach woman to endure – her chief lesson in this life! – and unselfishly to support others'.[52] This highly didactic agenda explains the selection of subjects, from the biblical figure of Ruth to Florence Nightingale. Owen represents Russell as 'one of the brightest examples of that unobtrusive feminine constancy, which softens greatness by the better qualification of goodness'.[53] This is, indeed, the dominant theme of her biography. Like other biographers, she stresses the perfect happiness of Rachel's second marriage to William Russell – 'it would, perhaps, be impossible to imagine a more complete affection than sprang up between these two young persons' – and 'her strong interest in political affairs'. While she acknowledges Russell's role in her husband's political career, Owen emphasises that 'her opinions [were] so diffidently yet so correctly formed' and that her influence was never exercised for 'an unworthy purpose'.[54] Her account of William Russell's trial and execution foregrounds the 'heroic resolution' with which Lady Rachel 'set about affording him all the assistance, as well as all the consolation, he needed'.[55] Owen's account of her widowhood stresses her pious resignation and her attention to her remaining domestic duties: the care and education of her children and those of her dead sister.[56] Owen's concluding reflection carefully qualifies celebration of her resolution of character:

> At home, a tender mother, a clinging associate, the almost timid dependent on her lord's love, she awoke to be transformed, in the hour of trial, into the fearless though sorrowing advocate, the untiring follower, the heroine of self-control. In some instances, great deeds are bruited about by men through generations ... yet it is in the fragrance of the unobtrusive flower which delights the sense, and not the gaudy glare of senseless blossoms.[57]

Elizabeth Rundle Charles's account of Rachel Russell in her *Sketches of the Women of Christendom* (1880) – as the title suggests – puts the emphasis on her subject's Christian piety.[58] The 'Preface to the English Edition' reminds readers that the text was 'originally undertaken at the request of a member of the Cambridge University Mission in Delhi' in order to give 'the women of India, some conception of what Christianity has done for the women of Christendom'.[59] Russell appears in chapter VII, 'Christian Women of Modern Times', after coverage of women in the Gospels, the Acts of the Apostles, and the early Church, and medieval figures such as Hilda of Whitby and Joan of Arc. In Charles's account, Russell is presented as 'an example of a noble Christian wife', struck by a 'terrible sorrow' which reveals a character 'which otherwise would have been hidden from us in the retirement of the home of which she was the light'.[60] She gives a brief account of the Russells' idyllic marriage, laying very little emphasis on Rachel's political involvement.[61] There is, indeed, no description of the political circumstances leading to William Russell's trial, which is, however, described in some detail.[62] So, too, is the couple's last meeting, and William Russell's last days and execution – at this point he is the central focus of the text.[63] After his death, the story shifts briefly to Rachel: Charles argues that 'her love she had for her husband, living and dying', deepened her faith and opened her heart 'in tender sympathy with all she could comfort or succour'.[64] She concludes: 'I have given this sketch of her life ... because [it shows] what a true Christian wife can always be: the most faithful counsellor and the dearest companion of her husband'.[65]

Sophia Goodrich Ashton's *The Girlhood of Celebrated Women: Women of Worth and the Mothers of the Bible* (1876), meanwhile, puts an emphasis on 'the relation of biography to every-day life', believing that the 'wholesome influence' of the examples detailed in this volume will be 'specially useful' to the young: her exemplars are particularly intended to help the 'enthusiastic young woman to settle into the harness of everyday life'.[66] Aiming to record the lives of more humbly born women, Ashton includes only modern and early modern women, all European or American, and only a few elite women. Her biography of Russell is an extremely brief one of ten pages, seven of which are quotations from Russell's correspondence after her husband's death.[67] The other three dwell mainly on William's trial, highlighting Rachel Russell's courage and resolution, her active role after his death in looking after her family, and her piety and freedom from a 'vindictive spirit'.[68] She sums up: 'Such an example shows the power of female influence to promote good and resist evil ... With such a guardian angel by his side, no wonder [William Russell] was strengthened to act his lofty part, and die a patriot martyr.'[69]

Margaret Bertha Synge's *Great Englishwomen: A Historical Reading Book for Schools* (1907), which would have enjoyed a working-class as well as a middle-class readership (and probably a 'captive' scholastic one), featured a short life of Rachel Russell among other brief biographies, including those of Queen Bertha, Philippa of Hainault, Lady Jane Grey, Elizabeth Fry and Florence Nightingale. Russell's was most definitely intended to offer a model of domestic virtue. Synge stresses that her second marriage is a domestic ideal: 'He [William Russell] consulted his wife about everything; he was guided by her advice in moments of extreme difficulty; he depended on her judgement, and found it just and good. On the other hand, she watched every event in which her husband's interest was concerned, with unwearying love.'[70]

She is also represented as a devoted sister and an affectionate mother – 'their [her children's] happiness and welfare was her great object in life'[71] – but it is her love and loyalty for her husband that is most fully emphasised. A highly sympathetic account of William Russell's opposition to the 'weak' and 'selfish' Charles II is given, culminating in his arrest and trial, at which the 'resolute wife' fulfils the role of his assistant.[72] Their final interview is touchingly described, with the information that, after the execution of her husband, Russell retires to the country to educate her children, trying to 'dismiss her sorrow for their sakes'.[73] Her 'calm but very sad' existence ends with burial beside the husband whom 'she had loved and served so devotedly'.[74]

While Rachel Russell appears repeatedly in Victorian didactic works of collective biography designed for young girls and women, Henrietta Maria seldom makes an appearance at all, a testimony to the difficulty of shaping her life into an exemplary narrative. One of the very few volumes in which she does appear, *Fifty Famous Women and the Lessons of Their Lives* (c. 1850), contains a motley collection of women who by no means suggest an agenda of exemplification. While some icons, such as Lady Jane Grey and Rachel Russell, do appear, so too do the Empress Josephine and Sarah, Duchess of Marlborough. This publication was repeatedly reissued (in 1864, 1876, 1879 and 1881), with some variation in the women subjects included. The 1881 edition included a two-page preface which explained that subjects had been selected on the grounds of their celebrity – and while some of the figures included did 'honour to their sex', others were remarkable for characters marked by 'errors and weaknesses'. The preface-writer continues:

> to find fifty persons of either sex for whom we must feel unqualified admiration would be difficult; but the lives we have selected for illustration are those of women whose careers may be profitably studied, and *many of whom* may be taken as models to be studied and imitated by the young.[75]

Victorian authors more bent on producing exemplary biographies than the writer of this work, however, simply did not include the queen at all. Perhaps unsurprisingly, her most frequent appearances tend to be in post-Edwardian works which focus explicitly on royal women, such as for example, Elsie Prentys Thornton-Cook's *Her Majesty: The Romance of the Queens of England*,

1066–1910 (1926) and the journalist Sidney Dark's *Twelve Royal Ladies* (1928).[76] Dark is very clear that his agenda (if he even has one) is certainly not one of exemplification:

> The personalities of the Twelve Royal Ladies are all interesting and suggestive. Some of them were great merely from the position into which they were born. One or two of them have been misunderstood and sometimes maligned. Nearly all of them were unhappy … on the whole, the moral of my sketches, if they have a moral, is it is better to be born and to live in comparative obscurity than in the palace of kings.[77]

Playing a role in the periodicals?: Rachel Russell and Henrietta Maria retain their reputations

Periodicals aimed at middle-class girls and young women, such as the *Girl's Own Paper*,[78] generally projected the same images of the two women as were portrayed in the collective biographies – even if they appeared in different generic contexts, including quizzes, competitions and other similar features. There is evidently a sustained continuity in the character of the representation of these two Stuart women, whether the publications in which they appear are aimed primarily at adult or juvenile audiences, middle-class readers and/or working-class ones, or in heavyweight educative or lighter literary genres or contexts. Reader contributions also suggest that the young readers of these periodicals and magazines (often, but not exclusively, middle-class) shared these conceptualisations of the two Stuart women, illustrating how successful and pervasive the exemplification of Rachel Russell as a domestic icon was. An 1873 sketch of Rachel Russell in *Chatterbox* – a weekly magazine for both boys and girls, edited by an Anglican clergyman and priced to reach a working-class as well as middle-class readership[79] – notes that 'she stands out among the records of the good and true women of the past as a devoted wife'. It deals entirely with the trial and execution of William Russell, emphasising at least equally the courage and Christian resignation of the husband, and concluding abruptly with a final paragraph which states that the grieving widow 'applied herself to the education and the conduct of her household with apparent energy, but that she never ceased to miss her deceased spouse'.[80] The article is accompanied by an illustration showing the devoted couple chastely embracing in a prison cell (Figure 6.2).

In the 'Varieties' column of 24 July 1873 in the *Girl's Own Paper* – a weekly periodical published (discreetly) by the Low Church Religious Tract Society, intended for both middle-class and working-class girls[81] – among other quotations, a double acrostic puzzle, a cryptic quiz entitled 'Buried English rivers', and the answers to an arithmetical problem, appears a quotation from Lady Rachel Russell describing 'The good wife'.[82] In an article in the *Girl's*

mouth sent a message to the imprisoned nobleman, offering to cast in his lot with him—an offer that was not accepted, Lord Russell making answer that he wished not his friends to die with him; and Lord Cavendish went so far as to propose to change clothes with him, and remain in prison in his place; to which generous suggestion he sent a smiling refusal.

One request alone he did not refuse, that from his heroic wife, begging to be present at his trial—'believing I can do you some service,' she wrote. And she was permitted to act as his secretary during his trial. But, alas! her fond heart was wrung by seeing that the case was going against her dear lord. She made one further effort to save

6.2 'Lord and Lady Russell', illustration to H. A. F., 'Lady Rachel Russell', *Chatterbox* (14 July 1873), p. 260. © Reproduced by kind permission of the Syndics of Cambridge University Library.

Own Paper of 7 November 1885, entitled 'Helpful wives' and written by the Rev. E. J. Hardy, 'Chaplain to Her Majesty's forces', Lady Rachel Russell is cited as an example of 'one of the many celebrated women who have encouraged their husbands to suffer and be strong'. Her support for William Russell during his trial and his imprisonment is briefly described, as well as her fortitude in concealing 'the agony of her grief under a seeming composure' at their last parting.[83] Although she is only an incidental figure in Nanette Mason's 1886 article on 'A girl's rambles through haunted London', the author of this piece of heritage tourism pauses to give Rachel Russell an exemplary write-up as 'one of the most famous women of history – pious, reflecting, firm, and courageous; alike exemplary in prosperity and adversity'.[84] As M. O. Grenby demonstrates elsewhere in this volume, heritage tourism literature aimed specifically at children played a key role in shaping their historical consciousness in the period through recreational practices.

Russell even appears in K. Thorne's commended entry for the stoutly pro-suffrage feminist journal, the *Woman's Signal*'s 'Illustrious Women Competition' of 1896.[85] Thorne divided her subjects into two categories, single and married women, the second including Elizabeth Barrett Browning, Fanny Burney and George Eliot. It was here that the life of Russell appeared, of course: 'In the history of our country, there are fewer nobler or more pathetic instances of love and devotion than that of Rachel, Lady Russell.'[86] Another example of a reader response reflecting the exemplary status of Rachel Russell can be found, by contrast, two years before in the highly conservative Anglo-Catholic *Monthly Packet*, aimed exclusively at middle-class girls and young women:[87] here, in the 'Second shelf' section, appeared a 'delightful list of heroines' supplied by Arachne. The historical section, featuring six women, included Rachel Russell as 'wife, widow, mother, always loving and constant'.[88]

In an example of the sort of historical games, puzzles and quizzes – which Rachel Bryant Davies demonstrates elsewhere in this volume to be a key component of late Victorian and Edwardian children's experience of historical cultures – reader responses were also invited in a prize competition announced in the *Girl's Own Paper* on 6 October 1883. This required entrants to create a 'Biographical table' featuring one hundred (named) 'famous women of the Christian era'. Thus they would, the advertisement suggested, 'become acquainted with the careers of women who hold distinguished positions in the history of the world'. The competition, however, did not focus entirely on potential role models: the list included not only women such as Lady Rachel Russell, Lady Jane Grey, Hannah More and Elizabeth Fry – traditional subjects for exemplification – but also women of more ambiguous character, including Mary Queen of Scots, Anne Boleyn, Catherine of Russia and Amy Robsart. Indeed, Henrietta Maria was also included. Similarly, in James Mason's

'September anniversaries of the girls' year', the author includes exemplary women and highlights their virtues for imitation – but he also features women more remarkable for celebrity than exemplary qualities. Rachel Russell appears as the entry for 29 September – the date of her death – and Hannah More is the subject for 7 September, but the Countess of Blessington, the Empress Matilda and Amy Robsart are obviously of more historical interest than exemplary character.[89] The author of 'Notes to the alphabet of celebrated women', where Rachel Russell appears as the subject of the letter 'R', also seems to have balanced inclusion of the edifying with the historically significant. Although exemplary women such as Philippa of Hainault and Lady Jane Grey are included, so too are the assassin Charlotte Corday and the contentious and autocratic Empress Matilda, both of them ambiguous figures.[90] So, while it is clear that Rachel Russell continued to feature as an exemplary figure in periodicals aimed at girls and young women, she also featured as a figure in educative historical competitions and quizzes. These included exemplary women (and added text highlighting their exemplary qualities), but did not exclude others arguably more remarkable for their historical impact than their virtues.

Henrietta Maria, meanwhile, did not appear as an exemplary figure in periodicals such as the *Girl's Own Paper*. References to Charles I's queen were generally incidental and related to such topics as past fashions or the history of culture – as, for instance, the passing reference to her wearing a mask while out riding,[91] the fact that she introduced to England the evergreen rose,[92] or her passion for dramatic exhibitions and masques.[93] When more substantial coverage is given of the queen, it is generally uncomplimentary in character: a discussion of the reign of 'King Charles the Martyr' in 'An hour with Mamma', which appeared in 1862 in the *Ladies' Treasury* – a largely (but not entirely) conventional domestic magazine aimed at middle-class women[94] – is decidedly critical. Kate Vernon, at an aristocratic gathering in 'the Library at the Castle ... Time, Quarter to Five', opines that:

> one great cause of Charles's misery in life, and of his cruel death, was the beautiful Henrietta Maria ... She was much under the influence of the Roman Catholic priests whom she had brought over with her; and Charles (doting on her as he did) was under her influence. She disliked the English, and ended up by making them dislike her. She was ill-judged, passionate, and very deficient in tact; and I believe that she was – what I am most certain Charles was not – both treacherous and insincere.[95]

No one else at this *conversazione* disagrees with this harsh judgement; indeed, Lady Lisburn adds the comment that the queen 'encouraged his [Charles's] aspirations after a despotism'.[96] Like Russell, Henrietta Maria also featured in James Mason's 'Anniversaries' series in the *Girl's Own Paper*, appearing as the subject for 10 August. But Mason makes it very clear indeed that she is not an exemplary subject, adding a highly negative commentary:

> It [the marriage of Charles I and Henrietta Maria] was an unhappy alliance, not only from the circumstances of the queen being a Roman Catholic, but also because she was a self-willed, intriguing and vindictive woman, fond of meddling in public affairs, who acquired unbounded influence over the mind of her husband, and always exerted it with a view to conform his regal government to the despotism of France.[97]

Similarly, the instalment of Sarah Tytler's Civil War novel, *A Young Oxford Maid*, which appeared in the *Girl's Own Paper* on 3 August 1889, opined that the queen's acts of bravery 'had a strong dash of the stagey and theatrical, which formed part of her amiable, excitable, shallowly clever character'.[98] That the Low Church *Girl's Own Paper* was highly critical of Henrietta Maria is hardly surprising, but it is notable that even the Anglo-Catholic participants in 'An hour with Mamma' shared a negative perception of the queen. Criticism focused, as usual, on the queen's faith and her French nationality, as well as her political influence over Charles.

The lack of pious adulation for Charles I's queen, however, may have made her fair game for more playful historical representation: in 'The comic lives of the English kings and queens: no. 32, Charles I', the same criticisms of Henrietta Maria as were voiced by Kate Vernon appeared in parodic form: 'Charles became king in 1625, and he and *Henrietta Marie-d* soon after. She was very French and very Romish, and brought over, oh such a lot of foreign priestesses [sic].'[99] Similarly, an article on 'Romantic attachments' in *Punch* in 1874 suggested that Henrietta Maria nurtured a secret passion for Oliver Cromwell.[100] Audrey Mayhew Allen's 'Horrid dates; or Molly's fairy history lesson' in the *Young Folk's Paper* of 1889 features a very young girl conveyed through the British past with a fairy as her guide, but this manages to project a negative image of the queen, despite the obviously juvenile audience which the author anticipated. A highly attractive description of Henrietta's appearance and costume is given when she first features in the text, but later on, young Molly notes that she is 'very haughty, in spite of her prettiness' and blames her for abandoning her husband and fleeing to France.[101]

If Henrietta Maria rarely appeared in collective biographies or the periodical press – and when she did, not as an exemplar of female conduct – she enjoyed a biographical revival in the Edwardian period, in works clearly aimed at adult readers of both genders. Concerns about women's political agency arising from the campaign for women's suffrage, and particularly Suffragette militancy, certainly seem to have re-stimulated interest in historical women whose political involvements had previously provoked debate.[102] If Strickland's life of Henrietta Maria is essentially an apologia rather than an exemplification of the queen,

Henrietta Haynes's 1912 biography – while exhibiting some of the same characteristics – attempts to achieve at a fully historicised account of the queen: it explores the context in which the queen lived and acted, rather than either celebrating or condemning her. In her introduction, Haynes presents a summative critical judgement:

> Had she [Henrietta Maria] been a Protestant and a woman of profound sagacity, she might have saved her husband. As it was ... she hurried him to his doom. She lived at a great moment, and she had no greatness to meet it. Herein alone is her condemnation. She has received more than her fair share of blame, for she has been made the scapegoat of Charles's faults. The tragedy of her fate rivals that of Mary Stuart or of Marie Antoinette, but she missed the historical felicity of a violent death, so that she has failed to touch the popular imagination. Had she done so ... [she] would have been saved from a verdict at the tribunal of posterity?[103]

In Haynes's opinion, therefore, the life of Henrietta Maria is meet material for neither an exemplary life ('no greatness') nor a romantic tragedy ('she missed the historical felicity of a violent death'). She is fully conscious of the problems which the queen's religious convictions as a Catholic and political instincts as a monarchist presented, given the historical context in which she lived, bluntly describing her life as 'a failure'.[104] Haynes's life – while acknowledging that Charles's unwise political decisions are his own – does not attempt to clear the queen of the charge of malign political influence to the extent that Strickland's did:[105] both king and queen receive a judicious amount of blame. Nor is she inclined to idealise the queen's family life in order to turn her into an exemplar of domestic virtue. In other words, the attitude which Spongberg identifies as characterising Strickland's biography of the 1840s is fully developed in this Edwardian biography.

Conclusion

This Edwardian biography of Henrietta Maria demonstrates what the earlier accounts of Strickland and Everett Green had suggested: the difficulty of treating Charles I's queen as an exemplar for girls and young women, rather than as the complicated subject of serious historical biography. The queen's previous historiographical reputation, her national identity, her Catholicism, and her political opinions and influence over her husband were too problematic for her to become an icon of domestic virtue, despite her happy marriage and family life. Even as a model of the heroic woman, she was suspect. In collective biographies and periodical articles, substantially aimed at girls and young women from c. 1850–1914, she was featured primarily as an historical figure, a parodic historical figure at times. However, even some playful appropriations of the queen in periodicals were unable to resist making disguised didactic points about her failings: too Catholic, too French, too bossy. Meanwhile, Lady Rachel Russell lent herself far more easily to the project of exemplification for the female child and teenage reader: her historiographical prestige as a Whig icon, her companionate marriage and domestic virtues, her Anglican piety and her limited political and public role all ensured her repeated appearance as an exemplar in collective biographies and periodical articles alike. Reader contributions in the periodicals and magazines suggest that this positive representation of Russell had been internalised by the young consumer of late nineteenth-century print culture. However, interestingly enough, she is not the subject of a full-length Edwardian biography. The very virtues which made her a Victorian domestic icon may have made her seem both less appealing as a role model, and of less interest as a historical subject in the age of Lytton Strachey's *Eminent Victorians* (1918).

Notes

1 Maitzen, "'This feminine preserve'"; Booth, *How to Make it as a Woman*. See also Mitchell, *Picturing the Past*, pp. 140–169.
2 Mitchell, 'The Nine Lives of the Nine Days Queen', and Maitzen, 'Plotting Women'; Dobson and Watson, *England's Elizabeth*; Lewis, *Mary Queen of Scots*; Mitchell, 'Edwardian Innovations'.
3 For brief lives of both women, see Hibbard, 'Henrietta Maria', and Schwoerer, 'Lady Rachel Russell'.
4 Although only Agnes Strickland's name appeared as the author of the *Lives*, she collaborated with her sister Elizabeth, who was, in fact, the author of the life of Henrietta Maria (Pope-Hennessy, *Agnes Strickland*, pp. 162, 319).
5 Strickland, *Lives*, VIII, pp. 108, 137, 153–177.
6 Spongberg, 'La Reine malheureuse', p. 747.
7 *Ibid.*, pp. 746–747.
8 For Everett Green, see Krueger, 'Mary Anne Everett Green', and Krueger, 'Why she lived in the PRO'.
9 Spongberg, 'La Reine malheureuse', pp. 750–751.
10 *Ibid.*, p. 749.
11 Strickland, *Lives*, VIII, p. 64.
12 *Ibid.*, pp. 65–71.
13 Spongberg, 'La Reine malheureuse', p. 756.
14 Strickland, *Lives*, VIII, p. 80.
15 *Ibid.*, pp. 89–90.
16 *Ibid.*, pp. 93–95, 98–103.
17 *Ibid.*, pp. 95–97, 113–116, 178–185.
18 *Ibid.*, pp. 194–210.
19 *Ibid.*, p. 259.

20 Everett Green, *Letters of Queen Henrietta Maria*, pp. v, xi.
21 *Ibid.*, p. 7.
22 *Ibid.*, p. 372.
23 *Ibid.*, p. 406.
24 *Ibid.*, p. 15.
25 *Ibid.*, p. 42.
26 *Ibid.*, p. 49.
27 *Ibid.*, p. 228.
28 My reading here of Everett Green's representation of Henrietta Maria is very similar to that of Spongberg's in *Women Writers and the Nation's Past*, pp. 210–244. We arrived independently at our conclusions, however.
29 Culley, 'Reading the Past', p. 34.
30 *Ibid.*, p. 35.
31 *Ibid.*, pp. 35–36.
32 *Ibid.*, p. 37.
33 *Ibid.*, p. 38.
34 *Ibid.*, p. 45
35 *Ibid.*, pp. 47–48. For instance, Culley argues that Louisa Costello's *Memoirs of Eminent Englishwomen* (1844) draws on Berry's account of her political activities, but these are 'carefully accompanied with a focus on her maternal duties' (Culley, 'Reading the Past', p. 48).
36 For an introduction to the historical thought of Guizot, see Crossley, *French Historians and Romanticism*, pp. 71–104.
37 Guizot, *Married Life of Rachel Lady Russell*, pp. 2–11.
38 *Ibid.*, pp. 17–18.
39 *Ibid.*, pp. 20, 22.
40 *Ibid.*, pp. 25–26.
41 *Ibid.*, pp. 30–31.
42 *Ibid.*, pp. 37–38.
43 *Ibid.*, p. 41.
44 *Ibid.*, pp. 41–50.
45 *Ibid.*, p. 50.
46 *Ibid.*, p. 55–59.
47 *Ibid.*, p. 71.
48 Booth, *How to Make It as a Woman*, esp. pp. 49–88. The targeted readership of the volumes is suggested by the appearance and likely price of the volumes.
49 *Ibid.*, p. 61.
50 Booth, *Collective Biographies*. It is difficult to ascertain the frequency with which Henrietta Maria is included, because her daughter shares the same name.
51 Owen, *Heroines of Domestic Life*, preface, pp. vi–vii. The copy which I consulted had formerly been in the Unitarian Chapel Sunday School library at Bury, suggesting that it was indeed intended for a juvenile readership.
52 *Ibid.*, p. ix.
53 *Ibid.*, p. 173.
54 *Ibid.*, p. 175.

55 *Ibid.*, pp. 177–178.
56 *Ibid.*, pp. 182–183.
57 *Ibid.*, pp. 184–185.
58 See Jay, 'Elizabeth Rundle Charles' for a brief life of this writer, best known for her religious historical novels, including *The Chronicles of the Schonberg-Cotta Family* (1863).
59 [Charles], *Sketches of rhe Women of Christendom*, preface, p. iii.
60 *Ibid.*, p. 207.
61 *Ibid.*, pp. 207–209.
62 *Ibid.*, pp. 209–211.
63 *Ibid.*, pp. 212–218.
64 *Ibid.*, pp. 218–219.
65 *Ibid.*, p. 219.
66 Ashton, *Girlhood of Celebrated Women*, prefatory note, pp. v–vii.
67 *Ibid.*, pp. 124–131.
68 *Ibid.*, pp. 121–124, quotation on p. 123.
69 *Ibid.*, p. 124.
70 Synge, *Great Englishwomen*, pp. 70–71.
71 *Ibid.*, p. 71.
72 *Ibid.*, pp. 72–74.
73 *Ibid.*, p. 75.
74 *Ibid.*, pp. 76–77.
75 Quoted by Booth, *Collective Biographies*, p. 293, emphasis added.
76 For a brief life of Dark, see Watson, 'Sidney Ernest Dark'.
77 Dark, *Twelve Royal Ladies*, introduction, pp. 1, 6.
78 There is now an extensive literature on the juvenile periodical press. Of particular use here is Moruzi, *Constructing Girlhood*.
79 See Lang, 'Childhood's champions', and Ellis, 'Influences on the availability of recreational reading'.
80 H. A. F., 'Lady Rachel Russell'.
81 See Moruzi, *Constructing Girlhood*, pp. 84–86. Also Rodgers, 'Competing girlhoods'.
82 Anon., 'Varieties'. I have been unable to establish whether the quotation is by or about Rachel Russell.
83 Hardy, 'Helpful wives'.
84 Mason, 'A girl's rambles'.
85 For the *Woman's Signal*, see van Arsdal, 'Mrs Florence Fenwick-Miller', and Tusan, 'Inventing the new woman'.
86 Thorne, 'Illustrious women competition'.
87 For the *Monthly Packet*, see Moruzi, *Constructing Girlhood*, pp. 21–52; also, Sturrock, 'Establishing identity', and Moruzi, '"Never read anything"'.
88 Anon., 'Second shelf'.
89 Mason, 'September anniversaries'.
90 Anon., 'Notes to the alphabet of celebrated women'. This appears to be the addendum to an earlier article, but I have been unable to locate this prior publication.

91 White, 'Chapter on pigments'. For the *Englishwoman's Domestic Magazine*, a domestic and fashion magazine aimed at middle-class women, young and older, see Beetham, *Magazine of her Own?*, pp. 59–88.
92 Loudon, 'The lady's own flower garden'.
93 Anon., 'About music and musical instruments'.
94 See Ridder, 'What? How? Why?', and Ridder and van Remoortel, '"Not simply Mrs Warren"', in which it is suggested that the periodical actually contained a wider and less gendered range of information than has previously been thought.
95 Anon., 'An hour with Mamma'.
96 Ibid.
97 Mason, 'August anniversaries'.
98 Tytler, 'A young Oxford maid', chapter XVIII. Sarah Tytler was the pseudonym for the prolific novelist, Henrietta Keddie: see Mitchell, 'Henrietta Keddie'.
99 Anon., 'The comic lives of the English kings and queens'. *Boys of England* magazine was intended for working-class boys and edited by a former Chartist, which might explain its detached irreverence for the monarchy: see Banham, '*Boys of England* and Edwin J. Brett, 1866–99'.
100 Anon., 'Romantic attachments'. Leary's *The Punch Brotherhood* is the best introduction to *Punch* during this period, when it had become largely socially conservative.
101 Allan, 'Horrid dates'.
102 See Mitchell, 'A Crisis of Representation', and Mitchell, 'Edwardian Innovations', where I argue that the Edwardian political context similarly affected interpretations of both Catherine of Siena and Lady Jane Grey.
103 Haynes, *Henrietta Maria*, p. xv.
104 Ibid., p. xiv.
105 This is acknowledged in White, *Henrietta Maria and the English Civil Wars*, which describes Haynes as a traditionalist who 'accepts the basic premise held by most seventeenth-century critics of the queen: that she exerted a powerful and malignant influence over Charles' (pp. 1–2). This judgement, perhaps, ignores Haynes's recognition of Charles's own role in his downfall.

References

Allan, Audrey Mayhew, 'Horrid dates; or Molly's fairy history lesson: XIV – the Stuart period', *Young Folk's Paper* (13 July 1889), p. 108.
Anon., 'About music and musical instruments', *Englishwoman's Domestic Magazine* (1 June 1870), p. 337.
Anon., 'An hour with Mamma', *Ladies' Treasury* (1 June 1862), p. 182.
Anon., 'Notes to the alphabet of celebrated women', *Girl's Own Paper* (18 November 1893), p. 111.
Anon., 'Romantic attachments', *Punch* (7 March 1874), p. 97.
Anon., 'Second shelf', *Monthly Packet* (1 January 1894), p. 118.
Anon., 'The comic lives of the English kings and queens: no. 32, Charles I', *Boys of England* (29 September 1867), p. 228.
Anon., 'Varieties', *Girl's Own Paper* (24 July 1880), p. 479.

Arsdal, Rosemary T. Van, 'Mrs Florence Fenwick-Miller, and *The Woman's Signal*, 1895–1899', *Victorian Periodicals Review*, 15:3 (Fall, 1982), 107–118.

Ashton, Sophie Goodrich, *The Girlhood of Celebrated Women: Women of Worth and the Mothers of the Bible* (New York: World Publishing House, 1876).

Banham, Christopher M., '*Boys of England* and Edwin J. Brett, 1866–99' (PhD thesis, University of Leeds, 2006).

Beetham, Margaret, *A Magazine of her Own? Domesticity and Desire in the Woman's Magazine, 1800–1914* (London and New York: Routledge, 1996).

Booth, Alison, *Collective Biographies of Women: Featured Women and an Annotated Bibliography*, at womensbios.lib.virginia.edu

Booth, Alison, *How to Make it as a Woman: Collective Biographical History from Victoria to the Present* (Chicago and London: University of Chicago Press, 2004).

[Charles, Elizabeth Rundle], *Sketches of the Women of Christendom* (London: SPCK, 1880).

Crossley, Ceri, *French Historians and Romanticism: Thierry, Guizot, the Saint-Simonians, Quinet, and Michelet* (London and New York: Routledge, 2002).

Culley, Amy, 'Reading the Past: Women Writers and the Afterlifes of Lady Rachel Russell', in Dew B. and Price, F., *Historical Writing in Britain 1688–1830: Visions of History* (Basingstoke: Palgrave Macmillan, 2014), pp. 34–52.

Dark, Sidney, *Twelve Royal Ladies* (New York: Thomas Y. Crowell Company, 1929).

Dobson, Michael and Watson, Nicola J., *England's Elizabeth: An Afterlife in Fame and Fantasy* (Oxford: Oxford University Press, 2002).

Ellis, A., 'Influences on the availability of recreational reading for Victorian working class children', *Journal of Librarianship and Information Science*, 8:3 (July 1976), 185–195.

Everett Green, Mary Anne, *The Letters of Queen Henrietta Maria* (London: Richard Bentley, 1857).

Guizot, François, *The Married Life of Rachel Lady Russell*, trans. J. Martin (London: Thomas Bosworth, 1855).

H.A.F., 'Lady Rachel Russell', *Chatterbox* (14 July 1873), pp. 260–262.

Hardy, E. J., 'Helpful wives', *Girl's Own Paper* (7 November 1885), p. 84.

Haynes, Henrietta, *Henrietta Maria* (London: Methuen and Co., 1912).

Hibbard, C. M., 'Henrietta Maria [Princess Henrietta Maria of France] (1609–69)', in H. C. G. Matthew and B. Harrison (eds), *The Oxford Dictionary of National Biography* (Oxford: Oxford University Press, 2004–).

Jay, Elizabeth, 'Elizabeth Rundle Charles (1828–1893)', in H. C. G. Matthew and B. Harrison (eds), *The Oxford Dictionary of National Biography* (Oxford: Oxford University Press, 2004–).

Krueger, Christine. L., 'Mary Anne Everett Green [née Wood] (1818–1895)', in H. C. G. Matthew and B. Harrison (eds), *The Oxford Dictionary of National Biography* (Oxford: Oxford University Press, 2004–).

Krueger, Christine. L., 'Why she lived in the PRO: Mary Everett Green and the profession of history', *Journal of British Studies*, 42:1 (January, 2003), 65–90.

Lang, M., 'Childhood's champions: mid-Victorian children's periodicals and the critics', *Victorian Periodicals Review*, 13:1–2 (Spring/Summer 1980), 17–31.

Leary, Patrick, *The Punch Brotherhood: Table Talk and Print Culture in Mid-Victorian London* (London: British Library, 2010).

Lewis, Jayne E., *Mary Queen of Scots: Romance and Nation* (London and New York: Routledge, 1998).
Mrs Loudon, 'The lady's own flower garden', *Lady's Newspaper* (18 August 1855), p. 106.
Maitzen, Rohan, 'Plotting Women: Froude and Strickland on Elizabeth I and Mary Queen of Scots', in L. Felber (ed.), *Clio's Daughters: British Women Making History, 1790–1899* (Newark: University of Delaware Press, 2007), pp. 123–150.
Maitzen, Rohan, '"This feminine preserve": historical biographies by Victorian women', *Victorian Studies*, 38:3 (Spring, 1995), 71–93.
Mason, James, 'August anniversaries of the girls' year', *Girl's Own Paper* (28 July 1888), p. 702.
Mason, James, 'September anniversaries of the girls' year', *Girl's Own Paper* (25 August 1888), pp. 755–756.
Mason, Nanette, 'A girl's rambles through haunted London; or, anecdotes of the streets of the great metropolis', *Girl's Own Paper* (26 June 1886), pp. 621–623.
Mitchell, Rosemary, 'A Crisis of Representation: Celebrating and Criticising Catherine of Siena in Victorian and Edwardian Britain', in O. Boucher-Rivalain, Yannicke Chupin and François Ropert (eds), *Tension, Evolution, Revolution in Nineteenth and Twentieth Century Europe* (Paris: L'Harmattan, 2015), pp. 45–73.
Mitchell, Rosemary, 'Edwardian Innovations: Adapting the Victorian Lady Jane Grey in the Age of the Suffragettes', in F. Baillet et al. (eds), *Tradition(s)-Innovation(s) en Angleterre au XIX Siècle* (Paris: L'Harmattan, 2017), pp. 75–86.
Mitchell, Rosemary, 'Henrietta Keddie [pseud. Sarah Tytler] (1827–1914)', in H. C. G. Matthew and B. Harrison (eds), *The Oxford Dictionary of National Biography* (Oxford: Oxford University Press, 2004–).
Mitchell, Rosemary, *Picturing the Past: English History in Text and Image, c. 1830–1880* (Oxford: Oxford University Press, 2000).
Mitchell, Rosemary, 'The Nine Lives of the Nine Days Queen: From Religious Heroine to Romantic Victim', in L. Felber (ed.), *Clio's Daughters: British Women Making History, 1790–1899* (Newark: University of Delaware Press, 2007), pp. 97–122.
Moruzi, Kristine, *Constructing Girlhood through the Periodical Press, 1850–1915* (London and New York: Routledge, 2012).
Moruzi, Kristine, '"Never read anything that can at all unsettle your religious faith": reading and writing in the *Monthly Packet*', *Women's Writing*, 17:2 (2010), 288–304.
Owen, Mrs Octavius (Emily) Friere, *The Heroines of Domestic Life* (London: George Routledge and Sons, 1861).
Pope-Hennessy, Una, *Agnes Strickland: Biographer of the Queens of England, 1796–1874* (London: Chatto and Windus, 1940).
Ridder, Jolein de, 'What? How? Why? Broadening the mind with *The Treasury of Literature* (1868–1875), supplement to the *Ladies' Treasury* (1857–1895)', *Victorian Periodicals Review*, 43:2 (Summer 2010), 174–195.
Ridder, Jolein de and Remoortel, Marianne van, '"Not simply Mrs Warren": Eliza Warren Francis and the *Ladies' Treasury*', *Victorian Periodicals Review*, 44:4 (Winter 2011), 307–326.
Rodgers, Beth, 'Competing girlhoods: competition, community, and reader contribution in the *Girl's Own Paper* and the *Girl's Realm*', *Victorian Periodicals Review*, 45:3 (Fall 2012), 277–300.

Schwoerer, L. G., 'Lady Rachel Russell [née Wriothesley; other married name, Vaughan] (bap. 1637–1723)', in H. C. G. Matthew and B. Harrison (eds), *The Oxford Dictionary of National Biography* (Oxford: Oxford University Press, 2004–).

Spongberg, Mary, '*La Reine malheureuse*: Stuart history, sympathetic history, and the Stricklands' history of Henrietta Maria', *Women's History Review*, 20:5 (November 2011), 745–764.

Spongberg, Mary, *Women Writers and the Nation's Past, 1790–1860: Empathetic Histories* (London and New York: Bloomsbury Press, 2019).

Strickland, Agnes and Elizabeth, *The Lives of the Queens of England* (London: Colburn and Co., 1845–48), first published 1840–1848.

Sturrock, June, 'Establishing identity: editorial correspondence from the early years of the *Monthly Packet*', *Victorian Periodicals Review*, 39:1 (Fall 2006), 266–276.

Synge, Margaret Bertha, *Great Englishwomen: A Historical Reading Book for Schools* (London: George Bell and Sons, 1911).

Thorne, K., 'Illustrious women competition: commended paper', *Woman's Signal* (27 August 1896).

Tusan, Michelle E., 'Inventing the new woman: print culture and identity politics during the fin-de-siècle', *Victorian Periodicals Review*, 31:2 (Summer 1998), 169–182.

Tytler, Sarah, 'A young Oxford maid', chapter XVIII, *Girl's Own Paper* (3 August 1889), pp. 694–696.

Watson, N. K., 'Sidney Ernest Dark (1872–1947)', in H. C. G. Matthew and B. Harrison (eds), *The Oxford Dictionary of National Biography* (Oxford: Oxford University Press, 2004–).

Mrs White, 'Chapter on pigments, patches, etc', *Englishwoman's Domestic Magazine* (1 April 1854), pp. 386–389.

White, M. A., *Henrietta Maria and the English Civil Wars* (London and New York: Routledge, 2006).

Part IV
Revived pasts

7

Tarry-at-home antiquarians: children's 'tour books', 1740–1850

M. O. Grenby

Mrs Markham's (unpublished) tour of England

In late 1829 and early 1830, notices appeared in the 'Literary chit-chat' and 'Works in the press' sections of several periodicals announcing the imminent arrival of a new book called the 'Kirby letters'.[1] These were to be published in three (later revised to two) octavo volumes, containing an account of 'A family tour from Yorkshire to Penzance'. The author was unspecified. No copies of such a book are now to be found. It seems highly doubtful that it was ever published. But previously unnoticed correspondence in the archive of the London publisher John Murray II, held in the National Library of Scotland, confirms that it was not entirely a phantom. This correspondence reveals the author of the 'Kirby letters', and that it was a project designed for the children's market. Moreover, the letters provide an intriguing, behind-the-scenes account of the making of a would-be entrant into one of the most crowded markets of early children's literature, what this chapter names the children's 'tour book'. By the time the 'Kirby letters' was being proposed, the children's tour book was already almost a hundred years old and constituted a coherent though interestingly ramified category of children's publishing. This chapter begins with an examination of how this particular children's tour book (almost) came into being, before surveying, taxonomising and interpreting the genre as a whole.

The letters in the Murray archive are to Murray from John Penrose Jnr (1778–1859), a clergyman, first in Cornwall and later Lincolnshire. Penrose was interested in education (his younger sister Mary married Thomas Arnold, the famous headmaster of Rugby School), and he was a well-published author, chiefly on theological subjects. But the proposed book, 'The Kirby letters', was not to be written by him, but by his wife, Elizabeth (c. 1779–1837). She was the daughter of the famous inventor of textile machinery Edmund Cartwright, but has herself come to be known by her pseudonym 'Mrs Markham'. Mrs Markham's *History of England* had appeared in 1823, followed by a *History of France* (1828), *The New Children's Friend* (1832), *Historical Conversations for Young Persons* (1836) and other titles.[2] Mrs Markham's histories were so widely read, so pre-eminent in their field, and so enduring, that they became proverbial, and parodied, even into the twentieth century.[3]

Penrose handled all his wife's dealings with Murray, and his letters allow us to reconstruct the history of the 'Kirby letters', which he described matter-of-factly as a 'Juvenile Tour in England'. It had its genesis, we learn, in a meeting at Murray's premises in Albemarle Street, London, and by August 1829 the Penroses had decided that this 'little work will take most naturally … the form of Letters' and would be ready within a year.[4] They were to be based on travels the author had actually undertaken – hence the particular itinerary, from York, near the Penroses' home in Lincolnshire, to Cornwall, where John Penrose had been born, raised and first employed. Their journey had presumably been made with their own three children, then aged about fourteen, thirteen and twelve (travelling *en famille* on recreational tours, whether domestically or in Europe, was not uncommon). Indeed, John Penrose was clear that his wife's book was to describe 'nothing but what she has seen', and 'to have as much the air of reality as any genuine correspondence could have'.[5] It seems likely that Elizabeth Penrose planned to include genuine correspondence, written during the journey, since her husband warned Murray that some were 'rather "broad farce"', and insisted, because 'there is a playfulness and unreserve in some of the letters', and because 'not a person either in her family or mine … has the least suspicion of her being engaged in any such matter', that the author's name should be concealed.[6]

The intended content of the 'Kirby letters' is revealed by a wonderfully succinct list, jotted in the blank space of one of John Penrose's letters. It reads: 'Machinery | Mining | Old Castles & Cathedrals | Monuments of Kings and celebrated persons | House in which remarkable persons were born | Mountains | Rivers | Lakes'.[7] His next letter, giving an indication of how an author might conceptualise and assemble a tour book, gave what was apparently a full itinerary (Figure 7.1): ten towns and cities, nine castles, five churches and cathedrals, five stately homes, three natural attractions, and probably three industrial sites (two Cornish tin and copper mines, and 'Ivy Bridge' in Devon, most likely for its paper mills).[8] Almost all of those sites that survive remain tourist attractions today. However, Murray was not entirely satisfied. He evidently suggested a more didactic strain, since in May 1830, John Penrose was promising him to 'introduce, and this to a greatly increased degree, *more* history, *more* fact & *more* anecdotes'. In addition, Penrose suggested that 'The mother of

Tarry-at-home antiquarians

> York
> York minster
> Sprotborough Hall near Doncaster
> Workshop Manor
> Newark Castle
> Bottesford Church, Leicestershire
> Belvoir Castle
> Warwick Castle
> Kenilworth
> Blenheim
> Oxford
> Donnington castle, Berks
> Bath
> Wells cathedral
> Palace at Wells
> Glastonbury
> Tiverton Church
> Tiverton castle
> Exeter
> Dawlish
> Teignmouth
> Ivy Bridge
> Plymouth
> Mount Edgcumbe
> Restormel Castle Cornwall
> Fowey
> Probus Church
> Falmouth
> Pendennis Castle
> Mount's Bay
> S.t Michael's Mount
> Land's End
> Logan Rock   ⎫ There are some lithographs of these scenes, published
> Botallack Mine ⎬ I know not where in London but which I have only
> Wherry Mine   ⎭ seen in the shops in Penzance, which if they can be
>   had and copied would be very illustrative.

7.1 John Penrose Jnr to John Murray II, 7 December 1829. Manuscript note of the itinerary for a planned children's tour book: ten towns and cities, nine castles, five churches and cathedrals, five stately homes, three natural attractions and probably three industrial sites (two Cornish tin and copper mines, and 'Ivy Bridge' in Devon, most likely for its paper mills). National Library of Scotland (MSS. 40,938, fo. 25r).

the family may be made to begin the series of letters with something of a more matronly & instructive stile than they possess at present, & other letters from her may be interspersed throughout the work'.[9] Later he offered more letters by Mr Kirby, *père*, perhaps to be more scientific in nature.[10] When a continuation was proposed, tracing the journey back from Cornwall to the north of England by a different route, Penrose requested that Murray send him published accounts of cathedrals at Bristol, Bath and Worcester to inform his wife's descriptions.[11]

Even though this proposal came from one of his star authors, Murray, it seems, was still not satisfied. The 240 pages sent in December 1830 do not survive. Indeed, they were apparently never printed, and no book matching the description given in the letters seems to exist. The correspondence does not explain why. What the letters provide, however, is an illuminating insight into how such a tour book might come into being and what an author and a publisher variously thought such a book should look like and achieve. The 'Kirby letters' represents Penrose's attempt to branch out into a different kind of historiography, not abstract and academic, but rooted in the material remains of the past, and communicated in the guise of a family's adventure. The correspondence with Murray highlights some of the sub-genre's most intriguing issues. What sites should be included in these tours? What balance should be struck between liveliness and didacticism? What purpose did such books serve? And what was the relationship between the writing of history, and of what we might now call 'heritage'?

Origins

From the early eighteenth century, a new kind of domestic travelogue had begun to be published, notable examples of which included Daniel Defoe's *Tour Thro' the Whole Island of Great Britain* (1724–1727) and later Samuel Johnson's *A Journey to the Western Islands of Scotland* (1775). In parallel there was a dramatic upsurge of interest in antiquarianism. Both were intellectual and often political enterprises – deploying eye-witness, empirical accounts of landscapes and sites of historical, cultural or economic interest to bolster a fragile sense of British unity in the period after the Anglo-Scottish Act of Union and the Jacobite Rebellions.[12] But increasingly, they also fired the growth of leisure travel and a literature to accompany it. Rosemary Sweet devotes a chapter of her study of eighteenth-century antiquarianism to its popularisation: the 'topographical tours, histories and guides', and the 'cheaper guides and abridgments' that disseminated antiquarianism to those beyond its initially chiefly male, patrician constituency.[13] What Sweet did not note is that antiquarianism also became an important element of the new children's literature that rapidly developed from the middle of the eighteenth century.

These children's tour books were similar in scope to those published for adults but, if anything, were more concerned with communicating historical and antiquarian information. In some ways, this fitted into a long tradition of literature giving advice on travel (sometimes called *Ars Apodemica*), published in many languages from the sixteenth century and typically including lists of places, things and personages to be visited, how to learn from what and who one encountered, how to classify and record this knowledge, and how to stay healthy while doing so.[14] Some of it was specifically directed at young people.[15] But, as this chapter will show, drawing on an analysis of more than seventy titles (see Appendix A), most of them offering domestic tours of Britain, its constituent regions or individual cities, principally London, the children's tour book was designed to function less as a guidebook for actual travellers and more as an exercise in nation-building. Moreover, as an element of an emerging children's print culture, these children's tour books constitute an important but almost entirely overlooked sub-genre of early children's literature, present from its very beginnings and embodying its fundamental principles.

The origins of the children's tour book might be dated to 1727, when a section called 'Curiosities in London and Westminster' was for the first time appended to William Mather's long-lived *Young Man's Companion*, which had been first published in 1681. Here, this new material sat alongside matters of more direct utility like 'Plain Directions for a Young Man to attain to Read and Write true *English*' and 'Easy Rules for Measuring of Board and Timber'. The new section gave historical details, listed impressive facts and pointed out matters of particular interest about buildings in the metropolis: what might now be called 'heritage education'. Information about the built historic environment began to appear in schoolbooks of the period too.[16] By mid-century, this kind of material had been expanded to fill a book, as in David Henry's *Historical Account of the Curiosities of London and Westminster*, published by John Newbery, the celebrated pioneer of children's literature, from 1753. It appeared in many editions both as a single volume and in its three constituent parts (the Tower of London, Westminster Abbey, and St. Paul's Cathedral).[17] It was not a children's book per se, but Newbery probably recognised that it would be used by young as well as old.[18] The *Historical Description of St. Paul's Cathedral*, for instance, pointedly informed its readers that at least the first 260 steps to the 'Golden-Gallery' ('you must pay Two-pence to gratify your Curiosity with a Prospect … of the River, City, and Country round') are 'so easy that a Child may ascend them'.[19] The empiricist imperative that would run through the tour book genre is clear here: a determination to observe, measure, count and report. Mather describes Westminster Hall, for instance, as 'One of the largest Rooms in *Europe*, not supported by Pillars: Tis about 228 Foot in length, 66 in breath, and 90 in Altitude, built by William Rufus'.[20]

From the 1740s, when a new kind of children's literature began to be published in London, written not only for instruction but also for children's enjoyment, texts based around the nation's built heritage were among the very first experiments. Indeed, it is notable that all three of the publishers usually congratulated for producing the incunabula of children's literature in the 1740s – namely Newbery, Thomas Boreman and Mary Cooper – numbered accounts of historical sites/sights in England among their earliest productions. What these publishers recognised was the potential of presenting historico-geographical information in an entertaining format, as communicated by engaging characters, or by embedding it within a loose narrative. Such a presentation might yield educative benefits and heighten these books' appeal, both of which might conduce to greater profits. Thus was the children's tour book born.

In 1740–1743, Thomas Boreman published his *Gigantick Histories*, a series organised around London's principal places of historical interest. The first, *The Gigantick History of the Two Famous Giants, and Other Curiosities in Guildhall* (1740), was chosen presumably because Boreman's shop was at the Guildhall, a complex of buildings in the City of London dating chiefly from the early fifteenth century. The book was an experiment, as Boreman admitted in a preface to a second part, born out of dire financial need. Yet he had stumbled on a ready market: '*Necessity* … has finish'd, left me, and sent *Success* in her stead', he wrote.[21] A second volume, a second edition and several sequels soon followed: *The Curiosities of the Tower of London* (2 vols, 1741), *The History and Description of the Famous Cathedral of St. Paul's* (2 vols, 1741) and *The History and Description of Westminster Abbey* (3 vols, 1742–1743). In each, in a tiny format (about 600 × 475 mm), Boreman set out the chief attractions, treasures and curiosities of each place, as well as its architectural splendours.

Mary Cooper was perhaps inspired directly by Boreman. Her *Travels of Tom Thumb over England and Wales* appeared in 1746, expanding the children's tour book in scale from the municipal to the national.[22] As in almost all of these early children's books, authorship remains a mystery, but whoever wrote *The Travels of Tom Thumb* was clearly aware of Boreman's slightly earlier attempts in the genre, mentioning the two Guildhall giants 'whose gigantic History hath some Years ago been published', and where Boreman had used friendly giants, employing the similarly fabulous and outlandishly sized figure Tom Thumb to introduce this tour to children. (Tom Thumb was a personage, moreover, whose demise Boreman had specifically prophesied would be the result of his own books: 'Tom Thumb shall now be thrown away'.[23]) Tom provides an appealing companion on the tour. 'After the many strange Adventures of my Youth, and the many Perils and Dangers I had escaped,' he explains, 'one would have thought I should have been very glad to have spent the

Remainder of my Days at Home in Ease and Safety.' But, he says, 'Ambition, and the Love of my Country, excited me to undertake the vast Design of travelling to distant Counties, and viewing all the Cities, Towns, and remarkable Places in the whole Kingdom of *England*, and the Principality of *Wales*.' His tour is a sort of playful geographical textbook, full of observations about the counties' topographical features, the healthfulness of their air, the principal settlements, distance from London, and their shape on the map ('Take a Piece of Dough or Glazier's Putty, as long again as it is thick, and squeeze it together a little in the Middle, and you will have pretty near the Shape of *Cambridgeshire*'). Its descriptions of England's built environment are concise but appreciative, and, as with the 'Kirby letters' list, map smoothly onto modern tourist trails. Tom wonders at the colleges of Oxford, for instance, and finds Blenheim Palace (completed just over twenty years earlier) 'most magnificent' though it 'has been censured by the Criticks in Building'. Although this empiricism is everywhere evident, Tom Thumb boasting of having been 'more careful and exact than even any former real Traveller' in the matter of 'the true Distance of their capital Towns from London', he seems particularly to value places with literary associations: Shakespeare's grave, for instance, or Warwick Castle where may be seen the sword of the Romance hero, Guy of Warwick, as well as 'the Chapel where he is said to have ended his Days piously, after hewing down so many Giants and Monsters'.[24] Three years earlier, Cooper had brought out *Tom Thumb's History of England*, a more conventional (though handsomely illustrated) exercise in historiography. Her *Travels of Tom Thumb* was an altogether more approachable venture.

Although they were the most intrepid and commercially astute of the early publishers for children, Newbery and his successors were relatively slow to make a contribution to the development of the children's tour book. It was left to Newbery's son and nephew, both called Francis, to develop a tour book specifically for the young. The son's was a guide to *Windsor, and its Environs*, 'containing the curiosities of the town and palace, the Royal chapel of St. George, and the seats in the neighbourhood', published in 1768.[25] The more successful nephew's first contribution to the genre was a much more extensive four-volume *Curiosities of London and Westminster Described*, which appeared in 1770. In addition to the Tower, St Paul's, and Westminster Abbey, it took in all the important sights of the metropolis, from London Bridge, the Bank of England and the British Museum to Bethlem, Bridewell, Christ's and the Foundling Hospitals. It had a friendly tone, and six engravings per volume, but gone were Boreman's and Cooper's attempts to mediate the historical information through fairy characters. Nevertheless, even selling at sixpence per volume, new editions appeared up to 1799, and possibly later, demonstrating the public's appetite for a children's antiquarianism.[26]

Proliferation and diversity

By the end of the eighteenth century, the children's tour book had become an established part of the market for children's books. In the preface to his own contribution published in 1788, John Aikin noted that 'Tours through England ... are publications sufficiently common and numerous', but regretted that 'they are, for the most part, works of a very low order in literature', full of 'tedious descriptions of objects ... relations become totally erroneous through length of time, and transmitted, unchanged, from one successive compilation to another; weak and illiberal partialities, local and national, with inelegancies and vulgarisms of every kind', all of which 'certainly render them little proper to be put into the hands of youth'.[27] Evidently this view was widely shared, and authors began to experiment with new modes of delivering their historical information.

At one end of the spectrum were children's novels such as the anonymous *Travels and Adventures of Timothy Wildman, in Europe, Asia, Africa and America*, published around 1790. Here was a picareseque narrative filled with exciting adventure, such as tiger-slayings, encounters with pirates, and condemnation by the Inquisition. But, true to the book's subtitle – 'Wherein many of the Principal Cities & Towns in the World are Faithfully Described' – the reader would also find detailed descriptions of places visited. Before the hero is allowed to begin his adventures at Venice, for instance, the reader is obliged to push through three pages of factual description: 500 bridges, 150 palaces, 115 towers, 70 churches, 17 hospitals, 2,000 canon, 64 marble statues, 23 of bronze, 'all master-pieces of art', and so on.[28] More integrated education and entertainment was to be found in a *London: A Descriptive Poem* (1811), a finely illustrated versification of the city's architectural wonders and commercial virtues, or *Instructive Rambles in London, and the Adjacent Villages* (1798) by the novelist Elizabeth Helme. In order to 'amuse the mind' at the same time as she worked to 'improve the understanding of youth', Helme introduced an agreeable family, the Richardsons, set in an appealing tale which saw a father re-engaging with his children after the death of his wife by embarking together on a restorative tour to the metropolis. The tour is a straightforward third-person narrative, with interpolated direct speech as Mr Richardson enters into in educative dialogue with his two children. The interpolation of historical and geographical information could still be crude however: 'I have long wished to see the Tower; will you favour me by taking us there?' says Charles. 'With all my heart [replies his father]; but as this is your first wish, you, doubtless, are informed by reading of every historic circumstance respecting it. Will you oblige me by relating a few'.[29]

Others sought to overcome this woodenness by couching the tour as fictional correspondence. *A Tour Through England*, first published in 1804, comprised a series of letters purportedly from a 'young gentleman' (travelling with his father) to his sister at home, the fulfilment of his promise that 'I would from time to time give you an account of our progress, that you might accompany us on the map, with such observations as would strike a JUVENILE TOURIST like myself, and would be most likely to please and entertain you'.[30] (As Richard Ansell has shown, this was a practice actually employed by real young travellers while on their tours.[31]) One preface admitted that the descriptions of a tour of the Alps that followed were 'copied, nearly word for word, from a journal kept by the author … except that it has been cast into the form of letters, the personages of which are fictitious'.[32]

Priscilla Wakefield perfected what we might call these 'epistolary family tours' in her *The Juvenile Travellers; containing the Remarks of a Family during a Tour through the Principal States and Kingdoms of Europe* (1801). Her fictional family, the aptly named Seymours, each have their own characters, interests and purposes. The book's success stems from her decision to separate these characters in space, so that they might write letters to one another describing what they have seen. As in an epistolary novel, this whole constitutes 'a narrative to engage the attention of young readers', as Wakefield put it, 'without too much diverting them from the main object in view' (which was to convey information about 'the prominent features in the character and manners of the inhabitants of other countries; with their chief cities, and most celebrated buildings').[33] It is a clear indication of the profitability of the tour book that Darton was willing to pay the extremely high price of £200 to Wakefield for the copyright, the highest price she was ever able to command for any of her highly successful works.[34] Seventeen further editions were published by 1842. *A Family Tour through the British Empire* followed in 1804, then *Excursions in North America* in 1806, *Perambulations in London, and its Environs … Designed for Young Persons* in 1809, *The Traveller in Africa* in 1814 and *The Traveller in Asia* in 1817. Each of these included the same set of characters, the Middleton family, adding an anchoring familiarity to the increasing foreignness of the books' settings, and Wakefield retained her familial correspondence format.[35] Penrose's 'Kirby letters' were evidently conceived under Wakefield's influence.

Over seventy children's tour books have been consulted for this study (see Appendix A), but many more were published in this period, particularly from the 1820s. Few children's publishers declined to attempt venturing into what was evidently understood to be a remunerative market. The majority eschewed Wakefield's more expansive scope and continued to focus on domestic locations. London remained a primary focus, with an emphasis on those of the city's locations that were connected with national events and imbued with ideas of Englishness, such as the Tower of London and Westminster Abbey. Examples include *Views of the Principal Buildings of London, With an Account of the*

Curiosities they Contain published by John Marshall in 1800, or *London in Miniature with Engravings of its Public Buildings and Antiquities from Drawings by Alfred Mills* published in 1814. John Harris added a similar title to his list with *A Visit to Uncle William in Town, or a Description of the Most Remarkable Buildings and Curiosities of the British Metropolis* in 1818, and *The Public Buildings of Westminster Described*, attributed to the historical novelist Christian Isobel Johnstone, in 1831. By then, the standard sights of London had evolved. In *A Month in London; or, Some of its Modern Wonders Described* (1832) by Jeffreys Taylor, for example, a New Yorker travels to England, land of his father's birth, to inform himself 'of the real progress of England in the grand improvements of the age'. What follows is his tour of London, with his two young English cousins, taking in such modern marvels as an 'aerostation' for 'balloon sailing', the city's recent gas lights, Marc Isambard Brunel's Thames Tunnel (then still unfinished) and the new discoveries showcased in the British Museum (notably 'meteoric stones' and other exhibits relating to 'the comparatively modern science of geology', plus the Elgin Marbles, on display since 1817). This was followed, as if by way of apology for the book's fascination with the new, by a thirty-one-page postscript giving of the city's history and an account of all the standard historical attractions.[36] Enterprising publishers were also keen to capitalise on current events to refresh their tour books. *Peter Parley's Visit to London, During the Coronation of Queen Victoria* (1838), for example, enlivened its description of Westminster Abbey by detailing the preparations for, and then the coronation itself, interleaving accounts of the history of the regalia and the coronation throne.

Other nineteenth-century tour books covered the provinces, and as the market for children's books became increasingly established, publishers evidently felt able to risk more chorographical tour books, concerned with describing only a specific region rather than full national coverage. *The Juvenile Tourist*, by the Rev. John Evans and first published in 1804, was originally sold as 'Excursions Through Various Parts of the Island of Great-Britain', but actually (as the subtitle to one of the later, expanded editions clarified) described 'Excursions Into the West of England; into the Midland Counties, with Parts of South Wales; and into the Whole County of Kent; Concluding with an Account of Maidstone and its Vicinity'. Louisa Weston's *The Cambrian Excursion, Intended to Inculcate a Taste for the Beauties of Nature* (1826) traced a family's tour only to Aberystwyth and then 'the interior of North Wales'.[37] The Religious Tract Society in the 1840s published titles such as *Wanderings in the Isle of Wight* (1846) and *Loiterings Among the Lakes of Cumberland* (1849), both by George Mogridge. Others went further afield, such as Sarah (Atkins) Wilson's *Relics of Antiquity, Exhibited in the Ruins of Pompeii and Herculaneum ... Intended for the Use of Young Persons*, published by John Harris in 1825. Equally, tour books diversified in terms of their format and appearance. The Rev. Samuel

Clark's Reuben Ramble books, published by Darton from the 1840s and advertised as 'Pictorial Instruction for Young Children', offered travels through the counties of England grouped by region with short textual accounts accompanying county maps, themselves surrounded by a decorative collage of sketches of the historical, sights to be found there (Figure 7.2, Figure 7.3). The toy books that became so popular from the 1840s – usually six or eight large, square pages of highly coloured illustrations, accompanied by a minimal text – also included tour book subjects alongside the usual traditional stories and rhymes, as for instance with *Tommy Trip's Tour through the Counties of England*, published by Dean and Co. in 1842, or *Grandmamma Easy's Account of the Public Buildings in London*, which Dean and Co. had brought out as part of a highly miscellaneous series, at sixpence each, by 1847. *London Sights for Little Folks*, published by Charles Tilt in c. 1838, compressed the usual sites into a miniature book, about 600 mm square.

The most sophisticated tour books enmeshed their accounts of historical sites in sometimes quite complex narrative frameworks. An influential model was Jean-Jacques Barthélemy's *Voyage du jeune Anacharsis en Grèce* (1788), published in English as *Travels of Anacharsis the Younger in Greece* in 1790–1791. Barthélemy was an accomplished antiquarian and classicist. He sought to communicate his expertise to a new audience by fictionalising an account of a Scythian boy's observations during a tour of Greece in the fourth century BCE, purportedly set down for posterity by the boy when he reached old age. The anonymous *Travels of a British Druid*, published in 1811, imitated this involution, purporting to be taken from a fifth-century BCE Celtic manuscript and recording the impressions of a young British druid's tour through France to Egypt, concentrating on classical Greece and Rome. Elynd sends home an account of his travels, hoping 'to remove from his countrymen the darkness under which they laboured'. Such a book did double duty, as contemporary reviewers noted, simultaneously providing 'a concise account of the different countries' through which Elynd travelled and educating readers about 'the character of the British Druids', and all 'in a pleasing and highly interesting narrative'.[38] The highly successful children's author Barbara Hofland also evidently came to recognise that children were expecting more narrative and less direct didacticism in their tour books. Her *Young Northern Traveller* 'was originally published [in 1813] in letters, the usual method pursued by travellers some years ago', explained a preface to a new edition of c. 1830, but 'Believing that it would be read with greater pleasure in the present more agreeable form, Mrs Hofland has carefully and entirely re-written it' (perhaps giving an indication of why the 'Kirby letters' was never published).[39] The novel that followed remained inexorably pedagogic in its eye-witness account of places and things (in Hull, for instance, the club with which Captain Cook was killed), but the renunciation of epistolarity in favour of a third-person narration

7.2 Frontispiece to [Samuel Clarke], *Reuben Ramble's Travels Through the Counties of England* (London: Darton & Clark, n.d.). Published by Darton from the 1840s. © British Library Board.

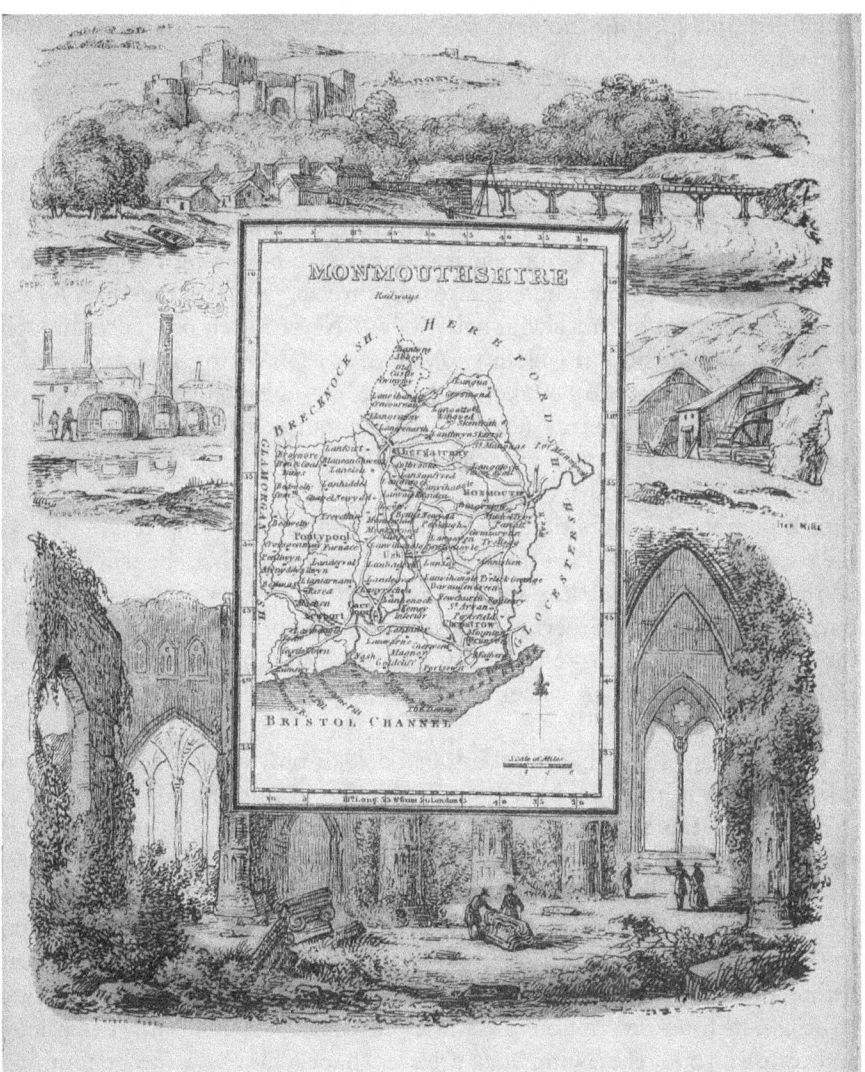

7.3 Illustration for Monmouthshire, [Samuel Clarke], *Reuben Ramble's Travels in the Midland Counties of England* (London: Darton & Clark, n.d.). Published by Darton from the 1840s. © British Library Board.

simplified and sped up the narrative, and removed a subjectivity that could sometimes interfere with these books' educative purpose.

Indeed, nineteenth-century tour books were inclined to moralising. In Agnes Strickland's *The Youthful Travellers* (1823), for example, while visiting Goodrich Castle, the heroine Emily decides to leave her family to explore a dungeon without her family. 'I left them ... and stole away, unperceived by any of the party to survey the ruins at my leisure, being too independent to stand in need of a guide', she says, but manages to ends up becoming trapped on the ruined steps to a tower where she requires rescue by her father. The lesson learned here is not historical, but behavioural: 'Never forfeit prudence through curiosity', he tells her.[40] In Helme's *Instructive Rambles* the very selection of what the children are to be taken to see becomes a moral choice. 'What are the objects *you* consider as worth seeing?' enquires Mr Richardson of his daughter. 'Bless me, papa, I can scarcely tell', replies Mary, before tentatively suggesting the 'fine shops, the park, the play, the opera, the concert, and ball; with a number of others that I have daily heard of, and long to see'. These, she soon learns, are not the proper sights of London. Rather, she will be cured of the erroneous education she has received by a tour of historical sites interspersed with moral narratives, each made to spring out of the other, as the chapter headings make clear: 'An Excursion to Chelsea – A Visit to the College and the Church – Uncommon Valour of Mrs Spragg – On the courage necessary for Females'.[41]

Equally, it was possible for the tour book to provide an overtly political interpretation of topography. When *The Travels of Tom Thumb* describes 'the Ruins of the famous *Pict's* Wall, built' (Hadrian's Wall), for example, it is explained as having been designed 'to restrain the Northern People, who have always been very troublesome to those of the South'. On one level this is a reference to the Picts threatening Roman Britannia; but there is a clear allusion to the Jacobite rebels who had invaded from Scotland in 1745, only a year before the book's publication. There are explicit references to the Jacobite Rebellion in Tom's description of Carlisle's city walls (not sufficiently defensible) and concern about the 'Number of private Chapels for *Papists*' to be found in London. Describing Temple Bar, he explains, apparently *en passant*, that this is where 'the Heads of State Criminals are stuck up after Execution', and he notes with a certain glee that 'many more are soon expected to bear it Company'. The Jacobite 'Rebel Lords' were indeed executed for high treason in 1746–1747.[42]

The specific political inflections of individual tour books are beyond the scope of this chapter, although critics such as Emma Major have shown how illuminating such readings can be – pointing out, for instance, how 'dissent is increasingly written into an Establishment landscape' in Wakefield's *Family Tour*, 'so that the number of Dissenting places of worship is noted alongside those of the Church of England', and places connected with Oliver Cromwell and the Glorious Revolution are given special prominence.[43] Above and beyond the political inclinations of individual authors, however, the children's tour book genre as a whole can be seen as contributing to a larger project: presenting a string of individual sites as part of a coherent national whole, and showing how the past could be read in its material remains, and understood as existing in a continuum that connected it with the nation's present, and indeed future, state.

Purposes and principles

For publishers, the financial advantages to be gained from the children's tour book were clear. If, from the second half of the eighteenth century, there were children's novels, children's verse, children's periodicals, bibles, biographies and books of science, why should there not be children's travel books? Whether, once sold, these books were intended to complement actual visits to the sites being described is a matter for debate. It was certainly not uncommon for children to be taken to see the sights of, say, London – as for instance when Isaac Bickerstaff in the *Tatler* (1709), took his three nephews to see the lions at the Tower of London, the tombs at Westminster Abbey, Bedlam Hospital 'and the other places which are entertainments to raw minds'.[44] Children also accompanied family members on domestic or foreign tours (or even travelled without their family at surprisingly young ages). Some tour books do seem to be designed to supplement and enhance this sightseeing, such as Newbery's *Historical Description of the Tower of London and its Curiosities* (1754) 'Written chiefly to direct the Attention of Spectators to what is most curious … and to enable them afterwards to relate what they have seen' (and which usefully lists the 'Prices of seeing the Curiosities'). But predominantly, the children's tour book appears to have been intended for those who would never visit the places being described – debarred by distance, class and perhaps gender – young people for whom (as Charlotte Brontë wrote to a schoolfriend in 1834) a great city like London was 'as apocryphal as Babylon, or Nineveh, or ancient Rome'.[45] Thus *A Visit to Edinburgh*, a novelised account of a family's visit to the city, was 'intended chiefly for the amusement and information of those young people, residing at a distance, who are desirous of becoming acquainted with some of its principal objects' (although, hedging her bets, its author also hoped 'it may prove an acceptable present to the juvenile inhabitants of this city').[46] Authors, such as Ann and Jane Taylor in *City Scenes: or, A Peep into London* (1809: see Figure 7.4) might even make a virtue of their book's surrogacy for actual travel:

Come, peep at London's famous town,

Nor need you travel there;

> For one foot up, and one foot down,
>
> In future, you may spare:
>
> At home, a hundred miles away,
>
> 'Tis easy now to look,
>
> At City Scenes, and London gay,
>
> In this my little book.[47]

Indeed, the famous 'Scenes in ...' series written by their father, Isaac Taylor, beginning with Europe in 1818, then Asia, Africa, America and England, was explicitly, and oxymoronically, advertised as being 'for the Amusement and Instruction of Little *Tarry-at-Home Travellers*'. The most astute authors knew that the careful build-up of verisimilitude offered an excellent means of engaging stay-at-home children with the locations being described. The Taylor sisters, for example, although avowedly writing for tarry-at-home travellers, offered site-specific advice to children visiting St Paul's ('mind how you go along the dark staircase .... Walk gently, and lay hold of the rail as you go along') and addressed them as if they were actual sightseers ('endeavour to remember all the curious things you have seen, and describe them to your brothers and sisters when you get home', so as to give readers the illusion that they were actually visiting.[48]

The idea of travelling without leaving home was of a piece with eighteenth-century children's literature more generally. Newbery promoted his books as providing education for those who could not afford formal schooling. His *Drawing School for Little Masters and Misses* (1773), for example, provided 'The most easy and concise Rules for Learning to Draw, *Without the Assistance of a Teacher*'.[49] In the same way, the tour book provided a knowledge of Britain, and the wider world, without the need to, or expense of, travel. So one could read this vicariousness as a kind of democratisation, providing encounters with situated history and geography to those who could never hope to live them. But it was also bound up with a valorisation of home. Chloe Chard has noted that eighteenth-century travel writings in general often 'simply take it for granted that the foreign and familiar are placed in a relation of rivalry to each other, and that the task of the traveller is to choose between them'.[50] Children's tour books presented this contrast, but generally were clear that Otherness was something that one ought to learn about, but, ultimately reject. Thus, in Barbara Hofland's *Young Northern Traveller*, when Frederic Delmar, aged thirteen, who has been sent on an extensive tour of northern Europe for the benefit of his health, returns to his home town of York and sees the Minster, he opines, 'Ah! there she is – I have seen nothing like her.' Moments later, he arrives at his family house, and we see that his 'home' is a moral as

7.4 Page from [Ann and Jane Taylor], *City Scenes: or, A Peep into London, for Good Children* (London: Darton and Harvey, 1809). © British Library Board.

well as geographical and cultural locus: 'I need not tell you, that my dear mother's kiss had never been so welcome, as on this eventful night ... and that I had met with no entertainment in hall or palace, equal to the tea, and brown bread and butter, of our own parlour.'[51] Indeed, tour books routinely present the return home as the happy denouement of the narrative and commend the protagonists not only for safe return, but also for remaining unchanged by their experiences. Characters who had made trips from the country to London were particularly praised for beholding 'the glare, and glitter, and dazzling display of London with dispositions so unchanged, heart so uncontaminated', as Charlotte Brontë congratulated her schoolfriend in 1834.[52]

Fundamentally, of course, children's tour books were intended to convey historical and geographical information in more palatable ways than could be achieved in a standard, often catechistical text book. A tour book would succeed, it was hoped, by linking historical data to physical space. As Aikin put it in his preface to *England Delineated*: 'I have been desirous of introducing historical matter ... as connected with some particular place; in order that, by such an association, the events might be forcibly impressed upon the memory of a young reader.'[53] It should be noted, though, that tour books were designed to supplement not supplant more standard historiography. 'In my choice of the historical sketches, I have selected such as I thought might interest young minds sufficiently to make them the more readily peruse the annals of their country', wrote Helme in the preface to her *Instructive Rambles*. The narrative exemplified her hopes. After visiting the Tower of London, eight-year-old Mary tells her father, 'though I have been greatly amused with what I have seen, and interested with what you have told us, yet I should like to know every particular respecting those remarkable characters'. This is the prompt for Mr Richardson to recommend his children to read their 'History of England'. '"My dear Sir [replies his son], [...] with your leave I will take it from your library to-morrow morning"'.[54] What Helme was expressing here is the tour book's conviction that the best way to enthuse children to study history is to anchor abstract history in real, recognisable places that one might, at least in theory, visit.

This is one reason to position these tour books as an early effort to provide children with what we might call 'heritage education', that is to say to introduce them not to history in the abstract but to the places in which history happened and its material remains in the hope that it would encourage a deeper engagement with the past. But heritage must also be understood as a social practice. In this sense the buildings, ruins, monuments, artefacts and antiquities that the books present 'become *devices*', as Emma Waterton puts it, 'that are imbued with meaning and used to trigger and guide a self-conscious dialogue between personal and collective memories and experiences'.[55] As those analysing how heritage sites work note, when visitors engage with sites, they find themselves inserted into a larger, collective story. This is precisely what the children's tour books sought to enable and encourage through print: the incorporation of the reader into a history, usually a national history, that was being represented synecdochally in the texts by those particular sites and artefacts. This had many advantages as a mode of engaging children with the past. First, as we have seen, it was hoped that embedding historical information in a narrative format, and emplotting it in geographical space, would render it more appealing to young readers. Second, as David Lowenthal has pointed out, heritage is different from history because, although it too 'uses historical traces and tells historical tales … these tales and traces are stitched into fables that are open neither to critical analysis nor to contemporary scrutiny'. It was, in other words, less requisite that historical stories told through that history's material remains should be corroborated or complete. Heritage, as Lowenthal puts it, is 'far more flexibly emended' than history.[56] The tour books embody this 'flexibility', offering a history that was often localised, detached from overarching chronologies and frequently based as much on supposition, story and myth as diligently collected evidence and careful historiography.

Third, historical sites featured in children's tour books were often presented as part of a seamless continuum with the present. This again is characteristic of how heritage (as distinct from history) is now understood: as 'the materials and practices through which the past is drawn into the present, stimulating reflection on our futures'.[57] The relationship between past, present and future is nowhere clearer than in the lithograph illustrations to *Reuben Ramble's Travels through the Counties of England*, each of which features a montage of old and new. Monmouthshire, for example, was represented by Chepstow Castle, the ruins of Tintern Abbey, 'Iron mills' and the smoking chimneys of 'Furnaces' (Figure 7.3). Cumberland was constituted by 'Carlisle Cathedral', a 'Lead mine', 'Lowdore water fall', 'Keswick Lake & Skiddaw Mountain' and 'Druidical remains'.[58] Similarly, in *Thirty-Two Remarkable Places in Old England, for the Instruction and Entertainment of Youth* (1818), a copperplate showing a picturesque ruin framing Norwich Cathedral faces a textual description explaining that the city is 'noted for making crapes, bombazeens, damasks, flowered satins, camlets, shawls, and various other stuffs'. The 'Old England' of the title can happily include cities such as Oxford and Bath, described in terms of their antiquity and beauty, and Birmingham, 'noted for its great foundries and hardware manufactures', most 'carried on by steam-engines, which are here in a high state of improvement'. ('By their means', the prosperous child reader is told, 'labour is so far diminished, that a few boys and girls work ponderous machines with ease and expedition.')[59]

To modern eyes this seems a curious combination of ancient and modern, industrial and picturesque. It would have horrified John Ruskin, whose vision of what was morally and aesthetically good, and worth observing and preserving

– a vision that became inordinately influential from the later nineteenth century – rigorously excluded any trace of mechanised industry. In the children's tour books of the eighteenth and nineteenth centuries, however, no contrast was intended between the remains of the past and the promise of the present. This is evident from the Penroses' letters to Murray setting out their plans for the 'Kirby letters'. The first outline flagrantly mixes ancient and modern: 'Machinery | Mining | Old Castles & Cathedrals | Monuments of Kings and celebrated persons'. The more detailed itinerary that followed included, with no particular comment, tin and copper mines and a paper mill alongside castles and cathedrals (see Figure 7.1).[60] Signalling how important Mrs Markham thought it that children should read about future prosperity as well as past glory, Penrose also complained about how difficult it was to come by information on the state and history of trade and manufactures that was not too technical to use in a book for young people.[61] A focus on the modern had been a feature of the tour book since Defoe, whose enthusiasm for new buildings, commercial activity and highly cultivated land has often been noted.[62] But children's tour books seem more obviously to have wedded this confidently progressivist and modern outlook to a concern to supply historical information. They offered readers an introduction to Britain's past, but as part of a continuum with its present progress, and from there, by implication, its future.

Some children's tour books even avowedly eschewed history. *The Travels of Tom Thumb* had begun the tour book genre with a notable contempt for antiquarianism, Tom insisting that 'I have touched very slightly upon those Particulars of old Ruins, Roads, and Camps, with which other Descriptions are so greatly swell'd'.[63] Forty years later, in his preface to *England Delineated*, Aikin warned readers that he too had excluded '*Antiquities*' from his 'Description of Every County in England and Wales', adding that nor had he 'given any notices concerning *family history, noblemen's and gentlemen's seats, pleasure grounds, prospects,* and the like.' Instead, he promised 'an accurate and comprehensive account of the present state of these kingdoms, under the several heads of natural and political history, agriculture, and commerce'.[64] Both authors were following Defoe, in whose *Tour* 'the looking back into remote Things' had been 'studiously avoided'.[65] Yet, despite their protestations, antiquarian and historical information was far from absent from these books. Tom Thumb might say that he wished to give 'a tolerable Picture of what every County and remarkable Town now is', not 'what it has once been', and he took evident satisfaction on the new buildings being erected, but in Wiltshire, for instance, he devotes a paragraph to Salisbury Cathedral, notices Wilton House (dating largely from the seventeenth century) and then gets to 'the greatest Curiosity in this County, and perhaps in the Kingdom', Stonehenge. Although Tom will 'not enter into a particular Description of this Antiquity, it having been already so often given by former Travellers', he does take some time to dispel 'what

Country People relate' (that the number of stones can never be counted: 'For I told them myself five Times over, and found them always the same') and to give his 'private Opinion on the original Design and Use of this wonderful Structure', in which 'I agree with Mr. *Aubry* and Dr. *Stukeley*, that it was the grand Heathen Temple of the *Druids* for the whole Country about' and that the surrounding barrows were evidently burial sites, as 'is manifest from the Bones and other Tokens found in them'.[66] Likewise, although the main theme of Aikin's account of Salisbury Plain was its 'fine grasses excellent for sheep', he too described Stonehenge, debated its purpose and quoted a depiction of it in verse. In fact the majority of locations on Aikin's tour have an entry divided evenly – as if in unconscious balance – between past and present. Of Durham, for example, we read: 'The cathedral is a large and magnificent edifice; the buildings of the city in general old. Durham possesses a manufactory of shalloons, tammies, and calamancoes [various kinds of cloth]: around it are grown large quantities of the best mustard, which yields very profitable crops.'[67]

Aikin's ambition for the tour book was 'to make my young countrymen better acquainted than they are usually found to be with their native land'.[68] This might stand as the manifesto for the genre as a whole. Even if some of the tour books focused on a single city or region, and thus operated more chorographically, their principal aim was to construct a particular understanding of, and indeed an association with, a collective national identity. The past was to be the foundation of this identity, but only as it linked to the present, and pointed child readers to an optimistic national future. How well it worked is open to debate. But, as one reviewer put it in 1803, speaking of John Evans's *The Juvenile Tourist*, 'in reading such a narrative it is impossible not to become more attached to our native country'.[69]

Notes

1 E.g. Anon., *Edinburgh Literary Journal* (26 December 1829), p. 444; Anon., *New Monthly Magazine and Literary Journal* (1 January 1830), p. 28; Anon., *La Belle Assemblée; or, Bell's Court and Fashionable Magazine* (1 January 1830), p. 45, and (1 July 1830), p. 44; or Anon., 'Works preparing for publication, by Mr. Murray', Anon., *Edinburgh Review*, 101 (April 1830), where it was listed as 'Nearly ready for publication'.
2 On Mrs Markham's histories see Mitchell, *Picturing the Past*, pp. 35–36, 67–70.
3 See for instance Nesbit's *Wet Magic*, and Belloc's *Mrs Markham's New History of England*; and perhaps Cooney and Chapman's farce *Move Over, Mrs. Markham*.
4 Penrose to Murray II, 20 Aug. 1829, NLS MSS. 40,938, fo. 19v.
5 Penrose to Murray II, 5 Feb. 1830, NLS MSS. 40,938, fo. 26r.
6 Penrose to Murray II, 7 Dec. 1829, NLS MSS. 40,938, fos 24r–v.
7 Penrose to Murray II, 2 Dec. 1829, NLS MSS. 40,938, fo. 22r.

Revived pasts

8 Penrose to Murray II, 7 Dec. 1829, NLS MSS. 40,938, fo. 25r.
9 Penrose to Murray II, 17 May 1830, NLS MSS. 40,938, fos 32v–33r.
10 Penrose to Murray II, 16 Mar. 1831, NLS MSS. 40,938, fo. 52v.
11 Penrose to Murray II, 7 Oct 1830, NLS MSS. 40,938, fo. 39r.
12 Schellenberg. 'Imagining the nation'; Smethurst, *Travel Writing and the Natural World*, pp. 109–127.
13 Sweet, *Antiquaries*, p. 330.
14 See *Art of Travel* database.
15 See Warneke, *Images of the Educational Traveller*.
16 E.g. Dufresnoy's catechistically formatted *Geography of Children*, which includes a question asking what are the 'places of note' in London (pp. 25–26).
17 See Roscoe, *John Newbery and his Successors*, pp. 333–335.
18 Roscoe notes that these travel narratives were several times included in Newbery's lists of books printed 'For the Instruction and Amusement of Young Gentlemen and Ladies' (*ibid.*, p. 274).
19 Henry, *Historical Description of St. Paul's*, p. 34.
20 Mather, *Young Man's Companion*, p. 470.
21 Boreman, 'To All my Kind Subscribers'.
22 On Cooper's precise role in publishing books bearing her name see Immel and Alderson, *Tommy Thumb's Pretty Song-Book*, pp. 14–19. On *Travels of Tom Thumb* see Connell, 'Paper Kingdom'.
23 Boreman, 'To the Author of the Curiosities in the Tower of London'.
24 Anon., *Travels of Tom Thumb*, pp. viii, 143, 1–2, 66, 62, 59, 45–46 and 45.
25 Anon., *Windsor, and its Environs*.
26 Roscoe, *John Newbery and his Successors*, pp. 93–96.
27 Aikin, *England Delineated*, p. iv.
28 Anon., *Travels and Adventures of Timothy Wildman*, pp. 63–65.
29 Helme, *Instructive Rambles in London*, pp. i. 52–53.
30 Anon., *Tour Through England*, pp. vii, 1.
31 Ansell, 'Educational travel in Protestant families', esp. p. 938.
32 [Clarke], *A Tour to Great St. Bernard's*, pp. iii–iv.
33 Wakefield, *The Juvenile Travellers*, p. iii.
34 Grenby, 'Pay, Professionalization and Probable Dominance?', pp. 123–124.
35 Graham notes that letters from female characters grow fewer and fewer as the geographical range expands, and it is only male characters who venture overseas. See: Graham, 'Juvenile travellers', pp. 379, 389 n. 39.
36 Taylor, *A Month in London*, pp. 8, 101, 151–182.
37 Weston, *Cambrian Excursion*, p. 4.
38 Anon., '*Travels of a British Druid*' [book review], *Gentleman's Magazine*, 'Supplement to Volume LXXXI, Part II', 81 (1811), p. 638; Anon., '*Travels of a British Druid*' [book review], *British Critic*, 37 (March 1811), pp. 314–315.
39 Hofland, *Young Northern Traveller*, pp. i–ii.
40 The book was also marketed as written in letters 'designed as examples of the epistolary style for children'. Strickland, *Youthful Travellers*, pp. 167, 170.
41 Helme, *Instructive Rambles*, p. 225.

42 Anon., *Travels of Tom Thumb*, pp. 93, 92, 135, 141.
43 Major, *Madam Britannia*, p. 227.
44 Steele, in *Tatler*, 30 (18 June 1709).
45 Charlotte Brontë to Ellen Nussey, 19 June 1834, in Brontë, *Letters of Charlotte Brontë*, pp. 1, 128.7.
46 [Simpson], *A Visit to Edinburgh*, p. iii.
47 [Taylor], *City Scenes: or, A Peep into London*, p. 1.
48 *Ibid.*, p. 13.
49 'Master Michael Angelo', *Drawing School for Little Masters and Misses*. Emphasis added.
50 Chard, *Pleasure and Guilt on the Grand Tour*, p. 42.
51 Hofland, *Young Northern Traveller*, p. 174.
52 Charlotte Brontë to Ellen Nussey, 19 June 1834, Brontë, *Letters of Charlotte Brontë*, pp. 1, 128.
53 Aikin, *England Delineated*, p. viii.
54 Helme, *Instructive Rambles*, pp. i, vi–vii, 65–66.
55 Waterton, *Politics, Policy and the Discourses*, p. 6. Original emphasis.
56 Lowenthal, *Possessed by the Past*, p. 121.
57 *Heritage Encounters* programme for the European Year of Cultural Heritage Exhibition and Conference. I am grateful to Chris Whitehead for sharing this definition.
58 [Clarke], *Reuben Ramble's Travels through the Counties of England* (London: Darton & Clark, n.d.), unpaged.
59 Anon., *Thirty-Two Remarkable Places*, pp. 3, 16–17.
60 Penrose to Murray II, 2 Dec. 1829, NLS MSS. 40,938, fo. 22r.
61 Penrose to Murray II, 17 May 1830, NLS MSS. 40,938, fo. 33r.
62 See Duckworth, '"Whig" landscapes'.
63 Anon., *Travels of Tom Thumb*, p. viii.
64 Aikin, *England Delineated*, pp. vii–viii, v. Original emphasis.
65 Defoe, *A Tour Thro' the Whole Island of Great Britain*, vol. 1, p. iv.
66 Anon., *Travels of Tom Thumb*, pp. viii, 13–14. John Aubrey's *Monumenta Britannica* discussing Stonehenge had been written in the late seventeenth century, but Stukeley's *Stonehenge* had been published in 1740, only six years prior to *Tom Thumb's Travels*.
67 Aikin, *England Delineated*, pp. 285–286, 46.
68 *Ibid.*, pp. vii–viii, v.
69 Anon., '*The Juvenile Tourist*' [book review].

References

Aikin, John, *England Delineated; or, Geographical Description of Every County in England and Wales: with a Concise Account of its Most Important Products, Natural and Artificial. For the Use of Young Persons* (London: J. Johnson, 1788).

'Master Michael Angelo', *The Drawing School for Little Masters and Misses* (London: T. Carnan, 1773).

Anon., *A Tour Through England, Described in a Series of Letters, from a Young Gentleman to his Sister* (1804; London: Tabart, 1806).
Anon., *Edinburgh Literary Journal* (26 December 1829), p. 444.
Anon., *La Belle Assemblée; or, Bell's Court and Fashionable Magazine* (1 January 1830), p. 45.
Anon., *La Belle Assemblée; or, Bell's Court and Fashionable Magazine* (1 July 1830), p. 44.
Anon., *The Curiosities of the Tower of London*, Vol. I, 2nd edn (London: Thomas Boreman, 1741).
Anon., *The Gigantick History, Volume the Second. Which Completes the History of Guildhall, London. With other Curious Matters*, 2nd edn (London: Thomas Boreman, 1741).
Anon., '*The Juvenile Tourist*' [book review], *Monthly Epitome; or, Readers Their Own Reviewers*, 2 (November 1803), p. 610.
Anon., *The Travels of Tom Thumb over England and Wales; Containing Descriptions of Whatever is Most Remarkable in the Several Counties* (London: R. Amey, 1746).
Anon., *Thirty-Two Remarkable Places in Old England, for the Instruction and Entertainment of Youth* (London: William Darton, 1818).
Anon., *Travels and Adventures of Timothy Wildman, in Europe, Asia, Africa and America; Wherein Many of the Principal Cities & Towns in the World are Faithfully Described* (London: J. Luffman and Champante & Whitrow, no date but 1789–1793).
Anon., '*Travels of a British Druid*' [book review], *British Critic*, 37 (March 1811), pp. 314–315.
Anon., '*Travels of a British Druid*' [book review], *Gentleman's Magazine*, Supplement to Volume LXXXI, Part II, 81 (1811), p. 638.
Anon., *Windsor, and its Environs* (London: Newbery and Carnan; Windsor: J. Blakeney, 1768).
Anon., 'Works Preparing for Publication, by Mr. Murray', *Edinburgh Review*, 101 (April 1830).
Ansell, R., 'Educational travel in protestant families from post-restoration Ireland', *Historical Journal*, 58: 4 (December 2015), 931–958.
Art of Travel 1500–1850, database of European travel advice literature forming part of the 'Transmission, and Cultural Exchange' project hosted at the Moore Institute at the National University of Ireland, Galway, online at https://artoftravel.nuigalway.ie/.
Aubrey, John, *Monumenta Britannica*, with notes by John Evelyn and Dr Thomas Gale 1665–1693, Bodleian Libraries, MSS. Top. Gen. c.24–25.
Belloc, Hilaire, *Mrs Markham's New History of England* (London: Cayme Press, 1926).
Boreman, Thomas, 'To All my Kind Subscribers', in Anon., *The Gigantick History, Volume the Second. Which Completes the History of Guildhall, London. With other Curious Matters*, 2nd edn (London: Thomas Boreman, 1741), pp. xvii–xviii.
Boreman, Thomas, 'To the Author of the Curiosities in the Tower of London', signed 'A.Z.' in Anon., *The Curiosities of the Tower of London, Vol. I*, 2nd edn (London: Thomas Boreman, 1741), p. vi.
Brontë, Charlotte, *The Letters of Charlotte Brontë, Vol. 1: 1829–1847*, ed. Margaret Smith (Oxford: Oxford University Press, 1995).
Chard, Chloe, *Pleasure and Guilt on the Grand Tour: Travel Writing and Imaginative Geography 1600–1830* (Manchester: Manchester University Press 1999).

Connell, Alyssa, 'Paper Kingdom: Travel Literature, Chorography, and the Writing of Britain, 1660–1770' (PhD dissertation, University of Pennsylvania, 2015).
Cooney, Ray and Chapman, John, *Move Over, Mrs. Markham; a Play* (London: English Theatre Guild, 1972).
[Clarke, R.], *A Tour to Great St. Bernard's and Round Mont Blanc … Intended for Young Persons from Ten to Fourteen Years of Age* (London: Harvey and Darton, 1827).
[Clarke, Samuel], *Reuben Ramble's Travels Through the Counties of England* (London: Darton & Clark, n.d.).
Defoe, D., *A Tour Thro' the Whole Island of Great Britain*, 3 vols (London: G. Strahan, 1724–1727).
Duckworth, Alistair M., '"Whig" landscapes in Defoe's Tour', *Philological Quarterly*, 61 (1982), 453–465.
Dufresnoy, Nicolas Lenglet, *The Geography of Children: or, A Short and Easy Method of Teaching or Learning Geography* (London: Edward Littleton and John Hawkins, 1737).
Graham, Ruth, 'Juvenile travellers: Priscilla Wakefield's excursions in Empire', *Journal of Imperial and Commonwealth History*, 38:3 (2010), 373–393.
Grenby, M. O., 'Pay, Professionalization and Probable Dominance? Women Writers and the Children's Book Trade', in J. Batchelor and G. Dow (eds), *Women's Writing 1660–1830: Feminisms and Futures* (Basingstoke: Palgrave, 2016), pp. 117–137.
Helme, E., *Instructive Rambles in London, and the Adjacent Villages. Designed to Amuse the Mind, and Improve the Understanding of Youth* (London: Longman and Rees, and E. Newbery, 1800).
Henry, David, *An Historical Description of St. Paul's Cathedral* (London: J. Newbery, 1753).
Heritage Encounters, programme for the European Year of Cultural Heritage Exhibition and Conference, Newcastle, UK, 3–6 July 2018 (at https://research.ncl.ac.uk/heritage-newcastle/conference/Heritage%20Encounters%20-%20Programme.pdf).
Hofland, B., *The Young Northern Traveller; or, The Invalid Restored. Containing a Tour Through Northern Europe* (London: A. K. Newman, n.d. but c. 1830).
Immel, Andrea and Alderson, Brian, *Tommy Thumb's Pretty Song-Book … A Facsimile Edition with a History and Annotations* (Los Angeles: Cotsen Occasional Press, 2013).
Lowenthal, D., *Possessed by the Past: The Heritage Crusade and the Spoils of History* (New York: Free Press, 1996).
Major, E., *Madam Britannia: Women, Church, and Nation 1712–1812* (Oxford: Oxford University Press, 2012).
Mather, W., *The Young Man's Companion: or, Arithmetick Made Easy with Plain Directions for a Young Man to Attain to Read and Write True English* (London: S. Clarke, 1727).
Mitchell, Rosemary, *Picturing the Past: English History in Text and Image, 1830–1870* (Oxford: Oxford University Press, 2000).
Nesbit, E., *Wet Magic* (London: T. Werner Laurie, 1913).
New Monthly Magazine and Literary Journal (1 January 1830), p. 28.
Penrose, John Jun. to John Murray II, 20 Aug. 1829, NLS MSS. 40,938, fol. 19v.
Penrose, John Jun. to John Murray II, 2 Dec. 1829, NLS MSS. 40,938, fo. 22r.
Penrose, John Jun. to John Murray II, 7 Dec. 1829, NLS MSS. 40,938, fos. 24r-v.
Penrose, John Jun. to John Murray II, 7 Dec. 1829, NLS MSS. 40,938, fo. 25r.
Penrose, John Jun. to John Murray II, 5 Feb. 1830, NLS MSS. 40,938, fo. 26r.

Penrose, John Jun. to John Murray II, 17 May 1830, NLS MSS. 40,938, fos. 32v–33r.
Penrose, John Jun. to John Murray II, 7 Oct 1830, NLS MSS. 40,938, fo. 39r.
Penrose, John Jun. to John Murray II, 16 Mar. 1831, NLS MSS. 40,938, fo. 52v.
Roscoe, S., *John Newbery and his Successors 1740–1814* (Wormley: Five Owls Press, 1973).
Schellenberg, Betty A., 'Imagining the nation in Defoe's *A Tour Thro' the Whole Island of Great Britain*', *English Literary History*, 62:2 (1995), 295–311.
[Simpson, Sophia S.], *A Visit to Edinburgh; Containing a Description of the Principal Curiosities and Public Buildings in the Scottish Metropolis* (Edinburgh: Fairburn and Anderson, 1818).
Smethurst, Paul, *Travel Writing and the Natural World, 1768–1840* (Basingstoke: Palgrave Macmillan, 2013).
Steele, Richard, Tatler, 30 (18 June 1709), in *The Tatler*, ed. D. F. Bond, 3 vols (Oxford: Clarendon, 1987), I. 223–224.
Strickland, A., *The Youthful Travellers; or, Letters Chiefly Descriptive of Scenes Visited by Some Young People During a Summer Excursion* (London: William Darton, 1823).
Stukeley, William, *Stonehenge: A Temple Restor'd to the British Druids* (London: Printed for W. Innys and R. Manby, 1740).
Sweet, Rosemary, *Antiquaries: The Discovery of the Past in Eighteenth-Century Britain* (London: Hambledon and London, 2004).
[Taylor, Ann and Jane], *City Scenes: or, A Peep into London, for Good Children* (London: Darton and Harvey, 1809).
Taylor, Jefferys, *A Month in London; or, Some its Modern Wonders Described* (London: Harvey and Darton, 1832).
Wakefield, P., *The Juvenile Travellers; Containing the Remarks of a Family during a Tour through the Principal States and Kingdoms of Europe: With an Account of their Inhabitants, Natural Productions, and Curiosities* (London: Darton and Harvey, 1802).
Warneke, Sara, *Images of the Educational Traveller in Early Modern England* (Leiden: E. J. Brill, 1995).
Waterton, E., *Politics, Policy and the Discourses of Heritage in Britain* (Basingstoke: Palgrave Macmillan, 2010).
Weston, Louisa, *The Cambrian Excursion: Intended to Inculcate a Taste for the Beauties of Nature; and to Direct the Attention of Young People to Sources of Mental Improvement* (London: Baldwin, Cradock and Joy, 1826).

8

Playing with the past: child consumers, pedagogy and British history games, c. 1780–1850

Barbara Gribling

The utility and tendency of this Game must be obvious at first sight; for surely there cannot be a more agreeable study than History, and none more improving to Youth, than that which conveys to them, in a pleasing and comprehensive manner, the Events which have occurred in their own Country.[1]

In 1803, London-based publishers John Wallis and John Harris produced a spiral race game for youth: *Historical Pastime or a New Game of the History of England from the Conquest to the Accession of George the Third*.[2] With the spin of a teetotum, players traversed a board, landing on 158 circular spaces of 'little prints' depicting key historical figures and events, including Robin Hood, John Locke, Magna Carta and the South Sea Bubble. Yet the game was not a straightforward journey to the finish: players moved forwards and backwards, paid fines, earned rewards and waited on various circles. These detours were designed to teach children about their nation through play and imbue a sense of familiarity and belonging. In the rulebook, the anonymous author hoped the game would 'excite a curiosity in the youthful mind' and inspire further learning.[3] One of the most popular educational games in the early nineteenth century, *Historical Pastime* underwent numerous editions and modifications between 1803 and 1850; its creation and subsequent adaptations offer a window through which to examine perceptions of the past and childhood through the shifting history market for youth.

The game's creation speaks to a vibrant educational market for history that emerged in the eighteenth century and flourished in the early nineteenth century, where commercial publishers vied for consumers' attention through new educational wares that combined pedagogy and play.[4] The period 1780–1850 saw unprecedented change in the history of childhood, shifts in teaching pedagogy and a renewed interest in British history as a subject that was most 'improving to youth' – integral to shaping character and forming good citizens. Alongside better-known book products, history-themed toys and games became a central part of a lively children's market, promoted and produced by publishers and penned by authors (who often remained anonymous). New puzzle, board, block and card games were created and became a hallmark of elite and middle-class British education. In Jane Austen's *Mansfield Park* (1814), Maria and Julia Bertram ridicule their cousin Fanny Price because she is unable to put together a puzzle map of Europe, showing, in their eyes, Fanny's intellectual as well as social poverty.[5] These games were used in both domestic and public settings, from parlours and nurseries to schools, and became a staple of early lessons.

The games were not intended merely to reinforce what could be gleaned through history books. Rather, this chapter will show that their experiential aspect was perceived as an integral and essential part of learning about the past through play. In doing so, it extends recent scholarship exploring childhood and education, illuminating the vibrant and innovative nature of eighteenth- and early nineteenth-century education and its use of play. Building on Linda Hannas's and Jill Shefrin's valuable work on educational toys and games and publishers, it brings into scholarly view a new perspective on the publishers of educational games, the use of games in children's education and their place in a wider commodity culture and a children's education market.[6] It highlights the Georgian era's new drive to incorporate play in children's education through a range of modes, engaging with Shefrin's emphasis on visual learning and interactivity; Michèle Cohen's on 'familiar conversation'; and M. O. Grenby's on the disjunction between prescribed use and engagement in the child reader, which applies equally to toys and games.[7] Yet only recently have scholars explored these games and toys as a tool to understand children's engagement with different subjects from science (e.g. astronomy games) to geography (games, puzzles, portable globes) to history, as explored here.[8]

Despite the abundance and significance of history-themed toys and games in eighteenth- and early nineteenth-century British childhood culture, little scholarly work exists on these games, which offer rich insights into the role of play in children's history education and their engagement with the past.[9] This chapter seeks to rectify this gap by revealing how history games illuminate children's engagement with the British past. The first section investigates the changing history market for children, exploring the intersections between history, consumerism and education by examining the major game producers and their new history-themed wares. Building on this overview, the second section offers a case study of Wallis and Harris's innovative and popular 1803 *Historical Pastime* game, analysing its debut as well as later editions and adaptations to illustrate how authors, publishers and children played with the past.

Early lessons: toys, games and the history market for children

Until the last quarter of the eighteenth century, educational games (largely either geographical or for teaching the alphabet) were the purview of map- and printsellers. However, in the 1780s, publishers who had already established a brisk trade in children's books extended into educational toys and games, and London became the centre of this vibrant new market.[10] By the early nineteenth century, the Wallis, Darton and Harris families (who had taken over from the Newberys) dominated the trade. To elevate the respectability of educational toys, in 1805, Wallis called his location (at 13 Warwick Street) an 'Instructive Toy Warehouse'.[11] These publishers were joined in the nineteenth century by others such as John Betts and William Spooner, who began work in the 1840s, and by numerous other manufacturers who produced a wide range of toys and games for purchase alongside other educational materials for children, including non-fiction books.[12]

In this competitive market, publishers shaped the key subjects thought to be essential to elite childhood education; alongside her failings in geography, Austen's Fanny Price was also derided for her lack of understanding of classics, philosophy, science and history. Increasingly English history became a pivotal subject, evident in the flood of materials from the 1780s. Catalogues overflowed with history wares, from miniature library books, alphabets, and charts of royal genealogies to games and toys such as Darton's *Pocket Tablet of English History and Chronology* (c. 1816).[13]

These toys and games reveal new thinking about the growing importance of play in historical learning. Authors and publishers promoted play as integral to juvenile understanding of history in their advertisements, illustrations (including box lids) and game rulebooks. For instance, the anonymous author of the rulebook to *An Historical Game of England* (1804) – published by Didier and Tebbett – noted its debt to the pedagogy of Abbé Gaultier (c. 1740s–1818).[14] Gaultier was in the middle of this pedagogical wave towards play and experiential learning, suggesting that children's histories of England were 'too complicated', and that games provided a 'concise' and 'instructive' memory aide.

Publishers also illustrated the important link between history and play through box lids, rulebook and slipcase covers that featured images of child players and historical events. For example, *An Historical Game of England* (1804) depicted an elite English pastoral setting where a mother or governess opens the game while two children watch with interest (Figure 8.1). Scenes showing child players emphasised the relationship between domesticity and play, and also presented history games as aspirational: Sallis's *Game of the Little Historian* (c. 1840s) depicts Victoria and Albert playing the game with their children. Box lids also illustrate the ubiquity of games in a variety of domestic and classroom settings. In 1815, the Dartons produced their dissected

8.1 Cover of *An Historical Game of England* (London: Didier and Tebbett, 1804). Courtesy of Princeton University Library.

Playing with the past

8.2 *Historical Amusement. A New Game* (London: N. Carpenter, 1850–1855).
© Victoria and Albert Museum.

puzzle *The Principal Events in the History of England, to the Reign of George III*, featuring a special educational price: 3 shillings for a sheet to be used in schools.[15] In the 1830s, *Historical Amusement – A New Game*, showed a group of boys and girls playing in a prosperous home (Figure 8.2).[16] And as a final nod to the purported improving power of history, under the box lid of a copy of *Historical Recreation; or, British History in Miniature* (c. 1800) is the mark for L. F. (London Female) Penitentiary, Pentonville, Middl[esex], which was established in 1807 and advocated reform for working-class inmates through education.[17]

Some of the earliest history-themed games focused on biographical learning, using particular characters as role models. These games proved popular into the nineteenth century, with card games and question-and-answer games such as *Historical Biographical and Geographical Cards: Intended as a Game for the Instruction and Amusement of Young Persons* going through multiple editions.[18] Biographical learning was also encouraged through biographies which accompanied games, rulebooks and on the game boards themselves, where 'significant' figures were represented, encouraging visual familiarity. These games were designed to teach children of all ages about the characters of individuals, reinforcing the concept in history teaching that viewing portraits of historical characters and learning about their lives was key to forming good character and citizens. Darton's *Instructive Conversation Cards* (1809) included portraits and information on a range of characters, from scientist Isaac Newton and architect Christopher Wren, to writers Geoffrey Chaucer, Samuel Johnson and Alexander Pope, and even the explorer Captain Cook. Some of these cards highlighted their figures' contributions to children's welfare; for example, Jonas Hanway was identified as a 'liberal friend to the Foundling hospital'.[19] This range of characters also illustrates how science and scientific discoveries were seen as integral to elite education alongside the arts.

Royalty featured heavily in history education as well. Children were asked to learn about the characters of their rulers, their genealogies, their images and the history of the nation through their reigns.[20] Some of the earliest history-themed toys and games were royal genealogies and chronologies which appeared from the 1780s and 1790s. These included dissected puzzles for children to reconstruct and put in order, and were often reworked and updated when a new monarch came to the throne. In 1787, Darton produced *Engravings for Teaching the Elements of English History and Chronology*, authored by biblical scholar and schoolmaster John Hewlett.[21] The puzzle showed the kings and queens of England from William I to George II, featuring a circular portrait as well as their birth and death dates and key events. Other royal games soon followed. In 1791, Newbery and Wallis produced their *Royal Genealogical Pastime of the Sovereigns of England*, which was designed to balance instruction and amusement. The game offered judgements on individual royal characters. Alfred was 'wise and good' and Elizabeth a great queen, but players who landed on 'bad prince[s]' such as Harold, Edward II or Richard III were instructed to 'put down two … counters for getting into such bad Company'.[22]

These toys and games also offer insight into changing reputations of royal figures and the popularisation of the past from the late Georgian era. For example, Wallis's 1788 puzzle *Royal Chronological Tables of English History* gave portraits from William I to George II with reigns, births, accession dates and remarkable events, and commentary on royal character. Henry VIII was projected as a 'fearless statesman, a tenacious disputant, and a cruel husband; fickle, vain, tyrannical and unfeeling'.[23] A hand-drawn card game from c. 1809 penalised and rewarded players based on a royal's character, lawful or unlawful succession, and events occurring in their reign: for example, players had to forfeit one token in response to Richard III, who 'usurped the crown', and three for the murder of his nephews, 'the lawful heirs' (Figure 8.3).[24] Royal games and puzzles continued to be produced into the reigns of William IV and Queen Victoria. For example, Darton's dissected puzzle *British Sovereigns from William the Conqueror to William IV* was adapted from an earlier version to the reign of George IV (c. 1830s).[25]

These puzzles accompanied other toys and games that promoted knowledge of royal figures through visual familiarity and biography. *Arrang'd in Bricks the Kings and Queens of England* (1840s) offered portraits of monarchs on one

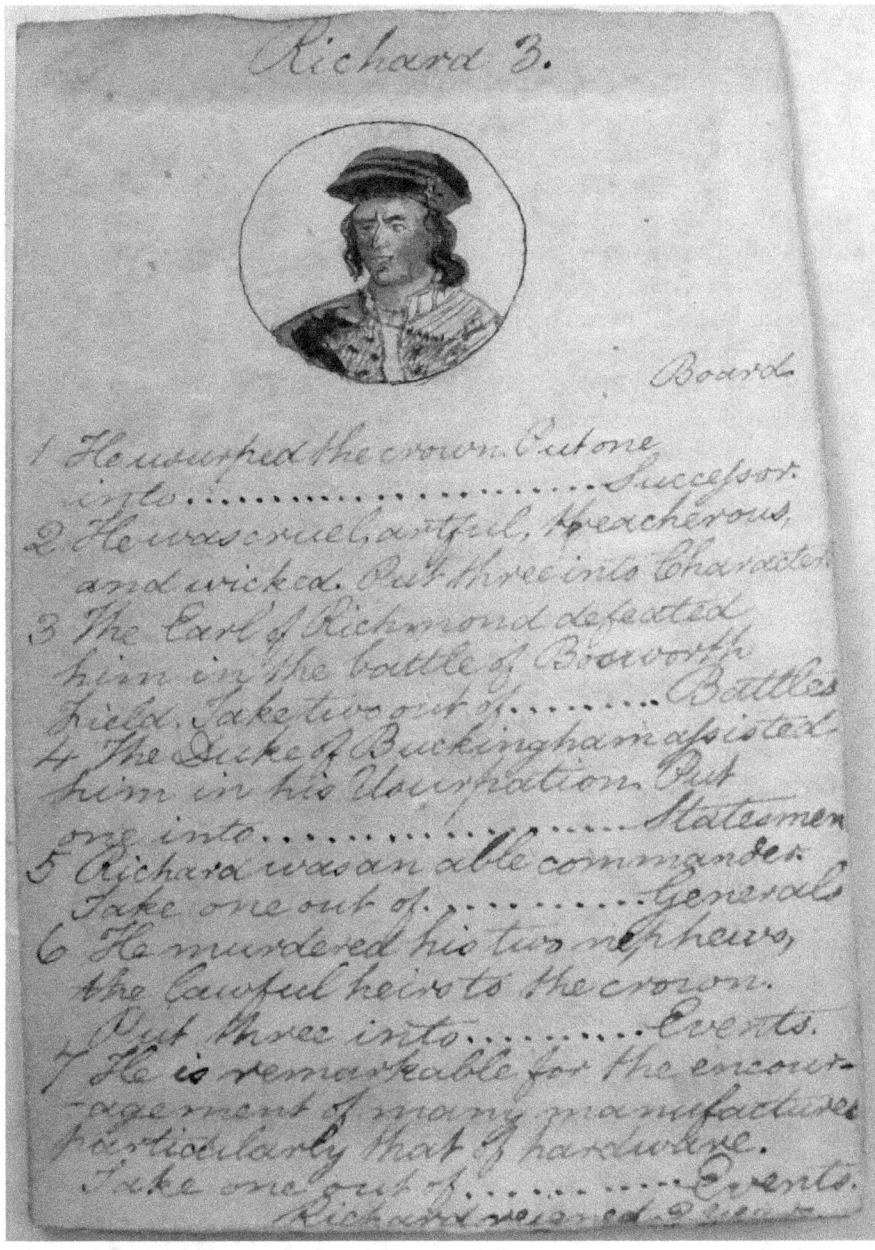

8.3 Anon., 'Richard III' card, *Historical Cards*, c. 1809. © Museum of Childhood, Edinburgh.

side and basic information on the other. Charles II's block noted that the king was 'wicked' and key events during his reign were the Great Plague and the Great Fire of London.[26] Edward Wallis's toy *Panorama of Kings* (c. 1830) offers up an image of Cromwell as 'brave, patriotic'.[27] These games often complemented existing narratives circulating in children's books. *Royal Revels, or, Game of Kings, for Learning the History of England* (1840s), a card game featuring portraits of England's rulers, offered a vision of King Edward II as 'weak minded and good natured', a stance promoted three years earlier in the widely popular Callcott's *Little Arthur's History of England*.[28] While the card by its nature limits information, *Little Arthur's* extends 'moral education' to include the public virtues as well as the private virtues of royals.

Publishers also capitalised on the pedagogical idea that learning about national historic events prepared children for their future roles and made them good citizens. Dissected puzzles were particularly popular as a way for children to learn about events while piecing together scenes in chronological order. The Dartons' 1815 board game *The Principal Events in the History of England, to the Reign of George III* incorporated Britain's ancient past as well, which distinguishes it from other games that saw English history as beginning with the Norman Conquest.[29] Instead, the first engraving features a family of Ancient Britons with Stonehenge and a wicker idol in the background. The game also illustrated its own technique of improvement through pedagogy, highlighting scenes of childhood and depicting King Alfred not as the great reformer of law or the unifier of kingdoms, but as a student listening to tales of heroes.[30] It still typified the early nineteenth-century intermingling of royalty, heroism and battles with renewed interest in constitutional development epitomised in the Magna Carta scene. The puzzle also included acts of violence such as riots in London, embracing the recent past which other histories glossed over.[31] These types of puzzles continued into the 1830s with *Wallis's Principal Events in English History from the Landing of Caesar to William the Fourth* (in a box shaped like a book – illustrating the pedagogical relationship between text and game).[32] Scenes were also created for younger children in blocks; the 1855 *Events of English History* contained coloured blocks with scenes on one side and text on the other, including the 'Death of Wat Tyler', the Great Fire of London, and King Charles I and his children before the king's execution (a domestic scene that was popularised in the Victorian era).[33]

Race, card and other board games (of chance) offered an opportunity for game-makers (and children) to play with different pasts. In Sallis's *Amusement in English History* (c. 1840s), players who landed on 'Magna Charta signed' (No. 22) jumped ahead to (No. 24) the first assembling of the barons (No. 64) – illustrating the latter half of the story, while those landing on James quitting the kingdom – when James II was deposed under the Glorious Revolution – had to quit the game.[34] Other games focused on a specific event such as the *Wars of the Roses: A New Game* (c. 1835–40).[35] The game plays with the idea of constant changing fortunes during the Wars of the Roses and the turmoil of the fifteenth-century fighting between royal cousins. It required players to choose a side – York or Lancaster – and then acquire more counters for their castles. Either side could be the winner, and in this sense, the game offers the chance to change historical outcomes through play.

How did players engage with these toys and games? Diaries and letters note the important place of history games in elite children's education.[36] Frederika Planta, a sub-governess for George III's daughters, writes in her letters that she designed a card game on the 'History of England' to teach her charges, seeing it as an effective tool alongside story telling.[37] Children often placed their names, ages and the date acquired on games as a mark of ownership. Ada Bridge, age twelve, signed her name on Darton's *British Sovereigns from William the Conqueror to William IV* (1830) while Emma A. Henborough signed the box lid of *Historical Amusement*.[38] Players would also modify the rules of the game, and this shaping of new narratives gives important insight into shifting notions of history. An 1814 edition of Wallis's *Universal History and Chronology* – which started with the creation of the world and ended with George, Prince of Wales (as regent) – contained a number of amendments to its rulebook. For example, those who landed on Charles I's beheading at Whitehall or the 'First Voyage round the world', which originally had no gameplay, were now instructed to go back to the Tower of London for the former and move forward to 'Longitude discovered' for the latter.[39]

Playing with history in Wallis's and Harris's *Historical Pastime* games

Before their collaboration on the *Historical Pastime* game (1803), John Harris and John Wallis had already proven themselves innovative and opportunistic in a competitive children's market. Harris had learned the trade under the Newbery firm.[40] He was adept at understanding the market and adapting to the growing demand for educational toys. In 1801, Harris purchased the business (with its stock) from Elizabeth Newbery and established his Juvenile Library, selling children's wares in the churchyard near St Paul's, the geographical centre of the children's publishing trade. The location provided not only a viable market, but an atmosphere that inspired innovation and competition. In contrast, John Wallis began as a bookseller for adults, but saw the growing market for juvenile wares and moved into children's publishing in the 1780s, where he became known for his ability to create new games or to adapt those of competitors to make them more appealing to child audiences.[41]

Both men had also produced best-selling history-themed children's toys and games. John Wallis had major success in 1788 with one of his earliest and most popular didactic toys, the *Royal Chronological Tables of English History*, which could be purchased as a dissected puzzle. The tables contained portraits of royals, emphasising royal and biographical learning and playing off the demand for English history. Wallis adapted his tables from Darton's 1787 *Engravings for Teaching the Elements of English History and Chronology* but his colourful version with clearer text proved a commercial success.[42] Wallis also saw the benefit in collaboration and had previously worked with the Newbery firm on games, including the 1791 *Royal Genealogical Pastime of the Sovereigns of England* (also sold as a dissected puzzle).[43] Collaboration was not unusual for games publishers – from co-producing games to allowing their wares to be sold in different shops. However, publishers were still wary of competitors, and certain publishers like the Dartons would not collaborate with their main rivals, the Wallis's. After Wallis's and Harris's early success in history games (both individually and collaboratively), and with Harris's newly established business, they embarked on a new collaboration. The outcome would be one of the most popular history games of the nineteenth century: the 1803 *Historical Pastime or a New Game of the History of England from the Conquest to the Accession of George the Third*.

The *Historical Pastime* game was both commercially savvy and innovative. While Wallis and Harris did not invent the spiral race game, they were successful at adapting it as an English history game. The game showed how they and the anonymous author had a keen understanding of the appetite for history in the early nineteenth century. It was innovative (for its time) in that it played with both visual and textual modes of historical learning, combined different aspects of design and gameplay that emphasised key concepts in popular pedagogy, and intermingled royal, biographical and key events. Alongside portraits and scenes, the game board utilised symbols and text to act as aide-memoires for historical events and objects. Circles on the 1803 board fell into three categories: portraits (sixty-five) of royals and other 'significant' figures and illustrated scenes of key events (forty-four) comprised the first two. The remaining circles featured symbols and text referencing both key figures and events (forty-nine).[44] The game's rulebook included royal biographies which gave further insight into the characters and events on the board – a nod to the continued popularity of royal biographies in historical learning.[45] The game also played with different modes of learning, in particular, the conversational question-and-answer format common in early history books for children. Some circles required players to answer a question and be judged by their peers. Thus, the author and publishers revolutionised features that had proved effective and saleable in earlier products to create a bestseller in their *Historical Pastime*.

The game used play and visual training to teach children about historical characters and to test their knowledge. It encouraged learning about royalty by featuring portraits of the kings and queens of England from William the Conqueror to George III.[46] The game presented William I 'the conqueror' as a consummate warrior in armour, and Henry VIII's image made reference to the widely circulated Holbein portrait (Figure 8.4). *Historical Pastime* helped shape the image of royals and contributed to a wider canon of images being promoted in juvenile culture whereby monarchs could be identified through a single iconic image. Likewise, the game-makers used the board to train children about historical events by creating a canon of key scenes for each reign. The choice of these events illustrates contemporary notions of history and values, with war scenes and royal stories featuring heavily. The board was peppered with great English victories at Crécy, Poitiers and Agincourt as well as the Battle of Hastings, the Armada, Naseby (a Parliamentarian victory) and Culloden (Figure 8.4). These taught children through rewards and merits how the battle was fought and who gained from it.[47] Royal celebrations, coronations and marriages as well as royal deaths and violence against royals were similarly popular. The game depicted the executions of Lady Jane Grey and Mary Queen of Scots and also featured the attempted assassination of Prince Edward in the Holy Land and the smothering of the princes in the tower (a scene immortalised by Shakespeare and associated with the loss of innocence).[48] It also highlighted instances of reigns that came to an abrupt end in abdications (James II) and executions (Charles I) (Figure 8.4). Charles I was offered up as an example of a royal who exerted too much power by disrupting the constitutional balance between monarch and Parliament. His story is told in portraits, symbols, and two scenes depicting his defeat at the Battle of Naseby and his execution. The accompanying biography emphasises his lack of respect for Parliament, whose members saw him as 'arbitrary' and 'despotic'.[49]

The game-makers also played with presumed and new knowledge and modes of learning history, layering genealogical learning, aide-memoires and the popular question-and-answer format to reinforce relationships between royals, spark knowledge and to test children on 'significant characters' and their contributions. It used play to highlight the relationship between particular royals: thus players who landed on Anne Boleyn were instructed to move forward to her daughter Elizabeth I, while players who landed on Catherine of Aragon were instructed to pass ahead to her daughter Queen Mary.[50] Texts and symbols acted as prompts. Forty-nine of the circles comprised text, symbols, or both, which provided visual clues about historical events and to aid in shaping a story of nationhood which highlighted Protestantism, royalty and constitutional balance. For example, children who landed on No. 121 were confronted with a glowing lantern and the words 'Gun Powder Plot' (Figure 8.4). In the eighteenth century, the lantern was a well-known symbol linked to Guy Fawkes who, it was believed, was holding a lantern when he was caught attempting to light gunpowder to blow up the Houses of Parliament

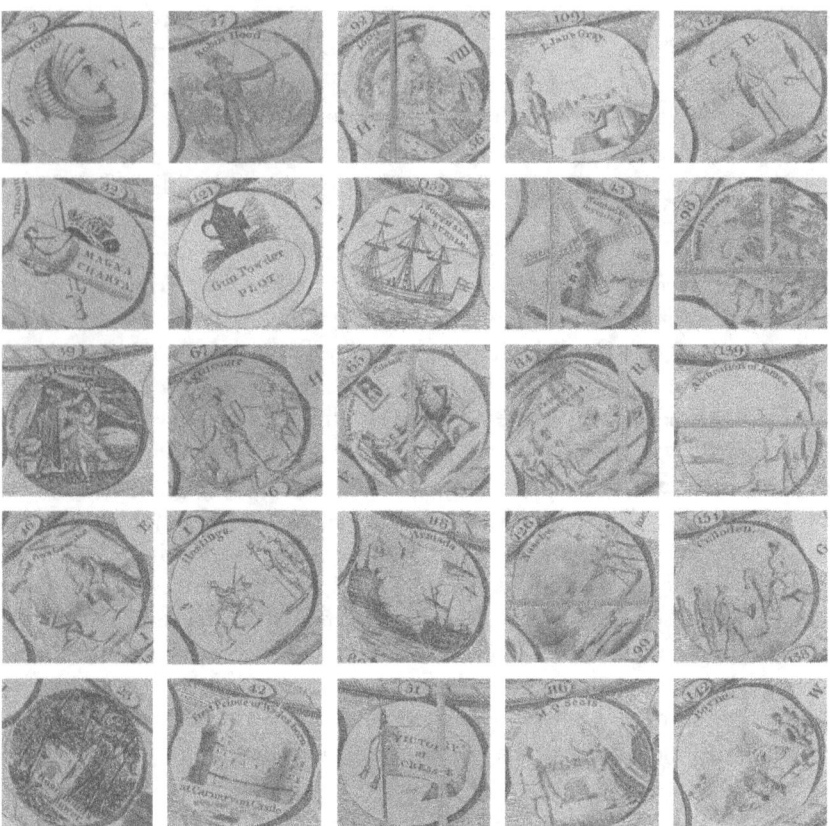

8.4 Close-ups of circles from *Historical Pastime or a New Game of the History of England from the Conquest to the Accession of George the Third* (London: J. Harris and J. Wallis, 1803). Courtesy of Princeton University Library.

as part of a Catholic plot. The story and the lantern were immortalised in the famous rhyme 'But by God's providence, him they catch, with a dark lantern, lighting a match!' Other objects made reference to England's development as a Protestant nation: players who landed on No. 102, the Holy Bible, moved on to No. 106, the Book of Common Prayer.[51] The aide-memoires could also show transformations or effects – No. 98 showed a ruined monastery as a result of Henry VIII's Reformation, reinforced in gameplay with players having to pay three tokens to the king (Figure 8.4).[52] Aide-memoires were also used to spark understanding of moments of national importance. No. 32, a scroll with Magna Carta on it (embellished with a crown, sword and the scales of justice) made reference to England's constitutional past – the restraining of King John's power by the barons was seen as a cornerstone of constitutional democracy (Figure 8.4).[53]

This negotiation between presumed knowledge and new knowledge is best expressed in the interactive question-and-answer part of the game, which only occurred when players landed on portraits of one of five figures: Roger Bacon (No. 44), William Shakespeare (No. 117), John Locke (No. 143), Isaac Newton (No. 145) and Alexander Pope (No. 156). The choice of these individuals is not surprising. By the time of the game's creation, they were celebrated figures in the arts, science, philosophy and education, and knowledge of them was seen to be a hallmark of learned society.[54]

The game played with the idea that children would or should be familiar with these figures. Players who landed on Roger Bacon were asked to 'Mention some Discovery of this Genius, or pay One to the Treasury' while those who landed on Newton were asked to 'Repeat any Circumstance from the Works of this Author, or pay One to the Treasury'. Landing on Locke required players to 'Repeat some Opinion of this Author, or pay One to the Treasury' while Shakespeare and Pope both required players to 'Repeat two Lines from this Author, or pay Two to the Treasury'.[55] Players were penalised if they failed to answer the question and, with no answers in the rulebook or biographies, their knowledge was judged by their peers, who would presumably be able to determine if the task was performed adequately.[56] Annotations made to an 1813 rulebook illustrate how gameplayers played with these ideas of presumed knowledge, creating their own rules. For example, players who failed to repeat any circumstance from the works of Isaac Newton may not have had to pay one to the treasury, but they did have to go back to Shakespeare, but those who failed to mention a discovery of Roger Bacon's had to pay not One, but two, to the treasury.[57]

The anonymous author of *Historical Pastime* used experiential learning to teach children about an event or deed by having them re-enact outcomes through gameplay. Those who landed on the 'Doom's-day book', No. 5, had to stop and wait to be counted (a play on William I's book wherein the king registered people and property), while players who landed on No. 58, the poll tax, were required to pay one token to Richard II (putting into action the unpopular medieval tax instigated by the king).[58] Players who landed on the South Sea Company circle, No. 152, were asked to take a chance with a second turn of the teetotum; if they 'turn more than Five, they receive One from each player; if Five, or under, pay One to each'. This action addressed the potential for the financial ruin when investing with the company, offering players the opportunity to gamble within the confines of respectable play (Figure 8.4).[59]

The game also played with rewards and losses to teach (and shape perceptions of) events and historical characters. For example, players who landed on key English victories against the French such as Agincourt would 'receive one from each player', as would players who landed on the Battle of the Boyne (Ireland), in which James VII and II invaded with the support of the French and was defeated by William III (helping to ensure the continuance of the Protestant succession) (Figure 8.4).[60] Players who landed on No. 72, Eleanor (the Duchess of Gloucester), had to 'remain here, till one of the players pass you', reflecting her long imprisonment due to accusations of sorcery. Players who landed on No. 99, 'Anne of Cleve[s]', were instructed that 'every player pays you Three, and you retire to the beginning of the Game'.[61] This instruction asked children to re-enact Anne's own story: she survived her divorce from Henry VIII and, according to the biography, 'retired on a pension of 3000 pounds per annum'.[62] Most interestingly, the author created new connections and historical stories through movement. For example, those landing on Guy Fawkes's 'Powder plot' were required to go back to Edmund Bonner (who, according to the game's biography, persecuted Protestants during the reign of Queen Mary): the two separate events and 'villains' (Bonner and the 'conspirators') were joined together.[63]

Following the game's success, Wallis and Harris each published spin-offs using *Historical Pastime* as a model. John Harris's game looked to the recent past and royalty. In 1810, he published *The Jubilee, an Interesting Game; Exhibiting the Remarkable Events, from the Accession of His Majesty, King George the Third, to the 25th of October, 1809; when he entered into the fiftieth year of his reign.*[64] Advertised as a 'continuation' of the *Historical Pastime* game, Harris's *The Jubilee* showed an astute understanding of the market by tapping into the larger demand for contemporary history alongside the patriotic fervour surrounding George III's golden jubilee in 1809.[65] The game began with George's proclamation and included royal births, wars (including the American War of Independence, French Revolutionary wars and the Napoleonic wars), relations with Ireland, riots, assassination attempts, executions, the king's illness and the abolition of the slave trade. The player who landed first on No. 150 was rewarded by receiving all the 'stakes' there and the fines in the treasury. They were also instructed to sing in praise of George 'God save the King', 'accompanied with a full chorus of all the Players'.[66] At 9 shillings, *The Jubilee* was a little more expensive than the *Historical Pastime* game.[67] It was successful enough for Harris to create a new edition in 1820 on the succession of the new king. He renamed the game *The Sun of Brunswick* and placed George IV in the central circle, updating it with recent events including 'Napoleon in exile' (No. 145), 'Arctic Expedition' (No. 147) and the 'Funeral of George III' (No. 149).[68]

In 1814, John Wallis published his own spin-off, the *New Game of Universal History and Chronology*, discussed in our Introduction to this volume. This game was a nod to the popularity of universal histories, charting a history of the world, in the late eighteenth and early nineteenth centuries. Wallis's game reworked the universal chronology format for juvenile audiences under a Christian and British nationalist framework, with players journeying from the 'Creation of the World' to George becoming Prince Regent.[69] The game was republished in 1840 by Edward Wallis, with updates including Queen Victoria's succession and a central circle featuring the modern railway moving into the future – a sign of Britain's technological progress.[70]

Further testifying to the commercial success of *Historical Pastime*, the game was reworked and updated throughout the early and mid-nineteenth century. While other games also saw new editions, the *Historical Pastime* game was exceptional in the sheer number of reworkings. Reissues of the game in 1810 and 1813 simply replicated the original edition, but major changes occurred in the 1820s editions (c. 1820, 1824, 1828).[71] These editions completely overhauled the illustrations, reduced pre-contemporary circles, updated the board to include current events and placed the new king, George IV, in the centre.[72] These newer versions were published by John Harris junior, who had taken over his father's business in 1824, and Edward Wallis who took over from his father John after his death in 1818.[73] The game was again modified in the 1830s when the central circle was changed to William IV. New editions in the Victorian era included portraits of the new queen and two new circles, and the last Victorian edition of the game was issued in c. 1850 by John Passmore, who had purchased Edward Wallis's stock in around 1847 (Figure 8.5).[74]

Who played *Historical Pastime* and what evidence do we have of the ways in which players interacted with it? The cost of the *Historical Pastime* game meant that it was marketed to upper- and middle-class boys and girls. The Ross children, an elite anglophone family living in Montreal, Lower Canada, were given an 1824 edition of the game by their father David Ross.[75] The 1803 game could be purchased either as a dissected puzzle or on linen at Wallis and Harris's shops. In Harris's Juvenile Library catalogue (1818) the *Historical Pastime* game was priced at 7s 6d, including the teetotum.[76] By 1825, consumers could purchase the game for 6 shillings, making it more affordable than the *Panorama of London: A New Game* and the *Sun of Brunswick*, which both cost 9 shillings.[77] One owner wrote out by hand a copy of the instructions for their 1824 version of *Historical Pastime*, perhaps to avoid paying for a new edition.[78] Players sometimes interacted with the game in other ways as well. In a child's hand on the back of the *Historical Pastime* game owned by the Ross children was written 'Cheer! Boys Cheer! ... Kissy-K ... And Gegge's Own Dear Game'.[79] An 1813 edition of the rulebook illustrates how players of the *Historical Pastime* game even created their own house rules, changing its lessons. For example, instead of paying one to King Richard II, those who landed on No. 58, the 'Poll Tax', had to 'turn backwards'.[80]

That these games could be easily adapted by publishers and players illustrates shifts in perceptions about popular culture and changes in the uses of the past. The new edition created during George IV's reign saw the removal of some circles, which shows a desire to refine the board while maintaining a coherent narrative. The exclusion of the ruined monastery was explained in later circles

Revived pasts

8.5 Close up of the central spiral including contemporary events added in the 1820s editions and additions made to the first Queen Victoria edition. *Historical Pastime. A New Game of the History of England* (London: J. Passmore, c. 1850). © Adrian Seville, private collection.

on the Reformation, and even though deleted, Becket's assassination was alluded to in the presence of his tomb. Other circles – such as the Invention of Windmills and the First Prince of Wales born at Caernarvon – were deemed not necessary knowledge and deleted, while the absence of Robin Hood and Fair Rosamond's bower (whose circles had been linked together in gameplay) speaks to shifting notions of the relationship between history and myth (Figure 8.4).[81]

Changes to the images on the board also highlight shifting ideas about the past and a widening of audience. The Poitiers circle changed from an image that highlighted chivalric character (the Black Prince welcoming King John of France to his tent after the battle) – a model of conduct prevalent in elite culture – to a scene that emphasised the connection between chivalry and military prowess through the depiction of arms, which signified the

Playing with the past

8.6 A comparison of circles in *Historical Pastime*, 1803 and *Historical Pastime*, 1824. Courtesy of Princeton University Library.

popular fascination and celebration of war in the post-Napoleonic period (Figure 8.6).[82] The game also reworked the images of Henry VIII's wives, who had previously been represented in portraits. The new images alluded to their fates: Anne Boleyn's head lies on the ground below the chopping block, her crown toppled off (No. 70); Catherine Howard's (No. 75) head is below the block but is partially covered with a cloth; Jane Seymour (No. 72) is represented with a coffin and 'Catherine of Arragon' (No. 68) and Catherine Parr (No. 77) have their names under a tent.[83] The increased emphasis on Tudor violence reinforced Henry VIII's reputation as a wicked character and underscores a wider interest in the Tudors that emerged in the 1820s and 1830s. This violence was stressed in the circle for Anne of Cleves (No. 73) where the game-makers have erroneously shown her beheaded – an error replicated in all later editions (Figure 8.6).[84] The game also included changes in the circle text as well as images. No. 157 'War with America', originally on a plain banner, was updated in the new edition to No. 125 'American Independence', which showed the American flag. When the game was produced in 1803, neutrality towards America suggested a kind of ambivalence and acceptance, but a humorous annotation in the 1813 rulebook required the player who landed on 'War with America' to return to George I.[85]

Revived pasts

The 1820s game also highlighted shifts in presumed knowledge. While previously children were simply confronted with portraits of Bacon, Locke, Newton, Pope and Shakespeare, by the 1820s they were offered clues about some of their contributions to aid players in recalling their discoveries or repeating lines from their works (Figure 8.6). Now, players who landed on 'Friar Bacon' (No. 28) were shown an open book reading *Opus Majus*, referring to his famous scientific and philosophical study. Those who landed on Pope (No. 123) were shown a lyre and an open book containing the words 'Homer' and '*Iliad*' (which Pope had translated), and players who landed on Newton (No. 114) now saw the divider and the telescope that enabled his astronomical discoveries. Perhaps less useful to children was Locke (No. 113), now just a book with indistinguishable writing, while Shakespeare alone kept a simple portrait with no clues.[86] The lack of clues suggests that children were still expected to recognise Locke and Shakespeare.

Alongside George IV in the centre, the game-makers also updated the game to account for recent events and changing perceptions. They added seven circles to the 1820 edition to include events up to the start of the new king's reign. These updates continued in later editions with circles added in versions of the game published during the reigns of William IV and, later, Queen Victoria. Thus the publishers did not shy away from confronting the recent past; instead, it was seen as important for children to know contemporary history, something that John Harris had advocated in his *Jubilee* game and the revised 1820 version, the *Sun of Brunswick*.[87] Yet the updates also shed light on how the *Historical Pastime* game helped to identify which recent events were significant.

The 1820s versions of the game highlighted the Napoleonic wars and also broached more controversial topics in its new circles. These included George III's 'lamented illness' (which eventually saw the future George IV as Regent) and the death of Queen Caroline, whose recent trial and conflict with her husband received major publicity. The game also offers insight into perceptions of contemporary events and characters' stories; for example, the coronation of George IV is celebratory, allowing players to 'spin again' with a chance to win the game, while the execution of Louis XVI meant that players must turn backwards.[88] The rulebook also contained a new biography of George IV which mentioned Queen Caroline's trial and its outcome, Napoleon's death, George IV's visits to Ireland and Scotland and 'the King of Spain restored to his throne'.[89] While the William IV edition of the game (1830) yielded only one major change – the new king's image in the centre – the first Queen Victoria edition (c. 1837) had two new circles: the first a bust of William IV (to mark the start of his reign in 1830), and the second with the text 'the Abolition of Slavery' (Figure 8.5).[90] Passmore's c. 1850 edition of *Historical Pastime* – the final edition published – offered four new images on the corners of the board: Seringapatam, Trafalgar, Waterloo and Navarino.[91] These events represented recent British victories on sea and land, from the gain of Indian territory in 1799 by the British East India Company at Seringapatam and the victories over Napoleon at Waterloo (1805) and Trafalgar (1815), to the more recent battle at Navarino in 1827, which saw the defeat of Ottoman forces. Thus, the game was now literally reframed as a story of British supremacy at war and empire-building.[92]

Conclusions

The *Historical Pastime* game offers a rich lens through which to examine the wider market for history-themed games and toys that emerged in London from the late Georgian era. A ground-breaking game for its time, it responded to new ideas about play and interactivity in learning and met a demand for respectable educational toys. It combined different forms of pedagogy and its diverse ways of presenting historical knowledge inspired new games. Yet it also provides a bridge between the late eighteenth-century history games market – with its chronological tables of royal figures and genealogical games modelled on earlier geographical puzzles – and the later games market of the early nineteenth century, which borrowed from earlier versions while also creating new games. The popularity of *Historical Pastime*, demonstrated in its numerous editions and modifications, is a prime example of how these early history toys and games enable scholars to chart changing notions of history and the place of historical knowledge in children's education. It speaks to the innovative role of publishers in popularising the past, drawing out trends circulating in historical knowledge produced in adult elite and respectable society in images and texts and recreating it for juvenile audiences in new forms. In doing so, the games run parallel to the emerging juvenile histories of England which began in the mid-eighteenth century and flourished in the mid-nineteenth with popularisers such as Mrs Markham and Maria, Lady Callcott.[93]

Publishers promoted history games as an integral part of juvenile education and highlighted their interactivity and playfulness, both as a way to teach children of all ages, and as a vehicle for imparting historical knowledge in new and diverse ways (for example, by creating connections between periods). As this chapter has shown, these games were anchored in a particular view that knowledge of British history was essential for children – thought to build character, create informed citizens and inspire patriotism. The prices of these games (though increasingly affordable) meant that they were primarily consumed by elite and middle-class boys and girls in home teaching and schools. *Historical Pastime* shows the impact of these games in wider geographical contexts beyond London and even in colonial British North America. By its

Revived pasts

c. 1850 edition the *Historical Pastime* game was a survivor of an earlier mode of education through play that flourished before the Education Acts. As *Historical Pastime* and the other fifty games consulted for this chapter have shown, playful interaction was a key part of late eighteenth- and early nineteenth-century children's encounters with the past. These games deserve a prominent place in the history of education and in the social and cultural history of childhood.

Notes

1. Advertisement in *Rules and Directions for Playing the Historical Pastime*, 1804.
2. For an image of a full spiral race game see Anon., *Wallis's New Game of Universal History and Chronology* (Figure 0.1).
3. Anon., *Rules and Directions for Playing the Historical Pastime*, 1804 [Ballam collection (Bodleian Libraries) hereafter B]; Anon., *Historical Pastime*, 1803 [John Johnson collection (Bodleian Libraries) hereafter JJ]. The *Historical Pastime* rulebooks often had different dates from the games. The earliest known rulebook is dated 1804. See Moon, *John Harris's Books for Youth*, pp. 144–145.
4. There were earlier examples of publishers producing history games. In the 1750s, Lady Barbara Montagu corresponded with Samuel Richardson about publishing educational cards on geography, chronology and history that she had designed. The letters discussing these cards – the difficulty a printer in Bath had in making them and their lack of commercial success – contrasts with the late eighteenth century when the games were made more effectively and were more commercially successful. Thanks to M. O. Grenby for a copy of this correspondence.
5. Austen, *Mansfield Park*, vol., 1, p. 33.
6. Hannas, *English Jigsaw Puzzle*; Shefrin, "'Adapted for and Used in Infants' Schools, Nurseries, &c.'"; Shefrin, *The Dartons*.
7. Shefrin, "'Adapted for and Used in Infants' Schools, Nurseries, &c.'"; Cohen, "'Familiar Conversation'"; Grenby, 'Delightful Instruction?'. For the intersection between visual and textual learning see Mitchell, *Picturing the Past*.
8. See Keene, 'Playing among the stars'; Norcia, 'Puzzling empire'; Norcia, *Gaming Empire*; Shefrin, *Neatly Dissected*; Carroll, "'Play you must'"; Dove, 'Geographical board games; Dove, 'The counties of England'.
9. *Playing with History* exhibition. History games were also featured in the *Game Plan: Board Games Rediscovered* exhibition.
10. Shefrin, *The Dartons*, pp. 7–8, 50–54.
11. Harris's shopfront (as depicted on his catalogue) showed a well-dressed woman and child peering at his window display which featured books, toys and games. Harris, *Harris's Juvenile Library* [Princeton University Library hereafter PUL]. Harris's catalogues in the 1810s and 1820s (including c. 1818) reveal how toys and games were a significant part of his business.
12. See Klemann's discussion of the book-toy hybrid in this period and their 'equal-footing' as educational materials: Klemann, 'The matter of moral education'.

13 Anon., *Darton's Pocket Tablet* [B; PUL]. For further information on pocket tablets see Shefrin, *The Dartons*, p. 76.
14 Anon., *An Historical Game of England*, 1804 [inside cover *An Historical Game of the Kings of England* [...] *adapted to the Juvenile Capacity*], Preface, pp. i–ii [PUL]. The wave began with John Locke's *Some Thoughts Concerning Education* and culminated in Richard and Maria Edgeworth's *Practical Education*.
15 Anon., *The Principal Events in the History of England*, 1815 [PUL].
16 Anon., *Sallis's Game of the Little Historian*; Anon., *Historical Amusement*, c. 1830s [B]; Booklet: Anon., *Historical Amusement*, 1830s [B]. The figure comes from a copy of the game in the V&A dated 1850–1855.
17 Anon., *Historical Recreation*, c. 1800 [B]. The game cover states: 'It is the duty of British Youth to study British History'. Mahood, *The Magdalenes*, pp. 75, 84. Most of these inmates would have been twenty-four or younger.
18 G. Darvall, *Historical Biographical and Geographical Cards* [PUL].
19 Anon., *Instructive Conversation Cards* [PUL]. W. and T. Darton produced the first edition in c. 1809.
20 This way of structuring history would be challenged by the historian J. R. Green in his *A Short History of the English People*.
21 Hewlett, *Engravings for Teaching the Elements of English History* [PUL]. On the puzzle the Directions began with 1. 'Learn to put the heads together in succession'. Shefrin identifies Hewlett as the author see Shefrin, *The Dartons*, p. 147.
22 Anon., *Royal Genealogical Pastime* [B; from the private collection of Adrian Seville, hereafter AS].
23 Anon., *Wallis's Royal Chronological Tables* [B]. The box lid gives the date 1788 but the puzzle inside is dated 1799. The box has a label for Jones's Toy & Tunbridge Warehouse. Ludgate Street.
24 Anon., *Historical Cards* [Museum of Childhood, Edinburgh].
25 Anon., *The British Sovereigns*, c. 1830s [B; PUL]. This was an updated version of the earlier Anon., *The British Sovereigns*, c. 1825 [PUL]. Darton also published a later version including Queen Victoria.
26 Anon., *Arrang'd in Bricks* [B]. For another royal-focused toy for younger children see Anon., *History of England* [round cards] [B].
27 Anon., *Panorama of Kings* [B].
28 Anon., *Royal Revels* [B]; Callcott, *Little Arthur's History of England*, pp. 89–92.
29 Anon., *The Principal Events in the History of England*, 1815.
30 This was a common trope in representations of Alfred for children. See Parker, *England's Darling*.
31 For attitudes towards the recent past in the Victorian era see Kingstone, *Victorian Narratives of the Recent Past*.
32 Anon., *The Principal Events in English History*, 1830s [B].
33 Anon., *Events of English History*, c. 1855 [B]. For the Victorian representation of Charles I and his family see Mitchell, 'Cavalier Children'. For an expanded form see Mitchell, *Household Histories*. For Wat Tyler's Victorian image see Badeo's chapter in this volume and Basdeo, *The Life and Legend of a Rebel Leader*.

34 Anon., *Amusement in English History* [AS]; Anon., *Amusement in English History* [Rulebook], pp. 6–7 [AS].
35 Anon., *Wars of the Roses* [JJ].
36 Hannas, *The English Jigsaw Puzzle*, p. 64; Shefrin, *Such Constant Affectionate Care*.
37 *Ibid.*, p. 56. Just as published books existed in a reciprocally influencing relationship with handmade texts, so too may have games. Mothers, fathers and teachers made handmade games which were picked up by commercial publishers and perhaps in turn influenced domestic production. Anon., *The History of England, on Cards* even marketed this concept: 'These cards were written by a lady, for the instruction of her children, and are offered to the public in the fond hope that they may prove useful to the rising generation'.
38 Anon., *The British Sovereigns*, c. 1837. This updated version of the c. 1825 edition was signed by Bridge [AS]. Anon., *Historical Amusement*, c. 1850–1855 [V&A] is signed by Henborough. The box lid of another version held in the Ballam collection is signed by the child owner Alice and dated 1841, Anon., *Historical Amusement*, 1830s.
39 Anon., *Explanation to Wallis's New Game*, pp. 14–15 [AS].
40 Shefrin, 'Harris, John'.
41 Hannas, *The English Jigsaw Puzzle*, pp. 30–35. For further on the location of these shops and their rise from the mid-eighteenth century see Grenby, *The Child Reader*, pp. 145–157. Wallis first sold the *Historical Pastime* game at his shop at 16 Ludgate Street. By 1812, he had moved to another hub of children's publishing, Skinner Street, which was home to William Godwin's Juvenile Library.
42 *Ibid.*, p. 31; Anon., *Wallis's Royal Chronological Tables of English History*, 1788; Hewlett, *Engravings for Teaching the Elements of English History and Chronology*, 1787.
43 Anon., *Royal Genealogical Pastime of the Sovereigns of England*, 1791.
44 Anon., *Historical Pastime*, 1803; Anon., *Rules*, 1804. Players aimed to land on No. 158 – the Treasury.
45 Anon., *Rules*, 1804, pp. 15–45.
46 A method that had proved effective in Wallis's earlier *Royal Chronological Tables*, 1788 [PUL].
47 Anon., *Historical Pastime*, 1803; Anon., *Rules*, 1804, pp. 7, 9–10, 13–14.
48 Orgel and Braunmuller, *Complete Pelican Shakespeare*, 4.3. 1–22. Anon., *Historical Pastime*, 1803; Anon., *Rules*, 1804, pp. 9, 11–13. The murder of Edward V and his brother Richard Duke of York in the Tower was a popular scene in both adult and children's culture in the late eighteenth and early nineteenth centuries.
49 Anon., *Rules*, 1804, pp. 18, 39.
50 *Ibid.*, p. 12.
51 *Ibid.*
52 *Ibid.*
53 *Ibid.*, pp. 8, 19.
54 Shakespeare deeply influenced the perception of historical events such as Agincourt, royal reputations (Henry V, Richard III) and myths, which can be seen on the

board game by the inclusion of No. 65 'Pr. Henry and Falstaff' showing the pair drinking (Figure 8.4).
55 *Ibid.*, pp. 9, 13–14.
56 Unlike some of the other historical figures on the board there was little information on these five characters in the biographies or rules.
57 Anon., *Rules*, 1813, pp. 11, 16.
58 Anon., *Rules*, 1804, pp. 7, 10, 15, 23. 'Where every player must enter before he can proceed' has been crossed out in an amended 1813 copy of the rules see Anon., *Rules*, 1813, p. 9. I am grateful to Adrian Seville for a copy of these pages.
59 *Ibid.*, pp. 14, 43.
60 *Ibid.*, pp. 10, 14.
61 *Ibid.*, pp. 11–12, 27.
62 *Ibid.*, p. 34.
63 *Ibid.*, 12–13.
64 Anon., *Rules and Directions for Playing the Jubilee* [PUL]; Anon., *Jubilee* [AS].
65 Anon., *Rules for Playing the Jubilee*, pp. iii–iv [Advertisement]. The advertisement states that 'it is hoped that the Events recorded (and surely an eventful Reign it has been) will create a lively interest in the breast of every JUVENILE BRITON; it is continued to the 25th of October, 1809, the day our revered Sovereign entered into the Fiftieth Year of his Reign, and a Day of *Jubilee* in every Part of his Dominions'.
66 Anon., *Jubilee*; Anon., *Rules for Playing the Jubilee*, p. 14.
67 *Harris's Juvenile Library*, 1818. *The Jubilee* is advertised under 'Amusing and Instructive Cards and Games'.
68 Anon., *The Sun of Brunswick* [V&A].
69 Anon., *Wallis's New Game*, 1814 [AS; PUL]; Anon., *Explanation*, 1814 [AS]. Whitehouse, *Table Games* cites Wallis's 1813 catalogue, 'Amusing Publications for the Improvement of Youth' which advertised the forthcoming game.
70 Anon., *Wallis's New Game*, 1840 [V&A]. For further information on this game see the introduction to this collection.
71 Marjorie Moon's work records a number of these editions: Moon, *John Harris's Books for Youth*.
72 For example see: Anon., *Historical Pastime*, 1824 [JJ]. The rulebook was also updated see Anon., *Rules*, 1824 [JJ]. The V&A has a copy of the 1828 edition of the game.
73 Shefrin, 'Harris, John'. Shefrin notes that in 1843 John Harris Junior 'sold the business to Grant and Griffith'. For Edward Wallis see Worms and Baynton-Williams, *British Map Engravers*, p. 696.
74 Anon., *Historical Pastime*, c. 1830 [AS]; Anon., *Historical Pastime*, c. 1837–1840 [British Library, hereafter BL]; Anon., *Rules*, c. 1837–1840) [BL]. The directions for gameplay goes to No. 135 'Victoria. Game. – Take the Treasury, and all Fines on the Game', while the biographies in the British Library edition only go to George III; Worms and Baynton-Williams, *British Map Engravers*, p. 697; Anon., *Historical Pastime*, c. 1850 [V&A].
75 Miller, *The McCord Family*, p. 57. Anon., *Rules*, 1824 [McCord Museum hereafter M]; Anon., *Historical Pastime*, 1824 [M]. The games were largely geared towards

British children, though they did travel in colonial contexts. Grenby makes a similar point concerning the geographical reach of juvenile literature by London publishers in Grenby, *The Child Reader*, p. 61.

76 Anon., *Harris's Juvenile Library*, 1818. The catalogue identifies it as 'An Historical Game, comprehending 160 principal circumstances in the History of England', and undoubtedly refers to *Historical Pastime*.
77 These are detailed in an advertisement for Harris's Instructive games at the end of Taylor, *Scenes of British Wealth*.
78 Anon., *Historical Game of the History of England* [PUL]. This handwritten rule booklet does not contain the biographies.
79 Anon., *Historical Pastime*, 1824 [M].
80 Anon., *Rules*, 1813, p. 12.
81 Anon., *Rules*, 1824 [JJ].
82 See also Gribling, *The Image of Edward the Black Prince*, pp. 101–103.
83 Anon., *Historical Pastime*, 1824.
84 Other historical errors were rectified through new illustrations – with the Black Prince's incorrect death date of 1372 being removed.
85 Anon., *Rules*, 1813, p. 16.
86 Anon., *Historical Pastime*, 1824.
87 Anon., *Jubilee*; Harris, *The Sun of Brunswick* [V&A].
88 Anon., *Rules*, 1824, p. 8.
89 *Ibid.*, p. 24.
90 Anon., *Historical Pastime*, c. 1830; Wallis and Harris & Son, *Historical Pastime*, c. 1837–1840.
91 Anon., *Historical Pastime*, c. 1850.
92 This is not to suggest that the inclusion of more topical content was a new development. From the eighteenth century, geographical games referenced recent events including war and empire building and this was also true of history games.
93 Penrose, *Mrs Markham's History of England*; Callcott, *Little Arthur's History of England*.

References

Anon., *Amusement in English History* (London: W. Sallis, c. 1840).
Anon., *Amusement in English History. Exhibiting the most remarkable events in each reign, from the time of the Britons* [Rulebook] (London: W. Sallis, c. 1840).
Anon., *An Historical Game of England* (London: Didier and Tebbett, 1804).
Anon., *Arrang'd in Bricks The Kings & Queens of England with Historical References* (place and publisher unknown, 1840s).
Anon., *Darton's Pocket Tablet of English History and Chronology* (London: W. Darton Junr., c. 1816).
Anon., *Events of English History* [Toy blocks] (place and publisher unknown, c. 1855).
Anon., *Explanation to Wallis's New Game of Universal History and Chronology* (London: John Wallis, 1814).
Anon., *Historical Amusement* (London: N. Carpenter, 1850–1855).

Anon., *Historical Amusement. A New and Entertaining Game on the History of England* [Booklet] (London: N. Carpenter, 1830s).

Anon., *Historical Amusement. A New Game* (London: N. Carpenter, c. 1830s).

Anon., *Historical Cards* [A game featuring royals from William the Conqueror to George III] (place and publisher unknown, c. 1809).

Anon., *Historical Pastime or a New Game of the History of England from the Conquest to the Accession of George the Third* (London: J. Harris and J. Wallis, 1803).

Anon., *Historical Pastime. A New Game of the History of England [from William 1st to George IV]* (London: E. Wallis and J. Harris & Son, 1824).

Anon., *Historical Pastime. A New Game of the History of England [from William 1st to William 4th]*, (London: E. Wallis and J. Harris & Son, c. 1830).

Anon., *Historical Pastime. A New Game of the History of England [from William 1st to Queen Victoria]* (London: E. Wallis and J. Harris & Son, c. 1837–1840).

Anon., *Historical Pastime. A New Game of the History of England* (London: J. Passmore, c. 1850).

Anon., *Historical Recreation; or, British History in Miniature. An entertaining Game, combining pleasure with improvement, and calculated to lead the minds of Youth to the love of true patriotism and virtue* (London: H. Teape, c. 1800).

Anon., *History of England* [round cards] (place and publisher unknown, 1840s).

Anon., *Instructive Conversation Cards, consisting of Thirty Two Biographical Sketches of Eminent British Characters* (London: W. Darton, Jun., 1813).

Anon., *Panorama of Kings [and Queens] of England from [William I to George IV]* (London: E. Wallis, 1830s).

Anon., *Royal Genealogical Pastime of the Sovereigns of England from the Dissolution of the Saxon Heptarchy to the Reign of His Present Majesty George the Third* (London: E. Newbery and J. Wallis, 1791).

Anon., *Royal Revels, or, Game of Kings for Learning the History of England, on a New Plan* [Box lid states *Royal Revels An Instructive Game*] (London: E. Wallis, 1840s).

Anon., *Rules and Directions for Playing the Historical Pastime; or New Game of the History of England; with a Short Account of the Principal Events which Have Occurred, from William the Conqueror, to the Accession of George the Third* (London: J. Harris and J. Wallis, 1804).

Anon., *Rules and Directions for Playing the Historical Pastime, or New Game of the History of England; with a short Account of the Principal Events which have occurred, from William the Conqueror, to the Accession of George the Third* (London: J. Harris and J. Wallis, 1813).

Anon., *Rules and Directions for Playing the Historical Pastime or New Game of the History of England* (London: E. Wallis and J. Harris & Son, 1824).

Anon., *Rules and Directions for Playing the Historical Pastime, or New Game of the History of England* (London: E. Wallis, c. 1837–1840).

Anon., *Rules and Directions for Playing the Jubilee, an Interesting Game; Exhibiting the Remarkable Events, from the Accession of His Majesty, King George the Third, to the 25th of October, 1809; when he entered into the fiftieth year of his reign* (London: J. Harris, 1810).

Anon., *Sallis's Game of the Little Historian* (London: W. Sallis, c. 1840s).

Anon., *The British Sovereigns, from William the Conqueror to George IV* (London: William Darton, c. 1825).

Anon., *The British Sovereigns, from William the Conqueror to William the Fourth, Designed to assist in Teaching the Elements of English History and Chronology, after the Manner of Dissected Maps, for Teaching Geography* (London: William Darton & son, c. 1830s).

Anon., *The British Sovereigns, from William the Conqueror to Victoria the First* [also called *Peter Parley's Royal Victoria Game of the Kings & Queens of England*] (London: Darton and Clark, c. 1837).

Anon., *The History of England, on Cards. Instructive Game* (London: W. Darton and J. and J. Harvey, 1807).

Anon., *The Jubilee An Interesting Game* (London: John Harris, 1810).

Anon., *The Principal Events in English History from the Landing of Caesar to William the Fourth* (London: E. Wallis, 1830s).

Anon., *The Principal Events in the History of England, to the Reign of George III. Dissected for Children* (London: William Darton, Josiah Harvey and Samuel Darton, 1815).

Anon., *The Sun of Brunswick a New Game* (London: John Harris, 1820).

Anon., *Wallis's New Game of Universal History and Chronology* (London: John Wallis and son, 1814).

Anon., *Wallis's New Game of Universal History and Chronology* (London: J. Wallis, 1840).

Anon., *Wallis's Royal Chronological Tables of English History on a Plan similar to that of Dissected Maps* (London: John Wallis, 1788, later edition 1799).

Anon., *Wars of the Roses. A New Game* (place and publisher unknown, c. 1835–1840).

Austen, Jane, *Mansfield Park: A Novel*, Vol. 1 (London: T. Egerton, 1814).

Basdeo, Stephen, *The Life and Legend of a Rebel Leader: Wat Tyler* (Barnsley: Pen and Sword History, 2018).

Callcott, Maria, Lady, *Little Arthur's History of England*, Vol 1, (London: John Murray, 1835. New edn 1880).

Carroll, Siobhan, '"Play you must:" Villette and the nineteenth-century board game', *Nineteenth-Century Contexts*, 39:1 (2016), 33–47.

Cohen, Michèle, '"Familiar Conversation": The Role of the "Familiar Format"', in Mary Hilton and Jill Shefrin (eds), *Educating the Child in Enlightenment Britain: Beliefs, Cultures, Practices* (London: Routledge, 2009), pp. 99–116.

Darvall, G., *Historical Biographical and Geographical Cards: Intended as a Game for the Instruction and Amusement of Young Persons*, 6th edn (London: Romsey Press, 1836).

Dove, Jane, 'Geographical board games: promoting tourism and travel in Georgian England and Wales', *Journal of Tourism History*, 8:1, (2016), 1–18.

Dove, Jane, 'The counties of England: a nineteenth-century geographical game to amuse and instruct', *History of Education*, 43:5 (2014), 691–707.

Edgeworth, Maria and Richard, *Practical Education*, 2 vols (London: J. Johnson, 1798).

Game Plan: Board Games Rediscovered. Exhibition. 8 October 2016–23 April 2017, V&A Museum of Childhood, London.

Green, J. R., *A Short History of the English People* (London: Macmillan and Company, 1874).

Grenby, M. O., 'Delightful Instruction? Assessing Children's Use of Educational Books in the Long Eighteenth Century', in Mary Hilton and Jill Shefrin (eds), *Educating*

the Child in Enlightenment Britain: Beliefs, Cultures, Practices (London: Routledge, 2009), pp. 181–198.
Grenby, M. O., *The Child Reader, 1700–1840* (Cambridge: Cambridge University Press, 2011).
Gribling, B., *The Image of Edward the Black Prince in Georgian and Victorian England: Negotiating the Late Medieval Past* (Woodbridge: Royal Historical Society, Boydell & Brewer, 2017).
Hannas, Linda, *The English Jigsaw Puzzle, 1760–1890* (London: Wayland Publishers, 1972).
Harris, J., *Harris's Juvenile Library the Following List of New and Useful Books for Young Persons, is Submitted to the Notice of the Public, by J. Harris (successor to Newbery,) at the corner of St. Paul's Church-yard* (London: J. Harris, c. 1818).
Hewlett, John, *Engravings for Teaching the Elements of English History and Chronology after the Manner of Dissected Maps for Teaching Geography* (London: C. Rington Bowles, C. Dilly and William Darton, 1787).
Hilton, Mary and Shefrin, Jill (eds), *Educating the Child in Enlightenment Britain: Beliefs, Cultures, Practices* (London: Routledge, 2009).
Keene, Melanie, 'Playing among the stars: science in sport, or the pleasures of astronomy (1804)', *History of Education: Journal of the History of Education Society*, 40:4 (2011), 521–542.
Kingstone, Helen, *Victorian Narratives of the Recent Past: Memory, History, Fiction* (Cham: Palgrave Macmillan, 2017).
Klemann, Heather, 'The matter of moral education: Locke, Newbery, and the didactic book-toy hybrid', *Eighteenth-Century Studies*, 44:2 (Winter 2011), 223–244.
Locke, John, *Some Thoughts Concerning Education* (London: A. and J. Churchill, 1693).
Mahood, Linda, *The Magdalenes: Prostitution in the Nineteenth Century* (London and New York: Routledge, 1990).
Miller, Pamela, *The McCord Family: A Passionate Vision* (Montreal: McCord Museum of Canadian History, 1992).
Mitchell, Rosemary, 'Cavalier Children: Sentimental History and the Stuarts', in Susan Anderson, Rosemary Mitchell and Karen Sayer (eds), *Victorian Childhoods* (Leeds: Leeds Working Papers in Victorian Studies, c. 2010), pp. 131–142.
Mitchell, Rosemary, *Household Histories: Gender and Domesticity in Victorian Historical Cultures* (forthcoming).
Mitchell, Rosemary, *Picturing the Past: English History in Text and Image, 1830–1870* (Oxford: Oxford University Press, 2000).
Moon, Marjorie, *John Harris's Books for Youth 1801-1843 Being a Check-list of Books for Children and Young People Published for Their Amusement and Instruction by John Harris and His Son, Successors to Elizabeth Newbery; Including a List of Games and Teaching Toys* (Cambridge: A Spilman, 1976).
Norcia, Megan A., *Gaming Empire in Children's British Board Games, 1836–1860* (New York and London: Routledge, 2019).
Norcia, Megan A., 'Puzzling Empire: Early puzzles and dissected maps as imperial heuristics,' *Children's Literature*, 37 (2009), 1–32.
Orgel, Stephen and Braunmuller, A. R., *The Complete Pelican Shakespeare* (New York: Penguin, 2002).

Parker, Joanne, *England's Darling: The Victorian Cult of Alfred the Great* (Manchester: Manchester University Press, 2007).

Penrose, Elizabeth [pseud. Mrs Markham], *Mrs Markham's History of England from the First Invasion by the Romans to the End of the Reign of George III* (London: John Murray, 1823).

Playing with History. Exhibition, 8 January–6 March 2016, Weston Library, Bodleian Libraries, Oxford.

Shefrin, Jill, '"Adapted for and Used in Infants' Schools, Nurseries, &c."', in Mary Hilton and Jill Shefrin (eds), *Educating the Child in Enlightenment Britain: Beliefs, Cultures, Practices* (London: Routledge, 2009), pp. 163–180.

Shefrin, Jill, 'Harris, John (1756–1846), Publisher and Bookseller', *Oxford Dictionary of National Biography Online*.

Shefrin, Jill, *Neatly Dissected for the Instruction of Young Ladies and Gentlemen in the Knowledge of Geography: John Spilsbury and Early Dissected Puzzles* (Los Angeles: Cotsen Occasional Press, 1999).

Shefrin, Jill, *Such Constant Affectionate Care: Lady Charlotte Finch Royal Governess and the Children of George III* (Los Angeles: Cotsen Occasional Press 2003).

Shefrin, Jill, *The Dartons: Publishers of Educational Aids, Pastimes and Juvenile Ephemera, 1787–1876* (Los Angeles: Cotsen Occasional Press, 2009).

Taylor, I., *Scenes of British Wealth, in Manufactures, and Commerce, for the Amusement and Instruction of Little Tarry-at-Home Travellers*, 2nd edn (London: J. Harris, 1825).

Whitehouse, F. R. B., *Table Games of the Georgian and Victorian Days* (London: Peter Garnett, 1951).

Worms, Laurence and Baynton-Williams, Ashley, *British Map Engravers: A Dictionary of Engravers, Lithographers and their Principal Employers to 1850* (London: Rare Book Society, 2011).

9

Re-enacting local history in the Stepney Children's Pageant, 1909
Ellie Reid

In May 1909, the Whitechapel Art Gallery (WAG) in the London borough of Stepney, was the venue for an historical pageant performed by 600 children from twenty-one local schools. Clad in historical costume, they danced, sang and enacted scripted episodes of local history to audiences drawn from East London and beyond. It was staged amidst a craze for historical pageants originated by the pageant master Louis N. Parker, and the organisers declared Stepney Children's Pageant 'the first Children's Pageant ever held'.[1] The art gallery where the pageant was held had been established in 1901 by Canon Samuel Barnett and the social reformers of his pioneering university settlement, Toynbee Hall. This 'House Beautiful' was to be the venue for inspiring educational exhibitions intended to improve the impoverished urban existence of East Londoners.[2] Stepney Children's Pageant brought 'living history' to the gallery in a project that gained the support and collaboration of civic and religious leaders, writers, artists, musicians, educationalists, teachers, parents and pupils.

This chapter examines how and why the fashion for historical pageants was embraced and made relevant to the children of London's East End. It describes how the organisers sought to immerse the child actors and their audiences in a locally grounded version of British history that aimed to provide exemplary models of citizenship from multiple pasts. It explores the children's experience of participation in a pageant that was promoted as an innovative educational project. This account also considers how the pageant reflected Edwardian perceptions of British history whilst confounding outsiders' perceptions of the inhabitants of London's East End.

Louis Parker and Edwardian 'pageant fever'

The Edwardian vogue for historical pageants drew large audiences to witness scenes of local history being re-enacted at sites of historical importance across Britain. The phenomenon was attributed contemporarily to the innovative work of the playwright Louis N. Parker (1852–1944). Formerly a music teacher at Sherborne School, Parker was invited to return to the Dorset town to stage an historical play to be performed in 1905 to celebrate the twelfth-centenary of the founding of Sherborne abbey, school and town.[3] In England, the staging of historical pageant processions and outdoor pastoral plays was not uncommon. Parker, however, partly inspired by continental community drama such as the Bavarian town of Rothenburg's annually performed folk-play, the 'Meistertrunk', created a 'pageant'. He re-defined the term to refer to the dramatic re-enactment of episodes of local history, performed outdoors on an historical site.[4] The Sherborne pageant was staged by enlisting local people to organise the event, create properties, make costumes and perform. Parker's infectious enthusiasm and adept publicity skills resulted in 900 'pageanteers' performing to audiences of thousands in an event that was so successful that it prompted a craze for similar events.[5] Feted as the originator of 'modern pageantry', Parker subsequently staged large pageants at Warwick (1906), Bury St Edmunds (1907), Dover (1908) and at Colchester and York in 1909. As 'pageant fever' swept the land, other historical locations held their own events, including Oxford and St Albans in 1907, and Cheltenham, Winchester and Chelsea in 1908.[6] It was not, therefore, surprising that the trustees of the Whitechapel Art Gallery turned to him, as the leading pageant master of the time, for some advice on staging historical tableaux in the art gallery. What was remarkable, though, was the eventual outcome – an historical pageant performed entirely by East London school children.

The performers in Parker's pageants usually played roles consistent with their age. He envisaged local people literally playing the part of their forebears, both as adults and children. At Sherborne the episodes included small children witnessing the founding of the school in 705 CE; King Alfred portrayed as a young boy in 860 CE; more than 100 Sherborne schoolboys playing their predecessors of 1550 CE, and young children maypole dancing in the final tableaux.[7] Similarly, his Warwick pageant of 1906 involved large numbers of school children, including a small boy who played the part of 'the druids's offering'.[8] Although children performed in them, these pageants were not seen as 'children's pageants'. That term was usually applied to events that included a procession of children in 'fancy' but not necessarily historical costume. Parker's redefinition of the word 'pageant', which already had a multiplicity of meanings, produced conflicting claims to the accolade 'the first children's pageant.'

The borough of Stepney: an historical pageant breaks new ground

Edwardian historical pageants tended to be staged in historical towns and cities with picturesque and touristic appeal that had a sufficiently affluent population to support the staging of these vast and costly events.[9] The borough of Stepney in 1909, notorious for its degrading environment, and its overcrowded and insanitary accommodation, was the antithesis of a tourist destination and therefore an atypical location for a pageant, though significantly the Tower of London came within its boundary. Located on the north bank of the river Thames, to the east of the City of London, the borough, which was established under the London Government Act of 1899, included the riverside from the City up to and including Limehouse and, north of the docks, the areas of Spitalfields, Whitechapel, Stepney and Mile End. The urban community had developed around the docks and the industries that supplied the city; population growth fuelled by migration from the countryside and waves of immigration of Huguenots, Irish and Jewish settlers. Between 1880 and 1914 around 100,000 of the Eastern European and Russian Jewish refugees who arrived in England settled amongst the existing Jewish community in London's East End.[10] The socio-economic deprivation experienced by East Enders was exposed by social investigators such as in Rev. Andrew Mearns's *The Bitter Cry of Outcast London* (1883), Charles Booth's series *Life and Labour of the People of London* (1891–1903) and Jack London's *The People of the Abyss* (1903). London's East End was a focus of national concern about both the living and working conditions of the poor, and the perceived impact of mass immigration; the latter precipitated the passing of the Aliens Act in 1905.[11] In Stepney, social reformers and philanthropists, Christian and Jewish religious leaders all sought to improve living conditions locally, and to provide social and educational opportunities for local people. Canon Samuel Barnett's Toynbee Hall and the WAG were two prominent organisations which pursued this mission.

In the autumn of 1908, the WAG trustees sought Louis Parker's advice on a proposal to stage some static tableaux illustrating scenes of London's history as part of their regular programme of educational exhibitions and events. During discussions, the idea of dramatic scenes that 'should live and move' emerged, suggesting a pageant.[12] The gallery had no outdoor space, which presented a potential obstacle to the scheme, as a dramatic re-enactment would require more space than tableaux. A solution to the restricted space indoors was found in a suggestion to use children as the actors as: 'It would have been almost absurd to entrust the scenes to grown-up actors, who would have occupied too much room on the necessarily small stage of the Art Gallery.'[13] It was also recognised that the active participation of children was likely to have a greater impact on them than passive spectating. The pageant would not only provide public education and recreation but would also enable the organisers to work directly with schools, supporting and supplementing formal education.

In October, at Canon Barnett's invitation, Parker gave an address on historical pageants at Toynbee Hall, and the proposal to collaborate with East End schools to stage a pageant in Stepney was publicly announced.[14] Parker agreed to supervise the pageant, although he declined the title 'pageant master', with the leading role in practice being taken by the vice-master, children's author and publisher, Frederick J Harvey Darton. Since this was the first pageant to be staged with Parker's assistance in which adult roles were played by children, Darton actively promoted it as the 'first Children's Pageant ever, and newspapers repeated Stepney's claim that 'it will be the first real children's pageant ever held'.[15]

Actualising the pageant

The Stepney Children's Pageant, although smaller in scale than large outdoor civic pageants, attracted a substantial group of influential figures keen to assist. In common with other Parkerian pageants, an extensive hierarchy of committees was established. The General Committee chaired by Canon Barnett had fifty-five members including: the mayor of Stepney, newspaper proprietor Harry Lawson; the Anglican rectors of the parishes of Stepney, Whitechapel and South Hackney; members of the London County Council including the educationist Cyril Jackson; historian Kenneth Vickers; professional musician Rosabel Watson; educator Amice Macdonell; Charles Aitken, director of the gallery; Parker; Darton; and thirty representatives of local schools. There were at least eight similarly constituted sub-committees covering topics such as costume, armour, music, ticket and stage arrangement which attracted specialists in these fields. Individual committees organised each of the eleven dramatic episodes of the pageant.[16] There were approximately 370 positions in total across the committees; dozens of men and women were involved, many of whom were participants in more than one committee. Examining how the pageant was organised and the role taken by selected individuals reveals the significant time and effort that volunteers devoted to realising the pageant. The preparations were also an important aspect of the pageant experience for the children involved.

Up to 600 children participated in the pageant, the majority as performers, but some as prop makers and others in back-stage roles. Two casts with understudies were selected, enabling different schools to perform on alternating nights, so maximising the number of children who could participate. Nearby schools were paired to work together on an individual episode. Twenty-one elementary schools took part, most of which were located within a mile or so of the gallery. They were both local authority and voluntary schools, and included non-denominational, Jewish and Church of England schools, though none was Roman Catholic.[17] In addition, the Jewish Lads' Brigade provided buglers. The organisers consulted with the Office of the Chief Rabbi to ensure that the dates and times of rehearsals and performances did not present any difficulties to the Jewish children who wished to participate.[18] Permission was also sought from the London County Council Education Committee for children to attend a few rehearsals within school hours.[19]

Each episode committee, which included the librettist, the designer and representatives of the relevant schools, selected its own cast. Singing, acting or dancing ability were not the only criteria for selection; there was to be only one set of costumes so the members of the two casts and the understudies needed to be of a similar size.[20] Two-thirds of the children had speaking parts. The organisers attempted to create equal opportunities for boys and girls, vice-master Darton reporting:

> The male and female characters are not evenly divided: history in the period covered did not allow much scope for the movements of women. But by allotting the dances to girls and allowing them to take ecclesiastical and similar parts, in which long robes were worn, some approach to equality between the sexes in opportunities of distinction has been made.[21]

The selection of the two pairs of 'Dialogue Children', who were to perform the dramatic links between the episodes, was competitive.[22] Each school put forward one boy and one girl for audition before Parker in February.

The children rehearsed in school prior to attending formal rehearsals at the gallery. Darton supervised a preliminary week of rehearsals in late March, Parker then supervised a fortnight of rehearsals in April, after which a final week of rehearsals was supervised by Darton.[23] The two casts watched each other rehearse, so not only did the children learn their own parts, but they saw the whole pageant (including their own parts) performed by others. The children were required to be word perfect for Parker's rehearsals. Darton reported that they were 'eager to learn their parts', were incidentally 'picking up a good deal of historical information' and would also ' learn elocution, to some extent'.[24] The organisers were keen to stress the children's enjoyment, one schoolmaster reportedly saying: 'The most dreadful threat that a master can use in these days is a threat to prohibit a refractory youngster from taking part in the pageant – it acts like a charm!'[25]

Historically accurate costumes were required for the children to 'live' the history they were re-enacting. During his address at Toynbee Hall, Parker emphasised that 'the costumes, armour, and all the properties should be made locally; thus, the educative value of a pageant was not confined to the mere teaching of picturesque episodes in history but was extended to the construction and design of beautiful objects'.[26] Creating the props and costumes communally

Revived pasts

was part of the pageant experience. The Dress Committee (with 'Boots' sub-committee) and the Armour Committee worked with the Central Dress and Training Committee to ensure each episode committee could acquire or create the costumes and props needed.

The Dress Committee was chaired by Amice Macdonell (later Lee, 1875–1964), author of two series of *Historical Plays for Children* which were described as giving 'the minutest and clearest details as to the production (at nominal cost) of accurate contemporary costumes, as well as the construction of simple illustrative scenery'.[27] One of eight costume designers acknowledged in the pageant programme, Macdonell contributed the design for the costume of the only adult actor, who was to play the part of the London chronicler John Stow (1524/5–1605). The use of historical research to produce 'authentic' designs was integral to pageants that sought to create a living illusion of the past. Pageant publications cited the source for Macdonell's design of Stow's costume as the memorial effigy commissioned by his widow, which was considered an accurate likeness.[28]

Funding the making of the costumes for the pageant proved challenging. Donations and sources of cheap fabric were sought, and volunteers recruited to cut-out the patterns. The children undertook most of the sewing, deemed by the organisers to be 'of an unusually interesting kind', during the winter months.[29] Weapons were made by the Stepney Jewish School, while spears,

9.1 'John Stow and London Children', Stepney Children's Pageant, May 1909, Whitechapel Gallery. © Whitechapel Gallery Archive.

Re-enacting local history in the Stepney Children's Pageant

crowns and similar properties were made at the Sir John Cass Institute. Although some costumes and accessories were loaned, costumes proved to be the single largest expense borne by the organisers: at £121 2s 9d they constituted more than a quarter of the total outlay for the event. Appealing for donations, Samuel Barnett and Harry Lawson explained: 'The children through this winter have been busy making the dresses of the fashion their fathers wore, and learning the words in which they declared their civic patriotism.'[30]

The constitution of the WAG prevented charging for tickets to the pageant, so funds had to be raised by donation or the sale of pageant publications. These included a series of eighteen postcards of the children in costume (Figures 9.1 and 9.3) which were sold by the 'pages' at one penny each.

Further preparations included the conversion of the art gallery into a temporary theatre by acquiring a stage, lighting, seating and erecting the scenery at a cost of £52 2s 11d.[31] The gallery was a relatively small (100 feet long and 48 feet wide) modern building rather than an open-air historical site but the organisers created scenery to mimic an outdoor pageant. Initially, the stage was set as a green pine wood, but at the end of the second episode, in which Bishop Gundulf plans the Tower of London, a backscene was revealed showing the completed tower. This remained visible for the rest of the pageant. The source for the backscene, painted by the Toynbee Hall settler and future WAG director, Gilbert Ramsey (1880–1915), was cited as Van der Wyngaerde's

9.2 'The Empress Maud. The Blind Beggar of Bethnal Green and his Daughter. The Coming of William the Conqueror', *Daily Graphic* (5 May 1909), p. 4. © The Bodleian Libraries, The University of Oxford, N2288 b. 17, v. 78.

Revived pasts

9.3 'Queen Elizabeth and Ladies in Waiting', Stepney Children's Pageant, May 1909, Whitechapel Gallery. © Whitechapel Gallery Archive.

sixteenth-century view of London, which had recently been reproduced in the London Topographical Society's *Maps of Old London*.[32]

The Music Committee was chaired by the musician Rosabel Watson (1865–1959), a popular music teacher and community music organiser. An active supporter of women's suffrage, she promoted equality for women in the music profession, organising a professional ladies' orchestra and other women's ensembles. Her initiatives in the East End included arranging classical chamber concerts at Toynbee Hall.[33] Her all-female Aeolian Orchestra performed the music for the pageant, which was especially written by Gustav Holst (1874–1934).[34]

In November 1908, the Arrangements Committee noted: 'Mr Gustav von Holst wishes to write all the music if he undertakes it.'[35] Holst, then a singing teacher at St Paul's Girls' School, Hammersmith, had begun composing for young people when he was unable to find music suitable for his pupils.[36] His involvement with the pageant coincided with preparations for the four hundredth anniversary of the founding of St Paul's School, for which he had been asked to write a masque for pupils of the girls' school by the high mistress, Frances Gray.[37] The masque centred on the founding of St Paul's School by John Colet in 1509 and depicted his mother in her garden in Stepney, dreaming of a great future for her deceased son's school. Despite Colet's strong associations with Stepney, this subject was reportedly considered but rejected for an episode in Stepney Children's Pageant, ostensibly on the grounds of lack of dramatic interest, but more probably because it did not accord with the main themes of the narrative.[38]

Holst's incidental music for the Stepney Children's Pageant (op. 27b) is known to have comprised: an overture, the opening chorus, music for the Morris dance and the blind beggar's daughter of Bethnal Green interlude, the choral ode, and music for the march past.[39] Only two songs, later published by Novello survive: 'Opening chorus' re-titled 'A song of London' and choral ode retitled 'O England my country' and later as 'What heroes thou hast bred' with the tune named 'Stepney'.[40] The words of both were written by G. K. Menzies, whose opening chorus, sung by pupils from Dempsey Street School, introduced the theme of London as the 'home of liberty', won by the daring deeds of its citizens in earlier ages.

Although Holst did not collect songs himself, he drew on traditional material for his compositions and collaborated with folk song collectors: Vaughan Williams, Cecil Sharp, Lucy Broadwood, and George Gardiner. The pageant programme acknowledged: 'Certain songs and dances are founded on English traditional melodies', and Imogen Holst suggested in 1974 that since 'the first of Sharp's volumes of Morris dance tunes had been published in 1907, one of the songs Holst used must have been "The blind beggar of Bethnal Green"'.[41] J. Harry Irvine, a pageant master himself at Chelsea the previous year, attended the Stepney Children's Pageant and recorded that 'Sumer is acumen in' and 'Dargason' were part of the performance.[42]

Dance was incorporated in historical pageants to provide movement and colour as a contrast to sombre or static scenes. Stepney Children's Pageant included three dances: the 'Morris dance' or 'old English dance' interlude after Episode III, 'a wedding dance' to conclude 'The blind beggar's daughter' interlude and 'Dargason' performed by citizens of Stepney to entertain Queen Elizabeth I.[43] No specific credits were given for the pageant's choreography, but a member of the relevant committees was Grace Kimmins (1874–1954).

Kimmins, a Wesleyan philanthropist and pioneering child welfare reformer, had established in Bermondsey in 1896 the Guild of Play, which provided sessions of organised play for disadvantaged children.[44] The children were taught old English songs, dance, games and fairy tales to perform at Guild of Play May day and yuletide festivals.[45] The guild avoided direct religious instruction and any element of individual competition, but used methods that promoted 'courtesy, unselfishness and gracefulness in deed and word'.[46] Kimmins endorsed the revival of national or traditional songs, dances and games as an educational resource that 'appealed very strongly to the children's sense of imagination'. She also advocated the development of a scheme for recreation and organised play to assist teachers. She used original sources selectively, aware of the debate about the appropriateness or otherwise of using some traditional materials with children, and considered Morris dancing ideal for 'disciplined recreation'.[47] She published two Guild of Play manuals of festival and dance as a resource for teachers, the second featuring the participation of 150 Guild of Play children in the English Church Pageant at Fulham Palace in June 1909.[48] Stepney Children's Pageant could be seen to be a practical expression of her ideas since children from twenty-one schools were being coordinated to produce the event. The new inclusion of traditional dance in the Board of Education's *Syllabus of Physical Exercises for Public Elementary Schools 1909* shows that this aspect of the pageant was at the forefront of current educational practice.[49]

Stepney Children's Pageant: the local reimagining of British history

Parkerian historical pageants typically combined a retelling of purely local events with episodes that showed how events of national history impacted locally. This reimagining of national history was combined with local folklore and representations of the pastoral idyll associated with the concept of 'Merry England'. Parker took personal responsibility for the scripts of his pageants, acknowledging antiquarian texts, literary works and local expertise as his sources. At Stepney, although he was not the author, Parker chaired the Libretto Committee. By the end of 1908, he had approved completed the 'book of words'.[50]

Stepney Children's Pageant was structured in a style consistent with Parker's large-scale pageants and comprised six numbered and dated episodes to be performed in chronological order. Three undated interluding performances and an overarching narrative linking the episodes. Since the pageant was entirely scripted, the historical narrative that the children were taught, and which they shared with their audience, was dictated by the authors of the libretto. The episodes and their authors were:

Episode I. *A.D. 61: The death of Boadicea*, by Charles Harrison Townsend (1851–1928), architect of WAG;
Episode II. *A.D. 1066: William the Conqueror's charter*, by *Punch* contributor George K. Menzies (1869–1954) of the Royal Society of Arts;
Episode III. *A.D. 1141: The rejection of Empress Maud*, by children's author and publisher F. J. Harvey Darton (1878–1936);
Interlude: Old English dance/Morris dance;
Episode IV. *A.D. 1191: The granting of the commune*, by Kenneth Vickers;
Interlude: The blind beggar's daughter of Bethnal Green, by G. K. Menzies;
Episode V. *A.D. 1381: The king's meeting with Wat Tyler [otherwise Rebels] at Mile End*, by F. J. Harvey Darton;

Re-enacting local history in the Stepney Children's Pageant

Interlude: *The Canterbury pilgrims*, by F. J. Harvey Darton and Emma L. Darton (b. 1876);

Episode VI. *A.D. 1588: The departure of the Stepney men to fight the Armada*, by F. J. Harvey Darton.

Kenneth Vickers (1881–1958), lecturer in London history for London County Council, was acknowledged as 'the mainstay of the libretto writers throughout'.[51] The libretto is a mix of prose, blank verse and rhyme, and its performance included music, song and dance. The pageant commenced with the overture and opening chorus, after which the characters of John Stow and the 'Dialogue Children' – an anonymous 'Girl' and 'Boy' – provide the links between the episodes and interludes. The pageant concluded with a final tableau and chorus followed by a procession through the auditorium of all the characters in chronological order to exit the stage.

It is apparent from the choice of subject matter that the authors sought not to teach an historically accurate chronology of local events but to enact, as Barnett described, 'episodes by which freedom has been advanced'.[52] In the first episode, the effects of Boudica's attack on London are acknowledged but the warrior queen is portrayed as a heroine whose fight for freedom commands respect even in defeat: Roman general Paulinus Suetonius paid the tribute: 'She lived and died a Queen and – free.' The second episode enacts the arrival of King William after his victory at Hastings, making peace with London and bestowing a charter on the city, confirming citizens' existing rights and privileges. The third portrays London's citizens fighting to defend their rights in the face of Geoffrey de Mandeville's tyranny. Failing to win the support of Empress Maud, Londoners welcome her rival, Queen Matilda, who guarantees London's laws and liberties. Kenneth Vickers' fourth episode, 'A.D. 1191: The granting of the Commune', describes another successful fight by Londoners against an oppressor, the Bishop of Ely, William Longchamp, effectively regent in the absence of King Richard I. Londoners decide to support Prince John, who pledges that Londoners' rights and privilege of self-government will be retained, recognising the city's mayor and council. The episode concludes with Henry Fitzaylwin, first mayor of London, foreseeing a prosperous future for the city as a centre of commerce. The fifth episode depicts Wat Tyler and his rebels taking their demands for social reform to the boy King Richard II at Mile End.[53] In the final episode 'The departure of the Stepney men to fight the Armada', the battle to defend citizens' rights moves from civil to national concerns, depicting the men of Stepney preparing to fight for their queen and country.

The episodes titled with specific dates, by implication, represented authentic historical events. The undated interludes, which were developed from literary and folkloric sources, could be interpreted as imaginary representations of an historical period.[54] However, the distinction was less clear than it appears, since the authors were candid about the questionable authenticity of some of the scenes enacted. The decision to place Boudica in Stepney was acknowledged to depend on little historical evidence and there was said to be 'no historical basis for the main incident' in the Armada episode, in which Queen Elizabeth addresses the Stepney contingent.[55] 'The king's meeting with Wat Tyler at Mile End', however, was declared to be 'all historical and authentically local', as were events in the second episode, which included a scribe reciting to the assembly the text of King William's charter.

Taking Boudica as an example, it can be seen that Stepney Children's Pageant incorporated national figures and historical fact into an imagined history which promoted to the children and their audience, values that could be applicable personally and locally. Historical pageants staged in south-east England commonly commenced with an episode referring to the Boudican revolt against the Roman occupation of Britain, and Queen Boudica's subsequent suicide. Martha Vandrei has examined the portrayal of Boudica in Parker's pageants at Bury St Edmunds (1907) – which depicted an imagined defeat by Boudica of a Roman general at a villa known to have existed in East Anglia – and at Colchester (June 1909), which included Boudica's liberation of Camulodunum and her departure for London.[56] Vandrei identifies Boudica as figure who represented heroic resistance and, in the case of Colchester, liberation. These themes are echoed in the imagined scene enacted in Stepney Children's Pageant which, set in the aftermath of Boudica's burning of London, shows Londoners and a wounded British warrior counting the cost of driving back the 'Roman tyrant'.[57] Boudica is portrayed proud and resolute in defeat, choosing death at her own hand rather than surrender to General Paulinus, declaring: 'Down through the coming centuries, shall run the story of the wrongs you wrought me. And History shall tell how – powerless to right them, even at the cost of torrents of my country's blood – I left my Britain and its conquerors, myself unconquered dying still a queen!'[58] While not depicting an actual attack, this episode was not sanitised history for children but laid bare the sacrifices that may be required in defence of citizens' rights and freedoms.

The intention of the authors was not only to impart their interpretation of the historical facts but also to stimulate the 'historical imagination' of the children. The three interludes drew on literature, legend and tradition to depict cultural history as a contrast to the political history of the main episodes. The first depicted Londoners celebrating with an 'Old English dance' or 'Morris dance', lightening the mood to provide contrast with the darker preceding episodes. The second, 'The blind beggar's daughter of Bethnal Green' interlude, based on an Elizabethan ballad included in Thomas Percy's *Reliques of Ancient English Poetry* (1765), presented in song and verse the local legend which had some foundation in the character of Henry de Montfort who was blinded at the Battle of Evesham in 1265. The third interlude, 'The Canterbury pilgrims', depicted the pilgrims setting out on their way to the shrine of Thomas Becket. This drew on Harvey Darton's *Tales of the Canterbury Pilgrims* (1904), an introductory illustrated retelling of Chaucer for young readers. Although the Tabard Inn, their fictional starting point, was in Southwark and Whitechapel would not have been on the route to Canterbury, Becket's status as the martyred son of a City of London merchant established a local connection to warrant the pilgrims' inclusion.

Literary figures also appeared as historical characters. Chaucer is introduced in person in the Wat Tyler episode and Shakespeare in the sixth, their presence justified on the basis that they could have been in the area at the time. Shakespeare's players enact part of *A Midsummer Night's Dream* (Act 3 Scene 1) in which Titania wakes in the forest and, falling in love with Bottom, commands her fairies to tend him. Here, entirely fictional content placed in a pastoral setting is imported into a dated although imaginary London scene, by being presented as entertainment for the queen. The final episode concludes with Queen Elizabeth calling up a vision of the past 'scene by scene' and Lord Burleigh declaring: 'Read London's glorious future in her past!', heralding the procession of performers in chronological order.[59] By the conclusion of the pageant, fact and fiction are inextricably entwined.

The episodes and interludes were framed by dialogue links in which two children engage in humorous exchanges with an adult portraying London chronicler John Stow. The author of the narrative links was the popular Cockney school novelist and humourist William Pett Ridge (1859–1930), known for his genial depictions of the lives of the East End poor. His choice of narrator was appropriate and topical. Stow was a London merchant tailor and self-educated antiquarian who, writing in English, became the most prolific historical writer of the sixteenth century.[60] In 1903 the monument erected by his widow in St Andrew Undershaft Church in the City of London had been restored at the expense of the Merchant Taylors Company, and in April 1907 the anniversary of his death was commemorated 'for the first time', with a wreath-laying ceremony there.[61] Stow's *Survey of London*, first published in 1598, and republished in a new edition in 1908, provided a topographical history of London derived from documentary sources and his personal observations.[62] His survey combined historical facts with details of custom and folklore, describing local communities as well as significant places and events, revealing him to be a patriotic Londoner and an appropriate local hero.

In the opening scene, 'Whitechapel, AD 1909' a boy and girl, described in one account as 'modern street children' given personalities 'racy of the pavement', wander the streets looking in shop windows.[63] The boy says he'd like to escape Stepney and see if there is anywhere better, and of history he says: 'Never been able to feel absolutely certain about history. Whatever it is, I don't suppose there was ever any of it about in Stepney.'[64]

A light reveals Stow, seated and writing, who offers to show them the great events that have occurred in the borough. Stow and the children then become onlookers of each scene. The dialogue links combine humour with instruction. For example, 'the blind beggar's daughter' is shown to refer to the legend rather than to the well-known eponymously named Stepney public house.[65] The device shows the children learning lessons from history; at the end they ask: 'Is that all that happens to Whitechapel?' Stow's reply spells out the message of the pageant: 'Be good, and brave; be proud of your town, and of those who fought for its sake. The future lies with you who are young; you, with a life to live. Afford to London your heart, your love, the best you have to give.'[66]

As well as a vehicle for the authors to promote participative citizenship and locally grounded patriotism, the pageant enabled the organisers to work directly with schools. This fulfilled Barnett's aim to supplement formal education and assist the professional development of elementary school teachers.[67] At this time, teachers were not required to follow a national curriculum or to adopt specific teaching methods, but visits to galleries and historical sites were encouraged. To support teachers of participating schools, an explanatory course of five weekly lectures on historical subjects represented in the pageant was arranged. Commencing in February 1909 at Toynbee Hall, the University of London Extension Board's lecturer S. K. Ratcliffe aimed to outline 'the leading events and personalities in the development of London'.[68]

The libretto, whilst delivering the historical narrative intended by the organisers, also reflected the guidance on history teaching in public elementary schools issued by the Board of Education in 1905. It suggested: 'The lives of great men and women, carefully selected from all stations in life, will furnish the most impressive examples of obedience, loyalty, courage, strenuous effort, serviceableness, indeed of all the qualities which make for good citizenship.'[69] Teachers were encouraged to present a rounded picture, detailing their subjects' shortcomings as well as their virtues, and to show how great personalities have influenced the past for evil as well as good. The guidance said that 'the scholars are not too young to be taught what a debt they owe to the forefathers who won the Great Charter of British liberties and sowed the seeds from which our modern Parliament has sprung' – so that they understood the history of the rights and duties that they would one day exercise.[70]

Making history: the performance

Between 4 and 20 May 1909, following months of preparations, the pageant was performed on eleven evenings and two afternoons. Each show lasted two hours without an interval. The logistics of organising the 300 performers, call boys and front-of-house 'pages' and their adult helpers in the confined space of the gallery required a detailed timetable for each performance and a printed list of twenty-two rules for participants and helpers.[71] The rules included stipulations that the performers were to come 'perfectly clean', ordinary clothes were to be hung on the allotted pegs, and 'no singing, shouting, running or stamping allowed'.

An incentive for the children to perform their best and behave as required was that one of the casts was to be selected for a royal performance, 'the better school in each episode' being chosen by the vote of the school representatives on the General Committee.[72] Through his connections, Barnett had arranged with the royal household that a performance should take place in the presence of the two children of the Prince of Wales (the future George VI), Princess Mary and Prince Henry, who, aged twelve and nine, were contemporary with the performers. The visit to Whitechapel of the royal siblings is perhaps echoed in Episode VI, in which Queen Elizabeth dismisses her advisers' warning not to go 'among the multitude' for fear of treachery, stating: 'I assure you, I do not desire to live to distrust my faithful and loving people'.[73] The royal parents in 1909 had no objection to their children venturing into London's East End, beyond a request that 'precautions are taken against infection'.[74]

Accompanied by their tutor and governess, the prince and princess were shown through the crowded audience and seated at the front, just below the stage, from where they witnessed Stepney's 'make-believe kings and queens'.[75] They were served tea by pages and after the performance the royal party were shown around the children's dressing rooms. Prince Henry was presented with 'a pair of splendid swords, of Roman model, with scabbards of hammered copper and hilts of bright steel; the belt boasted a buckle that bore in enamel a picture of an ancient ship in full sail, with the Red Cross of St. George blazoned on the canvas.' These had been made by pupils of the Sir John Cass Technical Institute and boys of Stepney Jewish School.[76] Three girls from the Stepney Central School gave the princess a bouquet, a book of words worked in colours by the girls of Myrdle Street School and a portfolio of photographs. The performers had been required to bring history alive and for those judged best, the reward was to witness living history themselves in the form of the royal children.

The pageant was not intended solely for the benefit of the participants. Barnett described its purpose as being 'to give the people of East London an interest in the past in which the present has its roots. Such an interest is likely to enlarge minds, to given them a better understanding of citizenship, and a more stable basis for patriotism'.[77] One performance was for the pupils of non-participating Stepney schools, but on most occasions the audience of 400 chiefly consisted of 'Whitechapel mothers and fathers, and little Whitechapel brothers and sisters'.[78] The pageant sought to promote locally based patriotism, yet for a significant proportion of the local community their cultural references were from elsewhere. A reporter for the *Jewish Chronicle* in an enthusiastic review of the pageant remarked: 'We had, too, a Jewish Queen Elizabeth – a live Jewish Queen. Beshrew me!'[79] Indeed, the Stepney Children's Pageant can be interpreted as an example of local initiatives that promoted acculturation.[80] The pageant was enthusiastically reported in national newspapers across the political spectrum and attracted visitors 'from the other end of town'. Those from the fashionable West End were seen to be surprised by 'the brightness, the vivacity, and the manifest artistic sense' of the 'children from sordid Whitechapel'.[81]

At the end of the first performance, Barnett spoke of 'his strong belief in the good effect which the children's pageant is bound to have'.[82] Yet the same report acknowledged that it was impossible to say how far the pageant's writers had succeeded in making the idea of citizenship presented in the various episodes 'sink into the minds of performers and audience'. Adults were keen to find evidence of the positive impact on the children, one teacher stating afterwards that the hundreds of children:

> are now looking back regretfully on the last few months of rehearsal and performance, months which for them contained more of novelty, of interest, and of excitement than their lives had ever known. For a few hours daily to become (as far as would be comfortable) a Saxon peasant or a Tudor queen, to be reported in the penny press, to receive the homage of family and friends among the audience, and finally to be visited by a prince and princess of royal blood – all these are events which give a glimpse of a life unknown in the daily round of Stepney streets.[83]

Parker himself, seemed clear on what had been achieved:

> unconsciously, while they thought they were playing, with laughter and good humour, the children performers will have been drilled in speaking good English clearly and with understanding; they will have been taught to move gracefully; they will have been taught the meaning and dignity and ordered liberty of good citizenship; and they will have learnt more history in a few days than I have in all my life.

It was, in his view, the ideal form of pageant, done by children, for children. 'Here is the right teaching of right patriotism: to love our home, to love our street, to love our city, and to love our country.'[84]

The children's own experience of the pageant has been difficult to discover. Although photographs survive, names of performers were not published. Parker's deliberate policy was that performers should be anonymous and so become the characters they were portraying. The success of this was noted by newspaper reporters on the first night, when a page repeatedly addressed an audience member, 'Mother, look! Mother!' and she, initially failing to recognise her son in costume, joined the calls of 'Sssh'.[85] The anonymity of the performers complicates any attempt to establish the effects of the pageant. One of the children, Kate Bartram of Red Coat School, who was 'Prioress' in the Canterbury pilgrim interlude can be identified by the survival of a copy of Harvey Darton and Hugh Thomson's abridged and illustrated *Pilgrims Tales from Chaucer* (1908) presented to her by Darton 'as a memento of the Stepney Children's pageant Canterbury Pilgrims Episode'.[86] Kate, the daughter of a hackney cab driver, was twelve years old at the time of the pageant. One of the boys who made and presented the swords to the royal visitors was Walter Stanley Hollyhock. He was born in July 1898, so was nearly eleven at the time of the pageant. He went on to serve as a private in the Royal Flying Corps during the First World War: a stark reminder that the pageant was performed by children who were of military age during the war years.

Conclusion

Children's performances are guaranteed audiences of friends and family members. Stepney Children's Pageant succeeded in gaining a wider and even national audience for its messages. Its legacy included an Historical and Pageant Exhibition held at the WAG in the autumn of 1909. Costumes, weapons and banners from Stepney and pageants held elsewhere were displayed in combination with original artefacts and historical paintings. Visits by groups of school children and public attendance at the exhibition were so great it was extended by one week. The artefacts from the pageant had become part of a new imagined past to educate and entertain the people of the borough of Stepney. Remarkable for its ambition, and the literary and artistic support which it received, Parker's first ever children's pageant inspired others.[87]

In creating the Stepney Children's Pageant, the social reformers of the borough of Stepney collaborated with schools to exploit the popular craze for historical pageantry. Teachers were aided to deliver a project that fulfilled some of the intentions of national guidance for teaching history. The organisers and contributors were able to use their talents, expertise and resources to promote active citizenship and improve, as they saw it, the quality of life of the people of the borough of Stepney. It was also an exercise in engendering pride in the otherwise deprived East End of London.

The children involved in the pageant became the educators and entertainers of adults and their own peers. Success for the performers was dependent on learning the script, improving their elocution and adhering to rules of conduct and behaviour. They were immersed in an imagined past that sought to give an impression of authenticity to validate its message of local patriotism and the responsibilities of citizenship. By shedding their own identities and enacting the fictional lives of the Stepney forebears, they became history-makers themselves.

Notes

1. Darton, 'Second article', 129.
2. Briggs and Macartney, *Toynbee Hall*; Anon., 'Lord Rosebery at the Whitechapel Art Gallery'.
3. Goodden, *Story of the Sherborne Pageant*.
4. Withington, *English Pageantry*, p. 197. In WAG, *Stepney Children's Pageant* [programme], p. 16, WAG director, Charles Aitken notes it was suggested that the Stepney pageant should become an annual or biennial event 'like the historical plays in some German towns, such as Rothenburg'.
5. Parker, *Several of My Lives*.
6. Historians have researched local pageants and the careers of notable pageant masters; references to these and previous work of historians of the pageant movement as a whole, together with an extensive database of research into Parkerian-style historical pageants can be found on the website of the AHRC-funded project Bartie *et al.*, *Redress of the Past*.
7. Goodden, *Story of the Sherborne Pageant*.
8. See the many postcards of Warwick Pageant produced by the Watercolour Postcard Co.
9. Yoshino examines tourism, commercialism and community in Yoshino, *Pageant Fever*.
10. Tananbaum, *Jewish Immigrants in London*; Arkell and Cook, *Street Map of Jewish East London*.
11. Stedman Jones, *Outcast London*; Cox, *London's East End*.
12. Anon. [Darton], 'The Stepney Children's Pageant', *Toynbee Record*.
13. *Ibid.*, p. 91.
14. *The Times* (5 October 1908).
15. Darton, 'Second article', p. 129; *Sheffield Evening Telegraph* (7 April 1909), p. 4. The organisers were seemingly unaware of the 1908 Dudley Historical Pageant which was enacted by schoolchildren. Bartie *et al.*, 'Pageant of Dudley, 1908'.
16. WAG, *Stepney Children's Pageant: The Book of Words*, hereafter *SCP Book of Words*.
17. Board of Education, *List of Public Elementary Schools*.
18. Whitechapel Gallery Archive, London (hereafter WGA), WAG/EAR/4/23/2, 'Minute book of Arrangements Committee', 2 December 1908; WAG/EAR/4/22, 'Correspondence'.
19. WGA, WAG/EAR/4/26, 'Stepney Children's Pageant 1909: list of rehearsals and performances', 20 March–3 May.
20. Darton, 'Second article'.
21. Anon. [Darton], 'The Stepney Children's Pageant', *Toynbee Record*, 92.
22. *Programme: Stepney Children's Pageant*.
23. WGA, WAG/EAR/4/26, 'Stepney Children's Pageant: time table' [poster]'.
24. Darton, 'Second article'.

25 Anon., 'Two pageants'.
26 Anon., 'Mr Parker on pageants'.
27 Macdonell, *Historical Plays for Children*; Anon., 'Historical plays for little players'.
28 *Programme: Stepney Children's Pageant*. The church was misnamed St Lawrence Undershaft; St Andrew Undershaft was meant.
29 Darton, 'Second article'; WGA, WAG/EAR/4/23/1, 'Minutes of the Dress Committee'.
30 Anon., 'The children's pageant', *The Times* (11 May 1909).
31 WGA, WAG/EAR/2/10, 'Stepney Children's Pageant: income and expenditure account and balance sheet'.
32 '*Programme: Stepney Children's Pageant*'; Mitton, *Maps of Old London*.
33 Briggs and Macartney, *Toynbee Hall*, p. 59; Gillett, *Musical Women in England*, pp. 60–62; A. J. R., *The Suffrage Annual and Women's Who's Who*, p. 388.
34 Holst was then known by his birth name Gustav von Holst. Short, *Holst: The Man and His Music*, pp. 14, 17.
35 WGA, WAG/EAR/4/23/2, 'Minute book of Arrangements Committee'.
36 Short, *Holst: The Man and His Music*, p. 33.
37 *Ibid.*, p. 48.
38 Anon., *The Vision of Dame Christian*; Anon. [Darton], 'The Stepney Children's Pageant', *Toynbee Record*, 91.
39 Short, *Holst: A Centenary Documentation*, p. 132; Holst and Holst, *A Thematic Catalogue*, p. 94.
40 Holst and Menzies, *A Song of London*; Holst and Menzies, *O England, My Country!*; Holst and Holst, *A Thematic Catalogue*, p. 94.
41 *SCP Book of Words*; Holst and Holst, *A Thematic Catalogue*, p. 94.
42 WGA, WAG/EAR/2/10, Irvine, 'Letter to C. Campbell Ross'.
43 *Programme: Stepney Children's Pageant*; WGA, WAG/EAR/2/10, Irvine, 'Letter to C. Campbell Ross'.
44 Koven, 'Kimmins, Dame Grace Thyrza'; Anon., 'The Guild of Play'.
45 Anon., 'An Historical Picture in Bermondsey'.
46 Kimmins, *The Guild of Play Book of Festival and Dance*, 1907, pp. ix, vii.
47 Kimmins, 'The use of folk-songs and games'; Kimmins, *Book of Festival and Dance*, 1907, p. x.
48 Kimmins, *The Guild of Play Book of Festival and Dance, Part 2, 1909*.
49 Board of Education, *Syllabus of Physical Exercises*.
50 *SCP Book of Words*.
51 Anon. [Darton], 'The Stepney Children's Pageant', *Toynbee Record*, 92.
52 WAG, *Stepney Children's Pageant* [programme], p. 3.
53 See Basdeo, *Life and Legend of a Rebel Leader*.
54 *SCP Book of Words*, p. 11.
55 Anon. [Darton], 'The Stepney Children's Pageant', *Toynbee Record*, 92.
56 Vandrei, *Queen Boudica*, pp. 189–196.
57 *Ibid.*, p. 196; *SCP Book of Words*, p. 9.
58 *SCP Book of Words*, p. 11.
59 *Ibid.*, p. 59.

60 Beer, *Tudor England Observed*.
61 Anon., 'Survey of London'.
62 Stow and Lethbridge Kingsford, *A Survey of London*.
63 Anon., 'A few days ago', p. 10.
64 *SCP Book of Words*, p. 6.
65 *Ibid.*, p. 31.
66 *Ibid.*, p. 61.
67 Briggs and Macartney, *Toynbee Hall*, p. 31.
68 Anon., 'News in brief', *The Times* (2nd February 1909), p. 3.
69 Board of Education, *Suggestions for the Consideration of Teachers*, quoted in: Keating, *Government Policy*.
70 *Ibid.*
71 WGA, WAG/EAR/4/26, 'Stepney Children's Pageant: time table' [poster] and 'Stepney Children's Pageant: rules for helpers and performers'.
72 WGA, WAG/EAR/4/26, 'Stepney Children's Pageant 1909: list of rehearsals and performances' [21 April–3 May].
73 *SCP Book of Words*, p. 58.
74 WGA, WAG/EAR/4/22, Letter from Mary Forbes Trefusis.
75 Anon., 'Royal children in Whitechapel', *Daily Mail*.
76 Anon., 'Court circular'; Anon., 'Stepney pageant: royal visit'; Anon., 'Royal children at Whitechapel', *Eastern Post and City Chronicle*.
77 *Stepney Children's Pageant* [programme], p. 3.
78 Anon., 'Stepney children's pageant', *The Times*.
79 *Ibid.*
80 See Tananbaum, *Jewish Immigrants in London*.
81 Anon., 'From the East End'.
82 *The Times* (5 May 1909).
83 *Ibid.*
84 *Stepney Children's Pageant* [programme], p. 2.
85 Anon., 'London poor children's pageant'.
86 Darton, *Pilgrims' Tales*. For Kate Bartram's copy see www.historicalpageants.ac.uk/get-involved/browse/image/793/ [accessed 24/10/2017].
87 Tonbridge Children's Pageant was organised in the wake of Stepney claiming to be 'the first great historical pageant to be enacted entirely by schoolchildren', presumably because it was performed outdoors. Anon., 'School Children's Pageant'.

References

A. J. R. (ed.), *The Suffrage Annual and Women's Who's Who* (London: Stanley Paul, 1913).

Anon., 'A few days ago', *Sphere* (22 May 1909), p. 10.

Anon., 'An Historical Picture in Bermondsey', *South London Press* (7 May 1898), p. 9.

Anon., 'Court circular', *The Times* (15 May 1909).

Anon., 'From the East End', *Jewish Chronicle* (14 May 1909), p. 28.

Anon., 'Historical plays for little players', *Contemporary Review (Literary Supplement)*, 545 (1911), 19–20.

Anon., 'London poor children's pageant', *Manchester Guardian* (6 May 1909), p. 8.
Anon., 'Lord Rosebery at the Whitechapel Art Gallery', *The Times* (13 March 1901), p. 11.
Anon., 'Mr Parker on Pageants', *Toynbee Record*, 21:2 (1908), 18.
Anon., 'News in brief', *The Times* (2 February 1909), p. 3.
Anon., 'Royal children at Whitechapel', *Eastern Post and City Chronicle* (22 May 1909).
Anon., 'Royal children in Whitechapel', *Daily Mail* (15 May 1909).
Anon., 'School Children's Pageant', *Coventry Evening Telegraph* (12 July 1909), p. 2.
Anon., 'S. Paul's Girls' School', *Kensington News* (31 July 1909). This article is in 'Gustav Holst's Scrapbook 1905–1910', held at the Holst Birthplace Museum.
Anon., 'Stepney children's pageant', *The Times* (5 May 1909), p. 10.
Anon., 'Stepney pageant: royal visit', *East End News and London Shipping Chronicle* (18 May 1909), p. 1.
Anon., 'Survey of London: tercentenary of John Stowe', *Morning Post* (8 April 1907).
Anon., 'The children's pageant', *The Times* (11 May 1909), p. 4.
Anon., 'The Guild of Play', Standard (19 December 1898), p. 7.
Anon. [F. J. Darton], 'The Stepney Children's Pageant', *Toynbee Record*, 21:4 (March 1909), 90–92.
Anon., *The Vision of Dame Christian: A Masque Presented by St. Paul's Girls' School July 1909 in Commemoration of the Four Hundredth Year of the Foundation of St Paul's School* (London: Chiswick Press, 1909).
Anon., 'Two pageants: old Whitechapel and historic York: history in tableau', *London Evening Standard* (7 April 1909), p. 9.
Arkell, George and Cook, Beverley, *Street Map of Jewish East London, 1899* (Botley: Old House Books and Maps, 2012).
Bartie, Angela, Caton, Paul, Fleming, Flemin, Freeman, Mark, Hulme, Tom, Hutton, Alex and Readman, Paul, *The Redress of the Past: Historical Pageants in Britain 1905–2016*, www.historicalpageants.ac.uk.
Bartie, Angela, Fleming, Linda, Freeman, Mark, Hulme, Tom, Hutton, Alex and Readman, Paul, 'Pageant of Dudley, 1908', *The Redress of the Past*, www.historicalpageants.ac.uk/pageants/1053.
Basdeo, Stephen, *The Life and Legend of a Rebel Leader: Wat Tyler* (Barnsley: Pen and Sword History, 2018).
Beer, Barrett L., *Tudor England Observed: the World of John Stow* (Stroud: Sutton, 1998).
Board of Education, Great Britain, *List of Public Elementary Schools (including Higher Elementary Schools) and certified in England (excluding Monmouthshire) on 31st July, 1909* (London: HMSO, 1907).
Board of Education, Great Britain, *Suggestions for the Consideration of Teachers and Others Concerned in the Work of Public Elementary Schools* (London: HMSO, 1905).
Board of Education, Great Britain, *The Syllabus of Physical Exercises for Public Elementary Schools 1909* (London: HMSO, 1909).
Briggs, Asa and Macartney, Anne, *Toynbee Hall: The First Hundred Years* (London: Routledge & Kegan Paul, 1984).
Cox, Jane, *London's East End* (London: Phoenix Illustrated, 1997).
Darton, F. J. Harvey [Illustrated by Hugh Thomson], *Pilgrims' Tales from Chaucer's 'Tales of the Canterbury Pilgrims'* (London: Wells Gardner Darton, 1908).

Darton, F. J. Harvey, 'The Stepney Children's Pageant: second article', *Toynbee Record*, 21:8 (1909).
Gillett, Paula, *Musical Women in England, 1870–1914: 'Encroaching on All Man's Privileges'* (Basingstoke: Macmillan, 2000).
Goodden, Cecil P., *The Story of the Sherborne Pageant* (Sherborne: F. Bennett, 1905).
Holst, Gustav von and Menzies, G. K., *A Song of London* (London: Novello, 1909).
Holst, Gustav von and Menzies, G. K., *O England, My Country!* (London: Novello, 1909).
Holst, Imogen and Holst, Gustav, *A Thematic Catalogue of Gustav Holst's Music* (London: Faber Music in association with G. & I. Holst, 1974).
Keating, Jenny, *Government Policy towards English Elementary Schools and History Teaching 1900–1910*, History of Education Project, March 2009, p. 12, www.history.ac.uk/history-in-education/project-papers/school-history.
Kimmins, G. T., *The Guild of Play Book of Festival and Dance* (London: J. Curwen & Sons, 1907).
Kimmins, G. T., *The Guild of Play Book of Festival and Dance, Part 2* (London: J. Curwen & Sons, 1909).
Kimmins, Grace T., 'The use of folk-songs and games', *Child Life* new series 44 (1908), 266–267.
Koven, Seth, 'Kimmins, Dame Grace Thyrza (1870–1954)', in *Oxford Dictionary of National Biography Online*, doi:10.1093/ref:odnb/34315.
Macdonell, Amice, *Historical Plays for Children* (London: George Allen & Sons, first series 1909; second series 1910).
Mitton, Geraldine Edith, *Maps of Old London* (London: A.& C. Black, 1908).
Parker, Louis N., *Several of My Lives* (London: Chapman & Hall, 1928).
Programme: Stepney Children's Pageant (Whitechapel: Whitechapel Art Gallery, 1909).
Sheffield Evening Telegraph (7 April 1909).
Short, Michael, *Gustav Holst, 1874–1934: A Centenary Documentation* (London: White Lion Publishers, 1974).
Short, Michael, *Gustav Holst: The Man and His Music*, revised edn (Hastings: Circaidy Gregory Press, 2014).
Stedman Jones, Gareth, *Outcast London: A Study in the Relationship between Classes in Victorian Society* (London: Verso, 2013).
Stow, John and Lethbridge Kingsford, Charles, *A Survey of London* (Oxford: Clarendon Press, 1908).
Tananbaum, Susan L., *Jewish Immigrants in London, 1880–1939* (London: Pickering & Chatto, 2014).
The Times (5 October 1908).
Vandrei, Martha, *Queen Boudica and Historical Culture in Britain: An Image of Truth* (Oxford: Oxford University Press, 2018).
Warwick Pageant Postcards, The Watercolour Postcard Co., 1906.
Whitechapel Art Gallery (WAG), *Stepney Children's Pageant* (Whitechapel: Whitechapel Art Gallery, 1909) [sixteen-page programme].
Whitechapel Art Gallery (WAG), *Stepney Children's Pageant, May 1909: The Book of Words* (London: Whitechapel Art Gallery, 1909).

Whitechapel Gallery Archive, London (WGA), WAG/EAR/2/10, J. Harry Irvine, 'Letter to C. Campbell Ross, 19/5/09 concerning performance on 18/5/09'.
Whitechapel Gallery Archive, London (WGA), WAG/EAR/2/10, 'Stepney Children's Pageant: income and expenditure account and balance sheet', 31st December 1909.
Whitechapel Gallery Archive, London (WGA), WAG/EAR/4/22, 'Correspondence'.
Whitechapel Gallery Archive, London (WGA), WAG/EAR/4/22 Letter from Mary Forbes Trefusis, 7 February 1909.
Whitechapel Gallery Archive, London (WGA), WAG/EAR/4/23/1, 'Minutes of the Dress Committee', 11 December 1908.
Whitechapel Gallery Archive, London (WGA), WAG/EAR/4/23/2, 'Minute book of Arrangements Committee', 2 December 1908.
Whitechapel Gallery Archive, London (WGA), WAG/EAR/4/26, 'Stepney Children's Pageant 1909: list of rehearsals and performances at the Whitechapel Art Gallery', 20 March–3 May.
Whitechapel Gallery Archive, London (WGA), WAG/EAR/4/26, 'Stepney Children's Pageant 1909: list of rehearsals and performances at the Whitechapel Art Gallery' [21 April–3 May].
Whitechapel Gallery Archive, London (WGA), WAG/EAR/4/26, 'Stepney Children's Pageant: time table' [poster] and 'Stepney Children's Pageant: rules for helpers and performers'.
Withington, Robert, *English Pageantry: An Historical Outline*, vol. 2 (New York: Benjamin Blom, 1926).
Yoshino, Ayako, *Pageant Fever: Local History and Consumerism in Edwardian England* (Tokyo: Waseda University Press, 2011).

Appendix A: A list of 'tour books'

M. O. Grenby

Listed below, in chronological order of first publication, are those 'tour books' consulted in the preparation of Chapter 7. Almost all of these books were published explicitly and specifically for young readers, but the list includes a wide variety of titles, published in a range of formats: some principally instructional, some novelistic or in verse, others largely pictorial. The majority were published in London, with some from provincial publishers (and one or two in America). Inevitably this is only a partial list, for children's tour books were published in very large numbers from the mid-eighteenth century onwards, with a huge proliferation from the mid-nineteenth century.

1710 R. B., *Admirable Curiosities, Rarities and Wonders in England, Scotland and Ireland*, 7th edn (London: Nathaniel Crouch). 'The Historical Remarks of London and Westminster, having found acceptation, I was encouraged to prosecute the same design upon every County in England'. Not specifically aimed at children.

1727 William Mather, *The Young Man's Companion: or, Arithmetick Made Easy with Plain Directions for a Young Man to Attain to Read and Write True English* (London: S. Clarke). Including 'Curiosities in London and Westminster'.

1740 Anon., *The Gigantick History of the Two Famous Giants: and Other Curiosities in Guildhall, London*, 2nd edn, corrected, 2 vols (London: Thomas Boreman).

1741 Anon., *Curiosities in the Tower of London*, 2 vols (London: Thomas Boreman).

1741 *The History and Description of the Famous Cathedral of St. Paul's, London*, 2 vols (London: Thomas Boreman). Volume II adds the subtitle: 'To which is added, An account of the monument of the fire of London'.

1742–43 Anon., *Westminster Abbey. By the Author of the Gigantick histories*, 3 vols (London: Thomas Boreman).

1746 Anon., *The Travels of Tom Thumb over England and Wales; Containing Descriptions of Whatever is Most Remarkable in the Several Counties* (London: R. Amey).

A list of 'tour books'

1753 David Henry, *An Historical Description of St. Paul's Cathedral* (London: John Newbery).

1753 David Henry, *An Historical Description of the Tower of London* (London: John Newbery). Although published by Newbery, Henry's three volumes were not exclusively designed for child readers, but were sometimes advertised as 'For the Instruction and Amusement of Young Gentlemen and Ladies'.

1753 David Henry, *An Historical Description of Westminster Abbey* (London: John Newbery).

1760–1780 Anon., *A Brief Description of England and Wales: Containing a Particular Account of Each County; With its Antiquities, Curiosities, Situation, Figure, Extent, Climate, Rivers, Lakes, Soils, Agriculture, Civil and Ecclesiastical Divisions, Cities, Towns, Palaces, Corporations, Markets, Fairs, Manufactories, Noted Places, Bays, Harbours, Products, &c.* (London: H. Turpin, no date). Essentially a miniature atlas, and curiously constituted of repurposed playing cards that had been first published by Robert Morden in 1676.

1763 Anon., *A Museum for Young Gentlemen and Ladies: or, A Private Tutor for Little Masters and Misses* (London: John Newbery, and Salisbury: B. Collins). First published c. 1750. Includes sections on 'The Seven Wonders of the World' and 'Historical and Geographical Descriptions of Several Countries'.

1764 Rev. George Reeves, *A New History of London, from its Foundation to the Present Year. Containing, Among many other interesting Particulars, I. A curious account of the foundation, name and extent, of London and Westminster. II. History of London bridge. III. An ample account of the tower of London and its curiosities, together with the prices paid for seeing them. IV. History of the cathedral church of St. Paul, and its curiosities. V. An account of the dreadful fire of London, and the Monument. VI. History of Westminster Abbey, with a circumstantial description of the tombs, monuments, and other curiosities to be seen there; with the stated prices for seeing them ...* (London: G. Kearsly, W. Griffin, J. Payne, W. Nicoll, and J. Johnson). Introduction describes the book as designed 'for the amusement and improvement of youth'.

1764? Anon., *The Beauties of Nature and Art Displayed, in a Tour through the World*, 14 vols (London: J. Payne, no date). Vols V and VI include the 'Particular Descriptions of the most remarkable Public Buildings, and other singular Productions of Art' and 'Curious Remains of Antiquity'.

1768 Anon., *Windsor, and its Environs* (London: Newbery and Carnan; and Windsor: J. Blakeney).

1770 Anon., *The Curiosities of London and Westminster Described*, 4 vols (London: F. Newbery).

1788 John Aikin, *England Delineated; or, Geographical Description of Every County in England and Wales: with a Concise Account of its Most Important*

Products, Natural and Artificial. For the Use of Young Persons (London: J. Johnson).

1789–93 Anon., *The Travels and Adventures of Timothy Wildman, in Europe, Asia, Africa and America; Wherein many of the Principal Cities & Towns in the World are Faithfully Described* (London: J. Luffman and Champante & Whitrow, no date).

1790 Anon., *A Fortnight's Tour through Different Parts of the Country, by Master Tommy Newton; including Original Anecdotes of Several Little Misses and Masters. Embellished with Cuts* (London: F. Power).

c. 1794 Mrs. Brook, *A Dialogue Between a Lady and her Pupils, Describing a Journey Through England and Wales ... Designed for Young Ladies and Schools* (London: Thomas Clio Rickman, no date).

1799 Anon., *The Curiosities of London Containing a Descriptive and Entertaining Sketch of the British Metropolis for the Amusement of Youth Ornamented with Numerous Superb Engravings* (London: Thomas Tegg).

1799 Anon., *The Wonders of the British Metropolis: Being an Instructive and Amusing Sketch of London* (London: Thomas Tegg).

1800 Elizabeth Helme, *Instructive Rambles in London, and the Adjacent Villages. Designed to Amuse the Mind, and Improve the Understanding of Youth* (London: Longman and Rees, and E. Newbery).

1800 Anon., *Views of the Principal Buildings in London: With an Account of the Curiosities they Contain* (London: J. Marshall).

1801 [Ann and Jane Taylor], *City Scenes: or, A Peep into London, for Good Children.* (London: Darton and Harvey, 1809).

1802 Priscilla Wakefield, *The Juvenile Travellers; containing the Remarks of a Family during a Tour through the Principal States and Kingdoms of Europe: With an Account of their Inhabitants, Natural Productions, and Curiosities* (London: Darton and Harvey).

1804 Anon., *A Tour Through England, Described in a Series of Letters, from a Young Gentleman to his Sister* (London: Benjamin Tabart).

1804 John Evans, *The Juvenile Tourist: or Excursions Through Various Parts of the Island of Great Britain; Including the West of England, the Midland counties, and the Whole County of Kent* (London: Thomas Hurst). First published in sections in the *Monthly Visitor*, 8 (1799), 18–30, 140–157, 263, 86; 10 (1800), 126–141; 11 (1800), 31–52, 149–174, 273–295, 368–396; 14 (1801), 41–59; and 15 (1801), 172–196, 264–276 and 391–403.

1804 Priscilla Wakefield, *A Family Tour Through the British Empire; Containing Some Account of its Manufactures, Natural and Artificial Curiosities, Histories and Antiquities; Interspersed with Biographical Anecdotes. Particularly Adapted to the Amusement and Instruction of Youth* (London: Printed for Darton and Harvey).

A list of 'tour books'

1805 S. W. [i.e. Elizabeth Kilner], *A Visit to London: Containing a Description of the Principal Curiosities in the British Metropolis* (London: Benjamin Tabart).

1805 Anon., *The Geographical Guide: A Poetical Nautical Trip round the Island of Great-Britain, with Entertaining and Illustrative Notes, in Prose, Descriptive of its principal Ports, Havens, Rivers, Creeks, and Inlets, Cities, Towns, Forts, and Mountains, &c. &c. &c and a Particular Description of the General Appearance of the Country, as Viewed from the Sea* (London: J. Harris).

1807 Anon., *Letters Written from London, Descriptive of Various Scenes and Occurrences Frequently Met with in the Metropolis and its Vicinity. For the Amusement of Children* (London: Darton and Harvey).

1808 John Campbell, *Walks of Usefulness in London and its Environs* (London: J. Burditt).

1809 Priscilla Wakefield, *Perambulations in London and its Environs; Comprehending an Historical Sketch of the Ancient State, and Progress, of the British Metropolis, a Concise Description of its Present State, Notices of Eminent Persons, and a Short Account of the Surrounding Villages. In Letters, Designed for Young Persons* (London: Darton and Harvey).

1809–17 Anon., *A New History and Description of the Tower of London and its Curiosities: Contained in the Royal Menagerie, Horse Armoury, Spanish Armoury, Small Armoury, Royal Train of Artillery, Jewel office, Mint, &c.* (London: G. Brimmer, no date). A 36-page chapbook.

1810 Mary Mister, *Mungo, the Little Traveller. A Work Compiled for the Instruction and Amusement of Youth … To Which is Annexed the Seven Wonders of the World* (London: Darton, Harvey and Darton).

1811 Anon., *London: A Descriptive Poem. Illustrated with Engravings* (London: William Darton Jr).

1812 Anon., *The Seven Wonders of the World; and Other Magnificent Buildings &c.* (New York: S. Wood, At the Juvenile Book Store).

1814 Alfred Mills, *London in Miniature. With Engravings of its Public Buildings and Antiquities* (London: Darton, Harvey and Darton).

1818 [Sophia S. Simpson], *A Visit to Edinburgh; Containing A Description of the Principal Curiosities and Public Buildings in the Scottish Metropolis* (Edinburgh: Fairburn and Anderson).

1818 Anon., *A Visit to Uncle William in Town* (London: John Harris).

1818 [Elizabeth Sandham], *Maria's First Visit to London* (London: Darton, Harvey and Darton).

1818 Anon., *The Young Travellers, or, A Visit to Oxford* (London: Williams and Co.).

1818 Anon., *Thirty-Two Remarkable Places in Old England, for the Instruction and Entertainment of Youth. With Several Copper-Plates* (London: William Darton).

Appendices

c. 1820 Anon., *Views in London, consisting of the most Remarkable Buildings with an Historical Description of Each* (London: R. Miller, no date).

1821 Anon., *A Tour through England: Described in a series of letters from a Young Gentleman to his Sister: with a New Map and Several Copper-Plates* (London: William Darton).

1823 Agnes Strickland, *The Youthful Travellers; or, Letters Chiefly Descriptive of Scenes Visited by Some Young People During a Summer Excursion* (London: William Darton).

1823 Agnes Strickland, *The Youthful Travellers; or, Letters Chiefly Descriptive of Scenes Visited by Some Young People During a Summer Excursion* (London: William Darton).

1824 Anon., *Pugs Tour Through Europe; or, The Travell'd Monkey: Containing his Wonderful Adventures in the Principal Capitals of the Greatest Empires, Kingdoms, and States. Written by Himself* (London: J. Harris).

c. 1824 Anon., *Papa's Tour through London with his Son Edward, or A Visit to St. Paul's, Westminster Abbey, Royal Exchange, Guildhall, Mansion House, Monument, Somerset House, Bethlem Hospital, Bank, Greenwich and Chelsea Hospitals, Windsor Castle. Embellished with Engravings* (London: D. Carvalho, no date).

1826 Louisa Weston, *The Cambrian Excursion: Intended to Inculcate a Taste for the Beauties of Nature; and to Direct the Attention of Young People to Sources of Mental Improvement* (London: Baldwin, Cradock and Joy).

1827 [R. Clarke], *A Tour to Great St. Bernard's and Round Mont Blanc … Intended for young Persons from ten to fourteen Years of Age* (London: Harvey and Darton).

c. 1830 Barbara Hofland, *The Young Northern Traveller; or, The Invalid Restored. Containing a Tour Through Northern Europe* (London: A. K. Newman, no date).

1831 Anon., *Papa's Tour Through London with his Son Edward. Or a Visit to St. Paul's, Westminster Abbey, Royal Exchange, Guildhall, Mansion House, Monument, Somerset House, Bethlem Hospital, Bank, Greenwich and Chelsea Hospitals* (London: D. Carvalho).

1831 Anon., *The Public Buildings of the City of London Described* (London: John Harris).

1831 Anon., *The Public Buildings of Westminster Described* (London: John Harris).

c. 1831 Anon., *A Month's Vacation; being an account of the manner in which a juvenile party passed their time in Baker Street. With an Entertaining Description of the Principal Places of Amusement they Visited in London* (London: William Cole, no date).

1832 Jefferys Taylor, *A Month in London; or, Some its Modern Wonders Described* (London: Harvey and Darton, 1832).

A list of 'tour books'

1832–33 Anon., *Dangers of Dutch-land: a Tale for Youth Descriptive of that Interesting Country* (London: Edward Lacey, no date).

1835 Anon., *Juvenile Researches; or, A Description of Some of the Principal Towns in the West of Sussex and the Borders of Hants … Interspersed by Various Pieces of Poetry by a Sister* (Easebourne: H. Dudley).

c. 1835 Anon., *The Youth's New Picture of London. An Interesting Account of the Rise, Progress and Present State of the 'Great Metropolis* (London: Edward Lacey, no date).

1836 Anon., *The Curiosities of Scarborough, Described in Verse for the Amusement of Juvenile Visitants* (Scarborough: C. R. Todd).

1839 Anon., *Peter Parley's Visit to London, During the Coronation of Queen Victoria* (London: Charles Tilt).

c. 1843 Mary Roberts, *Ruins and Old Trees Associated with Memorable Events in English History* (London: Harvey and Darton, no date).

c. 1844 [Samuel Clark], *Reuben Ramble's Travels through the Counties of England. With Maps and Historical Vignettes* (London: Darton & Clark, no date). This volume collected the separately Travels in the 'Eastern', 'Northern', 'Southern', 'Western' and 'Midland' counties of England, each published c. 1843–1844.

1845 [Samuel Griswold Goodrich], *The Travels and Adventures of Thomas Trotter* (London: Darton and Co.). A fictionalised account of travels through Italy.

c. 1850 Anon., Tommy Trip's Tour Through the Counties of England (London: Dean and co., no date).

1855 S. G. Goodrich, *A Pictorial History of Ancient Rome, with Sketches of the History of Modern Italy*, revised and improved edn (Philadelphia: E. H. Butler).

1856 'Peter Parley', *The Balloon Travels, or Robert Merry and his Young Friends, Over Various Countries in Europe* (London: William Tegg & Co.). First published in New York by J. C. Derby & Co. in 1855.

Appendix B: A list of British history-themed toys and games

Barbara Gribling

The list below includes the British history-themed toys and games I examined when writing Chapter 8. They represent only a small selection of the toys and games produced from the eighteenth century as part of a wider pedagogical drive to instruct children about the past. The majority of the games consulted were produced by London-based publishers. They are by date so that readers can see the development of the market for these educational games and toys, and because many were created by anonymous authors. While I have noted when games were reprinted with no changes under the first known publication date, I have also included separate entries for those games – like *Historical Pastime* – that were modified and updated. These entries illustrate the commercial success of these works and reinforce how the games industry became an offshoot of children's publishing.

Post 1760 Anon., [History cards: a set of letterpress cards on British history from Queen Boadicea to George III] (place and publisher unknown).

1787 John Hewlett, *Engravings for teaching the elements of English History and Chronology after the manner of dissected maps for teaching Geography* (London: C. Rington Bowles, C. Dilly and William Darton, 1787).

1788 Anon., *Wallis's Royal Chronological Tables of English History on a Plan similar to that of Dissected Maps* (London: John Wallis, 1788). Also consulted the 1799 edition.

1791 Anon., *Royal Genealogical Pastime of the Sovereigns of England from the Dissolution of the Saxon Heptarchy to the Reign of His Present Majesty George the Third* (London: E. Newbery and J. Wallis).

1800 Anon., *Historical Cards Exhibiting the History of England* [showing the kings and queens of England from William the Conqueror to George II] (London: John Wallis).

c. 1800 Anon., *Historical Recreation; or, British History in Miniature. An entertaining Game, combining pleasure with improvement, and calculated to lead the minds of Youth to the love of true patriotism and virtue* (London: H. Teape).

A list of British history-themed toys and games

1803 Anon., *Historical Pastime or a New Game of the History of England from the Conquest to the Accession of George the Third* (London: J. Harris and J. Wallis). Rulebook: *Rules and Directions for Playing the Historical Pastime; or New Game of the History of England; with a Short Account of the Principal Events which Have Occurred, from William the Conqueror, to the Accession of George the Third* (London: J. Harris and J. Wallis, 1804). Also consulted the 1813 rulebook.

1804 Anon., *An Historical Game of England* (London: Didier and Tebbett). Rulebook: *An Historical Game of the Kings of England; including the Memorable Events of their Reigns, adapted to the Juvenile Capacity* (London: Didier and Tebbett).

1807 Anon., *The History of England, on Cards. Instructive Game* (London: Harvey and Darton). Rulebook: *The History of England, in Cards, by way of Question and Answer* (London: W. Darton and J. and J. Harvey).

c. 1809 Anon., *Historical Cards* [A hand-drawn game featuring royals from William the Conqueror to George III] (place and publisher unknown).

1810 Anon., *Jubilee An Interesting Game* (London: John Harris). Rulebook: *Rules and Directions for Playing the Jubilee* (London: J. Harris, 1810).

1813 Anon., *Instructive Conversation Cards, consisting of Thirty Two Biographical Sketches of Eminent British Characters* (London: W. Darton Jun.). The first edition was published in 1809.

1814 Anon., *Wallis's New Game of Universal History and Chronology* (London: John Wallis and son). Rulebook: *Explanation to Wallis's New Game of Universal History and Chronology* (London: John Wallis, 1814).

1815 Anon., *The Principal Events in the History of England, to the Reign of George III. Dissected for Children* (London: William Darton, Josiah Harvey and Samuel Darton).

c. 1815 Anon., *The Royal Game, of British Sovereigns, exhibiting the most remarkable events in each reign, from Egbert to George 3rd* (London: J & E Wallis and Sidmouth: J. Wallis Junr). Rules for the c. 1815 edition were printed on the board. Rulebook: *Explanation to the Royal Game of British Sovereigns; Exhibiting the most Remarkable Events in each Reign, from Egbert, the First King, to that of His Present Majesty*, 3rd edn (London: E. Wallis, c. 1840).

c. 1816 Anon., *Darton's Pocket Tablet of English History and Chronology* [Egbert to George III] (London: W. Darton Jun.).

1820 Anon., *The Sun of Brunswick a New Game* (London: John Harris).

c. 1820 Anon., *Three New Interrogatory Games on English History, Arts & Sciences and English Grammar* (London: E. Wallis).

1824 Anon., *Historical Pastime. A New Game of the History of England [from William 1st to George IV]* (London: E. Wallis and J. Harris & Son). Rulebook:

Appendices

Rules and Directions for Playing the Historical Pastime or New Game of the History of England (London: E. Wallis and Harris & Son, 1824).

1825 Anon., *History Made Easy. Genealogy since the Conquest* [Genealogies First from Egbert to William the Conqueror; the Second from William to George the Fourth] (London: G. B. Whittaker).

c. 1825 Anon., *The British Sovereigns, from William the Conqueror to George IV. Designed to Assist in Teaching the Elements of English History and Chronology after the manner of Dissected Maps for Teaching Geography* (London: William Darton).

c. 1828 Mrs. O'Sullivan, *A Genealogical and Chronological Game of the History of England*, 4th edn (London: Bowdery and Kerby).

1829 Anon., *The Interrogatory Historical Game of England, Accompanied by a Chronological stream of time, on an entirely novel principle* (London: John Betts).

c. 1830 Anon., *Historical Pastime. A New Game of the History of England [from William 1st to William 4th]* (London: E. Wallis and J. Harris & Son).

1830s Anon., *Panorama of Kings [and Queens] of England from [William I to George IV]* (London: Edward Wallis).

1830s Anon., *The Principal Events in English History from the Landing of Caesar to William the Fourth* (London: E. Wallis).

c. 1830s Anon., *The British Sovereigns, from William the Conqueror to William the Fourth, Designed to assist in Teaching the Elements of English History and Chronology, after the Manner of Dissected Maps for Teaching Geography* (London: William Darton & son).

c. 1830s Anon., *Historical Amusement. A New Game* (London: N. Carpenter). Rulebook: *Historical Amusement. A New and Entertaining Game on the History of England* (London: N. Carpenter, undated). I also consulted a later edition of this game, 1850–1855.

c. 1835–1840 Anon., *Wars of the Roses. A New Game* (place and publisher unknown).

1836 G. Darvall, *Historical Biographical and Geographical Cards: Intended as a Game for the Instruction and Amusement of Young Persons*, 6th edn (London: Romsey Press).

c. 1837 Anon., *Panorama of English History* [begins with a Saxon] (London: William Sallis).

c. 1837 Anon., *The British Sovereigns, from William the Conqueror to Victoria the First* [also called *Peter Parley's Royal Victoria Game of the Kings & Queens of England*] (London: Darton and Clark).

c. 1837–1840 Anon., *Historical Pastime. A New Game of the History of England [from William 1st to Queen Victoria]* (London, E. Wallis and J. Harris & Son). Rulebook: *Rules and Directions for Playing the Historical Pastime, or New Game of the History of England* (London: E. Wallis).

A list of British history-themed toys and games

1840 Anon., *Wallis's New Game of Universal History and Chronology* (London: Edward Wallis).

c. 1840 Anon., *A Chain of Events in English History* (London: John Betts). Rulebook: *Key to Chain of Events in English History* (London: John Betts).

c. 1840 Anon., *The Royal Game of Contemporary Sovereigns* (London: John Betts).

c. 1840 Anon., *Amusement in English History* (London: W. Sallis). Rulebook: *Amusement in English History. Exhibiting the most remarkable events in each reign, from the time of the Britons* (London: W. Sallis, 1840).

c. 1840s Anon., *Arrang'd in Bricks. The Kings & Queens of England with Historical References* (place and publisher unknown).

1840s Anon., *Royal Revels, or, Game of Kings for Learning the History of England, on a New Plan* (London: E. Wallis).

1840s Anon., *History of England* [round cards] (place and publisher unknown).

c. 1840s Anon., *A New Game of Wellington's Victories* (London: E. and M. A. Ogilvy).

c. 1840s Anon., *Sallis's Game of the Little Historian* (London: W. Sallis).

c. 1845 Anon., *British Sovereigns or The Circle of English History A Game* (London: David Ogilvy and E. & M. A. Ogilvy). Rulebook: *The Circle of British History* (London: David Ogilvy). The rulebook contains instructions for two versions of the game – one intended for younger players.

1845–1847 Anon., *Crowned heads or contemporary sovereigns* (London: David Ogilvy).

1846 Anon., *The Game of English Blood Royal* (New Orleans: Wm. Chauncy Langdon).

1847 Anon., *Spooner's Game of English History, Comprising a chain of Memorable Events from the Invasion of the Romans to the Present Time* (London: William Spooner).

1848–1855 Anon., *The Bugle Horn, or Robin Hood & his Merry Men. A Mirthful Game* (London: David Ogilvy and E. & M. A. Ogilvy). Also consulted a later edition c. 1850–1865.

c. 1850 Anon., *Historical Pastime. A New Game of the History of England* (London: J. Passmore).

c. 1850 Anon., *Historical Tetotums. A New Game* (London: J. R. Barfoot).

c. 1855 Anon., *Grandmamma's New Game of English History. Interesting & Instructive* (London: J. R. and J. W. Barfoot).

1855 Anon., *The Sovereigns of England* [dissected puzzle] (London: John Betts). Rulebook: *The Sovereigns of England, including Thirty-Six portraits, with the Principal Events in Each Reign* (London: John Betts).

c. 1855 Anon., *Events of English History* [toy blocks] (place and publisher unknown).

Index

Adam and Eve 1, 3, 128
Agincourt (Battle of) 203, 205, 214n.54
Aikin, John 174, 184, 186–87
Ainsworth, William Harrison 133, 135
Albert (Prince) 49, 53, 195
Alexander the Great 110, 112
Alfred (king) 198, 200, 213n.30, 222
America (USA) 4, 174–175, 182
   American 13, 31, 36, 80, 100, 104, 150
   War of Independence 206, 209
Anglo-Saxon 2, 127–128
   Victorian glorification of 127–128, 134
antiquarianism 35, 170, 186
   antiquarian 12, 171, 177, 186, 230, 233
   for children 9, 12, 167, 173
   see also tour books
archaeology 34, 59
Argonauts 8, 71–81, 83–85, 87–88, 91n.17
   Apollonius of Rhodes, *Argonautica* 71–72, 75–79, 84–85, 89–92
   Orphic Argonautica (*OA*) 8, 72–81, 83–87, 89, 90n.10
Armada (Spanish) 4, 203, 231–232
armour 15, 105, 109, 203, 224–226

Babylon 58, 181
Bacon, Roger (also 'Friar Bacon') 205, 210
Ball, John 125, 128, 130, 136, 137n.2
ballads 99, 128, 232

Barnett, Samuel (Canon) 221, 223–224, 227, 231, 234–236
Becket, Thomas 208, 233
Bible 1, 6, 25–26, 31–33, 35, 51–52, 57, 91n.33, 115, 138n.29, 150, 181, 204
   Creation (of the world) 1, 201, 206
   Genesis 32, 34, 38, 51
   see also Noah's Ark
biblical 1, 7–8, 12–13, 23, 26, 28, 31–35, 38, 42–43, 50–51, 66n.6, 112, 149, 198
   see also scriptural
biography 9, 10, 34, 104, 109, 136, 142–158, 181, 197–198, 202–206, 210, 215n.56, 215n.74, 216n.78
   biographers 90n.11, 149
   biographical 143, 154, 156, 197, 202
Black Prince (Edward of Woodstock) 133, 208, 216n.84
Blind beggar of Bethnal Green 227, 229, 230, 232, 234
Boleyn, Anne 154, 203, 209
Boreman, Thomas 172–173
Boudica (Boadicea) 230–232
Britain *see* imperialism; Roman Britain
   see also England
British Museum 41, 48–54, 57–59, 61, 65, 110, 173, 176
Brontë, Charlotte 181, 184
Budge, Ernest Wallis 50, 59

Caesar, Julius 3–4, 99, 109, 118n.64, 200
Callcott, Maria, Lady 200, 211

Index

Canterbury Pilgrims 231, 233, 237
castles 168–169, 173, 180, 185–186, 201
cathedrals 56, 168–171, 182, 185–187
Caxton, William 71, 73, 77, 89n.6
Charles I 142–145, 155–157, 200–201, 203
Chaucer, Geoffrey 89n.6, 198, 233, 237
children's writing 27–28
    in periodicals 14, 96, 102–105, 112
    marks of use 14, 201, 207
    see also interactive play
Christianity 57, 150
    Church of England 180, 225
        Anglican 80, 143, 152, 158, 224
        Anglo-Catholic 154, 156
    Catholic (Roman) 143–144, 146, 155–158, 204, 225
    Huguenot 143, 223
    Protestant 80, 126, 157, 203–205
    see also muscular Christianity
Christian 8, 32, 57, 74, 91n.33, 112, 127, 148, 150, 152, 154, 206, 223
Church 143, 150, 152, 156, 225
    historical building 168–169, 174, 180, 201, 230, 233, 239n.28
citizenship 221, 234–237
Civil War (English Revolution) 125, 143, 146, 156, 161n.105
classical reception (as discipline) 6, 14–16
Cleopatra 49, 75
costume 15, 156, 221–222, 224–227, 237
Cromwell, Oliver 143,156, 180, 200
Crystal Palace, Sydenham 4, 7, 35
    Egyptian court 49, 52–54, 65

Darton, Frederick J. Harvey 224–225, 230–231, 233, 237
Darton publishing family 7, 175–177, 195, 197–198, 200–202
democratisation of the past 10, 12, 182
Dickens, Charles 25, 27, 38, 48, 97, 135
dinosaurs (antediluvian) 34–36
domestic 9, 13, 25–26, 33, 41, 43, 48–66, 142–158, 161n.91, 170–171, 194–195, 200, 214n.37
druids 177, 187, 222

Education Acts 19n.24, 101, 135, 212
Edward II 198, 200
Edward III 129–130
Edward V 71, 203, 214n.48
Egan, Pierce the Younger 126, 137
Egypt 1–3, 6, 8, 11, 13–14, 17n.6, 48–66, 177
    mummies 13, 49, 54, 57
Egyptian Hall 49, 53–54, 62–65
Elizabeth I (Queen Elizabeth) 4, 142, 203, 228–229, 232–233, 235–236
Emmett, George 126, 129, 131
England 19n.24, 52, 54–58, 61–65, 89n.6, 104, 118n.49, 135, 143, 145, 147, 151–152, 155, 167–187, 193, 195–198, 200–204, 208, 211, 222–225, 229–230, 232
    history of 147, 168, 173, 184, 193, 195, 197, 200–204, 208, 211
    Merry (Merrie) England 133, 230
Europe 2–3, 9, 35, 168, 171, 174–175, 182, 194
evolution 8, 11, 39, 41

Fawkes, Guy 203–204, 206
Fry, Elizabeth 151, 154

games 1, 7–8, 10–12, 14, 26, 31–32, 73, 76, 84, 97, 101, 115, 154, 193–212, 229
    see also interactive play
Garibaldi 110, 112
gender 9–10, 17, 49, 104, 142, 181
genealogical 195, 198, 202–203, 211
geography 84, 93n.72, 182, 194–195, 212n.4
    geographical 9, 12, 17, 85, 173–174, 184–185, 188n.35, 195, 197
geology 34–35, 176
George III 197, 200–203, 206, 210, 215n.65
George IV 4, 198, 201, 206–207, 210
Glorious Revolution (1688) 148, 181, 200
Greece (ancient) 4, 13, 15, 110, 177
Greek (ancient language) 9, 72, 74–76
Green, Mary Anne Everett 143, 146, 157

Index

Grey, Lady Jane 142, 151, 154–155, 161n.102, 203
Guizot, François 147–148

Hack, Maria 49–50, 55–57, 59, 65
Harris, John 176, 193–194, 201–202, 206, 210
  see also Wallis, John, *Historical Pastime*
Hastings (Battle of) 4, 203, 231
Hawthorne, Nathaniel 72–78, 80–81, 84–87, 89–90, 91n.18
Haynes, Henrietta 157, 161n.105
Helme, Elizabeth 174, 180, 184
Henrietta Maria 9, 142–147, 149–152, 154–157, 161n.105
Henry VIII 198, 203–204, 206, 209
Henty, G. A. 66n.6, 133–135
heritage 170–171, 184–185
  see also tour books
heroism 10, 13, 71–89, 147, 200
Hofland, Barbara 177, 182
Holst, Gustav 228–229
Homer 2–4, 18n.7, 87, 103, 108, 112–113, 210
  Homeric 15, 71, 110
  Iliad 72, 74, 103, 107–108, 112, 115, 210
  Odyssey 72–74, 76–77, 87, 113

imperialism 13, 17, 26, 42, 62, 65, 87, 89
  ancient 87, 110
  British Empire 36, 80, 93n.72, 175, 211, 216n.92
industrial sites 4, 168–169, 185
interactive play 194–195
  Guild of Play 229–230
  in periodicals 8, 10, 30, 100, 142–158
  see also children's writing; games; Noah's Ark
Ireland 205–206, 210

Jacobite Rebellions 170, 180
James VII and II 200, 203, 205
Jason (and the Argonauts) 8, 13, 71–81, 83–91
Jewish (community) 32, 223, 225–226, 235–236

John (King) 127–128, 204, 231
Juvenile Library 201, 207

Kingsley, Charles 8, 12–13, 40, 71–91
  The Heroes 8, 12, 71–76, 78, 81–88, 91
knights (medieval) 3, 15, 106, 133–134

Latin 44n.13, 75–77, 89n.6, 90n.10, 113–114, 116, 118n.39
  language learning 9, 11, 96–97, 99–100, 102–109, 116n.6, 119n.83, 128
Locke, John 193, 205, 210, 213n.14
London 8, 10–13, 15–16, 26, 49, 50, 52, 54, 58, 61–63, 65, 72, 125, 133–135, 154, 167–168, 171–177, 180–184, 188n.16, 193, 195, 200, 206–207, 211, 216, 221–235, 237
London Bridge 3–4, 130, 173

Magna Carta 193, 200, 204
maps 12, 84, 173, 175, 177, 194–195, 228
Marc Antony (Roman) 109–110
Mary Stuart (Queen of Scots) 154, 157, 203
Maud (Empress) 221, 227, 230–231
Medea (Medeia) 13, 71–73, 75–81, 83–86, 88–89, 90n.9
medievalism (as discipline) 6, 14–16
miniature books 172, 177, 195
monuments 51, 168, 184, 186, 233
morality 9–10, 50, 57, 73, 80–84, 89, 104
  education 79, 135, 180, 200, 212n.12
  lessons 8, 26, 32, 59, 83–84, 89, 91n.33, 113–114, 146, 152, 180, 182
Morris, William 72–73, 76–77, 79–80, 83, 85–89, 90n.13, 136
Murray, John II 167–170, 186
muscular Christianity 73, 84–85, 90n.15
museums 6, 8, 11–12, 26, 39, 54–55, 62
  see also British Museum; Crystal Palace, Sydenham; Egyptian Hall

Napoleon 48, 206, 210–211
Nesbit, Edith 28, 50, 58–63, 65, 66n.6
Newbery, John and Elizabeth 7, 172–173, 181–182, 195, 198, 201–202

256

Index

Newton, Isaac 198, 205, 210
Noah's Ark 1, 3, 8, 11–12, 14, 25–43, 90n.7
  see also interactive play; toys
Norman Conquest 4, 200
nursery rhymes 49, 64, 100

Odysseus 72, 77, 79, 88–89
  see also Ulysses
Old English 128
  dance 229–230, 232
Orpheus 72–76, 81, 83, 85, 110

pageants (historical) 6, 7, 10–14, 221–238
  Stepney Children's Pageant 10–12, 221–238
palaeontology 8, 36
Parker, Louis N. 221–225, 230, 236
Parliament 129, 203, 234, 129, 145
Passmore, John 207–210
Peasants' Revolt 9, 130, 137n.2
penny dreadfuls 125–128, 134–137
Penrose, Elizabeth (Mrs Markham pseud.) 167–170, 186, 211
Penrose, John Jnr 167–169
periodicals 7–9, 11–12, 14, 17, 26, 28, 32, 96–116, 125–137, 142–143, 147, 152–158, 167, 181
  Beeton's Boys Own 98, 101, 103, 107, 112
  Boys of England 98, 101, 102–104, 112, 127, 135, 137
  Boy's Own Magazine 97, 128, 139
  Boy's Own Paper (BOP) 96–98, 106, 109, 111, 113–116, 117n.19
  Chatterbox 108, 152–153
  Girl's Own Paper (GOP) 9, 152, 154–156
  Our Young Folks 36, 97, 108, 110, 128, 130, 138n.13
  Punch 38, 99, 116, 156, 161n.100, 230
  St Nicholas 38, 97, 100, 104, 112
Poitiers (battle of) 203, 208
poll tax 125, 205, 207
Pope, Alexander 198, 205, 210

portraits 1, 4–5, 15, 19n.28, 144, 197–198, 200, 202–203, 205, 207, 209–210
poverty 40, 194
  deprivation 223, 237
  poor 63, 99, 126–127, 136, 223
publishing market (children's) 1, 4, 10, 167, 172, 201, 212n.4
  for history 193–201
puns 41, 59, 97, 100
  see also riddles
puzzles
  dissected puzzles 62, 194, 197–198, 200, 202, 207, 213n.21, 213n.23
  in periodicals 97–98, 102–105, 110, 112, 152, 194

recent past 41, 63, 200, 206, 210, 213n.31
Reformation (English) 204, 207
Religious Tract Society 28, 101, 152, 176
Richard II 128, 205, 207, 213
Richard III 198–199, 214n.54
riddles 9, 11, 28, 97, 100, 104, 110, 114–116
  see also puns
Robin Hood 128–129, 131, 133–137
role models 13, 72, 142–143, 149, 154, 158, 197
Roman 76, 85, 87, 109–110, 113, 235
Roman Britain 2, 4, 13, 17n.6, 23–32, 63, 87, 180
Rome (ancient) 2, 4, 13, 17n.6, 87, 91n.20, 109, 177, 181
royal 5, 78, 128, 144, 151–152, 195, 198, 200–204, 206–207, 211, 213n.26, 214n.54, 235, 236–237
royalty 10, 198, 200–206
Russell, Rachel 9, 142, 147–155, 158
Russell, William (Lord) 142, 147–148, 150–154

St Paul's Cathedral 56, 171–172, 182
school 6, 12, 34, 49, 56, 72–73, 99, 110, 115, 134, 182, 225
  curricula 9, 96–97, 103, 105, 115
  East London school children 12, 222, 225–226, 229, 235, 237

Index

grammar school 99, 119n.83
public schools 99, 100, 114, 116, 118n.59, 167, 222, 228, 237
school stories 9, 81, 92n.57, 96–7, 108, 114, 116, 233
Sunday School 11, 134, 159n.51
science 27, 39, 55–6, 96, 102, 176
scientific (knowledge) 8, 39, 61, 101, 110, 114, 118n.57, 170, 210
scientific discoveries 13, 198
Scotland 15–16, 17n.5, 104, 146, 167, 170, 180, 210
Scott, Walter 127–128
scriptural 8, 11, 26–27, 35–36
  see also biblical
Shakespeare, William 101, 203–205, 209–210, 214n.54, 233
Sheppard, Jack 135–137
slavery
  abolition of the slave trade 206, 210
  Spartacus (slave revolts) 112
social reform 126, 135, 197, 229, 231
Stonehenge 186–187, 189n.66, 200
Stow, John 226, 231, 233–234
Straw, Jack 9, 125, 129–130, 132, 134, 137n.2
Strickland, Agnes 144–145, 158n.4, 180
Strickland, Elizabeth 143–146, 157
Stuarts 142–144, 152, 157
suffrage (women's) 156, 228

Taylor, Ann and Jane 56–57, 181–183
theatre 6, 71, 109–110
  Astley's Amphitheatre 15, 16, 101
  toy-theatre 1, 15–16,19, 28
Tom Thumb 172–173, 180, 186, 189n.66
tour books 9, 11–12, 167–187
  see also heritage
tourism 154, 238n.9
  'juvenile tourist' 168, 175–176, 181, 187
Tower of London 4, 129, 171–172, 175, 181, 184, 201, 223, 227

Toynbee Hall 221, 223–225, 227–228, 234
toys 7–8, 10–12, 14, 26, 28, 30–34, 39–42, 44n.15, 115, 194–195, 198, 201, 211, 212n.11
  see also Noah's Ark
Troy 3, 87–88, 101, 107, 112–113, 115
  Siege of Troy 6, 15, 100, 110
  Trojan Horse (wooden horse) 3, 44n.15
  Trojan War 2, 88
Tudor 25, 142, 209, 236
Turpin, Dick 135–136
Tyler, Wat 9, 125–126, 128–130, 134–137

Ulysses 99, 112
  see also Odysseus

Vickers, Kenneth 224, 230–231
Victoria (Queen) 4, 5, 176, 198, 208, 210
Virgil 79, 87, 113
  Aeneid 72–73, 77, 110, 113, 213n.25

Wales 19n.24, 136, 172–3, 176, 186, 201, 208
Wallis, Edward 200, 206–207, 215n.73
Wallis, John 1, 193, 201, 206
  Historical Pastime 10, 193–194, 201–203, 205–212, 215n.72, 215n.74
  Wallis's New Game 1–5, 8, 11, 14, 17, 34, 90n.7, 206
  see also Harris, John
Wars of the Roses 14, 201
Westminster Abbey 171–173, 175–176, 181
William I 198, 203, 205, 227, 231–232
William IV 198, 200, 201, 207, 210
Wilson, Sarah (Atkins) 49, 55–59, 65
working class 12–13, 48, 99–100, 108, 112, 130, 134–136, 150, 152, 161n.99

zoological past 26, 36, 38–41, 43

EU authorised representative for GPSR:
Easy Access System Europe, Mustamäe tee 50,
10621 Tallinn, Estonia
gpsr.requests@easproject.com

www.ingramcontent.com/pod-product-compliance
Lightning Source LLC
Chambersburg PA
CBHW070321240426
43671CB00013BA/2325